A GLOBAL ODYSSEY

The Autobiography of

JAMES K. MATHEWS

To: Jim Mitchell

God's best!

+James K. Mathews

ABINGDON PRESS
Nashville

A GLOBAL ODYSSEY: THE AUTOBIOGRAPHY OF JAMES K. MATHEWS

This book is printed on recycled, acid-free, elemental-chlorine–free paper.

Library of Congress Cataloging-in-Publication Data

Mathews, James K. (James Kenneth), 1913–
A global odyssey : the autobiography of James K. Mathews.
    p. cm.
Includes index.
ISBN 0-687-08926-3 (alk. paper)
    1. Mathews, James K. (James Kenneth), 1913–   2. United Methodist Church (U.S.)—Bishops—Biography. I. Title.

BX8495.M343 A3 2000
287'.6'092—dc21
[B]   00-021505

Scripture quotations noted NEB are from The New English Bible. © The Delegates of the Oxford University Press and The Syndics of the Cambridge University Press 1961, 1970. Reprinted by permission.

Scripture quotations noted KJV are from the King James Version of the Bible.

Scripture quotation noted Moffatt are from *The Bible: A New Translation*, by James Moffatt.

00 01 02 03 04 05 06 07 08 09—10 9 8 7 6 5 4 3 2 1

MANUFACTURED IN THE UNITED STATES OF AMERICA

To all who have pointed the way;
And who have lent a hand along the way; and
To those whom I have served on the way,
And to my family who paid a price for my
  following the way.

Acknowledgments

One might suppose that an autobiography is, by definition, the undertaking of one person, the writer. This has not been my experience. One is always indebted to many others who are of help along the way, but also to those who have assisted in putting together the story of one's journey. This is an effort to thank some of these friendly helpers.

First and foremost, I must mention my wife of sixty years, Eunice Jones Mathews. My first draft was in longhand. She is one of the few who can decipher my handwriting. In fact, she often is able to grasp some passages which I myself, after a lapse of time, can only read with difficulty. Far beyond that, she has been my constant companion and constructive critic. Often our stories have been so tightly melded together that our separate experiences are hard to distinguish. She has transferred my scrawl to the computer and seen it through many revisions. All this is a mystery to me for I confess to being a computer-illiterate. For all this and much more I record my deep appreciation.

Likewise, I acknowledge my indebtedness to Bishop Earl G. Hunt, Jr., colleague in the episcopacy for more than thirty-five years. He it was who was kind enough to read an early draft. He saw some worth in the effort and encouraged me to refine it. Beyond that he has undertaken to write a foreword. For all that he has done and is: Thanks.

Then what would I have done without the skilled and critical editorial eye of my friend and sometimes colleage, Dr. Alan Geyer, at present Canon-Ecumenical of the National Cathedral? As a former editor of *The Christian Century* he was especially helpful on matters both of fact and style, for he read the manuscript with meticulous care. How can I thank him adequately?

Much the same goes to my friend of many years. Dr. J. Robert Nelson, scholar, theologian and ecumenist. In fact, I was in company with him on many ecumenical ventures. He examined my effort by reading the manuscript with care—not once but twice—and supplied me not only with factual material, but corrected a number of faulty passages.

For fully fifty years I have walked the missionary road with Dr. Tracey K. Jones, Jr. He and his wife, Junia, both read this work-in-progress. Their interest and encouragement was particularly helpful.

Then a cousin, Nancy Ernsberger Copley of Watkinsville, Georgia, was good enough to scrutinize what I have written. Her aid on genealogical matters was very useful indeed. My long-time executive assistant and secretary, Faith Richardson of Newtonville, Massachusetts, read an early draft and her critique is appreciated. Having worked with me closely for nearly twent-five years in Boston, Washington and Albany, she has helped me to be accurate and honest. She has increased my indebtedness to her by preparing an index for this volume.

———— *Acknowledgments* ————

The Reverend Edwin A. Schell of Lovely Lane Museum in Baltimore reviewed a draft. Few matters having to do with historical accuracy are likely to escape him, so I felt encouraged that he did not fault me badly.

Years ago I went to seminary with the Rev. Dr. Luther Waddington King who retired to Spotsylvania, Virginia. We were fellow-members of the New York Annual Conference. I am particularly moved and pleased that he devoted a good deal of time and energy during the last months of his life to a critical examination of my book. He is well remembered and his constructive suggestions are all included—and with gratitude.

Our three children, Anne, Jan, and Stan, were also helpful in two ways (Their full names appear in the volume). They made critical suggestions. Beyond that, all three are expert on computers and were of great help to their mother as they probed the mysteries of these devices. Even our teen-age grandcson, Nicholas Younes, was able to overcome a stubborn machine. My sisters, Alleene Mathews Watson of Houston, and Alice Mathews Neill of Norwich, New York, came to my aid at times when only they could recall early details. To all these and others: Thank you very much.

The dust cover of this book is from a portrait painted by Glenora Whitman Hill of Silver Spring, Maryland. "Glenhill," her professional designation, was commissioned to do this by the Baltimore and Peninsula Annual Conferences upon my retirement. I was pleased with her work, for she caught, I think, the essence and focus of my ministry.

The publishers, William B. Eerdmans, have kindly

granted permission for use of some previously published material which appears in the final chapter. This, I appreciate. During my account of my military service I quoted a poem titled, "Conversation Piece" by Sergeant Smith Dawless. It appeared during World War II. My source does not indicate any copyright and it is from a booklet prepared by the Office of Public Relations of the CBI Theater. Having failed in my search for its publisher, I nevertheless record my thanks.

Life goes on, thanks be to God. If we are to believe, as I do, God's promise of life everlasting, surely the best of Life lies ahead.

—James K. Mathews
One of the bishops of The Methodist Church

CONTENTS

FOREWORD

More than a century ago, in Boston's old Trinity Church, Phillips Brooks reminded us that "Every true life has its Jerusalem to which it is always going up." These words suggest the ultimate role of a compelling and controlling purpose in structuring the real meaning of an individual's earthly pilgrimage. Fortunate indeed is the man or woman who achieves this focus in his or her career, particularly if the stimulus for such motivation has a Divine origin. The pages that follow chronicle the life of one who has made and continues to make the long journey to his Jerusalem with happy abandon and sacred commitment.

James Kenneth Mathews, as his colleagues in the Council of Bishops and many others in the United Methodist and ecumenical worlds see it, has brought both effectiveness and honor to God's church through his adventurous and distinguished life.

There is something almost massive about this venture in autobiography—its immense sweep, its rich detail, its cast of characters both famous and obscure, its frequent unstudied stylistic elegance, and its vast array of topics. The bishop reviews his long career with candor and without the disenchanting guise of false modesty. He writes with no sense of *denouement* and makes it quite clear that he has never believed in retirement for a Christian minister.

Sitting near Bishop Mathews in a meeting of the Council of Bishops, as I have done upon many occasions, provokes both reflection and appreciation. He presents an impressive image of buoyant health and easy, undiminished vigor. His native dignity befits his office and equips him to move gracefully among both the elite and the ordinary in any setting. There is about him a gentle and pleasant austerity that never quite abridges the gracious warmth of genuine cordiality. He follows the agenda closely, as he did before his several retirements, and courteously ignores points of trivia in discussions, quickly identifying major issues and, with fair frequency, interjecting illuminating and insightful comments that often guide the Council's thought toward wiser conclusions. That he is in the latter half of his ninth decade rarely occurs to his colleagues and perhaps never to him. He remains, after four retirements, an episcopal figure of strong and constructive influence.

Let me suggest an important point which the author himself makes repeatedly in this book. One can never assess the varied and substantial accomplishments of Jim Mathews in either the missionary or the episcopal eras of his life without acknowledging the far more than usual role played in it all by his brilliant and extraordinary wife, Eunice Jones Mathews, the only child of Dr. and Mrs. E. Stanley Jones, perhaps Methodism's premier missionary couple of the twentieth century. Born in India, she met Jim during his early days as a missionary pastor in what was then the city of Bombay. To catalog the multiple gifts and accomplishments of this proudly independent and charming lady would be a major challenge. It is enough to say that the lovely threads of Eunice's own creative life are interwoven with those of her husband's to compose a rich tapestry of thoughtful meaning in modern Kingdom history.

Bishop Mathews' career has earned him a cluster of ecclesiastical appellations: missionary, evangelist (the two he prefers), social activist, ecumenist, scholar, author, preacher, teacher, and bishop. In all of his roles he has exemplified a rare and remarkable balance between personal and social religion. His intimate and treasured knowledge of Jesus Christ as his personal Savior and Lord reflects the best of the ancient orthodoxy whose theology glorified the New Testament church. Yet his keenly sensitive social conscience has made him acutely aware of every human deviation from Divinely designed standards of right and wrong in earthly relationships. His effort to stand vigorously and with intelligence and courage for Heaven's norms has been lifelong and uncompromising. Both the personal and social poles of the Christian religion have been safely ensconced within the shelter of his broad and vibrant evangelical faith. Unfortunately this has not always been an accurate description of Christian leadership. It may well be that the church's historical failure to equate its profession of faith with its passion for social action, and vice versa, is the most reasonable explanation for the Gospel's long deferred total victory through the so-called Christian centuries. We have had our splendid periods of creedal emphasis and equally our splendid eras of social activism—but we have never seemed able to combine the two in adequate balance at any one time.

Possibly excepting the instance of the bishop's famous father-in-law, I have not seen, during my years, as satisfying and inspiring an example of this kind of theological balance in a Christian leader of recognized distinction as that embodied in the life and work of James K. Mathews. He is at once a devout personal evangelical (to use this word properly and in its classic sense) and an articulate social activist.

The range of Bishop Mathews' knowledge, as this volume clearly reveals, is startling. It reaches deeply into the realms of religious, cultural, historical, political and sociological scholarship. He and his wife are understandably influenced by the vivid lore of two vastly dissimilar traditions: India in the East and America in the West, both enormously important cultures on this planet. It may not be a verbal extravagance to suggest that Bishop Mathews approaches being a true Renaissance man as much or more than any modern person who has carried the bishop's staff in our church.

Perhaps because of my wife's and my own long-time appreciation for Jim and Eunice Mathews, and the fact that we view with awe the incredible accumulation of their involvements and achievements, I have set these paragraphs in what may appear to be a context of rather consistent seriousness. This is not a complete picture. Friends of the Mathews are aware that the bishop and his spouse are pleasant, charming companions for any occasion, intimately familiar with laughter and light-hearted conversation. Their hospitality, always warm and comfortable, nevertheless has an unmistakable touch of elegance about it. This does not mean, however, that it cannot become, when appropriate, quite gala. As an example, some of us recall an impromptu festivity at the close of a recent Council of Bishops evening session when Jim surprised the entire Council and its guests with a lavish, multi-flavored ice cream party to honor Eunice on her birthday!

Bishop Mathews makes it very clear that he elects to think of himself as a missionary and evangelist, choosing these designations even above that of bishop (which in no way diminishes in anybody's mind the splendid episcopal leadership he has given). The typical Christian missionary (who is always in the best sense an evangelist as well) exemplifies a unique and extraordinary excellence among those who undertake vocational service to the church. The basic selflessness of the "missionary mind" across the centuries has proved to be a major factor in conserving the motivational purity of the Christian ministry. Both Jim and Eunice Mathews have provided significant documentation for these observations. His has been a life of authentic eminence and telling impact in the history of twentieth century Christianity.

Throughout this volume there is the very evident and stimulating flavor of a forward look, the exciting hint of future tasks and better things to come. Jim Mathews tells about the yesterdays but still lives deliberately in the tomorrows. He is, indeed, a "pilgrim of the future," to borrow Pierre Teilhard de Chardin's fascinating self-description.

Once, years ago, I heard Bishop Mathews' distin-

guished brother Dr. Joseph Mathews address an episcopal audience and refer to his listeners as "princes of the
church." Not many of us have deserved that lofty title. In
my opinion, James Kenneth Mathews does.

—Earl G. Hunt, Jr.

1

GETTING STARTED

I mean to tell my story as I remember it. This means that I accept the shortcomings and inaccuracies of memory. There are, of course, papers—letters, records, some journals. These will be used as prompters' cards or for quotations where they may help the narrative.

We all like to talk about ourselves, although we are skilled at overlaying this pleasure with an appropriate mantle of modesty. Some friends have suggested that I record this story, so I have some excuse for lifting that mantle. As I have reflected about my journey thus far, it has seemed to me unremarkable in most ways, but such as I am or have experienced, I share with others.

It was on a cold wintry day, I am told, that I made my entrance into the world. This (for me) indispensable event occurred at about 6:00 P.M. on February 10, 1913, in Breezewood, Pennsylvania. For those who pay heed to such matters, 1913 was the year when the Federal Income Tax was inaugurated. It saw also the first Rose Bowl football game. My birth was about three weeks before Woodrow Wilson's first inauguration. I was born in an upstairs bedroom in the parsonage of the Methodist Episcopal church. My brother Joe had been born in a downstairs bedroom about eighteen months earlier.

Breezewood is now an interchange on the Pennsylvania Turnpike from which a spur runs to Washington, D.C. It is a place at present marked by service stations, motels, and fast-food establishments. Then it was a tiny village with not so much as an inn of any kind. One born in Breezewood has no cause for airs.

My father was a supply pastor there at the time. He served not only Breezewood but also four other small congregations. In addition, he was in charge of a summer camp meeting at nearby Crystal Spring. His hands must have been very full indeed.

Our family had a strong religious bias that had been in our blood for generations. Of my great-grandmother, Rebecca Donaldson Mathews, it was said that she walked with God for more than seventy years and never missed a step. She was a shouting Methodist, though originally a reserved, pious Presbyterian.

The Mathews were of Scotch-Irish extraction. Before that there were roots in England and in Wales, where the line can be traced back to a king in the tenth century. Preachers seem to have been abundant in our ancestry. At the same time there is evidence that some of our forefathers were hanged for stealing sheep!

The Scotch-Irish people were essentially lowland Scots who toward the beginning of the seventeenth century were sent by the English to colonize Northern Ireland (Ulster) and to lend stability amongst the rebellious Irish in that region. They were a stalwart lot, staunchly Presbyterian. Already a hardy people, they were toughened even more as they were ground between the English rulers and Irish resisters. "Stern," "self-reliant," and "adventurous" are adjectives that apply to them. They excelled not only in agriculture in general but in sheep-raising in particular. It was only a step from producing wool to the manufacture of cloth. Here too the Scotch-Irish settlers showed talent and enterprise.

Soon English pressures were visited upon these immigrants. Legislation favored English over Irish woolen textiles. This greatly depressed the economy in Ulster as well as that of other parts of Ireland. At the same time absentee English landlords raised the rents of their Irish tenants. Moreover, the right to vote was denied non-Anglicans. It was such economic, social, religious, and political oppression that prompted Scotch-Irish migration to the American colonies in successive waves throughout the middle of the eighteenth century. They sought freedom, self-government, and a new opportunity. Furthermore, they prized education for their children, a characteristic of Scotch-Irish immigrants.

Our roots in America reveal that there was frequent intermarriage between the Mathews and Donaldson families. This latter name was an anglicization of "MacDonald." We are part of the Clan Donald whose roots go back through Northern Ireland and Scotland. The stories coming from the misty past of Scottish history are no doubt a mixture of fact and fiction, but they sound good to the ears of the MacDonald clan. From the annals it is not difficult to gain the impression that they were possessed of immense force of character, considerable leadership talent, great energy, and ambition, combined with a large measure of political sagacity and prudence! One would like to think so. However, its members do not seem to have been endowed with excessive modesty or given to understatement.

Some of the Scots came directly to America, but our particular MacDonald line came by way of Northern Ireland to Maryland and Virginia in the 1730s. As they made their way up the river valleys of Pennsylvania, they purchased land from the Indians. Their rights were later disputed by William Penn's heirs, who tracked them down, evicted them, and burned their houses (1743). They then bought land from John Penn, Jr., and settled in Huntingdon County, Pennsylvania along the Juniata River.

Thus we find our more immediate ancestor, Moses Donaldson, in the Pennsylvania wilderness. His first wife and two of his three children were killed in 1778 in a British-inspired Indian raid. He married again and lived in Huntingdon, where he seems to have been a prominent citizen and an elder in the Presbyterian church. His surviving son moved to Ohio to live and die in Richland County. From this family came my great-grandmother, Rebecca Donaldson, who was born in 1816 and died in 1904.

Our more immediate forebear was William Mathews. He arrived from Northern Ireland before the Revolutionary War and went to Washington County, Pennsylvania. In 1776 he enlisted at Pittsburgh in the 8th Pennsylvania Regiment of the Continental Army and served under Washington for three years. After his military service he became one of the earliest pioneers of Trumbull County, Ohio. He carried the designation of "Deacon." He received a Revolutionary War pension in the 1820s amounting to eight dollars a month! His earthly possessions were few, as an inventory recorded late in life reveals. He had a son, William Jr., who was the first Presbyterian missionary sent to the Wyandot Indians in Upper Sandusky, Ohio.

Another son, Isaac, settled with his wife, Nancy Hamilton, near the Scioto Marsh in Hardin County, northwestern Ohio. The area was then heavily wooded. Game was abundant so meat was plentiful. Occasionally bears, wolves, and wildcats were noted. Friendly Indians roamed the region. Isaac and Nancy Hamilton Mathews were ardent Presbyterians of true pioneer stock. They had ten children, among them the father of Jonathan Mathews, my great-grandfather and husband of Rebecca Donaldson. While Presbyterian preachers were in short supply, Methodist circuit riders led a great revival in which my ancestors were soundly converted. They helped found Methodist Episcopal churches in Huntersville and nearby Ada.

Naturally, I have not told the whole story, only something about my paternal line. My mother was a Wilson. Her forebears also came from Ulster, apparently during the late 1700s. My mother's father, Hugh Wilson, was born in Sunbury, Ohio, in 1836. His grandmother was a Cadwallader from the vicinity of Philadelphia. My grandfather and his brothers were big and powerful men. He married Mary Ellen Algire (German or Dutch descent) of Marysville, Ohio. She was the only grandparent I ever saw. They lived in Delphos, Ohio, where my mother and her siblings were born. Hugh Wilson was a maker of staves and barrels. He was strong of limb, a man to be reckoned with. He was one of Lincoln's first 75,000 volunteers and served throughout the Civil War in the 25th Ohio Volunteer Infantry and one year beyond on garrison duty in the South. Twice he was wounded in the conflict, once at Gettysburg. Wartime deprivations undermined his health and undoubtedly contributed to his fairly early death. During the last two years of his life he was blind, the result of severe diabetes, from which he died in 1887.

My father's father, Joseph by name, was also blind as it happened. In 1860 he too volunteered for the Union Army. He was a Second Lieutenant in the 135th Regiment of the Ohio National Guard. During a battle on a hot day he jumped over a small stream but tripped on his sword. He was pitched onto stubble, which put out one eye. Developing sympathetic ophthalmia, he subsequently lost the sight of his other eye. He could no longer practice as a pharmacist, but he did own a drugstore and also farmed.

My Parents

It is frequently observed that one form of immortality is this: parents continue to occupy a vital role in one's thoughts. This has certainly been true in my experience and in the experience of my brothers and sisters. It has been particularly lively with regard to my father. Both of my parents, however, are present daily in my mind, and thus I join with William Faulkner in observing that for me "the past is not dead; it is not even past." We called them Mama and Papa and would have thought it stilted to address them more formally.

My father was a kind of walking genealogical table. He used to refer constantly to such ancestors as I have mentioned as if they were present—this reaching back several generations. My mother could do much the same. I wish now that I had paid fuller attention to their recollections.

James Davenport Mathews, my father, was born at Huntersville, Ohio, on November 16, 1869, the same year that Mahatma Gandhi was born. Huntersville was a tiny settlement established mostly by various branches of the Mathews family. The small cemetery there is filled with my ancestors' graves.

Papa was born in a log cabin. When we were boys he took us once to his birthplace. There were still a few logs lying around. We were deeply impressed. We used to joke about why he did not go from this log cabin to the White House, as American lore would suggest!

Soon after his birth, his mother, Margaret Davenport Mathews, died of what was called childbirth fever. It always seemed to me that Papa somehow blamed himself for his mother's death, occasioned by his birth. Those were insensitive days, and I gather that some family members also blamed him for this. He was deeply scarred by this circumstance.

In 1871 my grandfather married a second time to a woman named Rosa Sparks, referred to as Aunt Rosie. She proved to be a shrew and a tyrannical stepmother after the classic mode, relentlessly abusing her two stepsons and my father in particular. On one occasion she threw a block of wood at Papa, knocking him unconscious. The abuse became so pronounced that the brothers ran away, making their way to Iowa to live for a period with an aunt. Later, they bummed their way by freight train back to Ada, Ohio, where they lived with their grandmother, the saintly Rebecca Donaldson Mathews. She was very kindly and, doubtless, overly indulgent.

Meanwhile, Aunt Rosie deserted her husband after taking advantage of his blindness and relieving him of most of his assets. The wonder is that Papa was not traumatized more than he was by these experiences.

Papa apparently had an adventuresome youth. During one period he raced on the old-fashioned bicycle—with big wheel in front and the little wheel behind. He came to be quite proficient at this sport, though he suffered a concussion from one accident. It was a dangerous diversion.

He and his elder brother, Finley, went through a period of being what were called dandies. They showed up one time during pre-game practice on the playing field of one of the Chicago big-league baseball teams, my father wearing a brown derby. One of the players hit a fly ball, which landed on and caved in the top of the derby. This did not dampen his ardor for baseball, and he instructed his sons in some of the refinements of the sport.

There is more than a suggestion that for a time Papa lived a little on the wild side. But then as a teenager he had what he called an educational "awakening" after which he displayed a great knack for learning and excellence. Later still, he had a striking religious conversion, which must have surprised the community and pleased his grandmother immensely.

Papa excelled in English and mathematics. At what was called "mental arithmetic" he was nothing less than a marvel. He could compute the most abstruse problems in his head and endeavored to train his children in the same discipline, although it never really "took" with us.

He loved grammar and rhetoric, an interest that he pursued until the very end of his life.

He was far better educated than most of his contemporaries. For example, one of the Ohio congressmen determined to make appointments to the United States Military Academy based on a statewide competition. As a Civil War veteran, Papa's father insisted on his sitting for the examination, although Papa had no particular interest in the military. He came out first and received an appointment to West Point. This was in the late 1880s.

He used to talk about his experience at the academy. For the "plebes"—the first year students—there was some mild hazing. For instance, upper classmen could call a plebe to attention at any time or place. They were asked to mark time in place and to "fin out," which meant they were to assume a fish-like posture and look generally stupid. Then they would be questioned about their names, place of origin, and "previous condition of servitude." The academic standards were demanding, the socializing pleasant, the discipline strict.

Papa liked the higher math he was exposed to. But he did not like the severe discipline of West Point and resigned after a year. Late in life he did attend class reunions and was well treated by his erstwhile classmates, most of whom by that time were high officers in the army.

He continued his higher education and was graduated from Ohio Northern University in Ada. Later he did postgraduate work at Taylor University, Upland, Indiana, and at Valparaiso University, also in Indiana, which is now an institution of the Missouri Synod Lutheran Church. Papa did not go to seminary. Rather he took an annual conference ministerial reading course; but he had about the equivalent of a master's degree level of training, unusual for his period.

Having stressed my father's intellectual endowments and training, the fact remains that professionally he never really "came off," as we might say. Why this was so mystified his children. Now it is clear to us that he suffered from severe, debilitating, and recurring episodes of depression that nowadays, alas, can be controlled by rather simple medical means.

He did not continue in the ministry, for his health broke. The doctors advised that he seek outdoors work. He eventually became a conductor on the railway, which was respectable but beneath his abilities. He must have thought himself a failure. I could never bring myself to talk to my father about this, but I think he must have suffered considerable inner hurt by the realization that he had somehow not made the fullest use of his abilities and did not attain success as this world might count it. On the other hand, if one casts aside conventional values, he did instill a great deal into his children, and maybe in some final reckoning that might count more than what this world would consider to be important, or successful.

In 1899 while still a college student in Ada, Papa married a young woman who, tragically, died a short time later. This was devastating for him. After two years J. D. Mathews began noticing another young woman who was also studying at Ohio Northern University while she worked in a boarding house for students kept by her sister and husband, the Rev. Franklin and Ida Ernsberger. On October 1, 1902, my parents were married.

Laura Mae Wilson was born in Delphos, Ohio, a town located on the Ohio–Lake Erie Canal. Mama was devoted to her father and deeply mourned his death, which occurred when she was nine years old. She had two sisters and two brothers, and the family was close, but they lived on a Civil War widow's pension together with such small additional income as could then be mustered. They must have felt the financial pinch considerably. Mama referred to having one Sunday dress and one school dress, which often had to be washed and ironed overnight. Yet there was family pride and she greatly prized her relatives.

Pictures of my mother as a young woman show her as attractive in every way. She had sharp features, dark hair, and a good figure. She was gifted as a musician, well trained in piano, and possessed of a lovely soprano voice. She studied music at Ohio Northern and attained about the equivalent of a junior college education. She had many beaux. One later became a very prominent American churchman. She might have had an easier life if she had gone in that direction. But again, in that event, I would not be penning these words now.

Mama was a strong, stable person, in many respects a truly remarkable woman. Endowed with an affectionate nature, she showered love upon her considerable brood. She did not need to be reminded to "hug her children," as seems necessary nowadays; for her, that came naturally. She was a peacemaker on occasion and always a good manager. How she could make ends meet on a small income, I shall never know. She could cook, sew, bake, make do, and do without. She made her own dresses and her daughters' too, as well as her boys' clothing when we were young. She cut her sons' and husband's hair. Indeed, she filled all the domestic roles to perfection. She was not a gourmet cook, but her noodles, dumplings, and creamed veal, as well as her cherry pie and bread had to be tasted to be believed.

Sometimes Mama fell ill. We believe she had to—to get some rest! Her contributions to her children were great in every way. So far as I am aware she played no favorites with her children, but gave them all about equal attention according to their particular need.

Mama had a good sense of humor and loved a good story—for hearing or telling. If there were an amusing side to a happening our mother was sure to find it. She was reared that way, for her sisters and brothers showed this characteristic and were each possessed of a hearty laugh. They laughed until the tears came!

She also liked to read and did a great deal of it, mostly fiction or magazine articles. She read aloud to us, which was something we kids could never get enough of. She was an excellent conversationalist and raconteur; things were lively when she was around. She never lacked for friends and seemed to cultivate them easily. She was a good mom, and other neighborhood children liked us to share her with them. This she did not seem to find onerous.

Papa's humor was more reserved and subtle. He was a master of timing and delighted in straight-faced over-statement or understatement for effect. He liked what in quiet fashion he called a pleasantry, but did not extend to so-called practical jokes. In mentioning this dimension of living I am not suggesting that success in marriage depends solely upon good humor, but it helps. It also depends on shared interests, similar cultural traditions, mutual understanding and respect, and I think upon God's goodness. Then, I would observe that every member of our family has had a rich endowment of humor and our life together has been marked by considerable merriment. That continues among our descendants; our gatherings have often been hilarious occasions. There is much to be said for the lighter side of life.

My Family

The book of Psalms reminds us that God places "the solitary in families" (Ps. 68:6 KJV). This is evidently true and advantageous in every way. A dreadful toll is often exacted when this is not the case. On this score I am exceedingly grateful. Ours has been a good family.

We were eight children. The firstborn was Daisy, who died a few days after her birth. Nevertheless, Daisy continued to be very much a part of our family, though not in a grim sense; she was simply there.

Then came Margaret, Mary Margaret to be exact. She took her role as eldest almost too seriously, as a sort of surrogate mother to the rest of us. The longer she lived the more extensive, in her mind, became the part she played in the rearing of the rest of us. She acted as a kind of inspector general, especially with her brothers. Margaret had a rather good soprano voice that she cultivated.

She had strong convictions, which she readily expressed, a real human touch, and a unique sense of humor.

The next sister was Elizabeth. She was born in Whitehall, Wisconsin, where our father was pastor at the time. She had a wonderful disposition as a child and became a really splendid woman. Making close friends seemed easy for her, and her girlfriends became like sisters to her younger brothers. She had a sweet voice, a lighter soprano than Margaret had. They often sang together, took part in choirs and choral groups, sang in cantatas and operettas. Elizabeth was a good student. Like Papa, she was graduated from Ohio Northern University and before marriage was a high school teacher. In a later age she could have excelled in management. She lived nearby us as our own children were growing up. They recall her as the very model of an aunt. She died much too young of cancer.

The firstborn son was Donald, whom we called Don. Don had real gifts of tenderness. Physical fitness seemed to come naturally to him, but life itself was not easy for him. He was bright enough, but he did not like school nor did he excel in academic matters. He did have one year of college training, after which he married and went into business: real estate, insurance, filling stations, and the management of a small hotel. Blessed with a loving wife, he had a good family and lived comfortably. Yet he could not handle alcohol well, and in his mid-fifties he died of cirrhosis of the liver.

Then came Joe—Joseph Wesley. I was closest to him in age and closest also in spirit. Of him I shall have considerably more to say later. Joe was smaller in stature than either Don or I, but he was also sterner in spirit than either one of us. He too was sensitive but in a quite different way than Don was. Joe was a natural and acknowledged leader; he forged ahead in any organization of which he was a part. He was also a born actor. He was a good student, but had his educational awakening a little later than I did. He was an athlete too, but not as natural a one as Don was.

Joe and I, of course, ended up in the ministry. In fact we trained together for much of the time and often in the beginning carried out our ministry together. He began his formal ministry in this country—in a fairly conventional way. Since I was by that time in India, he had to shoulder family burdens that I escaped. His work was soon interrupted by World War II, in which he enlisted and served as a chaplain. He went through exceedingly fierce action in a succession of battles in the South Pacific. This experience changed his whole life course. After the war, the GI Bill and a devoted wife made possible his theological study in Yale. To this pursuit he was able to give undivided attention. He became a disciplined scholar and later a superb teacher. Finally, his leadership in the church renewal movement was almost without parallel, and for this he is well remembered throughout the United States and across the globe. Unfortunately he was a very heavy smoker. It is my belief that this habit prematurely hastened his death.

Then came I. We three brothers were separated in age overall by only three and a half years, so we were close. Don, Joe, and Ken Mathews attracted attention wherever we went. We played together, worked together, studied together. In World War II we all served in the military: Don in the navy, and Joe and I in the army.

For seven years I was the "baby boy"; this reign ended March 6, 1920, with the birth of my sister Alice Louise. We awoke that cold morning to the surprising news that we had a new baby sister. My father arrived in Ada, Ohio, by train about noon that day. We three brothers met him at the station and apprised him of this happy development, supposing he would be as much taken by surprise as we were.

Alice was a beautiful child. She was a quite serious girl, a good sport and playmate. Her brothers delighted in "furthering" her education, a role for which we thought we were superbly fitted by our more advanced years and experience. She did not always accept this kindly.

She showed particular aptitude in speech and theater. She could have become a fine actress, I think. At about midstream she earned a master's degree and became a teacher of high school English, at which she highly excelled. Alice taught not just a subject; she taught students to prize the demands of authentic personhood.

It cannot always be an easy experience to be the last child of a large family. That lot fell to Virginia Alleene (we called her Alleene). She too was a surprise to me, for at that time young children were not informed of such coming events, and their powers of observation noticed no revealing changes in their mother's contour. She was a pretty child with blondish hair. In many ways she was the most sensitive of all of us. No wonder she became an artist—and a gifted one at that. Her paintings delve into the depths of the human experience.

A great deal is made nowadays of sibling rivalry. Intense competition for parental approval does not linger in my mind as a serious problem among us. Mama was skilled in equitably sharing her affection. She seemed able to engender in each one of us a sense of being "special" to her without appearing to be partial.

One is astonished at the individual differences that are manifested among siblings, all of whom share the same heredity and are shaped by the same environment. A part of this must be in the mystery of individual response to these givens. Some would say that brothers and sisters do not grow up in the *same* family; it constantly changes. This could be understood as significantly true in our case, where sixteen years separated the eldest from the youngest. The mood or style of a family can change with this expanse of time. Or perhaps the difference lies in varying perceptions at separate stages. In any event, siblings share an immense store of common experience, possibly more than that which accrues even between spouses. The fact is that sibling rivalry in our experience was not notably destructive; we managed a full measure of mutual sharing and help.

Our family of ten were all together only *once*. It must have been in the summer of 1924 when we went on pilgrimage to Dresden, Ohio, where our firstborn sister, Daisy, was buried. It was for us a highly meaningful moment when we, the living, gathered around a grave marker at the foot of a tree of modest size.

I did not see that little grave again until I was about sixty years old! Nearly fifty years had passed. During the intervening years the tree had grown to about two feet in diameter, but I was able to recall the location of the grave and walked directly to it. I raked off the leaves to reveal the little stone and on it the one word, "Daisy." It was an awesome moment.

It occurred to me that by that time there were only three people in the world who could remember that single time our family was together. The time would come when there would be nobody who cared a thing in the world about that little grave. I know that this is a sentimental story, but I told it to my colleague, the late Bishop Fred Holloway, soon after it occurred. When I said that the time would come when no one would care, he corrected me and said, "No, there will still be One who cares and cares eternally," which was a lesson both in family solidarity and of the everlasting love of God.

I visited the cemetery again in 1993. I was alone. Once more I found the tree and the grave and the marker. But the letters marking Daisy's tombstone had weathered away.

There was a family portrait taken in front of the parsonage of our parents and their then five children. Margaret and Elizabeth wore their hair with braids hanging down to the shoulder and tied on either side by hair ribbons. We all look well scrubbed and well turned out. It reveals that I was not facing the camera but was gazing over my shoulder in admiring fashion at the rest of the family—my support group.

Papa owned a horse and buggy while he was a rural pastor. The horse, a mare named Nellie, was chestnut colored and had a gentle disposition. We five kids would mount or be placed on Nellie's back. I was at her neck, followed by Joe, then Don, then Elizabeth, and then Margaret. We must have made quite a sight as Nellie was led down to a nice stream behind our house for watering.

In the summers we would play in that shallow stream under the watchful eyes of our parents. The little town was a most pleasant place to live, and I feel good just thinking about it. I can recall my father preaching in the pulpit and remember vaguely his conducting a funeral. We delighted in seeing him hitch Nellie and go out to perform his pastoral duties. We did not, however, live there long.

We moved frequently; first to nearby Wellsville, Ohio, then to Upper Sandusky, then to Ada, where my father had grown up. Why these moves? First of all, Papa was an itinerant preacher—subject to frequent moves—after the Methodist Episcopal manner. Then his health deteriorated, and doctors recommended outside work. For a time he worked as a salesman. Finally, during World War I, since he was too old to serve in the army, he was employed by the Pennsylvania Railroad, where he worked, interrupted by periodic illness, until his retirement.

Vital religious practice was encouraged and cultivated in our family, especially during our younger years. We were brought up in the fear of the Lord, yet ours was not a home of stifling spirituality. Some of my earliest memories are about family prayer, which we devoted ourselves to consistently.

In those days houses usually had what we might call living rooms or family rooms and there was a parlor, which often was set off from the rest of the house by sliding doors. This room was equipped with our best furniture. The parlor was set apart for special times such as entertaining guests. It is rather pleasing to be able to recall that when we had family prayer, we went to the parlor. My father usually would read the Scriptures. Sometimes my mother or Papa would recite from the Bible. He liked Proverbs 4:18: "the path of the righteous is as a shining light, that shineth more and more unto the perfect day." Or 2 Corinthians 5:1—"For we know that, if our earthly house of this tabernacle were dissolved, we have a building of God, a house not made with hands, eternal in the heavens." All of us had a part, and after general intercession we would close with the Lord's Prayer.

I remember one time my father was in a hurry and did not read the Bible but went directly into prayer. It is still very vivid to me. I began snickering and laughing during the solemnities. I must have been about three years old at the time. At the completion of prayer, I was rebuked somewhat and questioned, "What's wrong, Kenny?" My reply: "Well, that was a funny one, without any Bible to it!" I have thought of that many times through the years. Such a short-circuiting did not seem acceptable to me. We try to do the work of the church and it is kind of funny: often there is not enough Bible to it!

Then we would gather around Mama and sing as she played the piano. She liked old-fashioned songs, which were of late nineteenth- and early-twentieth century vintage. We also liked Civil War songs and some of the more lighthearted music of the First World War and following. Most of these we knew by heart. The same was true of hymns. Charles Wesley's were favorites. My father enjoyed Cowper's "God Moves in a Mysterious Way," while I insisted on "The Little Brown Church" or "O, For a Thousand Tongues to Sing." Sometimes as we sang, Papa would get "happy." (If I have to explain that, you probably would not get it anyway.) I should say that Papa "could not carry a tune in a basket." Neither could brother Joe. The rest of us had better voices, but regardless of quality we all sang lustily and enjoyed ourselves immensely.

Our mealtimes frequently were celebrations. When Papa was present he would often deliberately direct the conversation in a useful direction. Both parents enforced strict manners. We were never allowed to sing at the table, nor were we ever to speak disparagingly of anyone. No racial or ethnic slur was acceptable, so almost never were derogatory terms voiced even indirectly. Profanity was, of course, proscribed—even the mildest expletives. Nor was slang tolerated. Moreover, mispronounced words or mistakes in grammar were immediately corrected. During the last conversation I had with my father—he was then nearly ninety-two—he corrected my use of the term "eleemosynary." In token of this tendency I note that Papa inscribed a book of grammar to us with these words: "May 1, 1949. Presented to James Kenneth Mathews and Eunice Jones Mathews, trusting that they and their children become users of the English language that need not be ashamed." When on rare occasions I happened to be in homes of friends where these practices were not followed, I was deeply shocked and was glad to be home again. I do not regard myself to have been at all hampered by our family restrictions.

Of course, the Sabbath was carefully observed. Until rather late in our family experience, we were not allowed to read a Sunday newspaper. Playing cards were never allowed in the house. We were, however, allowed on Sundays to play "Bible cards." These involved biblical questions and answers, which seemed to concentrate on the various kings of Israel and Judah. So far as I know no harm ever resulted from this modest pastime.

We managed to enjoy life in simpler days. It is remarkable how little one misses what had not yet been invented. This meant that we often devised our own games and needed little or no equipment. Then, of course, in a large family one never lacks playmates.

In fact, a big family is fun. There is no better training ground for the wider society. It allows free social development in a more or less controlled environment and is a school that prepares us for effective living and working with others.

Papa always encouraged solidarity among us. Very often he would tell the moral tale from McGuffey's reader—about a large family in which *dissension* ran rampant. The father asked each of his sons to give him a stick. He demonstrated how individually the sticks could easily be broken; but when bound together they were unbreakable! Mama too had cautionary advice. Typically, she would say, "Look the devil in the eye, and he will disappear!"

Christmas among us was celebrated modestly. While honoring its religious significance, presents were not frivolous, but emphasized the practical and the necessary—for economy's sake. Mama had a very special Christmas morning song that she would invariably sing to open the happy day. I can hear it still.

We were, I suppose, poor; yet, as Dwight Eisenhower said of his own family, "We didn't know it." When this is so, families do not become captives of poverty: the very smell of poverty does not attach to them. In fact, they could experience themselves as rich, as in many ways we were. We had good breeding, a cohesive family life, pride, self-respect, adequate housing, clothes and food, and many cultural advantages. We were well regarded in the community. Is all this not a form of riches? Moreover, most of our neighbors must have been rather poor too.

In the beginning of this chapter I gave short pen portraits of my sisters and brothers. I realize that I have said very little directly about myself, except as I participated in the family life I have described. Perhaps a little about me is now in order.

I am named after my father. How I came to be called Kenneth instead of James I have no idea. Frankly, I have never liked the name Kenneth, but I did like to be called Ken or Kenny, as I was during my early years. My mother used to try to reassure me by saying that Kenneth was an Anglo-Saxon name that meant "leader." While that did have a nice ring to it, it did not console me very much. When I went away to college I began signing my name *J. K. Mathews*. Then, my friends would call me "J. K." I knew to whom they were referring but did not really like that very much either. Later, in India, I started signing my name *James K. Mathews*. Then, of course, I became Jim, and that has stuck pretty much ever since. But when I would go home, it was still Ken or Kenny.

Meanwhile, as parents will, Mama and Papa called me Kenneth, to which I answered readily. Sometimes when I was guilty of an offense, my mother would address me rather directly and specifically, "James Kenneth Mathews!"—the full treatment! There are probably few others who have that exact name. This was a summons; this meant me! Years later my wife adopted this same unhappy practice, addressing me with my full name, stripped of all affectionate usages and titles. She still means me.

I was a shy child, and even today a measure of shyness is a part of me. I felt close to my mother. Mine was always an affectionate nature, and perhaps I got this from her. As I have said, Mama did not play favorites and had the knack of making each of her children feel special. As the youngest for seven years I was often home alone with her. She liked to have me brush her hair. This helped especially when she had what she called a "sick headache." She managed to see to it that each child's particular tastes were attended to. I was very picky about food; the list of my dislikes was long. Through the years I have overcome most of my dislikes, except for liver.

I do not recall either of my parents ever urging me to enter the ministry. Probably they did not want to be seen as having over-persuaded me. Yet years later, after I had been elected bishop, my mother told me of an experience while she was pregnant with me. She sat in an upstairs room—the same room in which I was soon to be born—and looked out on the Allegheny Mountains, which surrounded her. In one of her meditational moments she dedicated me to the service of God. I was glad to hear this and to realize that God had accepted this offering. This has reminded me that, like Jeremiah, I was called while still in my mother's womb, and God possessed me long before I acknowledged it.

I am glad that I can remember my baptism, for it did not occur in infancy, but when I was three and a half years old. It was at an evening prayer service in the First Methodist Episcopal Church in Wellsville, Ohio, on September 8, 1916. There together with my brothers, Don and Joe, I received the sacrament of holy baptism and formally entered the family of God. This was to be confirmed experientially and liturgically later on.

Fully seventy years later I was driving through Wellsville and went to the church and then to the very spot where we three were set apart for the kingdom of God. It made a deep impression on me then and still does. I am glad that Christian sacraments make specific that the material touches the spiritual, as through water, bread, and wine.

There are other golden moments. How is it that they remain indelibly impressed on our memories? One summer morning when I was about five, I woke up at dawn and went out to sit on the curbstone facing the brilliant sun. To this moment I can feel its caressing rays embrace me. I was barefoot, and today I can still see the print of my feet embossed on the dusty road in front of me. Suddenly, I was overcome with the beauty of the world and with how good it was to be alive! That moment has never left me, nor have I ever doubted the validity of that small epiphany. It would not have occurred to me then to call this Presence, but I gladly do so now. I knew what creature-feeling is. From that time I was possessed of an immense longing that I now know was for God.

In many respects I have always been naive; not excessively reflective, not overly self-aware or given to deep self-analysis. The significance of events has almost always dawned on me after the fact, not in anticipation. Yet I must have been not entirely lacking in self-reflection. For instance, when I was six I wrote a small poem. The following may be more self-revealing than I know even now, a part of my early search for self-identity:

> It is I, just little I
> It is only little me.
> If little me would only try—
> How happy I would be!

I do recall a good measure of intentionality in my makeup. Also at age five I very consciously made a decision that I would never use profanity. Of course I had good training in this respect but never any insistence on it. It was my decision: profanity was not for me. And it never has been. At almost precisely the same time I made the firm decision never to smoke, and I never have. Sometimes I wish I had made other laudable decisions too, but these two stand out strong and clear. To mention such things may suggest that I have been an insufferable person, pious, "holier-than-thou." Yet I think not. I recall this to show that at a very early age firm decisions can be made.

What is it like to be Kenny? Pretty good, I should say. I have been able to live comfortably with myself. Through more than fourscore years I have looked out with these same eyes upon the world and have identified all along with the same essential person inwardly. There has been scarcely any sense of aging within. When I look out on the world and at those who live there I can affirm them "good" and know that God does too.

2

GROWING UP:
ADA, HOUSTON, AND MANSFIELD

I have always thought and still think of myself as a small-town person. I lived the first twelve years of my life in villages. Then we lived in a fairly large city, Houston, Texas. After that, we moved to a small city, Mansfield, Ohio. In sum, my small-town or country sojourn has amounted to about sixteen years. All the rest has been in cities: New York, Boston, Bombay, Karachi, Washington, D.C., Harare, Albany, New York, even a three-month stint in Jerusalem. Still, I have remained a small-town person at heart.

There is a kind of symbiosis between our dwelling places and us. Somewhere the philosopher José Ortega y Gasset states that if we would tell him the landscape in which we live, he would be able to tell us who we are. The truth of this insight has often been noted with respect to mountain people. For example, there is a striking difference in every way between Himalayan people and their counterparts on the plains of India. This is even more pronounced among island dwellers, whether in Nantucket or the South Pacific. It is observable with those who inhabit peninsulas such as the Delmarva. It is marked among plains dwellers, and in the tension between inhabitants of town versus country. Where we live makes an indelible stamp on us. For me this is especially true of my childhood years in Ada, Ohio, whence came my formation as a person, for we lived there from my fifth through my twelfth year.

I subscribe to the virtue of small towns. In them and on the rural scene generally one's outer space is immense, no matter how confined the inner space may be. The experience of time there is, or was, more leisurely—one experience at a time, in contrast to the frantic pace of urban living. In a town, life is not piled up on life. There is more space between bodies, but there is room also for deeper acquaintances and mutuality. In small towns one's experience is rooted more deeply in the past; in cities it is likely to be more future-oriented. In towns, one's close relatives are likely to be there and linkage with a more remote past is afforded by a visit to the nearby cemetery or by listening to the tales of elders. There, in little communities, foundations are laid, ideals and values shaped.

Ada, Ohio, is the home of Ohio Northern University. Let me also sing the praises of a college town. A certain cultural atmosphere permeates a college community. We kids grew up knowing the college students, some of whom were from remote corners of the world. We knew the college president, the professors, and their families. We went to school with their children. We had access to sporting events, to cultural events, to musicals, to lectures, to religious programs, and to great moments when dignitaries on occasion visited our community. To grow up in a college town is to experience the early desire to go to college one's self—to take this for granted. It was almost as if we were already enrolled in college when we were very young.

During my early childhood the most common vehicles on our streets were horses and buggies. It was an exciting event when a car drove by. My own parents never had a car but owned a succession of four horses. Nellie, to whom I have already referred, is the only one I recall—and that with affection. I've seen the evolution from that point to supersonic jets and rockets. When an occasional airplane would fly over, we kids would all run outside to glimpse the sight.

The main line of the Pennsylvania Railroad passed through Ada. Two trains a day stopped there, one each way. Gathering at the station to see the train come in was an event. More important were the trains that did not stop. In our imaginations, we could easily escape Ada on these trains, for passing "flyers," such as the *Broadway Limited,* would arrive in Chicago or New York City a few hours later.

Radio emerged also during the first decade of my life. I can still see us hovering around a crystal set listening to station KDKA, Pittsburgh. How we thrilled to hear pianist Harry Snodgrass, "King of the Ivories!" He was an inmate of a Pennsylvania penitentiary. He became so popular that the governor of Pennsylvania, in response to thousands of pleas, pardoned him.

So Ada was for us an exciting place. There we went to Sunday school, joined the Boy Scouts or Campfire Girls, marched in Memorial Day parades, celebrated the Fourth of July, attended the annual farmers' and merchants' pic-nic, and swam in Grass Run, Hog Creek, and abandoned stone quarries. We played childhood games, learned to sing lustily the high school and college songs even before we could read their texts, fought our friends and quickly made up, got into mischief, and in general, learned life by living it. We did not experience being deprived of anything.

On Sunday afternoons we took part in what was called the "Chewing Gum and Candy Club." That name—bound to be attractive to kids—was bestowed upon the club by a boy in our neighborhood, Mark Warren. He was possessed of great good humor and was the friend I most admired. The club did not have much substance about it, I suppose, but it furthered a close bonding among us.

We made our own toys and made up our own games. My brothers and I imagined ourselves cowboys. Our steeds were small wheels or hoops that we pushed along on the crossbar of a T-stick. It was great fun, and we rode our "horses" everywhere. We would stage dramas in the haymows of barns that were a part of almost every residential property. I recall a brief selection from one of Shakespeare's plays in which my brother Don excelled as an "actor."

Every summer roving theatrical groups would come to Ada. In those days there were still "Tom Shows," which put on *Uncle Tom's Cabin*. The Shannon Shows would present melodramas and, on the lighter side, was the Kinsey Komedy Kompany. More serious was the annual Chautauqua, which brought us variety music, famous lecturers, and drama. These were tent shows, and we kids would help put up and dismantle the tents in exchange for free admission. They also had a children's program. During one of these I was chosen "mayor of Junior Town"—my first and only venture into elective office!

Years later when I was in India, I was impressed by what is called the Hindu undivided family, in which the grandparents, parents, and families of male descendants all lived together or in close proximity. They even paid income taxes as one entity. The Muslims had a similar tradition. It has occurred to me that we were not simply a nuclear family. Some vestiges of the extended family were present with us. It was a very positive arrangement.

I have referred to the one grandparent I ever saw, Grandma Wilson, my mother's mother. She was the very picture of what a grandmother should look like. She filled this role to perfection, and it was a great experience to visit her. During her last months she lived with us and died in our house—my first experience with death.

There were aunts and uncles for whom I had a particular affection. In my view, important parts of our training are not parental but avuncular. These relatives love you yet do not exercise the same restraint upon you as a parent does. A child might rebel against a father or mother, but not against an uncle or aunt. Something is lost in a society when at least some relatives do not live in our household or nearby.

An example of this stands out in my experience. My favorite uncle and aunt, Frank and Ida Ernsberger, lived about half a mile from us. Aunt Ida was a renowned cook, a reputation she richly deserved. She and my mother baked their own bread (I can smell it now) but on alternate days. When I was four or five, my job was to carry the "starter" (yeast) in a mason jar between our homes. It added greatly to my feeling of importance and had certain fringe benefits as well. Aunt Ida had not only mason jars but a cookie jar too.

Then there were Aunt Em (my mother's sister, Emma) and Uncle Tom Mullins. Aunt Em too was a great cook. Our fascination with Uncle Tom was that he was a broom-maker, a kind of one-man industry. We loved to see him at work—for children, it was a great spectator sport. Then there was Aunt Marie, a widow and a Roman Catholic, and Aunt Frances and Uncle Cliffie Wilson. Of course, uncles and aunts also meant cousins, and cousins meant kids, and kids meant family reunions and fun. All this meant that life was for living.

Speaking of cousins, I refer to three of them in particular: Dale, Paul, and Lloyd Ernsberger. They were all older than me and my siblings. All three were officers in the First World War, though only one went to France. We were fascinated with his letters home to our aunt and uncle. Dale was a captain who served for months on the Western Front. He was wounded and gassed in the conflict. These three cousins were our idols. We recall also the frequent troop trains that passed through town. The soldiers would throw hard tack out of the windows to the kids. It really was hard—and inedible. Then came peace. Armistice Day was celebrated twice; a false armistice was announced about a week before November 11, 1918.

This same Ernsberger family had India connections. Several members were missionaries there, and I even met one of them who was retiring from service the very year I arrived in Bombay. Earlier on furlough she gave my brothers and me a little bull carved out of black stone. Long afterward I realized this was Nandi, the animal associated with worship of Shiva.

We got to know nearly everyone in town. The mayor

was a familiar figure, so was the town constable. There was only one. We knew the merchants, lawyers, preachers, druggists, grocers, and doctors also. Our doctor was named Neiswander, and he was a splendid physician— young, vigorous, and caring. As a family doctor he made house calls, of course. He dispensed medicines directly, not ordinarily through prescriptions. His very presence was therapeutic. He did minor surgery in his office with the help of a nurse. On one day in rapid succession he removed the adenoids and tonsils from me and from my two brothers and two sisters. Then he drove us all home, where we recuperated.

This doctor was one who inspired in me the desire to become a surgeon, a vision I maintained for a number of years. He wore himself out in devoted healing service to the community. He was one of those people to whom the Bible refers when it mentions persons "of whom the world is not worthy." It is a pleasure to recall him.

Now I must mention a little of my educational odyssey. There was no kindergarten in Ada, and I felt frustrated in the delay. How eager I was to start school! How neglected I felt when I saw my brothers and sisters leave for school without me. But my turn finally came.

We walked to school. This happy practice continued through high school. There were no school buses and no student had a car. Often we walked four miles a day. It was good exercise. We carried our lunch, or when times were tough we went without lunch. Very often I would walk to or from school alone. I recall that as I did so I often engaged in highly vivid daydreaming. For example, I dwelt repeatedly on the possibility of transmitting electric power wirelessly over great distances. Of course, this soon became technologically possible. As far as I know, I suffered no harmful results from my flights of fantasy.

Once in New England I saw a bumper sticker that read: "If you can read this, thank a teacher." Immediately I tested myself. I could name all of my elementary teachers and was grateful for them. I loved them all; indeed, I was secretly "in love" with some of the younger and prettier ones. They were all women. The school superintendents and principals were kindly in my experience. It was a delight later in life to be asked to send greetings to one teacher and one principal when they celebrated their one-hundredth birthday.

As I remember, I did fairly well as a student. During the first years I was not very much aware of this. I simply did the work and did not think much more about it. Then in the third grade a remarkable thing happened. My elder brother Don, then in the sixth grade, for some unknown reason showed enough fraternal interest in my welfare to visit my classroom. We were engaged in some activity at the blackboard—spelling or arithmetic. Apparently I was the star pupil, invariably completing my task first. Until then I was utterly unself-conscious about this, but Don carried home the word that Kenny was excelling and was a very bright boy, a fact that had hitherto escaped my notice. Thus alerted, I determined to make the most of it.

Years later I was attendant at Don's deathbed. Life had been hard for him; he must have thought himself a failure. He looked out of his severely jaundiced countenance with haunting eyes as I was about to leave him for the last time. Then I turned back and told him this story, adding that if in any degree I was succeeding, it was largely due to him. His eyes brightened and I could tell that he was greatly pleased and comforted.

This was the beginning of my own intellectual awakening or conversion. I skipped the fourth grade. There are some social disadvantages to skipping a grade. Then, too, I missed certain elements, such as long division. I remember a wonderful teacher, Laura B. Hutchinson, who coached me for a while on this subject until I caught up— a most considerate thing for her to do. After that, throughout the rest of my schooling, I had nearly all 100's or A's with an occasional B. If I had ever gotten a C or below, I would have been heartbroken. It would have been utterly unacceptable.

Not all education was in school; it continued at home with parents and siblings. As I have noted, my father insisted on excellence. He was a born teacher and was concerned about his children. At one stage he secured a roll-up blackboard on which we were drilled on the multiplication tables, spelling, grammar, and geography. He often repeated the adage "the roots of an education are bitter but the fruits are sweet."

He would take us afield. His sons, particularly, went with him on long jaunts in the country. He taught us to swim the breast or "dog" stroke. He showed us how to collect edible mushrooms and puffballs—neither of which I have ever liked. He gathered watercress and hunted snapping turtles, for he loved turtle soup. He taught us to identify trees, flowers, and rocks. He *knew* things and imparted them to us. He did not take us hunting, however, for he detested the use of firearms.

If it is essential that parents impart sex education, then my father must be commended. At intervals he instructed us at appropriate levels in these matters and we are extremely grateful that he did, for he did so in a way that was not embarrassing to him or to us. Mama did likewise with our sisters.

Our parents believed also in corporal punishment and practiced the same. We were advised that if we were ever punished in school, we would be punished again at home. Actually neither ever happened. Mama would use a stick—a switch she called it. Moreover she would insist that we choose the instrument of our reproof. We would usually return with a mere twig. Sent out again, we would bring a club. By this time she would be so amused that when the proper-sized implement was found, her ire had subsided and the outcome did not amount to much. If our shortcomings were judged of sufficient magnitude, Papa would administer reproof with a belt or razor strop that would sometimes leave small welts. Yet we would never have dreamed of thinking we were suffering from child abuse. Reciprocal love would soon assert itself and all was set right again.

Let me turn now to a little more on my faith journey. I like this particular metaphor: the journey still continues. John Calvin used to say that all their lives Christians go to school to Jesus Christ. I concur entirely. We are not born Christians. We are led along the way as a part of the community of faith.

Sunday school attendance was insisted upon. I should like to acknowledge a debt to my teachers, some of whose faces come to mind at this moment. One was Mrs.

McDowell, who was our Sunday school superintendent. She continues to be for me the image of a saint. Another is a teacher named Ben Smith, son of the president of Ohio Northern University, and later himself a preacher. Others were a Mr. Henderson and a Mr. Kramer. These and many others I hold in honored memory.

We all went to Sunday school and church every Sunday. We had no car, so we walked to the church. Alice and Alleene, who by now had entered the family, would lead the procession, followed by me, usually walking alone. Then came Don and Joe, Margaret and Elizabeth, and finally our parents. It did not create any remarkable sensation, because other families did the same thing.

I also can recall when I was about six years old going to a series of meetings, what we would call revival meetings. I would wander off by myself to these, and even at that age I was greatly impressed and moved by what I heard. I noticed that my elder brother, Don, who was three or four years older than I was, would also go, but he too would go off on his own. We would not go together. In a sense I don't think he wanted to be seen as interested. But he was and one time he very visibly responded to the messages by going forward to the altar when invited to commitment.

A time or two at a very early age we also went to camp meetings with our parents, and at a later stage we attended some on our own. The church had a great meaning to me throughout my life. We were brought up in the life of the church. I would have to date anything like a conversion experience later on.

Privately, I would say my prayers daily before retiring.

They were rather perfunctory and narrowly focused, but earnest in spite of all. Some people would aver that only the committed, "born again" Christian's prayers are heard. Surely this is nonsense. God hears the searching and pleading of even the most wayward person, and in the economy of God no one is left out.

Already I have mentioned that in a college town the growing child does not lack for entertainment. Much of this was available free of charge. Liberal arts colleges in those days had what were called literary societies. They were like nonresidential sororities or fraternities without the Greek letters. Every Friday evening they would meet to put on an entertainment, such as a recitation, monologue, or musical recital. Sometimes they held intercollegiate debates. One learned the rules of debate so that years later in college it was relatively easy to undertake this form of public speaking.

Ada afforded one small movie theater, and we often attended the Saturday afternoon matinees. Admission cost was ten cents. You could get a lot of entertainment for a dime in those days. In addition to the feature film, there was a newsreel, a comedy, coming attractions, and above all, the serial. These were about one-half hour episodes of some very exciting continuing dramas. They had the annoying characteristic of ending abruptly at the most exciting and perilous moment. They were real cliff-hangers. Of course, this was calculated to woo the viewer back the following Saturday. The leading ladies were beautiful, and I remember two quite well: Pearl White in *Plunder* and Ruth Roland in *The White Knight*. Tom Mix was in those days every boy's hero, a real cowboy. Like all boys my brothers and I enjoyed westerns—then called "cow-boy movies." These we regarded as necessary training for our intended life-time vocations as cowboys, for we were certain that at age twenty-one or thereabouts we would transport ourselves to Colorado and enter this exciting and dangerous field of endeavor.

Years later in 1981 I did become a cowboy for a day, not in Colorado but Wyoming. My wife, Eunice, had a college friend who was married to a cowboy. We went there for a visit. There must have been anxiety on the part of us all as we anticipated our meeting. What was the cowboy Ernie to do with a bishop? And what was I, a bishop, to do with a cowboy? As it transpired, everything worked out; we all enjoyed one another immensely. I was invited to join about twenty cowhands in branding five hundred head of cattle. I became able to throw young steers with the best of them. This necessitated getting right down there in the dirt, manure and all. So, you see, my basic training at Saturday matinee westerns paid off after all.

As it happened our father enjoyed westerns too, but none so much as one of Zane Grey's features, *The Last of the Duanes,* to which we were taken. It had all the neces-sary ingredients: the hero, "Buck" Duane—a good guy, a beautiful heroine, a community at peril, saloons, people "dying with their boots on"—everything was right there. For years afterwards we three boys vied for the honor of being called "Buck." At that time none of us, probably including Papa, grasped the theological significance of a cowboy movie, so well portrayed much later by Gary Cooper in *High Noon,* but the story of redemptive deliv-erance was somehow present in *The Last of the Duanes.*

Thus it was that from this unlikely source came help not only for my fantasy career as a cowboy but for my actual career as a shepherd.

We somehow got into college football, basketball, and baseball games free. We attended track and field events and we witnessed college and high school dramatic presentations. Our older sisters were in operettas—*The Walrus and the Carpenter,* and *The Pinafore.* As they learned the songs so did we, and the music swirls around in my mind to the present day.

So far as our family was concerned we kids would work at anything. We delivered newspapers: the *Columbus Dispatch,* the *Cleveland Plain Dealer,* the *Toledo Blade.* Our routes took us all over town. Once I was at the train station, the *Broadway Limited* made a flag stop to pick up a prominent citizen who had just attended the funeral of a former president and founder of Ohio Northern University. He was one of Ohio's senators, Frank B. Willis, a former governor of the state. He asked me for a paper. He gave me a quarter, and I duly counted out for him his twenty-two cents change, failing to hear him say, as I had hoped, "Keep the change." Nevertheless, I still cherish this brief brush with greatness.

We always had a vegetable garden, and my father schooled us in some of the mysteries of tilling the soil. We raised good green onions or scallions and peddled them door-to-door. My first really hard work was toiling in the onion fields in one of two nearby drained swamps—the Scioto or Hog Creek marshes. My brothers and sisters and our friends would be transported on early summer mornings to these expanses some five miles away. There we would crawl on our hands and knees all day long weeding onions. We were paid one dollar a day for weeding one row; two dollars for two rows; three dollars for three. It was hard, backbreaking work. We would become sunburned, and the fine black soil would cake under our fingernails until they ached. Sometimes boils would develop on our knees. Other people engaged in this work too. They were vastly underprivileged people whom we later learned were migrant laborers. All my life I have felt a strong empathy, almost kinship with them.

We were willing to work at anything, and we were seldom without small jobs. The money we earned made it possible to attend the movies, have a small amount for Sunday school collections, and have a little pocket money. Mostly our income went into the family coffers, for we all pitched in to keep our family together.

At the same time I do not wish to overstress our financial stringency. As a worker for the railroad, my father was entitled to free passes for himself and his family. Imagine a pass for two parents and seven children! We did go on some long trips together that proved to give us a distinct advantage over some of our friends. Papa also belonged to his appropriate railway union: the Order of Railway Conductors. This helped protect his job, so I also have always had a great partiality for the labor movement.

The Houston Interlude

In the early fall of 1925 I was brokenhearted for a while. We were moving from Ada and I realized how deeply I was rooted there. The painful lump in my throat is still very real to me as I experienced the breaking of ties with friends and teachers.

We moved to Houston, Texas, where my father's brother lived. He was a physician, Finley Mathews, whom we called Uncle Doc, a pleasant and affectionate man. His wife had the unusual name of Keturah. We called her Aunt Kit. She was a bit stern on the surface but had a caring nature underneath.

Houston in the mid-1920s was beginning to be a burgeoning metropolis. It was exciting to live there in those days. A ship canal had been dug from the Gulf of Mexico to Houston so that the city was becoming a seaport. Its leaders were very aggressive in business and trade. The city had a large radio station designated as KPRC, an acronym for *Kotton Port Rail Center*. It used to proclaim that this urban center was "where twenty-three railways meet the sea and ships of all nations find a friendly port." Cotton was king and oil followed close behind it. Jesse Jones and Will Clayton were prominent citizens. "Ma" Ferguson and then Dan Moody were governors of Texas.

The city boasted three major newspapers: the *Houston Post-Dispatch*, the *Houston Chronicle*, and the *Houston Press*. Experienced newsboy that I was, very soon I found a paper route for the last and some modest income. Years later Walter Cronkite told me that he worked for the same paper at the same time. Meanwhile my brother Don dropped out of school for two years and got a job as office boy in the Kirby Lumber Company. The next year Joe dropped out also and worked for the same firm. Once again we all worked to support the family. My eldest sister entered nurses' training and the second one was in senior high school.

I alone of the three brothers stayed in school for both of these years. The transfer from Ohio to Texas schools occasioned no great difficulty, and once again I excelled in my studies. The teachers were superior and I still remember some of them with great affection. One of them, with the wonderful name of Lula B. Simms, taught me music appreciation. This I liked much better than basic harmony. I never did get to the point of actually reading music. Nevertheless I had an ear for music, and having once heard a classical number I could readily identify it the next time it was played. My school was named Travis after one of the early Texas military heroes, Colonel Travis. In this new setting I related well with my schoolmates.

About midyear Travis School was closed and we were all transferred to a brand-new building named the James S. Hogg Junior High School. It was a wonderful building, well appointed in every way, with fine classrooms and library, a large assembly hall and gymnasium.

James S. Hogg had been an outstanding governor of Texas. He was reputed to have had three daughters: Ima, Ura, and Whosa. This trio may have been apocryphal but I *did* meet Miss Ima Hogg, who once spoke to our school assembly. She was a social leader and philanthropist in the city.

We learned the special songs that relate to that great state: "The Eyes of Texas Are Upon You," "Texas, Texas, Pride of the South," "The Yellow Rose of Texas," and others. These songs I can still sing with appropriate gusto.

Texas does elicit large-mindedness, and I doubtless bene-fited in this sense. In the Hogg School I first studied Latin, won a prize in this subject, and attended a statewide meeting for the winners. I studied shop also for the first and only time, making one or two small articles of furni-ture, which were around the house for some years; then they disappeared. Is it not remarkable how things simply drop out of sight?

Looking back, I sense that I was something of a leader in school during Texas days, but I was largely unaware of it at the time. For instance, there was a school drama enti-tled *Under Six Flags* in which I played the role of Sam Houston! What greater honor could have been bestowed upon an Ohio boy! My mother made me a rather authen-tic-looking costume of blue and purple cambric. Even I was impressed by this outfit.

We did have a considerable financial struggle during these two Houston years, but we made it somehow. To give some idea about our experience, we had a spell in which our food, though adequate, was monotonous. My daily job was to go to a nearby bakery early in the morn-ing to get a supply of "yesterday's bread." One had to arrive there early or it would be gone. I bought ten loaves of bread daily for five cents a loaf. Then canned tomatoes were cheap as was alphabet pasta. Thus our staple at least one meal a day was plenty of bread and alphabet soup!

The Texas years were not notable, religiously speaking. Possibly economic restriction and poor clothes had some-thing to do with it, but during those years I scarcely dark-ened the door of a church. Maybe it was religious rebellion of short duration and mild intensity. It was not rooted in any great intellectual perplexity. Why it should have occurred I have never really analyzed in depth. It must have been more family-related than inner-related. My spiritual rootage was, however, of sufficient depth that I readily sprang back to my rightful heritage. This brief wilderness wandering did not appear to have damaged me much, and I trust it did not do damage to others. Maybe there was some value in not being a practicing Christian for a while.

MANSFIELD, OHIO

In the late summer of 1927 we moved back to Ohio, this time to Mansfield. It is located almost exactly in the north central part of the state. The surrounding territory of Richland County is shaped by rolling glacial hills, marked by good farmland and prosperous agriculture. Many of my ancestors had been pioneers in the region. The city itself had a population of about 40,000 and extensive industry: a steel mill, the Ohio Brass Company, a large Westinghouse plant, a tire factory, and various foundries. It was a major commercial nexus for a large area. At one time in the 1940s it ranked as the number one small urban center in the country.

Generally the community spirit was good. It also had a considerable presence of racial and ethnic minorities. All in all, it was a good place to live. The "feel" of Mansfield was a mixture of the progressiveness that characterized Houston, with just a remnant of the small town atmosphere of Ada. It was not difficult to adjust to living there. The schools of the city were excellent. Our two younger sisters enrolled at the primary level. Joe and I were in senior high school; Don was in junior high. I have always admired Don who, although he had dropped out of school for two years, was prepared to return at a class lower than his two younger brothers. Joe had worked only for one year, so we were in the same class for the rest of high school. We studied together and this was the beginning of a collaborative relationship that was to continue for the rest of his life.

Once again I was privileged to be a part of the first classes in a brand-new school building. The facility was located in the western part of the city, about two miles from our rented home. We walked back and forth daily. Having commented on the physical benefit of this, I will now only take note of its social values. We walked usually with friends; walking together is a splendid way of bonding with one's fellows. We all had great pride in this new school, and we engaged together to carve out appropriate traditions and to develop a genuine *esprit de corps*. M.H.S., as the school was familiarly called, was blessed with an outstanding principal, Jesse L. Beers, and a number of stellar and memorable teachers.

My brother Joe and I were classmates. We began to be leaders. We both did well and had records of nearly all A's. In those days they did not have SAT tests or scores, but there was a statewide test of high school juniors. I came out well toward the top and was the representative of Mansfield High at a reception for students of high achievement held in Columbus and hosted by Ohio's governor. That sort of thing boosts one's morale and self-esteem.

It will be no surprise to anyone who knows me that I did not possess much athletic prowess, not nearly as much as my brothers did. I did, however, win a letter during my senior year in football, which was the only competitive sport for which I tried out. We had an excellent coach, Russell Murphy, who is still the talk and toast of Mansfield. He was of small stature, wiry and entirely dedicated to the sport. He had an unusual ability to inspire his charges to give their very best to football. In those years the great Notre Dame coach Knute Rockne conducted summer football seminars for high school and college coaches. Murphy always attended these and we, in turn, benefited from the very latest in techniques. We were thoroughly drilled and encouraged to master solidly the rudiments of football, and we did. To this day as I follow professional football, I engage in a lively critique of the players, though without the skill of, say, a John Madden.

There were plenty of extracurricular activities in high school. For instance, they had a first-class marching band and a good orchestra. Unfortunately, I had never mastered music nor could I play any instrument. This is a matter of great regret to me, for I have always liked good music and listen to classical renditions often. Indeed, for years as I have driven along the highways, I have "conducted," without score, as I listen to radio presentations of the great orchestras. My long-suffering wife tolerates this activity, as she does so much of my behavior. Sometimes, when my "baton" falters, I explain to her that I have not conducted the number for some time.

My extracurricular activities included public speaking

and debate. On occasion I was allowed to preside at school assemblies. One time, though all went well, I "brought down the house" when I ventured to dismiss the audience with this: "We will all now arise and *pass out!*"

Drama always interested me, but it was my brother Joe who excelled in this field. He had a real gift for histrionics and could get into character and really sway an audience. I can see him yet as he played the leading role of Captain Jack Absolute in William Brinsley Sheridan's *The Rivals.* He was a stunning figure clothed in the scarlet and crimson regimentals of a British army officer. He also played the lead in our senior class play, *Rollo's Wild Oats,* a contemporary comedy that on Broadway had starred Roland Young.

In this same play I played a minor role. Joe's prowess had doubtless spurred me on to try out. For the first time I showed what I could do in this field. I memorized a striking passage from a currently popular play, *Disraeli.* I must have done well, for my teacher, Miss Emma Waring, could not believe that so timid a person as I could actually give himself over to the part of an English prime minister. Incidentally, that experience sparked a lifelong interest in Disraeli himself. Later on I did take part in other plays, in religious drama. I even coached a drama or two and have had a considerable continuing interest in the field.

Our last year in high school (1929–30) coincided with the beginning of the Great Depression, and by the end of the school year financial stringency was becoming increasingly evident. The strain became visible among our fellow students and even teachers. Meanwhile, my brother Joe was president of the senior class. It fell to his lot to assemble a planning committee for the senior prom.

I was the master of ceremonies for this signal event. The *Disraeli* episode had largely eliminated my excessive shyness. There was I, decked for the first time in a tuxedo, armed with appropriate patter and monologue, leading the whole show. And it *did* come off. More than that, I had sufficiently overcome my reserve that I took along a date. This must have been as much a surprise to her as it was for me. The dam was broken and I finally had begun to relate to girls close up, if that is the proper term. I did not have much trouble in that respect in the years that ensued, though I never really thought of myself as a ladies' man.

Though I do not intend to enlarge much here on the religious dimension, I do recall that the wilderness years that Houston represented, spiritually speaking, came to an end. When we returned to Ohio we resumed regular church participation. There was a sequence of able pastors who reawakened our interest. One of them was Dr. Earl Brown, with whose children I went to school and followed in later life. Dr. Brown was later head of the National Division of the Methodist Board of Missions during the early years of my service as an executive in the Foreign Division. Other pastors who helped me were Edwin Corwin and Oscar Adam. There were also challenging church school teachers and inspiring youth leaders. We became thoroughly involved in church programs, and it began to make all the difference with us.

I remember that during my senior year in high school I

had three jobs simultaneously. One was work after school for two hours in a men's clothing store where I would do janitorial service and occasionally wait on customers. For these duties I received five dollars a week. Then, I sold Real Silk hosiery and lingerie. This was after the manner of the Fuller Brush man. We were given a short course in salesmanship that impressed me immensely with its psychological effectiveness. One usually sold to one's friends and relatives; I think this was the company's idea. It was a good product and I found, after a time, that I was my own best customer. This finally persuaded me that I probably did not have a great future in the business world, but it taught me that you have to be convinced by experience of the soundness of your product if you would commend it to others. This goes for religion too!

My third part-time job was later in the evening when I served as an usher in a local cinema, the Ohio Theater. I felt important in the somewhat dashing uniform I wore. From time to time my brother Joe and I alternated on this job, once again not very lucrative. We did get to see the latest films free; *Hell's Angels* comes to mind, a real thriller. It seems that I also used to let my younger sisters in free, which pleased them a great deal.

Earlier I mentioned a movie theater in Ada. At that time there were silent movies, accompanied by mood music played on a piano. Apparently the music sheets were sent out with the films themselves. It was a marvel to observe and hear the piano player at his/her art. In Mansfield talking-pictures came into vogue. The first one, I believe, was *The Jazz Singer* with Al Jolson. By this time the piano was displaced by a pipe organ, a Wurlitzer. It was a gaudy instrument that would rise out of the floor for an organ interlude. All quite impressive!

My brother Joe and I were graduated from Mansfield High School in June 1930. Neither of us went on immediately to college. For nearly another decade Mansfield was our home, though with the passing years we went there with less and less frequency. A number of times I have returned for class reunions—the most recent one was the sixty-second. Some loyal spouses attend as well. Surely, they should have some special reward for this devotion. Mansfield is one of the places I look back on with real nostalgia, although I would observe that this all-American city did not afford the overall cultural advantage of a college town like Ada.

3
Days of Preparation

Since early childhood I knew I would go to college, but when and where I did not know. Having been graduated from high school in June 1930, normally I should have entered university the following September. But those were not normal times. The Depression was on, and I had no money. Moreover, at that time even in an outstanding secondary school good educational counseling was not readily available. Looking back, I am surprised that I was not more earnest and enterprising in search of a good scholarship. Yet, once again, my father was unwell and could not help. Both my brother Joe and I decided that we must go to work for at least a year before entering college.

During that year I worked for the Bissman Company of Mansfield, wholesale grocery distributors for a large section of north central Ohio. The two of us had already worked there the summer following our junior year in high school. It was hard physical labor—unloading freight cars and stacking the commodities in a warehouse, then loading shipments on trucks for distribution to retail grocers.

A carload of sugar, for example, typically consisted of 400 or 500 one-hundred-pound bags—burlap sacks. For years the employees there had taken a day and a half to unload a car and warehouse the product. Young, strong, and innocent, we did this easily in half a day. This made us popular with management but unpopular with our fellow workers. In time this tension was diminished and they all enjoyed having silly kids around. This work is done in pairs. Two persons unloading sugar develop a kind of rhythmic, swinging motion, each grasping either end of a bag and tossing it onto a trolley and then again stacking it in the warehouse. Salt bags weighed 150 pounds and green coffee bags even more. It was burdensome toil. For this work we received $21.80 a week, which seemed a lot at the time. Things are relative: we could get a full lunch for a quarter in those days—soup, main course, and dessert.

There were unanticipated advantages in such work. For instance, it was good physical exercise. Along the way, one learned a great deal about the business. We could have engaged in any part of it, including roasting and blending coffee. We learned also how to drive large trucks—semitrailers. Backing them up into a narrow space is an art that is not easily mastered. When we drove these vehicles and delivered the goods, we came to know the countryside thoroughly and gained the acquaintance of retail merchants as well. Best of all, we profited by serving side by side with men who were a part of the labor movement.

This "lost" year was not encouraging in any social way. My best friends had gone on to college while I felt left behind and left out. We continued to be very active in the youth group of the church, where we developed some friendly ties. We also spent a good deal of time in the public library, where I read widely but particularly in the field of medicine and psychology, in which I had a continuing vocational interest. About this time also I ventured into the writer's realm. I wrote what was called a short, short story and was bold enough to submit it to *Collier's* magazine. In due course I received a rejection slip. Upon re-reading this effort recently I have concluded that the editor's judgment was sound.

There was a good drama group in our church. One rather engrossing play was titled *The Violin Maker of Cremona,* in which I played the leading role. There was also a civic Little Theater group in which Joe was deeply involved and where he developed quite a local reputation for his acting skills. Because of this, in January 1931 he set out with a high school chum to hitchhike to California with the intention of trying to get into the movies.

When he departed, once more I was left behind, but I continued with my wholesale grocery job. During late winter I suffered from an accident in which I broke my right arm. I was delivering a heavy wooden case of ginger ale to a local residence. Apparently I had snow caked on the heel of my shoe and slipped on the cellar steps. Down I tumbled with the whole weight of the box, which I was carrying on my shoulder, landing on my right elbow. It was an inconvenient fracture, slow in healing, though I managed for six weeks to cope with full use of only my left arm. During that period I went on workmen's compensation insurance, which was fifteen dollars a week, about two-thirds of my pay.

The following summer I met with another accident. I was diving from the limb of a tree into a swimming hole, in a small, murky river, and my head struck a rocky ledge.

My nose was broken and I was banged up generally. Because of the severe blow on the head I lapsed into unconsciousness some days later. I might have been killed, but was somehow spared.

Never in my whole life did I experience time dragging on in seemingly endless duration more than I did during this interlude, the year after high school. My income during that period was supposed to have been put aside for college expenses. As it happened it actually went toward family support. I did not resent this. It was just a fact of life for me. Nevertheless, I was determined to get university training somehow, somewhere. A boyhood friend of my father was chancellor of Lincoln Memorial University in Harrogate, near Cumberland Gap, Tennessee. He invited me to study there. This college was founded by Civil War General Otis O. Howard, who had also been a founder of Howard University in Washington, D.C. Just as the latter school afforded opportunity to African American students, so the former gave a chance to southern mountaineers. Legend has it that President Lincoln himself had suggested to Howard that following the war the general should establish such a school. He did so and named it for Lincoln.

One could attend Lincoln Memorial University tuition-free and work to cover all expenses, a little after the manner of Berea College in Kentucky. This appealed to me, for I arrived on campus with only one hundred dollars to my name. Thirty-three months later (for I took no school holidays) I emerged with a bachelor of arts degree and thirty dollars in hand.

It was tough going. Through that period I worked at all

manner of things for an average of four hours a day, for which I was credited with thirty cents an hour toward my expenses. Most of the other students had to do much the same. We quarried limestone, an exhausting and dirty task. We also dug ditches, did farm work, mowed lawns, scrubbed floors, made soap, washed windows, baked bread, served as butchers, made jam and apple butter, washed dishes, and waited tables (at one time or another, I did all of these). Finally, I attained the exalted position of headwaiter. I shudder as I recollect these activities. Social recreation was minimal, nor had I time to engage in sports. I was either insufficiently skilled or too exhausted to engage in it anyway. No cities were nearby to invite temptation to youthful spirits. Most of the time I had no cash at all. One whole summer I made do with *one dollar* for incidentals!

All this theoretically is supposed to be useful in the development of strong character. I have my doubts. The fact is that during my whole period of undergraduate and graduate study I had to work to support myself almost entirely. One manages. My academic record was good, for I was graduated from college as valedictorian and became known as something of an orator. Prizes came my way in speech, debate, and premedical studies. The fact is, however, that in most subjects I did not attain the thorough mastery of material that would have been desirable.

Lincoln Memorial University was no top-drawer institution. Nevertheless, if I did not go to an Ivy League institution, the fact of the Depression brought the Ivy League to me. Some of our professors were of that caliber, offering excellent teaching in English, chemistry, physics, mathematics, social science, and philosophy. As in primary and secondary schools, so in regard to college I feel lasting gratitude to my professors.

This must be said about my college: it was set in a countryside of unsurpassed beauty. Considerable historical significance was attached to the region. The mountain people were as solid and unpretentious as they were reputed to be. I developed good friends among both genders, but since my subsequent work took me far afield, these friendships were not to be lifelong. The total enrollment of LMU had always been small; as might be expected its alumni did not boast many people of eminence. One exception was the poet Jesse Stuart, with whom I later became acquainted. Yet many persons, prominent in politics and arts, found their way as visitors to our campus. It was a people's school—devoted to training ordinary people like me.

I fully intended to become a surgeon and pursued studies to that end. That was to change radically during my second year. I was then redirected toward the Christian ministry. Several persons influenced me in this change.

One was my brother Joe. He had many adventures during his hitchhiking trip to Hollywood. One concerned Langtree, Texas, home of "Judge" Roy Bean—"the law west of the Pecos"—and Lillie Langtree, a famous English singer much admired by Bean and after whom the town was named. Joe and his friend found few generous drivers among the very few motorists at all who were touring West Texas at the time. The two camped out one night on what proved to be the bed of a dried-up stream. All went well until near midnight when a sudden thunderstorm broke out in remote mountains that lay on the horizon. A flash flood suddenly descended upon them and they were scarcely able to reach higher ground with their few belongings. Thus, miserable, soaked to the skin, they made their way into Langtree, where they found shelter in an empty freight car on a siding and settled down to a restless sleep. Years later, I drove my wife and children through Langtree. It became a part of the story of our whole family.

The next morning they discovered to their dismay that cement had just been unloaded from that car. Their wet clothing had now become impregnated with cement dust. As they dried out the cement set and their clothes resembled suits of armor! The weather became milder at noonday, and they washed their clothes in the Rio Grande and contemplated their prospects. My brother's friend proposed that they take a freight train to California. Joe reported that it was as if a voice within him cried out, "Don't go, Joe. If you do you will be a bum." Hitchhikers can keep their self-respect. After all, no one has to give them a ride. To accept a motorist's hospitality does the host no harm. When they resumed their "thumbing a ride" the following day, the very first driver who came along took them all the way to Los Angeles!

As it transpired Joe did not get into the movies. That was possibly Hollywood's loss, for he was a good actor.

Apparently God had other plans for Joe. It so happened that the Olympic Games were held in Los Angeles in that summer of 1932. At the same time the churches of the region organized what was called "The Olympiad of Religion," with the nation's outstanding preachers and evangelists taking part. One of these was the outstanding Bishop Arthur J. Moore of the Methodist Episcopal Church, South. Somehow the Christian message, as the bishop conveyed it, penetrated my brother's spirit-depths. He forthwith responded to its appeal. His was a classic conversion experience: his life was renewed and entirely redirected. This was followed by a clear call to the Christian ministry, to which he responded with genuine ardor.

Then he returned home and told me the story. At first his excessive enthusiasm and quite dogmatic beliefs put me off, but slowly I too yielded. There were other influences also, such as a concerned and appealing college pastor and a kindly woman evangelist who helped me in my struggle and search for forgiveness. So earnestly did I seek that I wrote out all the sins I could recall having committed, filling four foolscap pages. Then she gently led me to see that God's word was what God had to say to us, that to believe the word is to believe God, that my part was to confess and God's part was to forgive. Finally, I came to see that faith is taking God at his word. Because I was a Methodist a conversion experience was part of my heritage, and I fully expected that sometime, somehow I was to be reconciled to God and incorporated into the Church. This was my conversion experience—as simple, yet as profound and far-reaching as Joe's, yet no Damascus road event, no blinding lights, no inner emotional upheaval. Martin Luther would have been proud of me, for it was by faith alone, by grace alone, by Scripture alone. But the great transaction was done. My brother, spiritually speaking, became my father, and Bishop

Moore, as I often told him later, was my spiritual grand-father.

In my instance also this episode was followed by a call to preach. Here again there was no great emotional upsurge, just a quiet and growing inner conviction that I would only be personally fulfilled as a minister and priest of God. *This* was authentic and convincing enough for me.

This meant that my vision, long entertained, of becoming a medical doctor slowly faded away. Sometimes I have amused myself by reflecting that there are probably many people now living who would not be had I become a surgeon. But no, I think I would have made a good doctor. Gradually I have realized that ministry is a healing vocation too.

In completing my college work I studied the Bible more carefully. For the first time I read the Bible clear through, the first of many journeys through the Book of books. We had excellent instruction in Bible from our college pastor. My first sermon was preached to a tiny mountaineer congregation that met in a schoolhouse in East Tennessee where students were often invited to preach. If my hearers were not edified they were at least polite and patient.

Other sermons followed, before the college and in surrounding communities. I was on the way. Yet when my brother and I solemnly announced our vocational intentions to our pastor back home in Mansfield, a somewhat severe and scholarly man, he entirely discouraged us. We were not deterred, though this may have been the decisive factor in our not going to a Methodist seminary at that time. I can only guess that he must have been discouraged in his own ministry and did not want us to pursue our aim. We were, however, highly motivated to do so.

Not everyone responded to our enthusiasm with discouraging words. Others, of course, helped us on the way. I remember the father of a close friend of mine who was pastor of a Methodist Episcopal church in Lafollette, Tennessee. He and his wife opened up their hearts, their home, and their pulpit to us. We began to take the first faltering steps toward the Methodist ministry. This was to secure a license to preach. This meant that we were local preachers or lay preachers. After examination, written and oral, a successful candidate is issued the appropriate certificate or license. This was in the Holston Conference. I recall the district superintendent counseling us especially to guard our relationship with women—always a word in season. He reminded us that Genesis records that Joseph had to flee from a woman, leaving his robe behind! It was good advice. This district superintendent knew the perils of improper gender relationships. Countless pastors have stumbled here. I appreciated his advice and caution.

I attended Biblical Seminary in New York, now known as New York Theological Seminary. My brother followed me there two years later. We were directed there by Dr. W. B. Guerrant, our university minister, a Presbyterian. He secured for us tuition-free scholarships with an opportunity to work to cover our other expenses.

Biblical Seminary was nondenominational but had a Presbyterian bias. It was neither conservative nor liberal. Its middle-of-the-road theological position was well suited to my own thought and disposition.

As the school's name implies there was strong emphasis on English Bible, which was studied systematically book by book. It was proud of its tradition of studying the Bible itself rather than merely books about the Bible. These latter were indeed studied also, and we were trained in critical scholarship. Methods of study and teaching were particularly emphasized. One did learn how to study systematically and to teach effectively.

We were taught an inductive method of Bible study and employed extensive charting. We could chart anything; it facilitated getting a grasp on any particular subject as a whole. Typically we would draw a chart from left to right. We could say that since we read left to right, we think left to right. It follows that if we were Semitic we might more effectively chart right to left, or if Chinese, up and down. The fact is that I have used this approach throughout my ministry. In the case of my brother Joe, he developed the method to a fine art, for he was a superb teacher.

It has always been my view that if we are to be effective in a professional field, we must come into touch somewhere along the line with highly proficient persons in that field. Specifically one must sit under great teachers, the more the better. We had that privilege at Biblical Seminary. One of these was Wilbert Webster White, founder of the school. He himself had come under the spell of William Rainey Harper, founder of the University of Chicago and a master teacher, particularly of Hebrew. White was also a product of Yale with a sound foundation in the theological disciplines. He became profoundly convinced that the greatest failing of preachers was that they did not really know the Bible. It became his mission in life to try to correct this, and he went far toward this goal.

There were other fine teachers too. We profited also from visiting professors such as Edwin Lewis and Karl Heim. Most of all I appreciated the lectures of Dr. Julius T. Richter, one of the great lights in the history of missions, a German who was at one time pastor to Kaiser Wilhelm in Berlin.

I could scarcely have had better training in Bible, especially the New Testament. I became a kind of walking concordance, and if someone would have cited a verse of scripture, I believe I could have located it by chapter and book in the New Testament. As to the Old Testament, I could certainly have located it by book. At the same time I gained a degree of facility in Greek and in New Testament exegesis. Unfortunately I cannot claim the same for Hebrew.

It was assumed that with such "raw exposure" to Scripture one would at the same time gain a working biblical theology. To a certain degree this was true and at the same time liberating, for sooner or later you must do your own theologizing. The weak spot in this approach was that the student suffered from not being adequately grounded in systematic theology. In my own case, this has had a crippling effect on my entire ministry, and all my life I have had to try to catch up in this respect.

Biblical Seminary was located at 235 East 49th Street, in the heart of Manhattan. The Waldorf-Astoria was two blocks away. The theater district was within walking distance. Years later the United Nations was built nearby. Across the street lived Katharine Hepburn whom we boys delighted in spying from time to time, and we also glimpsed such visitors as Anne Harding and Spencer Tracy. The violinist Efrem Zimbalist lived next door. The subways were near at hand and we could travel any-where in the city for a nickel! We students took full advantage of all this.

We would systematically be taken on escorted tours to significant places all over New York. This included the New York Public Library and the offices of the *New York Times*. Other excursions led us to the Cloisters, to the Metropolitan Art Museum, and to the Metropolitan Opera. It was interesting to visit Sailors' Snug Harbor, a heavily endowed retirement home for merchant mariners located on Staten Island. One of its notable buildings there was the chapel built on the model of St. Paul's in London, but on half-scale. We went to settlement houses, mental institutions, and hospitals, as well as to the great churches—Riverside, St. Patrick's Cathedral and St. John the Divine, Christ Church (Methodist), and Fifth Avenue Presbyterian church. We heard all the great preachers of the day, a rare privilege. We also occasionally attended theater, the symphony, and the opera. The city then as now afforded unparalleled opportunity for outstanding cultural fare.

My scholarship cared for my tuition cost. To cover board and room I waited tables. As field work and for pocket money I taught at Five Points Mission on the lower East Side, an institution run by the Methodists for under-privileged children, mostly of Italian extraction in that part of the city. Each Sunday afternoon throngs of young people descended on the place. Discipline was hard to enforce and serious teaching impeded, but through it all

God was glorified and his people heard the good news. My own work there continued for one year only.

During my last two seminary years I served as a student assistant pastor at Metropolitan Temple Methodist Episcopal Church, situated at the corner of Thirteenth Street and Seventh Avenue in Manhattan. Here I worked with children and young people, coached basketball, coached dramatics, did some pastoral calling, and occasionally preached or led prayer meetings. The senior pastor was quite elderly but a first-rate preacher, once the mentor of Dr. Ralph Sockman. His name was Dr. Wallace McMullen. I learned a great deal from this experience.

During my first summer I returned to Ohio for further hard work in the wholesale grocery firm. The second summer was quite different, for I engaged in evangelistic preaching with my brother Joe. This was in three different coal-mining communities in Lee County in the extreme southwestern corner of Virginia, wedged between Tennessee and Kentucky. It was not far from LMU, by this time familiar terrain for us.

In many respects we were ill prepared intellectually, but what we may have lacked in this respect we made up for in energy and zeal. We were a team, and we would preach in turn every other night. This fact in itself was helpful, for we had precious little material in the form of revival sermons, but that was not all. Joe was made of sterner stuff than I was and his manner tended to emphasize the wrath and judgment of God, whereas my inclination was to stress the love of God. Between these two poles a fruitful ministry seemed to develop. It was a kind of "Divine Pincer Movement," which had the effect of embracing everyone.

One of our church bulletins listed an "alter" call (rather than an "altar" call); we always thought that quite apt.

Nor did we leave attendance to chance and response to the posters that announced our meetings. We proceeded also to make personal calls on every home in the community. Then we did the same thing in the surrounding countryside. Sometimes we would walk because we had no car, or we would borrow horses and ride from door-to-door. As we recorded at the time: "We walked until we could not stand up and rode until we could not sit down!" Having been earnestly invited, the people responded in large numbers; the churches were crowded to the doors with people of all ages and of all denominational backgrounds. Our first series was held at St. Charles, Virginia, a small mining town. Finally, everyone in town confessed conversion and we moved on to the next place, but not before we had baptized those who newly confessed their faith. This was partly a "precautionary measure," for the Baptist notion of adult believers' baptism was highly prized in that vicinity. We took the further step of baptizing by immersion in a nearby river. Thus there was no more a possibility of another evangelist following us insisting that baptism by sprinkling was invalid. They had already been as thoroughly baptized as they could possibly be!

The evangelistic effort was further enhanced by our holding vacation Bible schools for the children in the mornings and Bible classes for adults as well. Fortunately the local pastors of all the churches were supportive and cooperative, and the laity worked together harmoniously. Having finished our work in St. Charles, we repeated the whole exercise in a rural community surrounding Robbins Chapel, a few miles away. The results were the same. We proceeded to a third church in a rural setting at the foot of the Cumberland Mountains. This was a more sedate center and although the response was encouraging, it was by no means as sweeping and enthusiastic as the former two. Meanwhile we were being shaped into effective evangelists—Methodist style. The memory of these experiences has not faded during the years that have followed and the influence has been positive and continuing. We learned that summer to declare the gospel in clear and convincing and, I trust, winsome terms also.

It was during this summer of evangelism that I had what was for me a remarkable religious experience. As I reported earlier, my "conversion" was not a dramatic event; it was a quiet transaction of faith meeting with grace—both of which were gifts of God. Yet somehow I must have felt cheated. Where was the inner assurance, the confirmation of the "transaction," the Witness of the Spirit of which John Wesley makes so much? This must have troubled me a good deal, for in the spring of 1935 I wrote to an elderly friend who was at that time my principal spiritual adviser.

His reply to me may warrant repeating here at some length:

> I recall your remarks last Spring with reference to the witness of the Spirit. It is not at all unusual for skepticism to spring up at that point, and for the struggle for spiritual victory to be retarded through unbelief, and that is the very barrier between the soul and God. Many of the Saints of old could not enter into their gracious estate

because of unbelief, the devil's favorite weapon, which he wields with dexterity and power. I want you to conquer this obstruction, and you can conquer it by studying the character of faith which is not "a conscious effort, but a conscious act," that is, faith is always a voluntary act, and never a struggle. If I promise you a book, or a coin on a certain day to assist you in your education, knowing me as you do, you take it by faith, or appropriate it in advance without doubting for a moment the integrity of my word. Well, if you could so easily take me at my word, a weak, unreliable mortal, why should you not take God at His Word, and settle down on the foundation of the Divine faithfulness, knowing that "The foundation of the Lord standeth sure, having this seal, that the Lord knoweth them that are His."

Pardon this rather lengthy communication, but I want you to keep out of the fog and cultivate faith and spiritual expectancy, and know that out of the thousands of promises written in God's Scriptural Check Book, not one has come to protest up to date, and while the grass may wither and the flowers of the field fade, the "Word of the Lord" endureth forever.

Then in the summer of 1936, during our "evangelistic foray," it happened! As a part of our evangelistic program, as I have said, we would hold Bible classes every morning, usually teaching whole books of the Bible, especially the Gospels or Acts of the Apostles. One morning after I had been teaching the Bible, I made my way, alone, back to a farmhouse where we were living. I recall that it was a beautiful summer morning. As I walked along the road, there suddenly came across me the profound awareness that I was a child of God. It was not an experience of explosive force such as Paul had along the road to

Damascus. My Methodist heritage came to my mind: could this be the witness of the Spirit? Then, I didn't walk, I *ran* the rest of the way to the farmhouse. When I opened the Bible to where Paul says the Spirit himself bears witness to our spirit that we are children of God, I was convinced that this was the witness of the Spirit. I have had this sense almost constantly ever since, however unworthy I have been at times. That has been very reassuring and meaningful to me to this very day. I have not needed much more than that inner reinforcement of a spiritual nature.

After the summer of evangelism we had a somewhat unique episode. We returned home to Mansfield. Our brother Don and his wife were visiting the parents there at the time. Since they were driving back to Texas, Joe and I accompanied them—our first visit after ten years.

When it came time to return to the East Coast we had to arrange some mode of transportation, probably hitch-hiking. Since Don lived in a port city we found an alternative. Looking back I can hardly imagine how we had the gall to do this. We found a freighter that was to sail for Wilmington, Delaware, where our sister Elizabeth McCleary lived. To our astonishment they were willing to let us serve as deckhands on the voyage in exchange for our passage.

This was our first venture upon the briny deep. Our passage took us across the Gulf of Mexico, around the Florida Keys, and up the East Coast. We experienced a heavy storm at sea, complete with seasickness, of course. We saw flying fish and waterspouts for the first time, observed sporting dolphins, and marveled at the florescent foam around the prow at night. It was all very new and thrilling. The food was good and abundant, available at any hour of the day and night. The older sea hands tolerated us to a point that almost resembled friendliness. One such man had apparently been everywhere. We asked him how he liked some of the cathedrals of Europe. His reply was that their silence and massive size were too much for him and he had to leave after a few minutes. Was he experiencing awe?

The work was hard and long. We earned our keep by swabbing and "holy stoning" the deck, by endless painting, and by being "go-fers." At night we were sometimes assigned to lookout duty on the prow of the freighter. We were to alert the bridge about any oncoming vessels, with a special ring of the bell for ships on the starboard or port side or dead ahead. I remember that one time we rang the bell for a star that was just appearing above the horizon. Such was our brief career as sailors. After about ten days we landed at Wilmington, Delaware, and were picked up by our sister who lived nearby. When war came both Joe and I chose the army instead of the navy!

From there we went to New York; I to complete my third year at seminary and Joe to enroll for his first. He brought his particular brand of zeal to the institution and soon made a place for himself. We were delighted to be fellow students and colleagues once again. Although I never asked him to assume the role, he rather took it upon himself to be in charge of my social life, freely passing judgment on my own choices in the realm of female companionship. It was probably just as well that he was not in India with me where I had to make my final selection all by myself. In fairness to him, I should observe that I also exercised a role in passing judgment on his preferences for companions.

My last year at seminary seemed to pass quickly. I enjoyed my studies and extracurricular activities. I sang in the chorus. Since I could not read music, I found it helpful to stand next to those with strong voices who could. We had on occasion to preach before our fellow-students and faculty members, always a trying task, but somehow we accomplished it. We had to write a thesis as a prerequisite for a divinity degree. My chosen topic was "The Religious Motive in American Colonization." Much of my research was done in the New York Public Library, where I spent many hours during my senior year. To study in that magnificent setting was a privilege for which I am grateful to this moment. Though the "book" I produced was something less than earthshaking, there was lasting benefit in the experience. For example, I became acquainted for the first time with the Spanish priest and scholar-saint Las Casas. In contrast with most of his compatriots, he was a friend and defender of the Indians. I *did* conclude that the religious motive in colonization was high, even though almost invariably the aboriginal peoples were oppressed. Moreover, this study, though unbeknownst to me at the time, was a significant part of my preparation to be a missionary. Then I remember with great appreciation the Ukrainian-American young woman who typed my dissertation.

I managed to earn my bachelor of Sacred Theology (years later elevated to the Master's) degree and was considered academically prepared for service as a Christian minister. In other respects I was still very immature and not well prepared at all. But I was still a *bachelor* even if I wasn't a very competent theologian.

During the last months of my study I successfully passed the prescribed examinations as a ministerial candidate for the Methodist Episcopal Church, and in May 1937 I was received on trial as a member of the New York Conference. At the same session of the conference Bishop Francis McConnell ordained me a deacon. I have always been proud of this, for he was not only a man of superior intellect but a bold social prophet. It was while he was bishop in Pittsburgh that he very likely did more for the struggle for the eight-hour workday than any other churchman, a fact that labor leaders have never forgotten. When a man of this caliber lays hands on you, you cannot help hoping that some of his spirit rubs off. Years later I met Bishop McConnell in New York and reminded him that he had ordained me. In all honesty I must report that he seemed utterly unimpressed.

During the ensuing summer my brother Joe and I engaged in a rather interesting enterprise in northern Ohio. We established about thirty Bible classes. These were scheduled in five or six counties in north central Ohio. We had an itinerary we would follow every week the whole summer long. We would move into a community and see a pastor, usually a Methodist, and ask if we could teach a Bible class. One pastor of the Evangelical Church later became a bishop and elder colleague of mine. I am now amazed at the receptivity we were given. They did not seem to take us as oddballs, but they took us at face value. We did, I think, a good job of teaching Bible by books, by methods we had learned at Biblical Seminary. I must repeat that Biblical did know how to teach Bible, and how to teach teachers to teach Bible. All together about six hundred people enrolled. We were especially proud of a class of children to whom we taught the Gospel of Mark; we found them particularly responsive.

At the end of the summer in Mansfield, Ohio, at the First Methodist Church, most of those hundreds of people came together for an all-day meeting under the tutelage of Dr. White, president of Biblical Seminary, who thought this a remarkable development. I found out twenty years later that some of those Bible classes were still continuing. I marvel at the way the people were willing to entrust themselves to us—as rather inadequately equipped teachers—but we grew in our ability to teach and grew in confidence as teachers. I have found this experience of lifelong value. My brother Joe repeated the undertaking the following summer.

So far in my pursuit of higher education, although I was a dyed-in-the-wool Methodist, I had not attended a Methodist institution. That changed finally in the fall of 1937 when I entered Boston University School of Theology to study toward a master's degree in theology. During our summer of Bible classes my brother and I had used an ancient Essex automobile for transportation. In this vehicle we headed eastward again. I dropped Joe off in New York City to continue his work at Biblical Seminary while I proceeded to Boston. On this journey I drove through a terrible storm and afterward learned that it was a part of the famous hurricane of 1937! In Boston I sold the car to a layman in New Hampshire for forty dollars. Years later, by chance I met the purchaser. He informed me that the Essex had not proved a bargain. At that late date I was not disposed to make good his losses, despite the fact that by that time I had become his bishop.

The School of Theology awarded me a partial scholarship. I secured a job waiting tables at a nearby restaurant, which provided me with a noon meal and a small stipend. The rest of my expenses I received by borrowing from the student loan fund of our church. My living accommodations were in a small apartment on Beacon Hill, which I shared with three other students, one an African American. We all got on well.

During the time I was at Boston I did not have a student pastorate. Once I was interviewed for a student assistantship at Chestnut Street Church in Portland, Maine, but they did not see fit to hire me. Twenty-two years later when I became bishop in Maine I reminded them of the wisdom they had displayed at that time, but that now I was one of their pastors, after all.

As implied before, my principal reason for going to Boston University was to make up for what I lacked in systematic theology. Unfortunately I found that that very year Professor Albert C. Knudson, dean and principal theologian, was on sabbatical in Europe. The visiting professor who replaced him did not at all meet my needs. In other respects I was more fortunate. Dr. Lowstuter was extremely helpful in New Testament and befriended me in a personal way. Professor Edwin Prince Booth was strong in Greek exegesis and church history. His colleague in the history of the church was Professor Richard

Cameron, who led a notable seminar on Saint Francis. In that particular course I met fellow students who were to be lifelong friends, Dwight Loder, Mack Stokes, Marvin Stuart, Charles Golden, and McFerrin Stowe among them. All six of us were to become bishops. I was able also with these friends to work under Richard Cameron's direction to complete a work started by Professor George Croft Cell of republishing John Wesley's translation of the New Testament as compared to the King James Version. The work had been interrupted by Cell's death.

Above all, I profited by my study under the brilliant scholar Professor Edgar S. Brightman, who taught philosophy of religion. To be under his tutelage proved in itself to be sufficient justification for having gone to Boston. He was an original thinker and an advocate of Boston Personalism, a school of philosophy stemming from Borden Parker Bowne, Brightman's (and Francis J. McConnell's) teacher. My debt to Professor Brightman is immense, for he helped to awaken my intellect more than anyone else I have ever met.

The School of Theology was at that time located at 72 Mt. Vernon Street, or Beacon Hill. A part of it was a beautiful chapel with superb stained glass windows. They were all moved to the new chapel of Boston University, now situated on Commonwealth Avenue in Boston. One of those windows impressed me very deeply and reinforced me more than once in the years that were to follow. It portrayed Moses, and below his picture were words from Scripture: "He endured as seeing him who is invisible."

Suddenly my studies at Boston came to an abrupt end.

I studied there for only the first semester of the academic year 1937–38. I did not earn my master's degree but did earn sixteen hours of credit toward it. Some years later these were transferred in full to Columbia University, where I received my Ph.D. in 1957. Meanwhile my life took a sharp turn that was profoundly to affect my whole future, a transforming event on my journey. The first quarter of a century of my life was nearing its end. I must say that I was raw, immature, and very much an unfinished Christian. Later on I was to learn that all of us are, at best, Christians in the making. The church, I knew, expected much of me. At the same time it had given me a readiness to respond.

4

To India

John Wesley speaks of how he went unwillingly to a meeting on Aldersgate Street in London on the evening of May 24, 1738. His whole life direction was changed then and there. One evening, October 31, 1937, I myself went willingly but unsuspectingly to Trinity Episcopal Church in Boston. There my life direction was drastically altered.

Trinity Church is a masterwork of the famous architect Stanford White. Together with the lovely Boston Public Library, it graces Boston's Copley Square. Outside the edifice is a notable sculpture by St. Gaudens of Phillips Brooks, prince of preachers, rector of Trinity and later bishop of the Protestant Episcopal Church. At first glance the observer of the sculpture does not sense its true force. Then suddenly it becomes apparent that there is another figure in the background with a hand on the preacher's shoulder. It is the Galilean—the source of his power.

That evening the church was crowded, for the preacher was Bishop Azariah of Dornakal Diocese in South India. He was an outstanding person, a fervent evangelist, a one-time delegate to the famous Missionary Conference in Edinburgh, 1910, and first Indian to be elected bishop of the Anglican communion in his homeland. He spoke of India and the work of Christ there. I do not know how it was with others present that night, but I know how it was

with me. It seemed to me that once again Jesus stood
behind that preacher, his hand on *his* shoulder and the
source of Azariah's power. Though not ordinarily much
given to this sort of thing, I knew then and there that I
must become a missionary to India.

The very next day the speaker at the chapel service in the
Boston University School of Theology was Dr. Thomas S.
Donohugh, a secretary of the Board of Foreign Missions of
the Methodist Episcopal Church. He was not renowned for
his eloquence as a speaker, but he simply remarked that
there was an immediate need for a pastor for an English-
speaking church in Bombay. I knew, of course, that I should
respond. I spoke to Dr. Donohugh after the service, applied
for missionary service, was interviewed and appointed.
Three months later I was on my way to India. In confirmation of this I have in my possession a Certificate of Missionary Appointment and a letter from the personnel
secretary—who informed me of the following minute:

> That Mr. Mathews be accepted for missionary service in
> India, in connection with Bowen Church, Bombay for at
> least three years, subject to final medical clearance.

To say that this disrupted my life plans would be a pronounced understatement. My theological studies were
interrupted, my family members were dismayed. There
were clothes to be purchased, packing to be done, and
farewells to be said. Nevertheless, I recall being filled
with great anticipation and even joy. I did enjoy a final
Christmas with my family in Ohio. Early in the New Year
I returned to Boston to complete my first semester of
studies. The last time I was to preach before sailing was

on January 16, 1938, at Newburyport, Massachusetts, where another missionary, George Whitefield, preached his last sermon and where he is buried. There I spoke on Paul's Letter to the Philippians, the "epistle of joy." My text was "Let your manner of life be worthy of the gospel of Christ." I earnestly trusted that this might be true of me.

In most ways I was ill prepared: no special training for India or for the missionary task; no language orientation, no anthropology, no nothing! Sometimes I have said that I was given a passport and a ticket and was told India was "thataway." So it was. To my mind it is a great tribute to the Indian people that they were prepared to receive a greenhorn like me, to love me, to overlook my many shortcomings, and then to help mold me into a servant of the Lord. Every untried pastor knows the feeling.

It was on the afternoon of February 9, 1938, that I sailed out of New York harbor on the *Queen Mary* to begin my first missionary journey. Members of my family and a few friends came to the docks and even came on board to see me off. It was a cloudy, dismal day. These lines are being written on Wednesday, February 9, 1994, just fifty-six years after what for me has continued to be a most memorable event; this too is a cold, miserable day. I was to have returned in three years. Actually my absence stretched for eight very long years.

In those days I was entitled to what was called an "outfit allowance," which amounted to $100. With this I had to equip myself for the tropics, with luggage and articles of clothing suitable for that part of the world. My passage by tourist class accommodations from New York to Bom-

bay was $255. I was given for the journey $40 in cash and
$105 in traveler's checks. I must have lived cautiously, for
I only spent $66 on the journey. This included a room for
three nights in New York prior to departure, $4.50; and
meals for three days, $3. In London I spent $4.05 for food
for four days.

We were supplied with a "Manual for Travel of Missionaries." One passage I found particularly helpful:

> Missionaries undoubtedly will meet prejudice in their
> travels, and sometimes, open criticism of themselves and
> their work. Especially is this true on shipboard, where
> many people of divergent views are thrown together for a
> long period of time. All missionaries are urged to exercise
> such a degree of tolerance and charity toward their com-
> panions on the journey and of care in deportment as will
> lessen, if not prevent, criticism.

During the voyage I kept a fragmentary journal. It
reveals that we sailed at 1:30 P.M.; that we had a fire drill
before we cleared the harbor, during which I had an interesting conversation on India with an Oxford professor;
that I had an interest in seeing the pilot off the ship; and
that I had a kind of sinking feeling as I saw the receding
lights of land, the last until the lights of France were to be
visible. We had a fine dinner and a quiet but foggy night.
My cabin mate was an Englishman from the Midlands, a
businessman named Bertram Newbold. Other interesting
passengers included Matty Leyne, a Presbyterian missionary bound for China, and a British motorcycle racer
whose name I have forgotten.

If the first night was calm, things changed the next day.
The North Atlantic was tossed into a fury. It was my

twenty-fifth birthday and I celebrated it by being seasick. I continued with this illness for much of the Atlantic crossing. A solicitous cabin steward was of some comfort. I was most at ease while reclining but could not enjoy reading, for that made me feel even worse. Such experiences cause one for a time to rethink one's missionary vocation. No wonder Will Rogers recommended this cure for seasickness: "Go out and sit under a tree!" For some days few people showed up for meals, and on only one day did the sun show itself briefly. Finally I could walk around deck a little, play Ping-Pong, and watch movies. An emissary from the captain asked me to conduct worship on Sunday, February 13. When he saw my youth and probable inexperience, I think he was considerably relieved that I declined. A more senior minister took the service.

We sighted Bishop's Rock and Land's End late on Sunday. The next morning, Valentine's Day, we touched at Cherbourg, where we were greeted with snow. The closest one to a "valentine" I had met was Matty Leyne. She debarked in France to proceed to China, by what route I do not know. Hardly had she departed when I met another young woman, who had escaped my notice earlier. She was named Dick, an attractive woman hailing from El Paso and a court stenographer. I was delighted to learn that she would be proceeding to Bombay on the same vessel on which I was booked, so I could look forward to seeing more of her. She was traveling with her mother and an aunt who was a Presbyterian missionary in the Punjab.

Meanwhile, we made the short crossing to Southampton. By the time of our arrival there the weather cleared and it proved to be a pretty day. We proceeded to London by boat-train. Aboard the train I encountered a person who was of some note at that time and familiar from his pictures. He was Jeff Davis, the "Hobo King." Though he had crossed on the *Queen Mary,* I had not met him on shipboard, so I concluded that he had luxuriated in a higher class of passage than was afforded to me. I met also a Methodist missionary by the name of Anna Harrod, whom I was to see fairly often in the years ahead—a splendid Methodist missionary she was too.

On the voyage across I chanced to meet another Englishman, J. D. Jardine, of the famous Jardine family whose various members served in business and government from Bombay to Shanghai. Mr. Jardine invited me to be his guest for my stop-over in London. He proved to be a generous host and had an excellent flat in Kensington. I was overwhelmed by his unstinting hospitality. Not only did he share his home and table, but he also saw to it that I saw the sights of London on this, my very first trip there. These included the usual visits to Westminster Abbey and St. Paul's, a glimpse of Buckingham Palace and the Houses of Parliament, Whitehall, the shopping centers, and monuments. He also treated me to a very British variety show at the Palladium and a concert in Albert Hall.

It seemed to me that I simply must visit Oxford, a short train journey from London. There I tramped around its streets visiting the colleges and museums. Christ Church and Lincoln Colleges were especially appealing to me because of the Wesley association with these places. In a real sense I felt that I was furthering my neglected education. Back in London I spent my last day visiting Wren churches, the British Museum, and Wesley's Chapel. In the latter I engaged in a practice that must have been followed by countless aspiring Methodist preachers, both before and after me. Finding I was alone in the chapel, I stole my way up into John Wesley's high pulpit and for the moment hoped that some of his spirit might also find residence in me. Little did I suppose that years later I would preach more than once from that pulpit.

My most lingering memory of my London visit was how cold and damp it was. The chill seemed to penetrate to my very bones and linger there. It was no disappointment, therefore, when after my fourth day in England it came time to leave. Boarding a boat-train again I was transported to Tilbury Docks, some distance down the Thames. There we boarded the P & O liner SS *Strathaird*, a 22,500-ton vessel. It seemed to me a really fine ship, painted white, with three stacks. It was a good thing I liked it, for it was to be my home for three weeks. At 1:30 P.M. we approached the mouth of the Thames, then out into the English Channel. It was still quite cold and would continue so until we got well into the Mediterranean.

My cabin mate was an Anglo-Indian named Flett, a somewhat strange man. We proved to have little in common, but we had no trouble rooming together. Since we were to be aboard for three weeks we almost completely unpacked.

Most of the passengers were British of every stripe of society. There were also a number of Indians aboard, as well as Australians and a sprinkling of other nationalities.

Some Americans I had seen before, for we had traversed the Atlantic on the same vessel. I remember a well-known medical missionary who, with his family, served a hospital in the Northwest Frontier Province. Of note also was the presence of a team that was to attempt an assault on Mt. Everest later in the spring. The team leader was a Mr. Smythe. I followed the course of their climb, which was unsuccessful. Years later, on a flight to India I conversed with Tensing Norkay, the Sherpa who, with Sir Edmund Hillary, was the first to conquer Everest.

By this time I was better adjusted to sailing and did not suffer from seasickness as much—just one day when we encountered heavy head winds on the Mediterranean. The meals were good. There was a good library aboard, games were available, and there were occasional movies and amateur shows. At the end of these entertainments we were introduced to the custom with which we were to become familiar: rising and singing "God Save the King." Six swings around the deck added up to one mile and that was my chief form of exercise. At times we played deck tennis and quoits. The ship's officers saw to it that passengers had a chance to visit the bridge and the engine room, both very interesting.

On Sundays church services were held both morning and evening and ministers on board were asked to lead. My turn came on Sunday, February 27, soon after we had passed by the volcano Stromboli—quite a sight. I remember that I preached on Acts 27, St. Paul's stormy trip on the Mediterranean Sea. We were then bucking the same kind of Northeaster called "Euroclydon," which had blown Paul toward the West and resulted in the shipwreck on Malta.

Sometimes on this voyage we would be well within sight of land—a bit of the French coast, some of Spain and Portugal, Tangiers, Italy, Corsica and Sicily. On Washington's birthday we touched at Gibraltar, which looked exactly like the insurance advertisements. Here we were allowed to go ashore. Dick and I hired a horse and carriage and were driven around the compact British settlement: churches, markets, flower gardens, government buildings, barracks, and an impressive cemetery. All was in good order, the landscape studded with pine and olive trees. We were taken up to the Spanish border, where we glimpsed a little Spanish town and the quaintly uniformed Spanish police, then under the rule of General Franco. Views from the heights afforded a wide panorama of a protected harbor where ships of many nations were anchored—and in the distance the continent of Africa.

Our next port of call was Marseilles, where we were allowed ashore to see the sights of that colorful city. Here we were joined by a number of passengers who came from London and journeyed across France by train, thus cutting nearly a week off their travel time to India. Other stops were at Port Said, where again we went ashore for shopping and for the first chance to get a taste of the East. The passage through the Suez was naturally intriguing. Later on we got a glimpse of the mountains of which Sinai was a part. Again we put in at another harbor, Port Sudan—a taste of the utterly new world of Africa. The same was true when we landed at Aden, my first contact with Asia and its bazaars.

The frequent stopovers made this voyage far more

interesting than, say, a three-week passage across the Pacific might have been. One could, as it were, gradually ease into a vastly different culture. It was possible to get acquainted with the British people who were aboard, for one was to see much of them in India. The Indian passengers I found to be quite aloof, and I regret that I did not get to know them better. Perhaps they were a little suspicious of missionary types. During the passage I did manage to do considerable reading and study. I have already mentioned a young woman, Dick. Another young man, named Jack, was also attracted to her, but by the time we came to the Suez Canal, I had won out! Like shipboard romances do, this one faded rather rapidly once we came to shore and to our senses. We corresponded for a while, but I never saw her again.

By this time we were in warmer climes—quite a contrast to the frigid days after we embarked. We brought out summer clothes, basked on sunny decks, and watched the flying fish play in the Arabian Sea. Ships were not air-conditioned in those days and could be very hot. Sleep was a misery. It is often noted that the word *posh* originated in this connection. Well-experienced travelers would book cabins on the port side (the shady side) on the way out and on the starboard on the way back; thus *Port Out, Starboard Home*. Needless to say, I did not enjoy POSH travel.

Four days from Aden brought the western ghats of India into view. We entered the harbor, saw the city skyline of Bombay, and glimpsed the Gateway of India. On the afternoon of March 10, 1938, we disembarked in Bombay. There I was met and welcomed by missionary friends Paul and Mabel Wagner and Gertrude Warner, wife of my district superintendent, the Reverend Ariel N. Warner. I was in India to dwell not just for three years, as originally supposed, but for eight long years. This was by no means the end of the road. Rather, it was for me a brand new beginning.

The formalities in clearing customs and immigration were not complicated in my case. I had no gifts for others to declare and only a few meager possessions. I am afraid that I shed a tear or two as we drew near the dock, just as I had a few weeks before as we pulled away from New York. The afternoon, I recall, was warm, pleasant, and very beautiful.

Strangely, I felt a little embarrassed as my new friends welcomed me. They were all kind and helped to interpret strange new sights I was viewing for the first time in the interesting city of Bombay. They took me by the church I was to serve. It does not strike me with particular force nowadays, but then it seemed very impressive indeed.

The Warners took me home with them and together with the Wagners we enjoyed a good dinner. This latter young couple had arrived in India about sixteen months before I did. We were close enough in ages that we considered ourselves contemporaries. We were to see a lot of each other in the years ahead. My notes remind me that we played a game of Lexicon, then very popular. We ate some watermelon (a fruit I have never much liked) and then I retired after a long day. For the first time I slept under a mosquito net. My reflections about all that had happened to me during the last twenty-four hours did not last very long, and I fell into a deep slumber.

The next morning I awoke early, or shall I say I was *awakened* early, for my first morning in India I was greeted by a cacophony of crow-calls—a sound that went with the territory. This was not to be the last experience of this kind, for that durable and noisy species of bird thrives throughout the country to the present. After prayer and breakfast Mrs. Warner volunteered to show me around that day.

We went to the famous Crawford Market, then in the heart of the city. It was a sight in itself—flowers, fruits, meats, and people, as well as various sounds and smells. One interesting event occurred during this trip to the bazaar when a Parsee woman beggar solicited us. Mrs. Warner said that never in all her forty-plus years in India had she seen such a sight, for the Parsees (Zoroastrians) usually care very well for their needy. Of course, we encountered dozens of other beggars, most of them unfortunately professional. One is saddened and embarrassed by this, and I have never really learned how to handle the situation. To give to them only seems to perpetuate the institution. Perhaps the best way is to give to organizations that minister to their needs. Writing as I am years removed from this incident I cannot but observe that through the years India has brought the beggar problem pretty much under control, and one seldom sees one there nowadays. Meanwhile, in the United States, where once the practice of begging was almost unknown, it has become a common sight.

On my shopping tour I bought a bedding roll (or *bistar*)—essential to travel in India—a canvas cover for a thin mattress, blankets, sheets, and a pillow. To this I added a mosquito net and an earthen water jug, which holds one's boiled water and at the same time cools the contents (don't leave home without it!).

Bombay was a comparatively modern city and at that time had a population of some two million people. It is not really a tourist city. It does have some fine gardens and public buildings, some *maidans* and palm-fringed beaches. There are universities and museums, Back Bay, Marine Drive, Malabar Hill, Hindu Burning Ghats, and the Parsee Towers of Silence, where the Parsees dispose of their dead by exposure to scavenging birds—in contrast to the typical practice of the Hindus, cremation, and of the Muslims, burial. The temples and mosques of the city are not particularly notable. It was and is still largely a commercial city. In those days there were no skyscrapers that now stud the skyline. Near the Gateway of India was the striking Taj Mahal Hotel, and across the harbor the famous Island of Elephanta with its fine caves and its colossal three-headed figure of Shiva, with this deity as central but incorporating the faces of both Brahma and Vishnu. These were some of the sights I saw with wide-eyed wonder on my first day in India.

At lunch that day I witnessed a sad occurrence. Mrs. Warner was handed a cable that announced the death of her father. She was a well-trained daughter of the American South, and received this word calmly and with genuine grace. As it turned out, both Dr. and Mrs. Warner had by then lost their parents while they themselves were in India. This was not a rare experience within the missionary fold. Later on I learned of the death of *my* father while I was on a visit to India, and I was in the Netherlands when I learned that my mother had died.

In the afternoon I went to a meeting of what was called the Methodist Episcopal Missionary Union (MEMU). We gathered in the bishop's residence. This group of missionaries and Indian pastors and their wives met regularly. I was introduced to my new colleagues. There were also Episcopal and Nazarene missionaries present. They asked me to speak briefly, which I did, using a passage from Isaiah. There too I met for the first time Bishop and Mrs. J. Waskom Pickett. She was a most gracious lady, daughter of one of India's greats, Bishop J. W. Robinson. Bishop Pickett was young and vigorous, a Christian statesman. Indeed, an Indian pastor reported on a new book by the bishop titled, *Christ's Way to India's Heart.* To this I shall return later.

Still later in the afternoon I was able to go bathing at a lovely "swimming bath" called Breach Candy. Dinner with yet another missionary family completed my day.

Quite early the following morning, a Saturday, I was taken with my baggage by Dr. Warner to Victoria Station, where I departed for Poona (now spelled *Pune*), a station at the top of the Western Ghats, about 100 miles from Bombay. Naturally, I traveled third class, called "missionary first class." Here I had my initial real view of India. The landscape was varied. Near the sea it was quite tropical and broken by coastal streams. Then we turned inland and began to climb. Some of the lower mountains were forest-clad but for the most part they were barren, resembling somewhat the mesas of our American Southwest. Here and there were villages whose homes were mostly of stone, with mud used for mortar. At stations there were crowds of people—a never-ending stream of them, clad in what seemed to me outlandish costumes that combined impossible color combinations that never seemed to clash. Seeing people in the mass in India has never ceased to be immensely fascinating for me.

Our electric engines drew us smoothly up the ghats, then past endless fields from which grain had recently been harvested. There were water buffalo here, goats there, and yokes of cattle yonder with birds nit-picking on their backs. There were temple towers lifted above the landscape, people carrying huge loads on their heads, women bearing water from the wells, and children in great abundance. All this I drank in.

At Poona, center of Marathi culture, I was met by Dr. and Mrs. Royal D. Bisbee, senior missionaries from Boston. He was the pastor of an English-speaking church in the city. I also met Dr. and Mrs. E. L. King of Jabalpur, head of the Epworth League in India. Missionaries constituted a great fellowship; one is always looked after very well by these friends. They welcomed me and saw me transferred to a crowded bus—they are always crowded, over-crowded. I found myself jammed into a hard wooden seat, concerned about my baggage, which was supposed to have been stowed in some invisible space on top. It was a slow, dusty, miserable journey over unpaved roads for the next four or five hours. We climbed steadily but gradually, rising from about 2,000 to 4,500 feet on the great mountain ridge along India's west coast called the Western Ghats. My discomfort was, of course, more than compensated by the ever-changing sights and scenery that awaited me around every turn of the road. I could see villages close up and observe the abundance of piles of dried cow dung, at one and the same time a fuel and an art form! Poverty and human deprivation were much in evidence.

Finally we arrived at Mahableshwar and I proceeded by tonga to my residence. The town was one of the many hill-stations that the British had established in many parts of the country. They were literally life-saving stations, affording welcome relief during the hot season from the searing plains below. Nearly every state or province had its hill-station, to which the whole government repaired annually for this season. Mahableshwar was not one of the larger ones nor as impressive as some, but it had its own charm. This was the Bombay governor's summer seat. The surrounding country was associated with one of the Maratha heroes, Shivaji, about whose legend I was soon to be fully informed. It was a heavily wooded region, filled with flowering trees, English-style gardens, and abundant vegetables and fruits—lovely strawberries and mangoes in season. There was a small golf course, tennis courts, riding trails, a bazaar, and an assortment of bungalows.

My reason for being there was to begin the study of the Marathi language. For most of the language areas of the country such a school was established by the missionary societies for the training of their recruits and others. In this case the compound and buildings surrounding the Anglican church were set aside for that purpose. Pandits—Brahmin scholars—were hired to teach classes and to give private tuition to the students. We used a phonetic approach, a direct method that was only then being introduced for this tongue. The director was a British woman, a professor of linguistics, Miss Lambert. She ran a very tight ship.

Marathi is a Sanskrit derivative. About 40 percent of its words are of that origin. It is one of the Indo-European languages, and there is a certain similarity among the languages of northern India. The languages of southern India—Dravidian they are called—are of more indigenous origin, though they are also filled with Sanskrit words in the religious vocabulary. Sanskrit itself comes from Asia—from the Caucasus—and is a kind of "mother of languages," thus akin to Iranian tongues, Greek, Latin, and of the languages of western Europe. India has hundreds of languages and dialects, but if one is acquainted with one of the languages of northern India a kinship with other languages there is noted. Marathi has a military flavor, for the Marathas themselves are a warlike people. Typically it is spoken with a rather sharp edge without undue attention to courteous forms of address. It is written in a script similar to Sanskrit, called Balbodh or Devanagiri.

In Mahableshwar I plunged into this study by this direct method. You simply dive in. Soon one uses simple phrases and is encouraged in progress. Some of the pandits were quite strict, some more considerate. Most were Brahmins, that is, high-caste Hindus; a few were Christian. One was an elderly gentleman, Pandit Harshe. He was a saintly soul, recently converted to Christianity and baptized. For this he had to endure a good deal of rejection by the Brahmins, but he was finally accepted. Others would never have dreamed of becoming Christian. One of my tutors was Pandit Chandavarkar, with whom I have kept in touch through all the subsequent years. We were of the same age and had much in common. Another was Pandit Vaidya (whose name meant "doctor"), who followed me to Bombay. I liked Marathi but, I fear, never truly mastered it, thanks in considerable measure to my being appointed to an English-speaking church. Nevertheless, I find that more than half a century later when I return to India, I can carry on at least simple conversations in Marathi. Along the way I also have picked up conversational Hindustani.

While in language school I had my meals at a large bungalow called Mt. Douglas, where a number of new missionaries stayed. My own quarters were in a hut or *chupper* made of corrugated sheet metal, the roof protected from the sun by a large shade tree. Also staying at Mt. Douglas were Dr. Stewart Fulton and his wife, Harriet, whom I had known at Biblical Seminary, where they had engaged in pre-field religious studies; Dr. and Mrs. Reid Graham, Presbyterians, soon to head a Marathi-language seminary in Poona; Bob Perkins, an Australian; a Canadian surgeon, Dr. Evelyn Fleming; a British nurse and an Anglican sister. In other bungalows were similar aggregations of missionaries of various nationalities and denominations, reaching across a broad theological spectrum. A very pleasant young American Congregationalist, Miriam Rogers, was another contemporary, as was an English physician, Dr. Nelson, an Anglican.

Life was full with morning and evening worship, with church services twice on Sunday, and with interesting and sometimes argumentative conversations at mealtime. For good measure my very first morning in this hill-station was punctuated by a small earthquake. We went for hikes—one particular one was to an ancient fortress named Raigarh. From its height, about 4,500 feet, one could see the Indian Ocean; but within its precincts was a spring that was the principal source of the Godavari River, which emptied into the Bay of Bengal. Another hike was to Chinamani waterfalls. There were teas, games of tennis, and tennis tournaments—my first opportunity to engage in this sport. There were lectures on Indian culture. One was by Dr. J. F. Edwards, Marathi editor and scholar, who was called the "Booming Englishman," a sobriquet he himself relished, and well deserved because of his robust voice. Also along was the Reverend Gabriel Sundaram, years later to become a Methodist bishop. He was a most amiable person, a South Indian of Telugu background. He advised me to read Gandhi's periodical, *Harijan,* and a liberal Christian magazine called *The Indian Social Reformer*; advice well taken. A lecture was given by Shri K. M. Munshi, a great nationalist leader, friend of Mahatma Gandhi and later governor of Bombay in independent India. Still another visitor was Dr. John MacKenzie, principal of Wilson College, Bombay, a very erudite Scotsman.

Unfortunately, I was not a photographer. I could not have afforded a good camera. Thus I do not have much of a pictorial record of this period. Instead, vivid impressions are stamped on my memory of lovely sunsets, incredibly brilliant moonlight, birds of exotic plumage and strange song, monkeys, and the spine-chilling calls of jackals at night. They are all still there. Even more do I recall the people often dressing and living in styles I easily associated with biblical accounts. I recall an interfaith conference, the first of its type I was to attend. It was a round-table discussion of religious insights as exchanged by adherents of the many faiths of India. This experience showed me how much I had to learn in order to be at all effective in my new surroundings.

As I look back over my notes recorded during my early days in India, I find that I was very introspective, morose, and self-critical. I did not reflect in this period the kind of joy and excitement that surely I experienced much of the time. It is apparent to me now that I had some trouble adjusting to a different climate, new foods, and a strange culture. One simply did things differently in India. If you needed clothes, you had them made for you; if sandals or shoes, a shoemaker would measure your feet, you would choose the leather, and in a few days the finished product was delivered to you. If you needed a haircut, the barber came to you; or for laundry, the *dhobi* or washerman would collect the garments from you and return them refreshed. There was much that you simply went without. I felt at the time that I was poorly disciplined, but in fact I lived according to a regular schedule. My devotional practices were fairly constant and public worship was frequent. I preached several times and sang in a choir. I read rather extensively. I engaged in stimulating conversation and made new friends. I became well aware of the political and social issues of the country and of the particular problems that confronted missionaries. Yet I had a certain restlessness about me, which finally I overcame. Almost before I knew it, it was time to return to Bombay.

As I have said, I was appointed as pastor of Bowen Memorial Methodist Episcopal Church in that city. It was located a short distance from the famous Gateway of India, erected to commemorate the visit of George V to India for the Durbar of 1911. The church itself was quite small and ministered to the needs of the Anglo-Indian community as well as English-speaking Indians, together with American, British, and other residents and visitors.

A word needs to be said about George Bowen, after whom my little church was named. He was a New Englander, born in Vermont. He came of a privileged family and was graduated from Harvard. He took a grand tour of Europe that extended for five years, during which time he mastered several European tongues. He had the resources and leisure to enjoy atheism. He was both an aesthete and a dilettante.

Then he was dramatically converted after the tragic death of his fiancée, and in due time entered and was graduated from Union Seminary in New York. He then sailed "before the mast" to India—a six-month's voyage around the Cape of Good Hope. Having arrived in Bombay he never departed India's shores. He chose the life of poverty and gave a remarkable Christian witness. He long edited the Bombay *Guardian*, which was considered the finest Christian journal in the world in his day. He wrote a number of books and Queen Victoria was one of his admiring readers, even sending her son to see Bowen and thank him when the Prince of Wales visited Bombay. Bowen was a fine musician and judged by Robert E. Speer to be the greatest devotional writer since St. Augustine.

I arrived in India just fifty years after his death and he

was still remembered. Indeed, fresh flowers often appeared upon his grave, brought by Hindus and Muslims. George Bowen was a saint. He welcomed the great worldwide evangelist William Taylor when he came to Bombay, and the two of them, though very different in temperament, became close associates.

It was no small matter, then, to be pastor of a church bearing this man's name. There were still a few persons around who remembered Bowen personally. Since 1938 marked the fiftieth anniversary of his death, we had a special service commemorating the occasion, at which the distinguished Bishop John Wesley Robinson was the preacher. The eminent Presbyterian missiologist Robert E. Speer, who had compiled a biographical volume on Bowen, wrote a message to be read at the service.

At the very beginning of my ministry there we had a service in commemoration of the two-hundredth anniversary of the conversion of John Wesley in London, May 24, 1738. The following year, 1939, we celebrated the reunion of American Methodism, which had divided nearly a hundred years before into three principal parts: The Methodist Episcopal, The Methodist Episcopal, South, and The Methodist Protestant Churches. Now once again they were one and the effect of this reunion was felt as far away as India. Each of the three years I was pastor we had special evangelistic services led by Annie McGhee, a visitor from America, and by the Reverend M. D. Ross and the Reverend E. A. Seamands, both warm evangelical missionaries from South India. This was the custom in those days, and these experiences had the effect of re-invigorating our congregation.

Otherwise, we had a fairly conventional program. I preached twice on Sunday and once at midweek. My mode in those days was to prepare extensive notes and memorize them so that I preached without notes. Manuscript preaching did not seem to suit my style, for I lost eye contact with the congregation. I kept all the notes and, although I cannot claim that it was great preaching, it was biblical and held the attention of people. Sometimes I would feel that I had failed dismally. Once I felt this way after speaking on Psalm l, only to be told by a member at the close of my pastorate that it was for him the most helpful message I had delivered while there. We are not always the best judges of our own work.

We worked hard on a youth program and it was fairly successful. I tried to be a good pastor, either walking to my parishioners' homes or going by bicycle. This latter mode had drawbacks because the Bombay climate was sultry and one would arrive soaked in perspiration. One of my parishioners was the most popular actress in Indian movies of the day. Her film name was Sabita Devi, but she was a Christian. After Sunday evening services I would cycle to the other side of the city to have good home cooking with my colleagues, the Wagners. Then I would spend the night with them. This I found very sustaining and a welcome change from my bachelor's existence.

Sometimes I have recalled with amusement the financial stringency under which I lived. It had never occurred to me to inquire in New York about the salary of a single missionary. In due time I learned that it was 150 rupees ($50) a month. Years later I asked my father-in-law what his salary was when he arrived in India just thirty years before I did. He informed me that it was fifty dollars a month. Thus I concluded that when the Board of Missions found a good thing they stayed with it! Then as a neophyte I determined how much I would contribute to the church. Naturally I had heard a tithe recommended. It seemed to me that a clergyman ought to double that, so I gave 20 percent of my income—only to find that I was the largest giver in the church. We have continued that happy practice through the years. When you find a good thing, stay with it!

Life in Bombay was interesting. Sooner or later all the great people of India would come to town, and when I learned of these visits I would turn aside to see these great sights. Thus, I saw the Viceroy, Lord Linlithgow, a man of immense stature, ride a white horse around one of the *maidans* reviewing the troops. Then, when Indira Nehru, daughter of Jawaharlal Nehru (later Indira Gandhi), returned in about 1939 from her lengthy studies in Europe she was greeted by the leading Indian nationalists, who turned out in hundreds to greet and garland her like the beautiful young "princess" that she was. One night with Bishop Pickett I stopped to hear Mohamed Ali Jinnah speak to a Muslim League rally. He was speaking in Urdu, then switched to English when we arrived. On another occasion I heard the fiery nationalist "Netaji," the Bengali Congressman, Subhas Chandra Bose, address a large rally. Frequently we heard the Bombay Symphony Orchestra, the most cosmopolitan assemblage imaginable play at Cowasjee Jehangir Hall. There were in the orchestra British, American, Indian, Japanese, and Chinese musicians from music schools, army bands, and churches. The conductor was a Parsee violinist, Mehla Mehta, father of Zubin Mehta.

Toward the end of 1938 a conference of the International Missionary Conference met at Madras Christian College, Tambaram, just outside the city of Madras (now Chennai). Here the theological "greats" from many continents gathered, and I met many of them as they passed through Bombay: John R. Mott, E. Stanley Jones, Bishop James C. Baker, Georgia Harkness, Toyohiko Kagawa, Bishop Azariah, Hendrik Kraemer, Henry P. Van Dusen, Constance Padwich, a number of German theologians, and many others. The whole world, for a time, seemed to be at one's door.

During Kagawa's visit to India he called on Mahatma Gandhi, as did a number of these visitors, all of whom have recounted the experience in their writings. I remember that when Dr. Kagawa was in Bombay he expressed a desire to visit Elephanta Caves, which lie six miles across the harbor on an island. We hired a *bandar* boat; that is, a country sailboat. Unfortunately, after sailing for a little while the wind fell completely and the boatmen had to resort to oars. It was dreadfully slow and even painful for our Japanese guest, who had a speaking engagement that evening. We had to hail a passing motor launch to return him to the Bombay side, thus he missed the caves.

I remember that during my first two years I suffered from many colds—almost every month. Maybe it was the climate or extremes of temperature. Maybe I was especially susceptible, or possibly I was exposed to new strains of viruses. Anyway, it was not pleasant. Otherwise, I kept well and walked a lot. At Christmastime the missionaries always arranged a fine outing at Juhu Beach. We often had picnics. The weather was reliable and one could schedule an outdoor function months in advance, but never during the rainy season, May through September. Then it might rain almost every day, sometimes *all* day, sometimes only brief, intermittent showers. But it was pleasant, for we liked to see the rains come. Things cooled down for a bit.

Most of all I found that I had arrived in India at an exciting time. First, I was a part of the last wave of missionaries who served toward one of the great missionary-sending periods in Christian history. Of that I am proud. Second, I went to India during the last decade of British rule. I could observe that rule in full-flower and then watch it begin to fade away. The fact is that I had a "grandstand seat" from which to observe the greatest struggle for freedom in history. I would not exchange this privilege for anything.

In retrospect I see that very early there began for me a kind of romance with India. Sometimes the relationship has been a kind of lover's quarrel, for India can be exasperating. It has produced towering figures such as Gandhi and Nehru. India has often served as a role model for other peoples who have sought freedom. It has had the courage to lead the Nonaligned Movement, determined not to be beholden to either of the adversaries in the Cold War. This has meant that she has risked misunderstanding, particularly from the United States, which has held India's neutralism suspect. Her economic policies and position on nuclear issues have earned her enemies among those who should have been her friends. India can be puzzling, and it has to be acknowledged that even after fifty years of freedom, India has not taken her rightful position among the family of nations nor has she been seen for what she is as the world's largest democracy. Nevertheless, I have thought of myself through the years as an interpreter and advocate of this great people.

5

An Extended Stay

It must be evident that I was thrilled to be in India. Sometimes I speak of my "love affair" with India. There has not been a single day since I first arrived there until now that I have not reflected gratefully upon that privilege. Never have I ceased to view the land and its people with wide-eyed, childlike interest—this after more than fifty trips to the subcontinent spread over more than half a century. Someone has said that India is not nearly as "homogenized" as Western culture; there is infinite variety to be found there. About the time you feel thoroughly acclimatized you are confronted with some entirely new dimension of life. The fact is that when we move in affection from the land of our birth to make room for another land, we become enlarged and take in the whole world. So it was then and is now that I am not anymore homesick, but at home everywhere.

Although I was a pastor of a small congregation, I began to reach out beyond its borders. Bombay (now Mumbai), for example, was and is a regular laboratory of religions. It is often reckoned that there are about a dozen principal religions in the world, with a great many subvarieties, and a person could meet adherents of, say, ten of these faiths during the course of a half day's walk around Bombay. It would be possible to meet a representative, as I have done, in the person of a tribesman from one of the possibly twenty-five million animists of the country. Hindus of all types abound and many branches of Muslim sects too. One could encounter a naked Jain monk surrounded by awe-filled disciples clearing a way for him.

The city is a center of the Parsees or Zoroastrians, often clad in distinctive dress. A turbaned Sikh taxi driver is sure to pass by, possibly with a passenger clad in a yellow robe, a Buddhist monk visiting from Ceylon (Sri Lanka). There are still a few Indian Jews in Bombay—Ben Israelites they are called. A Chinese community resides there, including Taoists and Confucianists. Among the bands of Japanese tourists are bound to be some Shintoists. One could pass by both Protestant and Roman Catholic churches. As St. Paul observed about Athens, so it may be said of residents of Bombay: "I perceive that you are a very religious people."

Among such people I experienced no difficulty in establishing acquaintance and even real friendship. This was true of some Muslims from various levels of society. It was and still remains the same with Hindus and others. As a pastor who often wore clerical attire I was treated with respect by devotees of many religions, for India is at heart a tolerant country—this in spite of not infrequent indications to the contrary.

Naturally, I made friends among Christians. This was true amongst Roman Catholics. I established a close friendship with an English Roman Catholic woman, Susan Bliss, who edited a Roman Catholic journal in Bombay. Similarly I became acquainted with several

Roman Catholic priests and bishops. When one works as a Christian in a country where there is a great preponderance of Hindus or Muslims, the distinctions among Christians become less pronounced. It seems to me that it is especially important for a missionary very early to form friendships with national colleagues. One of these for me was P. C. Benjamin Balaram, later a bishop. He was like a brother, and I always felt that I could share anything with him. Such a level of mutual trust I was able to develop with others too.

Bonds within the missionary community itself are very close, and the network extended throughout the country. If, for example, you found yourself a stranger in some out-of-the-way quarter, you could soon locate a missionary colleague and be assured of a place to stay. One became an "uncle" or "aunt" for the children of missionary associates. This extended beyond one's own denomination and became international in character as well. This was particularly true when one had children in one of the schools established mainly for missionary families. The two principal schools were Woodstock in Landour, Mussoorie, in the foothills of the Himalayas, northeast of Delhi; and Kodaikanal, a hill station in the heart of South India, southwest of Madras. At one or another of these places missionaries vacationed in order to be with their children, who were away from their homes most of the year. These were centers for physical, social, and religious renewal— great places to become acquainted with missionary colleagues across a broad denominational spectrum.

All of this may seem very cozy. What of the fact that India was then under colonial rule by an imperialistic power, Great Britain? Were not missionaries and Indian Christians after all "running dogs of imperialism," as often charged? Whatever truth there may be in this allegation is no more than a half-truth. The fact is that in the early days of the East India Company barriers were placed in the way of missionary work. No Christian Indians were allowed to be company officials. Added to this was the fact that the East India Company actually subsidized some Hindu temples and Muslim mosques. On the other hand, while the British at later stages were officially neutral toward religions, some officers privately supported missionary efforts. Still, the British connection as such was not used to further the Christian enterprise, and the conduct of many Europeans was a scandal—a real stumbling block to Christianity. Of course, the Marxist interpretation of missionary work would have the church a bedfellow of imperialism—to my mind an unfair and exaggerated judgment.

Much reference was made in those days to what was called the "missionary pledge." It was supposed that each missionary had to sign a statement in which he or she forswore political activity while implying that it would be appropriate to exercise influence favoring the constituted authority. In operation, the individual missionary, to the best of my knowledge, did not actually sign such an instrument; rather, a given mission board would take this responsibility on the missionary's behalf. The mission board was backed up by the Foreign Missionary Conference of North America, as certifying authority. This may seem a distinction without a difference; nevertheless, battle lines were often drawn on this issue.

Of course, some missionaries crossed the line and involved themselves directly in political issues. This struggle seemed to heat up in the autumn of 1939, particularly after war was declared. This latter exacerbated the whole matter, for to many it added insult to injury. Not only did Britain exercise political domination, but it took India into the war without its consent. This was more than some missionaries could take, and two couples and two individuals in the Methodist family alone were asked to leave India after stoutly protesting this policy. Both the religious and secular press were filled with accounts of this struggle. It may not be charitable to suggest that some missionaries seemed to relish the notoriety that was generated by the controversy. For my part, I concluded that I could be more helpful by continuing to serve in India rather than by taking stands that would ensure that I could not do so. Was this a coward's stand?

In spite of this public stance, privately my sympathies were entirely with the Indian people and their struggle for independence. It is only fair to observe that some of the older missionaries, but by no means all, sided with the British in their sympathies. We younger ones were generally great admirers of India's emerging leaders. We read their books and articles, followed their careers, and did what we could to encourage our Indian friends in their nationalist struggle. In those days there was generated in one an intense interest in Indian culture and politics, which has continued unabated to the present.

What galled India's people, especially in the latter years, was the air of superiority that many of the English adopted toward them. This contempt was at the root of the inevitable resistance. At the same time the Indians had a tremendous admiration for the British, if for no other reason than the latter's ability to subject them to docile rule. Indians borrowed much from the West. This fact, mingled with intense pride in their own culture, set up a tension in the Indian mind that has continued even since independence. It accounts for some of the Indians' extreme sensitivity at present—almost to the point of paranoia.

Indian nationalist sentiment began to gather force about the middle of the nineteenth century. The abortive and bloody attempt to overthrow foreign rule in 1857 is well known in history and fiction. Termed by English writers as the Mutiny, Indian historians regard it as "the first war for independence."

The group that finally won India's independence was the Indian National Congress. Founded in 1885 by an Englishman, Allan Octavian Hume, it was originally a rather mild and polite political debating society. It commanded interest from many religious groups, though it was predominantly Hindu. In the early years of the present century the Congress began to agitate for dominion status like Canada. Finally its aim sharpened to complete severance from Britain. On January 26, 1930, Congress declared India independent, though as in our own history, it took several years to realize that goal.

A great Indian nationalist, Tilak, said: "*Swaraj* (home rule) is my birthright, and I will have it!" This became a battle cry. George Bernard Shaw pointed out once with regard to India that a man without his freedom was like a man with cancer: "He can think of nothing else."

By the middle 1940s it would be fair to say that all

major groups in Indian life wanted freedom—the Congress party, orthodox Hindus, Muslims, moderates, and the princes—but their definition of freedom would have been qualified in various ways. Even the British overlords could point to a mounting series of declarations of intent to allow home rule. Increasingly government responsibility was shared with Indians, who nevertheless retained doubts about the ultimate sincerity of British promises of full freedom. (Of Mahatma Gandhi's movement I will write later.)

Perhaps I should say that my own interest in India's freedom movement was stimulated by my acquaintance with one of the principal actors. He was Dr. B. R. Ambedkar, a member of the viceroy's cabinet as independence approached and later law minister in Nehru's cabinet. As principal author of India's Constitution, he might properly be called the James Madison of India.

Dr. Ambedkar was born an Untouchable, and as a lad he suffered sorely under the strictures of the caste system. Possessed of a brilliant mind, he came to the notice of the Gaekwar of Baroda (a prince or ruler of a Native State) who saw to his education. Finally, he earned doctorates both in Britain and in the United States, then began the practice of law in Bombay. It was there that I came to know him. At the time he was a widower, yet he enjoyed the company of cultivated women. He was especially drawn to one of our missionary ladies. She frequently invited him to dinner in her residence. To make things "proper" I was invited at the same time. It was a great privilege to come to know him in this way. He was not a member of the Congress Party, nor a follower of Gandhi, although he was an ardent advocate of independence and of genuine freedom for his oppressed community. In 1935 Dr. Ambedkar, a principal leader of the Untouchables, renounced Hinduism in a speech and invited his followers to do likewise. There was much speculation at the time as to whether or not there might be an even greater influx into the church of this group, a development for which the church was ill prepared. About that time the great bishop of Dornakal, Azariah, conferred with Ambedkar. The latter said in substance, "If you are suggesting that my people should unite with the church, with *which* church shall they unite?" Thus he pointed to the scandal of our divisions. Thereafter Bishop Azariah was more than ever convinced that fuller Christian unity was not an elective but a necessity for the church in India.

In 1946 in Delhi I called on Dr. Ambedkar, with whom I had by then been acquainted for a number of years. At that time he was Minister of Labor in the viceroy's cabinet. While I was waiting for him at his residence his secretary showed me about the house. There were two large living rooms with an office in between. Above the mantelpiece in one room was a picture of Buddha, an Indian. Above the mantelpiece in the other was a picture of Christ. Above the desk in the study was a picture of Christ before Pilate. When Dr. Ambedkar came out, I took him on a tour of his own house to view in turn these three pictures. As we stood finally before the latter picture, the trial scene, I asked, "Dr. Ambedkar, isn't that about where you stand, thinking what you will do with Jesus?" He replied: "Yes, I guess you're about right."

Four years later I called at his office again. Dr. Ambedkar was then law minister of independent India, equivalent to our attorney general. I recalled the earlier scene. Dr. Ambedkar remembered the occasion and then added, "You may be interested to know that last week I became a Buddhist!"

I was called in as an "extra male" at more than one dinner for Dr. Ambedkar. Single men were in short supply in Bombay, so I was invited to a great many events—dinners, banquets, musicals, theatricals. In New York I had been advised to bring a tuxedo and forthwith obtained this valuable article for covering the male form for the unbelievable sum of $22.50. The advice was sound, for evening dress was at that time very much in vogue in British India. It was not uncommon for me to have to dress for dinner three times a week. This made for interesting conversational contacts with business and community leaders to whom I would not otherwise have had any real access. It enlarged my horizons and helped me to overcome my shyness so that I was at home in British as well as Indian society. It had the further advantage of partially providing me with excellent food, which on my small salary was in short supply.

My story must not be extended too far, but I have been recalling how my exposure to India reached well beyond the tiny Bowen Memorial Church. For example, I had to take part in activities of the Bombay Annual Conference, of which I was a member. All Methodist pastors are members of such an organization that in other polities might be called a diocese or presbytery or synod. Each conference was divided into districts, and each was presided over by a district superintendent who was rather like an assistant bishop. Then the missionaries had some organization, though of lesser importance than the conference. Very soon I was assigned to the role of mission treasurer for the Bombay Conference. It was not a role of very great importance. It did involve a moderate amount of bookkeeping, about which I knew nothing and had to learn as I went along. The mission treasurer also had to cultivate support from the United States, both soliciting and acknowledging gifts from donors. By the third year I was also elected as conference secretary, a more important role that of course involved keeping minutes of conference proceedings and editing the journal each year. I think I may say that I did this very well.

Earlier I reported that in 1936 I had been received as a probationary member of the New York Annual Conference of the Methodist Episcopal Church. Soon after going to India my membership, as was the custom, was transferred there—to the Bombay Annual Conference. The next session of that conference was held in December 1938. Since I was a newcomer they wanted me to appear before the conference as preacher, for all wanted to "size up" the newcomer; hence, I was scheduled to preach at the Sunday morning service. Later it was planned for the ordinations to take place at that time. Naturally, I tried to withdraw, but this was refused. Thus I found myself in the unusual position of preaching my own ordination sermon. It was delivered the second Sunday before Christmas, and the biblical text I chose was St. Paul's highly theological way of telling the Christmas story: Philippians 2:5-11, the famous *kenosis*, "emptying," passage. My own translation from Greek follows:

Concentrate upon having an attitude among you such as Christ Jesus Himself demonstrated to us who although He had always possessed the nature of God, yet He did not conclude this equality to be a trophy greedily to be grasped, but divested Himself of His divine privileges and took on the nature of a bond-slave, appearing in the likeness of a human being. And being found thus in appearance, He stooped down even more unto death; yes, the meanest kind of death—crucifixion. In consequence of this God exalted Him to the highest rank and station and graciously bestowed on Him a title which is above every other name, so that in the name of Jesus, every knee—every creature of the universe—should prostrate itself and every tongue freely confess that Jesus Christ is Lord, to the supreme end that God the Father might be glorified.

My topic was "Ministry Is Servanthood." Apparently the effort was well received, and following it I was ordained elder or presbyter in the Universal Church, as I believe, though I was to exercise this ministry under a Methodist discipline. Bishop Brenton Thoburn Badley ordained me. He was of a second-generation missionary service and a great authority on the Himalaya Mountains. Indian ministers also laid hands on my head, as I am happy to recall. Servanthood has remained a continuing emphasis of my ministry.

Meanwhile, I was lonesome. That was soon to change. Already I have reported both my shyness and my admiration of members of the opposite sex, though mostly from a distance. I had a number of girlfriends but was serious about none. This was in striking contrast to most other young male missionaries, who were already married to women with whom they had grown up or met in college.

In March 1939, just over a year after I had arrived in India, I learned that the famous missionary evangelist Dr. E. Stanley Jones was to hold meetings in nearby Poona. His reputation was already firmly established in India and beyond. His first book, *The Christ of the Indian Road*, had already taken the Christian world by storm and had been translated into many languages; his friendship with Gandhi and other Indian national leaders was also well known. He had adopted the practice of carefully preparing five lectures each year. He took about three months to do this. Then he would travel widely in India delivering these addresses on current topics of great social interest but with a distinctive Christian focus. They were directed toward educated and thoughtful Hindus, Muslims, and adherents of other religions. The lectures excited widespread interest and were followed by lengthy periods of penetrating and far-reaching questioning from the audience. India loved this sort of thing, and Jones became very adept at it.

These meetings were not held in churches but in public halls, for many of his hearers would not have dreamed of entering a church. Such meetings were held five days a week under the chairmanship of some distinguished citizen or official. Saturdays and Sundays Jones would give to churches, and Sunday night he would entrain for another city to repeat the procedure. Through the years he did this in virtually every Indian city of more than 50,000 people.

He was booked for Gokhale Hall in Poona. My friends Dr. and Mrs. Royal D. Bisbee invited me to Poona for these meetings. This may have been a little calculated on their part, for they had not informed me that Dr. Jones and his daughter, Eunice, were also to be guests in their home. She was traveling with him as his secretary. It was on March 24, 1939, that I was first to meet her there. I recall the very spot where first I saw her. More than fifty years later I returned with Eunice to that living room of the parsonage, and with the somewhat surprised pastor we thanked God for that first meeting.

As I have implied, up to that time I had formed no attachments. This time it was different. It was almost as if till then I had been restrained from commitment. Now I felt prompted toward one. I was almost immediately smitten when Eunice walked into the room and into my life. How she felt, I have no idea; that was not a major concern for me then.

I did attend E. Stanley Jones's lectures, immensely impressed by their range and delivery, amazed at his skill in responding to the most searching questions. Likewise I attended a round table conference that he led and during which he drew out from representatives of all the major religions their most authentic accounts of religious experience. All this I did most faithfully, but I also found time to get to know Eunice Jones a little better. I went bicycling with her. We visited Mahalakshmi Temple, situated on a prominent hill overlooking Poona. I greatly enjoyed the view from there. In a borrowed car we toured a bit in the countryside. We determined to meet again, and again, and again.

Soon I returned to my post in Bombay. Far from being cured from my loneliness in Poona's salubrious climate, I found that I was more lonely than ever. I wrote to Eunice, of course, and then waited hopefully for a reply. By this time I learned to no particular surprise that other young men, British and Americans, were interested in her too. Thus I hardly expected a return letter. Still a reserved type of person and not wishing to assume anything, I kept my distance and addressed her formally as "Dear Miss Jones." How was I to know that she would share my missives for her father's help in deciphering my scrawl and that both of them enjoyed a good laugh at my expense?

As May 1939 approached I had a decision to make. The original intention was that I should return to Mahableshwar for another month of uninterrupted language study. Another door also now opened to me. I was invited to attend the Sat Tal Christian Ashram for a month's retreat under the guidance of Dr. E. Stanley Jones. I confess that I did not wrestle very much with the matter; I decided on the latter course of action, for Eunice was to be there too.

So it was that I ventured out on my first journey to North India. May can be very hot in Bombay before the rains begin; the interior of the country is hotter still. Traveling by third class accommodations can be a real trial in India, but you cannot beat the price. The round-trip, totaling approximately 3,000 miles, cost the equivalent of about ten dollars. I broke journey in Agra, site of the Taj Mahal. It was my good fortune to be there on a full moon night, and it was thus that I first saw this marvelous structure. The scene is very vivid to this moment: there was an ethereal beauty about the building, as if the whole were covered with flowing gossamer silk. One traveler said that Muslim art is "geometry set to music." The Taj then is a symphony—just as one dreams it should be. The following morning I visited the monument once again and saw it in an entirely different light. During ensuing years I have repeatedly visited the Taj during all seasons and circumstances, have seen it from the air, from the opposite side of the river that borders it, and from the fort. It never disappoints.

From Agra there is a meter gauge railway called the *chotti* (small) line. An overnight trip leads from Agra to a station bearing the marvelous name of Kathgodam at the foot of the Himalayas. From there a three-hour bus trip takes one to a town called Bhowali, a fruit-growing and trading center lying at about 5,000 feet. From there, in those days, one walked the four miles to the Ashram. A *Bhotiya* coolie was hired to carry baggage. By wrapping a rope around a load that is carried on the back by an attached cloth or leather strap across the forehead, these men could carry very heavy burdens; but my baggage must have been only about thirty pounds.

The word *ashram* (pronounced ah-shrum) is of Sanskrit origin. The word *shrum* means hard work; the prefix *a* is either a negative or an intensive. Thus, an ashram is a place where work ceases or where the most intense work is emphasized—namely, prayer. It is a place of disciplined devotion and study looking toward inner religious renewal or leading to some form of community service. During recent years a number of Christian ashrams have been established in India. Sat Tal Ashram was the first or one of the first of this type. It is situated on a 450-acre plot at nearly 5,000 feet in the Himalaya foothills, a region characterized by pine, oak, and rhododendron forests, the latter growing to full-sized trees. Sat Tal means seven lakes; three of them are now dry or seasonal, but one of them is a perfect little gem—*Panna* (Emerald) Lake. It affords fine swimming and on occasion splendid fly fishing to the experienced angler.

E. Stanley Jones bought the property, gave it to the church, and established his ashram in 1930. By that time he had served in India for nearly twenty-five years. Something of his approach and work I have already alluded to, but after years of evangelism he observed the need for more emphasis on group discipline. A kind of skeleton ashram continued throughout the year, but a concentrated program was offered in May and June, the hottest season on the plains. To this place repaired each year Indians and Westerners, missionaries, British officials and seekers of many nations for what was sometimes called a "vacation with God."

At the session in May 1939 some 150 persons were in attendance. It was a most interesting group. One example was "Father" Kandaswamy Aiyer of Madras. His designation, "Father," was out of affectionate regard for his age. Though a Brahmin, he was thought of and indeed thought of himself as being a "Christian Hindu" and would take communion with Christians. In some instances a venerable person such as he can take this position and not have to suffer persecution and rejection by his family and caste. Another was Dr. Paul Santamurti, also born a Brahmin but married by his specific and somewhat rebellious choice to a woman of outcaste origin—very much a thing that was "not done." Three English participants came from the Christa Sevak Sangh Ashram in Poona. One, a Jewish convert, contributed richly to our fellowship. Another was a recent convert from Islam, a prince of Turkestan's royal family. There were several who called themselves Christian radicals; that is, they had strong nationalist commitment and leftist leanings. There was a good representative missionary presence from many denominations and national backgrounds. Fully half of our numbers were Indian Christians. And, of course, there was I and—not incidentally—Eunice Jones. Her mother was also there. Both of her parents kept watchful eyes on us!

We had a full and disciplined program. We would arise at 5:30 in the morning, have a period of private and shared devotion, eat breakfast at 7:00, and follow that with an hour's work period that involved everyone. We would gather wood for cooking, clear paths of pine needles, and clean rice. Some, including myself, would act as sweepers, with responsibility for cleaning latrines. Others would paint and generally tidy up the premises. Then there would be a study session. That summer we had read to us Brother Stanley Jones's manuscript for a new book titled *Along the Indian Road,* which we would then discuss chapter by chapter. This was particularly helpful to me for it afforded a broad survey of the whole national situation. The discussions were critical, lively, and sometimes contentious. Other sessions involved Bible study. There was rest in the afternoon, followed by swimming, tea, and then evening vespers at the lakeside at which Brother Stanley was usually the preacher, with a challenging evangelistic message. We were all addressed as "Brother" or "Sister," which not only generated a family atmosphere but also promoted a kind of sanitizing effect on relations between the genders. Meals were simple but adequate, and conversation was good, with just enough relaxation and fun as to leave a pleasant memory of the experience.

This was my first venture into the Himalayas (the word means "abode of snow") and it was all very exciting to me. We went a time or two to nearby Naini Tal where from a high prominence one could glimpse the very lofty snow-clad peaks of 25,000 feet and more, superbly beautiful although nearly 100 miles away. We either hiked to "Naini" or hired horses. One such beast was a retired racehorse named "Shaitan" (yes, you guessed it, it means "Satan"). He ran away with me on a narrow mountain path and I was nearly thrown. On another venture Eunice was actually thrown from her animal. I had then the not altogether unpleasant task of rubbing her wounded back with Ellerman's Horse Embrocation, a trusty British liniment, equally effective on man (or woman) and beast. Naini Tal was then a beautiful hill-station surrounding Naini's (a Hindu goddess) Lake. Legend had it that she exacted a sacrifice each year and anyone unfortunate enough to drown in her lake was considered an offering to this deity. As a girl, Eunice had gone to the Wellesley Girls School in Naini Tal, a British type boarding school under Methodist direction.

Without going into detail, I record that Eunice and I became much better acquainted with each other during this period and looked forward to other meetings. Before either of us was ready for it, May came to an end and I descended again to the plains. It was hot! On the way to Bombay I stopped over at Mathura and Vrindaban, both centers of Krishna devotion and located south of Delhi; and in Vrindaban I visited for twenty-four hours with Dr. A. C. Chakraverti at the Christian ashram he had established there. This holy man had been a Brahmin priest and devotee of Durga, the Hindu goddess of destruction, consort of Siva. His conversion to Christ was dramatic and thorough, his new devotion strong and consistent. His book, *How I Found God and God Found Me*, is an intriguing account of his spiritual journey. His readiness to live as a Christian convert in a great Hindu center showed extreme courage on his part and restraint on the part of Hindus in Vrindaban. Chakraverti and I remained friends until his death.

From Vrindaban I returned directly to Bombay and took up my usual round of responsibilities there. The city and its people were so interesting that it was impossible to be bored. With the Taj Mahal Hotel near at hand, a steady stream of visitors came there to stay and sometimes I would visit them. A P&O liner put in every week. The Anchor Line's ship arrived fortnightly, with *Lloyd-Tristino* and American ships calling periodically. These occasionally brought visitors to my little church. Several times young Americans would drop by Bombay and I would put them up in my small "digs" located above the church. I was given a membership in the American Club, and although very few of the members were related to my church, when illness, death, or marriage occurred I was from time to time called into service.

The afternoon following a mail ship's arrival there would be prompt delivery of post from abroad. I have kept all the letters from my family members during this period. At the time it seemed to me that I heard from them only infrequently. In retrospect, however, I find that they were faithful in correspondence and this sustained me more than they could have imagined. Sometimes several family members would write to me about the same happening. Far from this being repetitious, I found that by their reporting from somewhat different perspectives, I was able to form a three-dimensional view of events. Likewise my family kept many of my letters, and although my handwriting left much to be desired, I managed to give them a fair picture of my situation.

Certainly I did not lack for material of great interest. Bombay itself was a cultural and anthropological museum. The local English newspapers were well edited and reported rather fully on the situation in the country, even accounting for the British bias that they undoubtedly reflected. Or there were short motor trips or hiking tours outside the urban limits. There was a perfect gem of a hill-station called Matheran about an hour from the city. It was approached by a kind of "toy" train that would lift the passengers along a narrow-gauge track to a 2,000 foot level. There were beaches, especially Juhu, which afforded convenient recreation. Breach Candy swimming bath and tea garden was a delight, although the kites, a kind of falcon, were not a delight as they swiftly dived upon the unwary, snatching a piece of toast from one's hand or leaving "calling cards" to those who did not expect such courtesy.

When opportunity presented itself I would try to visit missionary work in the rural areas where the "real India" lay. One such excursion took me to southern India, to the Kanarese language area. Here a senior missionary, Dr. E. A. Seamands, gave three of us a delightful tour, part of which we walked and part of which we rode on camels. This was, of course, exciting, but one was to discover that after sitting on the backs of these "ships of the desert," one began to suffer from *seat*-sickness. It was not desert country but rather through jungle, which is not a forested area as the word may suggest, but rather semi-arid terrain, marked by scrub trees and cacti. It was desperately hot, and I was to discover how cooling a hot cup of tea could be since it called forth perspiration and consequent evaporation—all most pleasant indeed.

We visited village congregations, which were numerous in that part of the country. Large numbers had been converted from outcaste Hinduism and were most earnest and ardent in the practice of their newfound faith. We came to a large village, Bhimanhalli, where an exceptional pastor, the Reverend H. Gnanamitra served. He led the people in daily worship, taught them Bible, and instructed them in the Christian life. He also helped them devise services of worship suited to their situation. For example, he found that the typical Christian marriage service was not at all congenial to their circumstances—consisting of a ceremony of one-hour duration at most. Hindu nuptial celebrations were much lengthier. With local Christians he developed a marriage service that would last all day. The actual vows were included in the proceedings, of course, but there was much emphasis on and instruction about family life, hygiene and sanitation, the rearing of children, family prayer, nutrition, and other topics that relate to serious matrimony. There was singing and dancing and joyful exuberance expressed in abundant measure. No longer did the former Hindus miss the jollity they left behind as non-Christians. The Christian life was a full and joyful life. This account is typical of the creative and intellectual approach that this pastor brought to his task. He had also a lively interest in sociology and anthropology. Pursuing these interests, he produced a number of fine monographs. One of them, I recall, had to do with the Hindu practice in that vicinity of "marrying" a village prostitute to a sword.

We proceeded through a number of villages, observing the joy of villagers being established in their newfound faith. We noted, too, that the Hindu leaders showed respect for these recently converted Christians, once regarded as untouchable. They could not but be impressed with their drastically changed lives. We worshiped with the people, often in open air under trees. Women would sweep the ground clean and draw a checkerboard-like series of lines in the earth. Each person sat within a square. It was all very orderly. We ate with them and sang with them. We observed their schools and walked through their fields. On one occasion we joined them in the annual practice of walking around the boundaries of their villages. We showed interest in their children and sometimes cared for their sick. As I have said, it was terribly hot. One night there was a sudden rainstorm, a regular torrent. We stood in the downpour clad only in shorts. We learned something about showers of blessing and were inducted into rural missionary work.

Among my papers I find a rather full account of another one-week trip to two of our church districts situated some 350 miles from Bombay: Nander and Udgir Districts. As mission treasurer, I had been writing letters to solicit financial support for work there but I had not myself actually visited the region. My friend and colleague Paul Wagner, pastor of another English-speaking church in Bombay, and I determined to tour this section together. We found that by leaving by train after our Sunday evening services we could make this trip mostly by rail and return at an early hour the next Sunday morning in time for our services. We slept in beds only two nights that week, the rest of the time on bedding rolls on trains. Several times we had to change back and forth between broad gauge and meter gauge railway tracks.

Our itinerary took us into the Nizam's Dominions, Hyderabad State. The Nizam was a Muslim ruler, a descendant of the Moghul Emperor, Aurangzeb. The Nizam was reputed to be the richest man in the world and certainly one of the stingiest. Only once did I see him; he was not an impressive man as he was driven by in the backseat of an ancient Ford touring car. His wizened presence was doubtless more suited to this vehicle than to one of the dozen Rolls Royces he was supposed to have owned. His rule was over a large Native State, second only in size to Kashmir. The state had its own railway and postal system and its own army. It was in every way sovereign except for foreign relations, but was also under the watchful eye and review of the paramount power, Britain.

I wrote a compact document about this tour, titled "Diary of a Tenderfoot Missionary."

On our journey we paused at a station called Aurangabad near which the famous Ellora and Ajanta caves are located. At this station a policeman followed me as I walked up and down the train platform to exercise. Suddenly he began to whistle a tune that I recognized. It was "What a Friend We Have in Jesus." I joined in and whistled with him. He proved to be a fellow Christian and a Methodist. He was trying to attract my attention by this tune, for since we were both friends of Jesus, we were friends of each other. Incidentally, we were both offending Islamic custom. We should not have been whistling. That practice, according to strict Muslim views, is reserved for the angels.

At noon we arrived at Nander, the headquarters of the district. Our colleague, the Reverend Abednego Barnabas, was suffering from a fever and sent one of the pastors, Navgire by name, to meet us. We "enjoyed" a hot curry for lunch, its fire somewhat tempered by eating a banana with it. During that period I was still becoming acclimatized and accustomed to local food. To this day I have never made my peace with food that was really highly spiced, but that particular week I gained lots of experience, for every meal was Indian. Breakfast was easy: chapattis, tea, and fruit, so this moderated the hotter meals.

When we arrived in a town we would hire bicycles to ride around and see the sights or take us to the people we were supposed to visit. Nander was the site of a Sikh temple, one of the most famous in the country. As always, once we removed our sandals we were allowed to be guided to all but its most sacred precincts. We had no church there at the time; the faithful would gather in a home for worship. In the whole district there were then only six hundred Christians. Today there are thousands. These scattered Christians were the ones we had come to visit. In one village literally named "Manure Town" we were welcomed by a dancing group to the tune of a familiar *bhajan* (ballad-hymn), "King Jesus Has Come." The people received us with great hospitality and even in the poorest homes we were served tea or lemonade or whatever their circumstances allowed. It is very touching indeed to receive of the poorest of the poor. In this place I preached (through an interpreter) my first village sermon. It was translated into both Marathi and Telugu. I hope the people were edified. Some of them were carpenters and of course this reminded us, and we reminded them, of the vocation in which Jesus was trained. Following our service we had a kind of roundtable discussion with the leading Hindus of this place.

Thus we went from place to place, to towns with strange names: Bhaisa, Mudhal, Khedgaon, Purna, Basar, Udgir, Bidar, Parli, Jalna. Each place had its own charm, each a distinct "personality." Some of them were walled towns, heavily laden with history—of the Maratha hero, Shivaji, and of the Moghuls. We were fortunate enough in two places to arrive on bazaar day, which brought in large numbers of people from all around. Farmers traded their goods, perhaps purchased yokes of oxen or had a cart or plough repaired. Sometimes the Lambharis, a gypsy-like people, were present and they were fascinating in every way. We two innocent Europeans must have attracted a certain amount of fascination, for we were the only ones of our background who were present. It was not uncommon to see a caravan of camels pass by, for they were widely used in Hyderabad State.

An entry from my diary highlights this excursion:

Dinnered on curry and rice again. We'd had it for the last six meals at least. It was reputed to be very good, but by this time I was tiring of it.

Then we were led through the darkness of the ill-lighted streets to a kind of barn-yard. Here a number of people were gathered. We sat on a cot and observed the proceedings. I had a girl beside me (5 years old)—Kusum, by name. Nearby was another pretty little girl, Lilavati. Soon a worker called Simon Nirmal came in. He started the people singing "bhajans" or ballad-hymns. Then he catechized them for us. They were our village-Christians who came from 10 or 15 miles to meet us. Their training and knowledge was amazing. He questioned them from creation through the life of Christ. It was excellent. At appropriate places they sang. Nirmal gets 10 rupees a month ($4.00), but has done a remarkable work as he lives among his people. Has taught many of them to read. They love him as we came to do. When they had stopped, we said a few stammering words of Marathi. Their language was so mixed with Telegu that we could hardly make it out.

To bed without mosquito nets. Slept on varandah. Had dreadful bout with mosquitoes and bed-bugs, who seemed to divide spoils over us. We won out finally, for we were still there when dawn came.

Before we knew it we were back in Aurangabad and proceeded by bus to the Ellora caves. Bus fare was eight annas—about twenty cents. I recorded the following in my diary:

The Caves are 34 in number. Twelve are Buddhist, 17 Brahmin, and 5 Jain. We started in with the Buddhist. Took no guide for we could not understand their Hindustani. Went around them for five hours by ourselves. The Buddhist caves were good. They were all carved out of solid rock. They usually consisted of large colonnaded walls. Around the walls were various figures of Buddha. At the extreme end was a kind of "sanctum sanctorum" in which was a big Buddha surrounded by other figures and symbols. Then there were little cells for the monks. All this was done at great labour and displayed considerable art.

We then hitchhiked back to Aurangabad with some salesmen. We had to wait four hours for a train. We had dinner at the station, which had three restaurants: European, Hindu, and Muslim. We chose the latter, which was cheapest, and talked over our sermons, which we had been composing at odd moments throughout the week. We caught the train at ten o'clock, changed trains at 1:00 A.M. and arrived back in Bombay at 6:00 A.M. in time for our Sunday services.

In September 1939 Dr. E. Stanley Jones came to Bombay for a week of evangelism under the auspices of pastors and missionaries of a number of denominations. Somehow I was chosen as chairman of a preparatory committee that was to report on the situation in the churches in the city at that time. It resulted in a considerable document entitled, "A Brief Survey of the State of the Christian Church in Bombay." Our committee worked hard in garnering data from existing papers and through original research and survey of a vast array of Christian enterprises throughout the city. Then a Malayalam pastor, the Reverend Frederick Lazarus, and I had the task of editing and writing large portions of the report. This was an exceedingly valuable exercise for me, because it enhanced my grasp of the total Christian witness in this large metropolis and brought me in touch with leaders of all types. Stanley Jones found our work helpful as he tried to witness effectively and relevantly in this urban context.

Of course, with the presence of Dr. Jones in the city, this meant that his daughter, Eunice, was also there, much to my delight. I had not seen her for three months and correspondence was only a poor substitute for the real thing. St. John in one of his letters makes this point when he wrote: "I have so much to tell you, but I do not want to do it with pen and ink. I hope to see you soon, and then we will talk personally." My exact sentiments! We did further our acquaintance considerably, and by this time I had come to the point of addressing her as "Eunice" rather than "Miss Jones." So one is emboldened by affection. She stayed with my friends Paul and Mabel Wagner, who kindly gave us use of their car to help the romance on. The week passed very quickly. While we were together in Bombay, World War II was declared, a reality that was to affect the world and us profoundly.

6
OF LOVE AND WAR

It was not until January 1940 that I again saw Eunice. Her mother invited me to their home in Sitapur, 52 miles north of Lucknow, for a few days. That gave her a better chance to observe me closely, which she did, a fact of which I was thoroughly aware. I can recall vividly how I arrived there on the morning of January 18, 1940. I was still clothed in the shorts and shirt I had been wearing in Bombay thirty-six hours before. My topcoat was checked in my baggage. How was I to know that North India would be so cold? I was still under the impression that India was a warm country. But not Sitapur in January!

Moreover, it seemed to be located "at the end of nowhere." Perhaps its affect on one can best be experienced by recalling the remark of an American visitor to Sitapur long ago: "What a beautiful sunset for such an out-of-the-way place!" I have heard that expression long enough to make it my own. In the economy of God there are no out-of-the-way places.

It was an eye-opening experience to be in this town. I saw the rather gracious house in which Eunice was born, once the residence of a British official. Adjacent to it was the boys' primary school that Mrs. Jones had established and nurtured through the years, where she had pioneered in having women teach young boys—quite contrary to the prevailing practice throughout the country. With the help of the boys she largely grew the food needed by the boarding department. Sitapur was a cantonment town; that is, British troops had been established there. It was involved in the Indian mutiny of 1857. Tombstones in the little Anglican churchyard bore witness to this. Likewise they recorded the grim record of the death of soldiers and civilians, young and old, who had succumbed to the ravages of India—cholera, malaria, sunstroke, snakebite, bee stings, or even trampling by an elephant.

All this Eunice showed me, as well as the girls' school, the bazaar, the miles of cantonments with their decaying barracks, and the first airfield in India, a grassy expanse used for training pilots in World War I. We also visited the Joneses' neighbors, both Indian and British officials. I recall too the incredible full moonlight—bright enough to read a newspaper—which pushed our romance on. I remember hearing Mabel Lossing Jones draw from her vast storehouse of Indian experience or recount tales of her Cornish and Canadian ancestors, or tell of the events of her daughter's growing up, this much to Eunice's distress. Moreover, I had the privilege of meeting Dr. Lillie D. Greene, a missionary neighbor and quite unique scholar, holding a double doctorate in Pali-Sanskrit and ornithology from Johns Hopkins and the University of Chicago.

After a few days we all went into Lucknow to attend the governing board meeting for Isabella Thoburn College, of which Mrs. Jones was a member. This, my first visit to Lucknow, was occasion to become acquainted with this great historic city with its Muslim Imambara, its marvelous palaces, and the ruins of the residency, center of some of the worst struggles of the Indian mutiny. We stayed at the Christian Ashram Eunice's father had established there in an old Muslim mansion called Nur Manzil, "Palace of Light." We were able too to see Mrs. Prem Nath Dass installed as president of Isabella Thoburn College. She was a remarkably gifted woman of a prominent Indian Christian family and a graduate of Wellesley College in the United States.

The big news, however, was that during that week Eunice and I were engaged to be married. Having been assured of her willingness, I even went so far as to ask her father for her hand. I knew that he did not like the ordinary Indian practice of arranged marriage, nor the Western custom of the young persons making the choice solely on their own. Instead, he advocated a joint venture of parents and the prospective couple, after the model of Mar Thoma Christians. As it happened, I chanced to ask his permission while he was getting his hair cut. The barber did not understand English, so this rather private conversation could take place in such a setting. Stanley Jones readily agreed, giving us his blessing. Under the circumstances he could scarcely have done otherwise, for the barber was poised with razor over him to trim his hair!

There was living in Lucknow at that time a German Jewish refugee who had fled from Adolf Hitler and had established a jewelry store. We went to him, and within twenty-four hours he had made up an engagement ring that still graces Eunice's hand. Not surprisingly, I did not have money to pay for it and had to borrow the sum. We were duly and happily engaged, and when I got back to

Bombay a few days later I sold my typewriter in order to pay back the loan. Besides, Eunice already had a typewriter, and while her father was to lose his secretary I was to gain one. If the truth be told she probably got the poor end of the bargain, for ever since she has typed out my papers from abominable handwriting, up to these very words.

The ensuing months passed for me at a very slow pace indeed. I did my work, which by now has been sufficiently described and need not be repeated *ad infinitum*. Eunice did come to Bombay for a few days in March and April—again, high occasions for me. We were able to find a wonderful apartment in which to live. One of my best friends, a young English bank executive, agreed to rent a room in our flat and to board with us to help make ends meet. This friend, Mowbray Mackie, I also asked to be my best man, a role he could not fulfill because demands of his work would not allow the long journey to North India for the wedding. As it happened I made that trip alone but I did not return alone. In late May of 1940 I went back to Sat Tal and had three or four days at the Ashram.

Now I must write a few words especially about Eunice. They say that some marriages are made in heaven and I tend to believe it. Along the way I had known and liked some other young women but none seemed quite the one for me. Then came Eunice, and she seemed almost immediately to be the right one. I write these words more than half a century later and am still as excited by her—by her sparkle and vivacity—as when first we met. Of her I cannot say, "she *was* the wife of my youth," but, "she *is* the wife of my youth," and I see her with eyes reserved for her alone.

She was an only child, but I do not believe that she has suffered from that by excessive pampering and coddling, nor has she become self-centered and maladjusted because of this. Rather, she has always struck me as being well-adjusted, poised, and normal. She grew up with a father who idolized her when he was present, but who was for the most part traveling in India or fields afar while she was growing up. Her mother, of Quaker descent, was not inclined to be overindulgent toward her one child and even exercised considerable restraint lest her offspring might be spoiled. On her mother's side she had English ancestors, the Treffrys. They were Cornish, from Fowey on the south coast of England, and of sound stock and lineage. Indeed the original John Treffry was knighted on the battlefield of Hastings. Another ancestor attended Queen Elizabeth I's coronation ball. Eunice also had some Dutch forebears: a great uncle was Benson J. Lossing, an outstanding American historian. Her father's background was, of course, Welsh, but so numerous are the Joneses that the precise line has never been sorted out.

Growing up in Sitapur, Eunice learned Hindustani before English and still commands proper pronunciation of that language. Whereas I was accustomed to dogs and cats as pets for children, Eunice had a deer, a monkey, a peacock, and a mongoose named Riki Tiki Tavi. Her grandchildren delight in hearing her tell of them. Her mother taught her at home until she was nine years of age, when her parents returned to the United States for their year's furlough. That year, in Dubuque, Iowa, was her first experience at attending a public school, an American school at that, with all its new experiences. On returning to India with her parents, she spent five years as a boarding student in Wellesley Girls' School in Naini Tal. Following that she transferred to Woodstock in Landour, Mussoorie, where she was graduated from high school. As in the case of other missionary children, she would be home for the long winter holidays, including Christmas, when weather was mild on the plains. The rest of the year she was in boarding school, with her parents taking accommodations nearby for a month's summer holiday in the hills. So it was that Eunice spent much of her early life in the Himalayas. She seems to have profited from this and became strong and athletic, though her earlier years were plagued by assorted illnesses. After high school she returned to the United States and was graduated from American University in Washington, D.C.

Following that she took a course in shorthand/typing to equip herself to act as secretary to her father. She spent a number of months as secretary not only for him, but also for other members of the National Preaching Mission of 1938, working with such persons as Howard Thurman, Arthur Compton, and Jesse Bader. At the end of 1937 she was to have joined her father in China, but the breakout of hostilities between China and Japan interrupted all that. She went back to India instead, arriving in Bombay in December 1938. Shortly thereafter was where I came in.

Our marriage took place on Saturday afternoon at 2:30, June 1, 1940, a date easy to remember, in the chapel of Wellesley School in Naini Tal. The Reverend Paul W. Wagner and the Reverend Roland W. Scott, both fellow missionaries, "stood by me." The chapel was a beautiful building finished off with teak panels and teak pews.

Behind the altar was a picture window that opened toward a chaste garden, affording a natural floral display. Eunice looked lovely in a white gown of Madras tissue shot through with silver thread and a darned net veil made by Belgian Catholic sisters in South India. Her attendants were her "cousins," Carol Titus and Mabel Wagner. People said it was a nice wedding, with beautiful music and a chapel crowded with Indian and missionary friends. The wedding was conducted by my saintly friend, Bishop John Wesley Robinson and by Eunice's father after he and Mrs. Jones had "given her away." There was a reception following the ceremony in the Wellesley parlor, but I must confess that looking back, the sequence of events is a bit blurred. We were, however, well and truly wed.

The next day we set out on our wedding trip to Kashmir, surely one of the loveliest spots on earth. This meant going from Naini Tal, at 7,000 feet, down to the plains at Kathgodam by car, then the meter gauge railway to Bareilly. Here we were met on a stiflingly hot day by a wonderful and thoughtful missionary, Edna Bacon from Clara Swain Hospital, who brought us homemade ice cream, which we enjoyed as we changed to the broad gauge rail. This train carried us to Lahore for a twenty-four-hour stay with friends. Then another overnight journey to Rawalpindi. From there we had a long journey by car through Murree, arriving at Srinagar (5,000 feet), capital of Kashmir State, late in the evening.

Kashmir was fabulous. Called an "emerald set in pearls," its lush green fields and trees are surrounded by the snowy Pir Panjal range. The city of Srinagar is situated on the banks of the Jhelum River and on Dal Lake. On both of these bodies of water are houseboats, some of them palatial in their proportions, and used by vacationers as their home away from home. These stunning houseboats came into vogue during early British rule. Since land was not available for purchase by British subjects in the Native State of Kashmir, elaborately appointed houseboats solved the problem. Ours was small and somewhat unimpressive. Still it was adequate, and though it may have been lacking in style it was right in price: nine rupees per day, about three dollars. This included room and full board for two, with attached cook-boat, servants, and a small paddle boat called a *shikari*. We soon had our boat towed or poled to Nagin Bagh, a beautiful landing south of the city. If we were supposed to get away from it all, we failed miserably. It seemed that hosts of our friends had also chosen to go to Kashmir that summer. In a nearby houseboat were Dr. and Mrs. Ralph Wellons, he the president of Lucknow Christian College. In another were Dr. Sarah Chakko, soon to be president of Isabella Thoburn college, together with two missionaries, Marjorie Dimmitt and Florence Salzer—all good friends. Then Bishop and Mrs. B. T. Badley were occupying the best houseboat on the lake, appropriately named "Buckingham Palace." They invited the newlyweds to tea on June 8. Staying with her mother, Lady Thomas, at the British resident's house, was Dr. Mary Thomas, a friend of Eunice from girlhood.

Life in a houseboat was charming. The food was good; tea, served on the roof, always exciting. Our little houseboat was visited by wallahs (merchants) with their wares—flowers, fruit, embroidered silks, carved walnut goods—all very tempting and very inexpensive by Western standards. We would take excursions on our *shikar,* paddled by our boatman. One day Bishop Badley took us to visit some of the famous Moghul gardens. They were works of art, laid out according to Persian design three centuries earlier, marked by terraces, waterways, falls, and flower beds designed to resemble oriental rugs. One was the famous Shalimar ("Abode of Love"), another was Nishat Bagh ("Garden of Excessive Delight"), and one little gem, Chasma Shahi—(the "King's Spring"). Since Bishop Badley was an authority on Kashmir, he was able to make this all come alive in memorable fashion.

One day we visited the renowned Dr. Arthur Neve, Himalayan trekker and climber and surgeon extraordinaire. He spoke of writing his memoirs and was examining his notes on the 40,000 operations he had performed and had concluded that the most important quality for a surgeon was *judgment.* On another day we visited Dr. Cecil E. Tyndale-Biscoe's school located on the Jhelum River. This English missionary educator loved boys and literally transformed the lives of thousands. He was a master in inculcating character in his charges: truth and honesty, discipline and devotion were his constant emphasis. All boys in school had to learn to swim. Though they lived on water's edge very few knew how to swim and many hitherto had drowned.

Our boatman and his crew went with us to Pahalgam, about 75 miles from Srinagar, where we hired pack ponies, horses, tents, and equipment for a trek up the Lidderwat River, via Aru to the Kolahoi Glacier. We hiked through mountain scenery of incredible beauty along a gushing mountain stream, whose singing lulled us fast asleep at night. It was during this trek that on June 19 we received the grim news of the fall of Paris. Up to that time the conflict that began in September 1939 was called the "phony war." We made two other trips to this area. We crossed from the Liddarwat Valley to the Sind Valley, touched on the border of Tibet, and climbed a small mountain that proved to be higher than any peak in all the Alps: 16,700 feet! To this day, I possess a rock that I picked up on the summit.

On yet another excursion from Srinagar we went by bus, horseback, and on foot to Gulmarg, (9,000 ft.) a mountain resort for British military officers and civilians alike, and boasting the highest golf course in the world. Years later we visited Gulmarg again and met the Dalai Lama there.

Needless to say this newly married couple experienced very full days as we probed the mysteries of matrimony. We were to discover, as hosts had done before us, that couples learn more about each other in days after marriage than they do in months before the wedding. With real regret we left the incredible beauty of Kashmir for the heat and dust of the plains and returned once more to Bombay.

Our apartment was in a brand-new building on Marine Drive, in one of the finest areas of the city and not far removed from my little church. We were the first family to move into the building. Our flat had a living or drawing room, a dining room, two bedrooms, two baths, and a kitchen. Most of the time a sea breeze made the atmosphere quite comfortable, aided by ceiling fans, which were characteristic of Bombay. The rent was 150 rupees ($50) per month, which we were able to swing because of the young Englishman who had room and board with us. We had sparse but adequate furnishings from my flat in the church, supplemented by some furniture I had built myself.

The congregation of Bowen Church welcomed my new wife. She had no specific training for church work, though she had, of course, been brought up in a mission-ary family. In fact her parents had been married in Bowen Church. The work went on much as it had before, but I could do the work with a lighter hand; after all, I had someone to stand beside me. Eunice was a good and thoughtful hostess and showed skills at management of a household. For part of the first year she worked as secre-tary to Bishop J. Waskom Pickett, and of course she did typing for me. We were invited out a great deal to all kinds of occasions, and we did considerable entertaining ourselves. Eunice says that there was a noticeable falloff of attendance of young single women after their bachelor pastor was married. Our paying guest and friend, Mow-bray, worked out splendidly. He was, by the way, a devout Anglican. He had a most unusual way of enter-taining himself. He would sit by the hour with the com-plete score of a symphony before him and was ecstatic at "hearing" the music as he read the notes. We were sad-dened when after some months he was transferred to Colombo, Ceylon. Fortunately for us his replacement at the bank decided to continue with us.

During this period I gave two addresses on All-India

Radio; one on U.S. history and one on the Philippines. Naturally, I could ring the changes on independence and tried to make the most of my opportunity. Another event was in October of 1940 when we helped Bishop J. W. Robinson celebrate his fiftieth anniversary in India. He was the one who performed our marriage ceremony, and incidentally would not accept a fee from me for the service. That same autumn we were visited by a terrific cyclone, which tossed the sea outside the apartment into a fury.

In late November I left for an annual conference session in Nagpur, and once again I served as secretary of the body. Paul Wagner and I went back to Bombay via Wardha, near which lay Sevagram (Village of Service) where Mahatma Gandhi had established his ashram—the unofficial capital of India. We spent the night in the railway station which had what were called retiring rooms set aside for this purpose. One would simply unroll a sleeping bag on a settee, or on the floor and enjoy free overnight accommodations; India in those days was well suited to low-cost travel. Early the next morning we set out before daylight to walk the five miles to Sevagram.

Just as dawn broke we arrived at the gate of the ashram. At that very moment who should appear but a little brown man carrying a bamboo staff, accompanied by a dozen or so of his colleagues as he set out for his morning walk. There was Mahatma Gandhi, father of his country. To our great delight, he invited us to go along. Only one other of the company did I recognize: the young Dr. Sushila Nayyar, with whom I was to become well acquainted later, and who was to become prominent in the medical world. When Gandhi asked who we were, we replied, "American missionaries." To this he responded, "I thought as much. Which church?" We said, "Methodists." Then he rather shocked us by stating, "I wonder whether if John Wesley were alive today, he would recognize you people?" A good question.

The following hour we walked and talked with him, and you may be sure that the experience has a treasured place in my house of memories. He talked of his projected renewed campaign of civil disobedience (the "Quit India" movement) and of the young Vinoba Bhave, who already had been arrested as he launched the effort. I remember having mumbled to Gandhi the question: "Do you not feel sorry that Vinoba Bhave is in jail?" He replied: "No, this is a part of it all. When one breaks the law, one suffers the consequences." This was a part of the discipline of *satyagraha:* nonviolence.

Sooner than we desired the walk was over. He graciously excused himself from us but invited us to stay at the ashram for as long as we pleased. We stayed until noon. During this period we had a chance of unhurried conversation with one of Gandhi's secretaries, Mahadev Desai, a devoted follower and fine man. We also caught a glimpse of Mrs. Gandhi, Kasturba. Then we saw Madeline Slade, daughter of a British admiral. By then she had adopted the name of Mirabehn, and had been a resident for some years at the ashram and a devotee of the Mahatma. She rather scowled at us I thought; she believed that she had a kind of monopoly on Gandhi and all other Westerners were intruders. We then had a lengthy conversation with Dr. Aryanaikan, a Christian who specialized in what was termed basic education. Our short sojourn at Sevagram was most exciting for us.

Later Eunice's mother visited us, and during this time we made a short visit to Dhulia. On the return trip to Bombay we had a frightening experience of finding that one of our fellow passengers had been murdered aboard the train that night—shades of Agatha Christie!

At the turn of the year, 1940–41, we went with Mrs. Jones to New Delhi to attend a session of the Central Conference of the Methodist Church, whose chief business was to elect two bishops. After repeated ballots two were elected: Shot K. Mondol of Bengal and Clement D. Rockey of North India. The record shows that I, junior missionary that I was, received two votes! While the conference met in the venerable city of Old Delhi, we were able to visit the brand-new capital of New Delhi. It was beautifully laid out and at that time consisted mostly of open spaces. Both cities probably did not have a population of more than half a million combined, as contrasted with more than ten million today.

We were able to observe some of the antiquities the city offered: the Red Fort, associated with the Moghul emperors, with its wondrous palaces, Diwan-I-Am and Diwan-I-Khas; that is, public and private audience halls. The latter featured fountains and baths carved of white marble in the shape of flowers. Centuries ago perfumed water would spray from these marble flowers. Around the ceiling was the oft-cited ascription in Persian: "If there is a paradise on earth, it is this; it is this; it is this!" Nearby was the tiny Pearl Mosque, also of startling white marble. Formal gardens abounded. Across from the Red Fort was the colossal Jumma Masjid (Friday Mosque). Not far away were Humayan's tomb and the Lodhi Gardens. All these sights may be enjoyed to this day, but then I viewed them with a sense of wonder. I was really getting accustomed to India, and to experience such things with Eunice, who felt quite at home in all these surroundings, simply doubled my pleasure. I should say that this particular trip from Bombay to northern India and back—about 5,000 miles in all—we made with a "zone ticket" good for three weeks unrestricted travel and costing about five dollars.

Time was marching on. By March of 1941 my three-year stint was up and I began to look forward to a trip home. My family in the United States looked forward to our arrival. During this period we made a trip back to Mahableshwar, where I had studied language, accompanying Dr. Stewart Fulton and his wife, Harriet, medical missionaries, both good friends. We even played a round of golf there and enjoyed a rare treat of strawberry shortcake, for strawberries abound in that hill-station. Another diary entry reminds us that Frank and Betty Kline, missionaries of the Free Methodist Church and longtime friends, visited us. They were establishing a seminary in Yeotmal in Maharashtra.

We were to have returned to the United States in the spring of 1941. My intention was to study for a doctor's degree at Princeton University. Then there came suddenly another dramatic change in our lives. Bishop Pickett proposed that we extend our stay in India for another year, for he wanted to appoint me district superintendent of the Dhulia-Puntamba District. For those unacquainted with Methodist polity, it should be noted that a district superintendent is a kind of assistant bishop and would be so designated in some other polities. The district superintendent is chosen to serve up to six years in this office. There were four districts in the Bombay Conference.

Dhulia-Puntamba, as its name shows, was a hyphenated district. Dhulia was the headquarters town to the civil district of West Khandesh. One cannot be very proud of living in Dhulia, another of those out-of-the-way places lost in India's spacious landscape. The very name means "dusty," and it was surely that. It is located on the banks of the Panjhra River, which flows into the Tapti River, which flows into the Narbada River, which empties into the Arabian Sea—part of the Indian Ocean. The district was mostly agricultural with related industries, of fertile soil, and well-forested in our time. Once it was the haunt of wild beasts: tiger, leopard, bear, various representatives of the deer and antelope families, even elephants. The population was relatively sparse, and in the 1940s Dhulia city was inhabited by about 40,000 people, three-fourths Hindus, about 20 percent Muslims, with Jains and Christians present in about equal numbers, five hundred. The Christian missionary work had been started by Roman Catholics, Scandinavian-American missionaries, and Methodist Protestants who in 1939 had become a part of the Methodist Church.

The other half of the church district was called Puntamba, a *taluka* or county of the Ahmednagar civil district. It was located just over 100 miles from Dhulia and could ordinarily have been reached by auto over the graveled or metalled roads (none of them black-topped), but during the war petrol (gasoline) was rationed and in such short supply, so the district car could not be used. There was also a small and ancient motorbike that was also out of commission. Therefore, to travel between the two poles of the district it was necessary to go by slow train. It would pull out of Dhulia at about sunset and proceed at a crawling pace the 40 miles that separated it from the main line of the Great Indian Peninsula (GIP) Railway at Chalisgaon, where there was a change of trains that carried one to Manmad, another 40 miles, arriving about midnight. There I would spread my bedding roll out on the station platform and sleep for three hours. A coolie would awaken me, and I would board a third slow train for 40 miles more to Puntamba.

This journey I made in one direction or another many times during the course of a year. It required a certain amount of hardiness. In those days at either end of the district "local" travel was by bullock cart, bicycle, bus, or foot. So it was that I conducted my last service at Bowen Church, ending three years of eventful service—the last one made more so by the fact that I now found myself side by side with Eunice. The church members were tolerant. They had accepted my pastoral service and although it was not, I believe, outstanding, it did contribute some new strength to an old congregation. I had gone to Dhulia several times for the turnover of the district to me from my predecessor, the Reverend J. F. Minnis, a jovial and easygoing missionary from North Carolina.

At Dhulia there was a small hospital with a wonderful physician/surgeon, Dr. Edith Lacey, and a little orphanage and a primary school, each under the charge of lady missionaries. Attached to it also was a farm of some 200 acres, a new town church, several rural preaching points, and three pastors or local preachers. In Puntamba the work was larger in scope: a middle boys' school and a middle girls' school with hostel, a small dispensary and some twenty-five churches and preaching points spread over an area of about 400 square miles. There again was a missionary doctor, two missionary educators, teachers and nurses, and twenty-seven pastors and local preachers.

I was twenty-eight when I was appointed, said to be the youngest district superintendent in the whole church. The fact is that I had a very imperfect command of the language and precious little experience. What I did have was energy and determination, drive, a lively imagination, and a clear vision of what could be. Some say that I was then and still am an "idea person." Also required was devotion to the One who empowers all Christian witness. But I had something more: a good Indian friend and mentor. He was P. C. B. Balaram, nicknamed Benji. I have mentioned him before. He was a Telugu of South India origin and had a wonderful wife from among the Syrian Christians of Travancore or Kerala. What a splendid couple they were! Well, Benji and I were a team. Together and with the cooperation of our fellow workers we began to shape a new program that would bring new faith and power to what Bishop Pickett called "the most spiritually backward area of Methodism."

As I write I have before me the minutes of our first district conference, which lasted for ten days. Actually, the

routine business of such a meeting could have been discharged in about half a day, but we had more serious
intentions in view. It was more like an extended in-service training session. I taught Bible. Our conference
preacher was a pastor from Vikarabad in the Hyderabad
Conference, the Reverend J. R. Luke, a flaming evangelist.
Then to lend maturity to the meeting I invited my colleague, the Reverend Abednego Barnabas. We all took
physical exams and blood tests, which revealed some
medical problems in time to remedy them. A specialist in
Indian music, a sitarist, and Christian educator, the Reverend R. S. Mandrelle, was with us. We became indebted
to him for composing a new tune for singing the Lord's
Prayer that became very popular and widely used in the
villages.

We also drew up a new order of Sunday worship to be
used in all our churches. Likewise a brief daily evening
worship service was devised, which a schoolteacher or
layperson could lead. Up until that time services tended
to be slipshod and irregular. Better worship makes for
better Christians.

We soon organized a District Planning Committee. Our
Discipline did not call for such a group, but it seemed necessary and proved to be valuable and fruitful. One of the
results of this procedure was the organizing and carrying
out of a Christian Mela or Jatra, which attracted some two
thousand village Christians (and some non-Christians)
from all over the district. As a kind of fair it included
games, contests, competition, display of choice domestic
animals, health programs, prize-giving, music, dance,
refreshments, as well as worship. This effort released

great new energies that affected all aspects of our work. We arranged for special training programs in women's work. We had made a brass Bishop's Cross for Christian Achievement, which would be awarded annually. This then would be used in the winning village for a year until the successor was designated. We set a goal of every Christian in the district becoming literate within the next ten years. Systematic vaccination programs were started. We instituted the practice of Christian greeting, "Jai Christ" ("Victory to Christ"), which helped to uplift morale and self-esteem of Christians. Finally, we inaugurated a Rural High School in Puntamba, which contributed vastly to the region during the years that followed. All in all, our efforts brought new life to the district. Young people were inspired to pursue Christian vocations; the new recruits tended to encourage the older pastors, some of whom had been relaxed for years or defeated.

A report I made at that time about the district concluded with these words:

> As I walked back to Puntamba, a thousand thoughts besieged my mind—of villagers' trials and triumphs, of new urgent opportunities, of transformed lives, of the past, of the future, of this: that God is with us. And then I thought appreciatively of colleagues who were laboring in excellent cooperation; of preachers and teachers and their sacrifices; of their plans for smokeless, windowed houses—for gardens during the coming year; of our district boys finishing their preparation for the ministry soon; candidates for ordination; of my wife who not only wrote numberless patron letters but also bore responsibilities at home during my trips about the district; of inter-

ested friends in America. It was easy for my thoughts to drift into dreams; but perhaps they were not dreams but visions to be translated into reality. Then it occurred to me that in many respects I was in the greatest work in the world and that I enjoyed my work. I think I must have broken into whistling our new tune for the Lord's Prayer. And the only thought which troubled me was that I should have to write a report of our doings to present at Conference time.

Every day seemed to bring excitement. My notes show, for example, a great alarm that arose one day when we heard the call, "Nag! Nag!" (Cobra! Cobra!) I dashed out of the house and with a walking stick I dispatched a cobra that had taken up residence under our veranda. Another entry recalls that once as I proceeded toward my bedding in the station platform at Manmad, a karait (a small but deadly viper) crossed my path. That one I killed with a blow from my sandal. It makes one reflective to be aware that had it bitten me, it would have killed me within fifteen minutes.

An entry tells of a journey from Dhulia to Aurangabad to see the Ellora and Ajanta caves again, this time with Eunice. Dr. and Mrs. Elbert M. Moffatt, lifelong friends of Eunice, accompanied us. They were great people, endowed with an acute sense of humor; both were marvelous raconteurs. We not only enjoyed the caves but also Elbert reading, as we drove along, from P. G. Wodehouse's *Jeeves*. Another friend, Hendrix Townsley, came to visit us and suffered a severe sunstroke while there. We played tennis at a local club, which afforded not only good exercise, but association with British and Indian officials not otherwise easily accessible to missionaries. Then there was the shocking announcement in early December 1941 of the Japanese bombing of Pearl Harbor.

As I look back, I find that I was gradually obtaining some grasp of the complex society in which we were living. We read more about our Hindu, Muslim, and other neighbors as we came to know them better in our daily association with them. I find evidence that we kept abreast of the political developments of the country, for this was reflected in a concise essay in which I analyzed the situation as of that time. Finally, my papers include detailed analysis and information of the Dhulia-Puntamba District for my successor. Re-reading it awakened astonishment of the grasp one can gain in a relatively short time. For we had only one year in Dhulia.

ARMY YEARS

The spring of 1942 was a period of turmoil. We had technically completed our term of service; that is, an extended year of service from three to four years. We were tentatively scheduled to leave in March on a ship headed for the United States that was to take a circuitous route around Africa to some American port. On March 6 Eunice had to go to Bombay to have a small cancerous growth removed from her lip—happily an entirely successful operation. Then on March 10 we had word that the ship to the United States had been cancelled. It needs to be recalled that a World War was on and shipping was both uncertain and risky. Meanwhile my attitude toward the war itself had undergone a drastic shift.

Though I had never been an absolute pacifist, I could have been described as having a leaning in that direction. For one trained during the 1930s it could scarcely have been otherwise.

A letter dated October 11, 1939, which I wrote to friends in the United States, contains the following views:

> When you get this it will be about Armistice Day. This year it will be a considerable mockery, I guess. I've often thought that the *children* of Israel were well named, for they acted so much like "children." But we act the same today. To think that the world seems to have learned nothing from the last war! Would that we would become sufficiently like little children that we would actually enter the Kingdom of God. But I think a good many did learn sufficiently in the last war, to know that war is foolish. Now at least we *know* we are fools for having wars. Perhaps this is a "war to end *peace*."
>
> Nevertheless one's sympathies are with Britain and France. But was there no other way? That question will doubtless be settled if and when there is a peace conference. If there is a just peace, then it will have been a just war. This is an encouraging fact, that little real hatred seems thus far to have shown itself. May that continue. And why should it not! I see little sign of real bitterness here. I remember how in the last war (I was five in 1918; thus I tell my age!) we used to say: "We *hate* Germans." Then we were reproved by our elders: "We do not hate Germans, but we hate their ways." We do hate the false philosophy which has been imposed upon them.
>
> We do not anticipate any immediate difficulty in Bombay. Nevertheless some precautions have been taken. I have stated that no bombs had better be dropped on me, for that would be an offense against American neutrality! I will not mention any details, for the censors may cut

them out, but one sees some evidence even here that a war is on in the Empire.

This week I received my first American letters for six weeks. But they were "pre-war" stuff. Some English friends are just getting letters from England too. They start amusingly: "Won't it be awful if there is a war?" But it had already begun.

Even in the autumn of 1940 I preached a sermon that was antiwar. This prompted a letter from a British friend who expressed these sentiments about Germans:

> I have not yet got within reach of the savages but I hope to soon. Their behaviour is reminiscent of early Asiatic conquerors. I am sending a pamphlet to a number of friends overseas, and some in this country who do not realize what evil people the Huns are. I think it is good for everyone to realize what we are fighting against. I am sure it is wrong for the Christian to sit idle and watch evil going on. What do you think?

In the months that followed I began to take a more and more Niebuhrian view, for I received *The Christian Century* regularly. By the spring of 1942 I wrote to my Board secretary in New York City:

> In March we decided it best to sail for home. We have already stayed a year longer than we had originally planned for. The Finance Committee gave its approval and we packed up. Then the boat was cancelled without prospect of another one for some months. That decided for us our next course.
>
> It was my intention to volunteer for the Army as soon as I reached America. The delay of sailing gave me an opportunity of joining up here. I felt that with my experi-

ence in India, they would probably send me out here again to serve. So I chose to stay and volunteered in India.

You may perhaps wonder why I took this step. It is difficult to state such a process of thought in a few words. Ever since the fall of France, the grave state of this crisis has been plain to me. It was so to a certain extent before that. And now, looking back, I can see that our consciences should have pricked us even more about China, Spain, and Ethiopia. We should have opposed force with force then, but somehow we felt that a black man or a yellow man was not quite so much worth our concern as a white man.

At any rate I do feel that the world and the ideals we hold more dear are terribly threatened. If this is true for the world in general, it is more true for the Church and for those who are engaged in Christian service. The very right of doing freely the work we are called to do is at stake.

If this is true, and I feel with many others, that it is; then, able bodied as I am, I have no right to ask another who may not have my convictions to risk his life in the defence of those ideals, without which, life would not to me be worth living. I have no right to ask special favours. I have no right to hide behind the "cloth." I must act as any other average citizen. For this reason I have joined the Army.

So quite apart from deserting the cause, I could not have felt faithful to the cause by acting otherwise. I do not hate anyone; I am not a war monger. Nor am I a lover of war; nor do I believe that we should resort to it if the end can be attained in any other way. Again, I do not believe the Allies are guiltless. There is, I think, an element of the judgement of God in this; we have all sinned, we all are suffering. May we learn what He has to teach us through it all.

The very reality with which we are faced has forced a re-thinking of the Christian attitude toward war. I believe it may bring a reality into all our social thinking. We have been wedded to ideals, half forgetting that to large numbers of people they were not ideals at all. The whole thing is a tragic paradox; pacifism has been a path *to* war. An effort to prevent suffering has indirectly led to more of it. Yet I believe He is able to bring forth good even out of all this evil.

I could say much more, but then this is not the place for that. You will understand my position. Many will doubtless misunderstand it. Dr. Jones will be grieved. I am sorry. But under the circumstances this seemed the wise thing to do.

Again, you may wonder why I did not join the Chaplain's Corps. My answer is an extension of what I have said before. I wanted to be willing to undergo what any other citizen would be asked to undergo. Not that I will shirk the Chaplain's function; for even today I am to preach in the local Methodist Church. I will do anything else of the kind as opportunity presents itself. Already several have spoken to me of the things that matter and said they would have hesitated if I had worn the Chaplain's insignia.

So I have asked for a leave of absence. One does not like to make too definite plans for the future. We would like, however, to return to America after the war, and I study for my Ph.D. and then, if agreeable to all concerned, return to India again.

Those may seem somewhat lofty sentiments, but looking back for more than fifty years, I believe they reflect accurately the convictions that prompted me at the time.

Moreover, I offer it as proof that I had not altogether lost my Christian perspective as some seemed to have alleged at the time. All my life from time to time, I have expressed myself in poetry, and during that period of wrestling I penned these words under the title of "Twentieth Century Vision":

As tired, alone I journeyed o'er rough ways,
    A vision came to me:
I looked and behold I saw a clenched fist,
Which is, by interpretation, Greed;
    And I was sad.

Again I looked and there appeared a mailed fist,
Which is, by interpretation, War.
    I was filled with despair.

Once more I looked and saw Bleeding Hands,
Which, when interpreted, mean Faith and Hope and Love.
    The vision passed—

Refreshed, I travelled on—yet not alone.

During the late autumn of 1941 and especially after Pearl Harbor, I began casting about to see what part I might take in the struggle. As a first step I inquired of British Army representatives who at the beginning discouraged me. Again broaching the issue I was invited to Bombay to the British Army headquarters. There I passed the physical and was directed to report to Belgium for induction into a unit of the tank corps that was to move to North Africa. I did not sign up at the time, for an officer advised me to explore what effect this might have on my American citizenship. This I did do, but before an answer came, the same officer advised me that an American unit had already landed in Karachi and that an American general was in Delhi. To spare details I shall simply say that I did visit General Raymond A. Wheeler at his headquarters in the Imperial Hotel, New Delhi, on April 24, 1942. He was most courteous and we seemed to "hit it off" well. Having supplied his office with details about myself, I returned to Sat Tal—about 200 miles northeast of Delhi, to await development. Meanwhile the FBI checked me out back home. On May 11 a telegram came to me from General Wheeler in which he appointed me a First Lieutenant in the United States Army and assigned to the Quartermaster Corps.

The following day I departed for Karachi, now a part of Pakistan. This involved a long journey over the arid expanse of the provinces of the Punjab and Sind. I was immediately put in uniform and posted as a supply officer in the U.S. Army Base Section No. 1, located in the city and environs.

The question may be raised as to why I was not made a chaplain. General Wheeler informed me that if I were to be a chaplain I would have to return to the United States and undergo special training. The fact was that he desperately needed some officers in India who knew something of the country. Since I was volunteering I saw no reason why I should not be ready to serve as and where I was needed. The truth was, however, that I often functioned as a chaplain, for there were occasions when no one else was available for preaching or for burying. I conducted a marriage, presided at Communion services and at one or two baptisms. My background was well understood, and I was sought out at times by fellow officers and GIs for spiritual counsel. So it was that I managed to serve in the army and at the same time not let the Christian cause down. One had to learn fast. I acquainted myself with military procedures by study of useful manuals. I learned the manual of arms and how to lead troops in close-order drill.

My entire service of more than four years was in the China-Burma-India Theatre. Sometimes it has been referred to as the "forgotten theatre." In every sense it was at the end of the line. Even so, something like three-quarters of a million American troops served in this sector and there is today a very active veteran's group for CBI. It was mainly a supply line for Burma and China where combat usually took place in cooperation with our British and Chinese allies. I myself was never in combat but could have been so assigned at any time and was indeed at times in what is called "harm's way." The CBI operation enabled China to stay in the conflict. We also pinned down two million Japanese troops in Southeast Asia, thus relieving pressure on General MacArthur's advance in the Western Pacific. So it was that our contribution toward victory was immense.

Karachi, as a seaport, was for three years an important base and later this was true of Calcutta as well as Bombay and Madras, though in lesser degree. There were also air-bases in many parts of the country, particularly around Calcutta and in the extreme northeast of India—Assam. Supplies were often shipped clear across India; sometimes transshipped two or three times as the railway gauge changed. Urgent supplies, of course, went forward by air or truck convoys, which moved from Calcutta to Assam and sometimes directly on to Burma or China. These could be trying and hazardous trips.

Bombing raids from India-based planes were made on Japanese-occupied Burma. In the upper Brahmaputra Valley of Assam there were a number of airbases from which supplies were flown over the Hump (the Himalayan Range) into China. This went on in round-the-clock fashion. It had to have been one of the most perilous flights in the world. Something like eight hundred planes were lost on this sector, many never to be found. In other cases, happily, tribal groups would rescue the crews and return them to safety. Meanwhile other troops were fighting in the jungles of Burma, combating not only a stubborn Japanese foe but also disease, tropical climate, insects, poisonous snakes, and wild beasts. The "forgotten theater" was forgotten only by those who did not take part in it. For those who did it was unforgettable.

Perhaps something of the "flavor" of CBI service can be conveyed by this poem, written by Sergeant Smith Dawless:

Conversation Piece
Is the Gateway to India at Bombay,
Really as beautiful as they say?

Don't rightly know, Ma'am. Did my part
Breakin' point in the jungle's heart;
Blasted the boulders, felled the trees
With red muck oozin' around our knees,
Carved the guts from the mountain's side,
Dozed our trace, made it clean and wide,
Metalled and graded, dug and filled:
We had the Ledo Road to build.

Well, surely you saw a burning ghat,
Fakirs, rope-tricks, and all of that.

Reckon I didn't. But way up ahead
I tended the wounded, buried the dead.
For I was a Medic, and little we knew
But the smell of sickness all day through,
Mosquitoes, leeches, and thick dark mud
Where the Chinese spilled their blood
After the enemy guns were stilled:
We had the Ledo Road to build.

Of course you found the Taj Mahal,
The loveliest building of them all.

Can't really say, lady. I was stuck
Far beyond Shing with a QM truck.
Monsoon was rugged there, hot and wet,
Nothing to do but work and sweat.
And dry was the dust upon my mouth
As steadily big "cats" roared on south,
Over the ground where Japs lay killed:
We had the Ledo Road to build.

You've been gone two years this spring.
Didn't you see a single thing?

Never saw much but the moon shine on
A Burmese temple around Maingkwan,
And silver transports high in the sky,
Thursday River and the swift Tanai,
And Hukwang Valley coming all green,
Those are the only sights I've seen.
Did our job, though, like God willed:
We had the Ledo Road to build.

My own service was largely administrative. Some of it was as a purchasing and contracting officer. This entailed extensive dealings with Indian merchants and entrepreneurs. We were under orders to obtain as many supplies and equipment locally as we possibly could in order to save shipping. Some things were in short supply and thus exorbitant prices had to be paid. Moreover this tended to lift prices for British and Indians who sought the same goods, which they clearly resented.

Karachi was located in a part of the country where a good breed of cattle (Sindhi) was available for beef. Even so vigilance had to be exercised by veterinary officers who inspected all meats. I moved also into subsistence and my warehouse experience back home in Ohio helped immensely. My four years' experience in India placed me in a position to render peculiar service. Sometimes I was designated temporarily as a graves' registration officer, one of the functions of quartermasters, though at the time and place that fortunately did not keep us very busy.

Army procedures were often strange to me. One was subject to temporary duty at all sorts of tasks. Once I was directed to fly to Agra to escort fifty new recruits to Karachi. These men had only just arrived in India and were very raw indeed. We traveled by meter gauge rail for forty-eight hours across the Indian Desert. They were filled with wonder at the experience. Another assignment was to explore the feasibility of shipping supplies by freight trains (goods trains, as the British termed them) across the country by meter gauge to Assam so that transshipment would not be necessary. To do this would have meant laying several hundred miles of new track, but this was finally judged not to be feasible.

Another assignment was to go with a refrigeration officer from Calcutta to Assam and to the head of the Ledo Road to see how refrigerated meat could be shipped forward to troops. We examined this problem thoroughly and were able to submit detailed recommendations as to how it could be done. During this trip we proceeded some distance down the Ledo Road, which was a marvel of engineering through incredible terrain.

In June 1943 I was ordered on another most interesting assignment: to purchase coffee in South India. Before I left I was able to study a good deal about growing coffee, helped by a close friendship with a longtime grower. Once again my Ohio experience helped because I used to unload coffee from boxcars and help grade, blend, roast, and grind the beans. Proceeding to Bangalore, a beautiful city in the south, I made my way to the Indian Coffee Board. The director was an Englishman, Sir John "something or other." I was informed that he was busy and could not see me. The clerk did consent to deliver a note to him. This I wrote out, informing him that I was there to purchase five hundred *tons* of coffee for the U.S. Army. The British knight put in an immediate appearance and the deal was done. Later we purchased another seven hundred tons of coffee. Meanwhile, back in Karachi we had improvised coffee roasters out of fifty-gallon steel drums, for more advanced roasting machines were not available. This "invention" was shared for use by our military installations all across India.

Officers serving at headquarters, as I was, had to take

turns as duty officers on post all night, touring installations at specified times to see that all was well. Of particular note too I would mention being appointed numerous
times to serve in special courts-martial. To equip myself
for this I had to master the Articles of War, a précis of military law that set forth the rules, privileges, penalties, and
procedures for military justice. It opened up a whole new
world to me, for I had never been particularly informed
about nor interested in legal processes. The role of prose-
cutor was usually left to army lawyers, members of the
Corps of Judge Advocate-General. The defense counsel
role was assigned to ordinary officers not necessarily
skilled in legal matters; quite frequently I was assigned
this responsibility. I took it seriously and did my best to
defend those accused. Sometimes I was successful,
though the word was out that compassion, when warranted, should be meted out by commanding officers.

One incident that I now recount had to do with a GI. An
African American was charged with the shooting and
wounding of an Indian coolie. The soldier was on guard
duty at a warehouse. He said the Indian was stealing, was
ordered to halt, and was then shot and wounded when he
failed to do so. The coolie was a man from the Northwest
Frontier whose language was Pushtu. This time I sat as a
member of the court-martial while an interpreter was
translating the testimony into English. There were apparently no eyewitnesses to the incident until the prosecu-
tion brought forward an alleged witness. He was asked:
"Did you see the shot fired?" His reply as translated from
Pushtu was: "Yes, I saw the shot fired." At this point I
interrupted the proceedings and challenged the inter-

preter saying that I believed the witness had not *seen* the shooting but had *heard* the shot fired. Although I did not know Pushtu, I did know enough of Indian languages to note that the witness had used a word that sounded somewhat like "soon"—related to "sonar" or "sound." Upon further questioning this proved indeed to be the case; his evidence was, as it were, "hearsay." Then it was a case of the GIs word against the coolie's, and the former was given the benefit of the doubt and was found not guilty. Months later I chanced to meet the soldier, who thanked me heartily.

A quartermaster officer often was confronted with unprecedented matters. I find among my papers a letter from one Ganga, daughter of Rukhsingh, stating, "I am a Prostitute belonging to Lahore and have come down to request yourself that I have eight beautiful girls with me . . . Fit and Gentlewomen . . . useful for the Purpose of Enjoyment of the Military . . . I guarantee to furnish the Fitness Certificate of a Doctor" etc. I must say that nothing in my past experience or training had equipped me to deal with such a delicate proposal, so I am afraid that her letter went without a reply.

Obviously my experience was varied and not quite like the soldier who wrote of building the Ledo Road, but I was involved in a large enterprise. After a little over a year I was promoted to captain, and two years later to major as my responsibilities increased. In the spring of 1945 I was assigned for six weeks of temporary duty in the United States. Thus after seven years of absence I returned home for a brief visit with my family. It was a happy experience. Later, I returned for another year's military service, this time in Chabua, Assam, at Base Section No. 3. Here I was directly involved in sending food supplies in particular across the Hump to China.

Meanwhile, Eunice was in India for three years of my time while in the army. As a highly trained and experienced secretary her services were in demand, particularly in a confidential role. So it was that she worked for the OSS organization, which finally became the CIA. Her work was of such a secretive nature that neither then nor since has she shared with me details of what she did; but she did do her part in the struggle. Our situation was, of course, exceptional, for we were allowed to dwell in an apartment while in Karachi and in the bungalow of a tea plantation in Assam. This we shared with an American civil surgeon who served the tea-workers. This episode in itself deserves a chapter, but the story is already too extended. Eunice returned to the United States in September of 1945, shortly after the war's end, while I continued for another ten months in India.

With the surrender of the Japanese there still remained much work to be done in the winding up of operations. Among other things many supplies and large quantities of equipment had to be disposed of in India. Vehicles and hospital equipment were particularly useful to the missions. I alerted Bishop Pickett to this. He and others were able to raise funds for obtaining these articles for mission hospitals—at greatly reduced prices.

Then came the time to depart for the home shores. My last night in India was spent in a tent at an American installation near Calcutta. Such a thing had never happened to me before, but that night I was robbed of wallet, passport, papers, and other valuable articles. Some of my fellow officers suffered the same fate. We had to scurry around to obtain the necessary documents for departure. This done, we embarked on May 6, 1946, from Calcutta aboard our transport, the SS Marine *Panther,* and sailed down the Hoogli River to the Bay of Bengal toward San Francisco. Some 2,200 passengers were on board. On the South China Seas a sailor fell overboard. After a fruitless search for an hour we were about to proceed without him, when suddenly through my binoculars I saw his head bob about a mile away. We were all pleased with his rescue. After a pause in Manila we proceeded to the United States after what seemed a very slow passage. We found that the Golden Gate Bridge looked mighty good. We disembarked on June 2, glad to be again on native soil. I was mustered out of the army on July 9, 1946— ready, once again, for an entirely new phase of my life's journey.

7

INSIDE METHODISM:
THE BOARD YEARS
1946–1960

In this chapter I refer to the fourteen years (1946–1960) during which I served as associate or corresponding secretary, and from 1952 as associate general secretary, of the Division of World Missions of the Board of Missions of The Methodist Church. Nowadays the organization is designated as the World Division of the Board of Global Ministries of The United Methodist Church.

The work was hard and demanding. One could never quite say that it was ever done. Later I will describe in some detail what exactly I did, but my work was not all that I did. Together with my wife, Eunice, we began to rear a family of three children. From the outset, if credit is due in our family experience, that credit must go mostly to Eunice. She bore the brunt of the responsibility, all too often without very much participation or even presence on my part. For good or ill her father too was often an absentee parent—doing "the Lord's work" throughout the world—so she was in some sense prepared for the experience.

To indicate how enterprising Eunice was, I must recount a little more of our story. For five years we had been married but no prospect of a family appeared. Then in September 1945 we learned that Eunice was pregnant. At the time we lived on a tea plantation in Assam. As a civilian employee of the U.S. Army she enjoyed good medical care. What was termed the "rabbit test" for pregnancy had only recently come to our notice. One of the army doctors used this method, and we therefore had rather early notice of our prospects.

I was visiting army headquarters in New Delhi at about that time. The war was already over but I had stayed on a number of months to help wrap up the supply operation. While there I met General Raymond Wheeler, who had commissioned me in 1942. He inquired about Eunice. When I told him, he remarked that she must fly to the United States without delay: "I will give this my immediate and sympathetic attention." This he did. She was given a high priority and duly arrived in New York in the fall of 1945. She stayed for a time with my sister and her husband in Montclair, New Jersey; and later with her cousins Howard and Georgeanna Jones, both physicians, in Baltimore.

During the winter of 1945–46 I was offered a job with the Board of Missions in New York to begin after I got out of the army. This necessitated that we have living accommodations, preferably in New York City. Needless to say, apartments were in short supply. My brother-in-law was not reassuring, stating that it would be impossible to secure housing.

Then suddenly Eunice was informed by friends that a flat had indeed come on the market in Manhattan in the vicinity of Columbia University. She quickly traveled to the city and sought the address: 54 Morningside Drive. She happened to take the wrong subway train and landed in nearby Harlem at Morningside *Avenue*. This address was separated from Morningside *Drive* by Morningside Park, which rested on a hilltop rising approximately two hundred feet to Morningside Heights. There had just been a severe sleet storm and the whole hillside was covered as if by a frozen sheet of ice. There was Eunice, seven months pregnant, crawling up this treacherous slope on her hands and knees! But she made it to the top.

She did more than that. She bought a cooperative apartment on the spot! Thus we became instant members of the Morningside Cooperative Association, Inc. The cost of apartment 5B was $5,000 for a two and a half bedrooms, one and a half bathrooms, and a living room–dining area. It afforded an unobstructed view toward the east across Harlem to what is now called LaGuardia Airport—five miles distant. Also required was a monthly payment of $40 for collective property taxes and upkeep expenses of the cooperative. The purchase was made from the widow of a former professor of Columbia University, who chanced also to be a sister of the magician Houdini. As if that were not enough, Eunice was able for an additional sum of $500 to purchase the complete furniture of the apartment. We are using some of it still—fifty years later. And as if *that* was not enough, she was able to sublet it for the four months until I returned home! My skeptical brother-in-law was completely nonplussed if not downright disappointed at her good fortune. Anyone who recalls the tight postwar economy of that period will be able to appreciate the coup my young wife had made.

Two months later our first child, Anne Treffry Mathews, was born on April 17 at Johns Hopkins Hospital in Baltimore. I did not see her until she was two months old, but she immediately became and continues to be the joy of my life, although subsequently she had to share with a sister and a brother that place in my affection. As I came out of the army I immediately had a wife, a family, a furnished apartment, and a job!

We were blessed also with good neighbors who also shared apartments in our cooperative. Next door was Dr. Wade Crawford Barclay and his invalid wife. He was a distinguished Christian educator and mission historian. On the other side dwelt Miss Laycock, retired school teacher and always a friend in need. Then there was Dr. Everett M. Stowe, former missionary to China. Most of all, we enjoyed Dr. and Mrs. Robert Goheen, medical missionaries from Maharashtra in India. I had known them there and came to know their son Bob, later president of Princeton University and then ambassador to India.

Our apartment was located just to the south of 116th Street on Morningside Drive. On the opposite corner to the north was located the elegant residence of the president of Columbia University. Before he went to the White House General Eisenhower was president of the University for a period. In the penthouse he used to engage in the recreation of painting pictures, an art in which Sir Winston Churchill encouraged him. Eunice used to hang the diapers on the roof of our building that afforded a direct view into Eisenhower's studio. When in the evening she collected our laundry, she could often view the general, sometimes stripped to the waist, painting. Our guests would on occasion accompany her in this activity. If perchance a reader should think ill of us for this, we beg absolution.

Now I see that I have managed to get far ahead of my story. Why was I starting this new job in the first place? Like most veterans my life after the war was bound to take a drastic change. As earlier stated, I had vague plans to study for a doctorate at Princeton University. I was still a kind of missionary on leave. Out of the blue came this offer of an important position at the Board of Missions of The Methodist Church. What to do?

Let me say that my response was by no means immediate. Rather, I resorted to a device that years before I had learned, as I recall, from Dr. John R. Mott, the renowned missionary statesman. His practice was, when faced with an important decision, to draw a line down the middle of a page. On the one side one would write down all the reasons for accepting one course of action rather than another. On the other side one writes all the reasons against the proposal. One simply "thinks one's self empty"—all this in a deliberate and prayerful fashion, usually extending over several days. Ordinarily this process leads to a clear indication as to what course of action one should take; the scales tip one way or the other. In this case, after some delay, I accepted the invitation.

This was not the first time I had used this method. For example, I went through this exercise when trying to decide to go to India in the first instance. It was even a part of my decision to marry, though doubtless I was directed by strong natural urges also in this latter instance. Nor was it the last time. Indeed, when some momentous personal decision, particularly a vocational decision, was to be made, I have invariably fallen back on this mode. Once having thus determined, I have not had to look back on or reverse my decision.

Having served in the army for four years, at the time I had a good deal of accrued leave coming to me. This could have been used for additional pay when I got out of the service. Rather, I decided to use it constructively by traveling extensively around India and what was later to become Pakistan to visit the churches and institutions in the area over which I was to exercise administrative care in the years ahead.

So it was that I made a rather wide tour in all parts of the country where our church had work. Normally I traveled by train, for civilian air travel was almost nonexistent. Over a few portions of the trip I was able to hitchhike a ride on military planes. Most days were spent in visiting the churches, schools, hospitals, and social centers that The Methodist Church in Southern Asia operated in eleven annual conferences and some ten language areas. I talked with Indian leaders and missionaries about their work, their needs, and their dreams. If I stayed overnight it was usually with missionaries, and I am deeply in the debt of hosts of them who proved hospitable to me. Otherwise, I would travel overnight by train and repeat the exploration the next day in a new setting. It was an eye-opening and mind-changing experience. In sum, I was afforded a broad perspective of missionary work throughout the subcontinent that proved indispensable to me in the days ahead. My conclusions and my own vision for Indian Methodism are recorded in the Board of Missions annual report for 1946. Such reports I wrote in detail year by year in what altogether would make up a sizable book in themselves.

As I look back it occurs to me that I must have been a strange and even suspicious sight to missionaries and Indian Christians alike. Here I was, a virtual stranger to many, appearing suddenly in a U.S. Army officer's uniform to observe and question them about what they did. If they had doubts about me, they successfully hid the fact, while I profited vastly from the experience. On one occasion I do recall one elderly missionary who took me to task for traveling on a *Sunday* afternoon from Lucknow to Cawnpore. This did not coincide with his views of Sabbath-day observance.

Some of my travel I did on military warrants. All of this was of minimal cost to the board, for I was not on board salary at the time. It was probably the least expensive secretarial tour on record.

In mid-June 1946 I took up my job as the secretary for India and Burma. The Board of Missions had its headquarters at 150 Fifth Avenue at 20th Street in lower Manhattan. From our apartment in Morningside Heights I could easily travel to and from the office by subway. My salary, by the way, was $5,400 a year, which seemed a lot to me.

For the first six weeks on the job I had to wear my military uniform because I did not have any civilian clothes. The clothes I had taken to India, eight years before, were either out of style or not suited to the climate or no longer fit me, or I had simply given them away. It must have caused a great deal of consternation in the minds of people to see in a missionary organization, largely peaceful in its outlook, one of its secretaries in uniform. My fellow workers were, however, tolerant.

It was weeks before I could buy civilian clothing—this due to postwar shortages. Then one day I noted a suit sale advertised in the _New York Times_ was thronged by young men likewise seeking civilian clothes but I managed to get one of my size. It was a tan (just short of khaki in color) wool cheviot garment. I never did like a brown suit, but it allowed me to enter ordinary life once again.

The practical administrative experience I had gained while I was in the army proved to be immensely valuable to me. I like to think that I had matured somewhat, but maturing seems a lifelong process. India and its people I knew well. I was acquainted with the missionaries and Indian Christian leaders, I loved the Indian people while being aware that they shared, with the rest of humanity, many shortcomings. After nearly sixty years, at this writing, I still do. Most important, I was able to continue my vocation of Christian ministry, though not in its usual form of a local pastorate.

Then I had the tremendous advantage of working for my first three years under the direction of Dr. Ralph E. Diffendorfer, executive secretary of the Board of Foreign Missions. Up to that time I scarcely knew him. We had met briefly when I was interviewed for missionary service in 1937, then again at the Central Conference in Hyderabad in December 1938. Oh yes, I did manage to recover and return to him a coat he had left behind. It is pleasant to recall that the young Timothy once rendered a similar service to St. Paul. Diffendorfer was considered a stern and even tough administrator. His whole life he had devoted to foreign missions, starting out as a worker in the mail room at the head office and working his way to the top. Born in Ohio, he continued an ardent alumnus of Ohio Wesleyan University, where he was a classmate of baseball great Branch Rickey. "Diff" completed his training at Drew Theological Seminary in Madison, New Jersey. By 1946 he was dean of missionary administrators. Despite his hard-nosed reputation, he had a heart of gold and was a thoroughly devoted Christian. He became my mentor. He had a most creative mind, was possessed of boundless energy, and was given to colorful, forceful, and persuasive speech.

How I should like to tell his story in detail, for it needs to be told. During recent years I have tried to find and complete the research material once compiled by Dr. Thomas S. Donohugh, but it seems to have been misplaced. "Diff," as his friends called him, was a man of vision, a skilled executive, a true missionary statesman, an articulate and eloquent advocate of the missionary venture and indeed, a great man. Quietly, I believe he tried to bring out in me whatever positive qualities I possessed, so I am ever in his debt for his encouragement. His colleagues could argue with him as long as they had the facts well in hand; he was solicitous about them, and with his penetrating mind and analytical power he was ready to help when needed and invariably pointed to the Christian way. One time I heard him say: "To know what God knows and not be what God is is the most dangerous thing in the world." Thank God that God is great, but also good.

Diff was literally saturated with missionary lore and Christian purpose. How often I have heard him tell of Bishop James M. Thoburn, *his* mentor and also a missionary statesman of the highest order, who frequently said:

"Tonight, one half the world will go to bed hungry.
Tonight, one half the world is beyond the reach of modern medicine.
Tonight, one half the world is illiterate and beyond the reach of modern knowledge.
There will never be peace in this world as long as these conditions prevail."

Now, that is missionary perspective! When such a view is linked with a solid commitment to Jesus Christ as the world's compassionate, healing, teaching Savior, a transforming missionary zeal is generated. This Dr. Diff possessed in eminent degree and passed on to others. I am actually writing these lines in the autumn of 1997, but I recall that the Quadrennial Program for The Methodist Church, "The Advance for Christ and His Church," approved by the 1948 General Conference, was largely the brainchild of Ralph E. Diffendorfer. The program has continued for nearly fifty years and $700 million has been raised for a host of missionary and relief purposes throughout the whole world, but I have not seen reference to its originator, a shortcoming I am pleased to correct.

Dr. Diffendorfer headed a team of which I was to become a part. There was a corresponding or associate secretary for each of the major areas: Frank T. Cartwright for China and later Southeast Asia; Raymond L. Archer, a scholar of Islam, for Africa and Europe; Thoburn T. Brumbaugh for Japan, Korea, and the Philippines; and Alfred W. Wasson for Latin America. There were also the treasurers, George Sutherland and Albert E. Beebe and their assistants, a legal counselor, and an array of support staff suitable for a large international organization. All of these persons became my close friends as well as colleagues. We were a congenial cooperative fellowship mutually supportive of one another in every way. Even in those days we reached our decisions by consensus, although this mode of operation did not widely commend itself to management groups until years later.

The corresponding or associate secretaries not only served the Board of Missions as a whole but also represented the field they administered. For example, my colleagues in India came to understand that I was "batting on *their* team." My task was to interpret the countries of India, Pakistan, and Burma to the Division of Foreign Missions and to the Church at large. I was also one of the main channels of *information* for conveying the emphases and trends of the Church in this country to the fields of my interest.

To perform the functions adequately, it was necessary to keep well informed about conditions on the field. It seems essential that the secretary visit the field at least once a quadrennium. An adequate visit took about six to eight months, for southern Asia was the largest mission field of the church. There was a constituency of more than half a million Methodists there—almost equal to the number in all other fields put together at that time.

Before I knew it I was involved with a heavy burden of correspondence both in the United States and abroad. Naturally I had a part in the formulation of policies and then responsibility for administering in accordance with them. Since mission board secretaries were also related to their counterparts in other denominations, abiding friendships were formed in the process. We had to speak widely, interpreting and promoting missions. We were in daily contact with the secretaries who had similar responsibility for work for the Woman's Division of the Board of Missions. We became known as "pairs of secretaries." My "opposite number" was Miss Lucile Colony, with whom I had the most harmonious and constructive association.

Mention must be made of the assistants and private secretaries assigned to each area administrator. In my own case, I was fortunate in having the devoted and competent assistance of Marjorie Koller. Her long experience meant that she was an informed and tireless co-worker who extended my usefulness, and who spared me many woes and pitfalls. She was a wise counselor who could make me look good even when I was not. After her retirement I was favored by being able to keep in touch with her until the time of her death. Her successors were also able and devoted in service.

One other matter I would note. Immediately adjacent to my small office at 150 Fifth Avenue was another of the same size. It was occupied by a man of whom I stood in awe, for he had been a college president (Ohio Wesleyan University) and had completed a long and distinguished episcopal career in East Asia. He was none other than Bishop Herbert W. Welch, who had retired long since but was still active at age eighty-three (I was thirty-three then) and served as executive director of the recently formed relief agency, the Methodist Committee for Overseas Relief. He welcomed me heartily and we formed a comradeship that became warmer through the years when I was to join him in the Council of Bishops. The same was true of his successor in MCOR, retired Bishop Titus Lowe. Until 1952 *all* bishops of our church were members of the Board of Missions, so at the annual meetings I gradually became acquainted with all of them.

Before I had even had a chance to visit my office, and immediately after I was discharged from the army, there was a Conference for Furloughed Missionaries and Executives held in 1946 at Albion College in Michigan. Here I met my colleagues for the first time. There were some three hundred missionaries of both the Foreign and the Women's Division present. This meeting of missionaries was the first of its kind after World War II and was important for that very reason. It afforded opportunity for missionaries from widely scattered regions to meet together, to report on their work, and to become acquainted with board policies and, indeed, have some part in their formulation.

There too missionaries home from India were enabled to meet with their secretary, in some cases for the first time. The preacher for the Sunday morning service was India's Bishop Shot K. Mondol. I had been present when he was elected in Delhi in 1941. He was a handsome man, gifted as many Bengalis are as wordsmith. He preached with great eloquence and I was proud of him.

Prouder still was I of our daughter Anne who had accompanied Eunice and me to this conference. It so happened that it coincided with Father's Day, the first time I had been qualified to be favored on such an occasion. At any rate our Anne, then two months old, possibly in consultation with her mother, gave me a Father's Day gift. It was a bottle of rather potent after-shaving lotion, which I wore proudly.

These meetings for missionaries on furlough became a regular part of the board's program, and they contributed greatly to the morale and equipment of all of us who were colleagues in the missionary undertaking. They lasted about a week and were occasions to which all participants looked forward; among other things, they were fun. After the Albion gathering subsequent sessions were held on the campus of DePauw University in Greencastle, Indiana. For years at these sessions a regular feature was my teaching various books of the Bible. I enjoyed doing this immensely and was well trained in method. Over a period of a dozen years I taught nearly all the books of the New Testament and the Psalms as well. Of great value to me in the process was the fact that it forced me to study and to keep up in the biblical field.

Among many other things at these gatherings missionaries trained one another in the skills of missionary cultivation. This included suggestions as to the most effective mode of making a missionary address. Some were very gifted in this art. Likewise they were trained in writing letters to supporters. Mabel Lossing Jones (Mrs. E. Stanley Jones) had mastered this art. Her letters were brief, about one and a half pages. In the open space below the duplicated portion she would add a personalized handwritten note. She never *asked* for anything; she merely stated an unmet need. And the money poured in— enough to keep a thousand boys in school with scholarships. She did this for fifty years.

As we have seen, mission board secretaries were

engaged in a multifaceted vocation. For example, we were deeply involved in the recruitment of missionaries. Sometimes in our travels we would meet prospective candidates. When they applied they were subjected to a careful screening and evaluation process, including physical and psychological tests. A dossier of some twenty pages was prepared for each candidate, and over a period of time scores of these were submitted. The area secretaries were supposed to read all of these and indicate whether or not they seemed acceptable for the current needs in any given field. We were often present when these prospective workers were questioned by the personnel committees prior to their acceptance.

The secretaries were members of various other committees within the structure of the board itself and in the denomination. For instance, I was for twelve years a member of and chairman of the Crusade Scholarship Committee. Arising out of the Crusade for Christ campaign of the 1944–48 quadrennium, which raised more than $25 million for postwar development, it provided scholarships for hundreds of students from all over the world to do graduate work in the United States. A whole generation of leaders from what were then called the "younger churches" benefited from this effort. Future bishops, professors, school principals, physicians, and leaders in public life were among the company that these scholarships made possible. We reached beyond The Methodist Church and provided six graduate scholarships for Greek Orthodox students, one of whom became world-renowned: Archbishop Makarios of Cyprus. It was certainly one of the most creative ventures in which

Methodists have been involved. The committee was made up of church leaders and college administrators from across the country. The work was exciting and exacting. For me it afforded an opportunity to become acquainted with leading educators in the United States. All of us did a conscientious job of immense benefit to both church and society.

Another organization in which I found myself involved was MCOR (later called UMCOR), the Methodist Committee for Overseas Relief. It was a program inaugurated by the 1944 General Conference to help meet the overwhelming human needs that arose out of World War II and that could only be met by a broad scale ministry of compassion. In 1946 I was assigned to be a member of this committee and remained so for eighteen years. I served as its chairman from 1960 to 1964.

MCOR prided itself in "traveling light." As originally conceived it was not regarded as a permanent organization, for it had to be newly authorized by successive General Conferences. It operated on a minuscule administrative budget so that nearly all contributions found their way to the needs for which they were given. Here again almost incalculable good was done in connection with emergency disasters and relief and refugee service. Sometimes this help was administered directly through Methodist churches and mission agencies; sometimes it was done cooperatively in conjunction with other churches or later through the National Council or World Council of Churches. Naturally I was delighted at being a cog in this ministry, just as I was distressed by the human suffering that occasioned its creation.

Mission secretaries were then involved in what was called the Foreign Missionary Conference of North America. There we became acquainted with men and women who served as our counterparts in other churches. Leaders I had only read about or heard about earlier became personal colleagues and some of them lifelong friends. Among these were Lesslie Newbigin, Charles Ranson, Charles Long, John Coventry Smith, Edward H. (Ted) Johnson, Gloria Wysner, Sue Wedell, and a host of others.

Within this overarching organization there were area committees for each of the major regions and countries. Thus I became deeply involved in the work related to India and southern Asia in general. Much missionary work was done in connection with other denominations, and it became almost a rule "never to do separately what we could do more effectively when acting together." During the 1940s and 50s one seldom heard the word *ecumenical* but we learned what it was by doing it. Naturally we advocated and lent support to the National Christian Councils in the various countries. For instance, just after World War II nearly fifty churches or organizations joined in supporting Vellore Christian Medical College in South India. This clearly illustrated the maxim that mission led to Christian unity.

We were also involved in various "functional missionary bodies." One notable one was Agricultural Missions, Inc., of which I served as chairman for several years. It represented an astonishing array of institutions that served rural and village people in many countries. Their approach was influenced by the grange movement and the county agent movement in the United States and sim-

ilar approaches in Europe. Notable was Allahabad Agricultural Institute of Allahabad, India, established by Presbyterian missionary Dr. Sam Higginbottom. He was a
very energetic and colorful person who became famous
for his emphasis on "the gospel and the plow" or "the
gospel and the cow," the latter for his crossbreeding of
bovines resulting in hardier stock. Mrs. Higginbottom
was a most interesting person and was a daughter of
"Buffalo Bill" Cody.

I still thrill as I think of such devoted leaders as Dr. John
F. Reisner, who was *Mr.* Agricultural Missions. Of no less
stature was Church of the Brethren missionary Ira W.
Moomaw, a quiet man but a genius in village work. At the
meetings of this little organization we were constantly
encountering outstanding rural missionaries and nationals from China, Africa, South America, and the islands of
the seas. One I recall vividly was Dr. Henry Loudermilk
of the U.S. Department of Agriculture (but a missionary
at heart, I think) who recounted the incredible venture of
exploring the headwaters of the Yangtse River for giant
sequoyah-like trees that were rumored to be there—and
he found them! I think too of Helen Fehr and her remarkable program of training village leaders in Central India,
or Mabel Sheldon's similar work in North India's United
Provinces, particularly her Brides' School, which sought
to strengthen the family. Presbyterian missionaries
William H. and Charlotte V. Wiser became justly honored
for their village work in India, reflected in their book
Behind Mud Walls. Other "greats" were Arthur Mosher of
Allahabad Agricultural Institute and Elbert Reed, who
contributed so much at El Vergel in Chile to develop the

fruit industry in that country. Lulu B. Tubbs was a most effective worker among rural women in what is now Zimbabwe. Then there was Frank Laubach and his justifiably renowned literacy work; Ruth Ure of World Christian literature; and Bishop Stephen Neill, of the World Christian Books Project.

To mention these is to fail to mention many no less worthy and stalwart people who labored in out-of-the-way places all around the world. One was privileged to encounter such folk all the time when they passed through New York City as they moved to and from their fields of endeavor. And what of those engaged in medical work: Dr. Douglas Forman, head of Christian Medical Missions; or Dr. Robert Hume, medical educator from China. Then there were those engaged in missions to people afflicted with Hansen's disease (leprosy). I have said that a board secretary's work was never dull, and such persons as I have mentioned and the work they represented became a part of one's stock-in-trade.

I have been recounting what mission board secretaries *did,* and it must be evident that their lives were busy. In addition, we all engaged in giving missionary addresses and were encouraged to do this as much as possible. My files are crammed with notes on the hundreds of addresses I gave. Ordinarily I spoke from notes, which seemed simpler and more effective for me, although for more formal occasions presentations were made from a prepared manuscript. The setting for these speeches ranged from Sunday school classes to preaching services, youth gatherings, annual conferences, retreats, colleges and seminaries, interdenominational meetings, and many more. This activity I enjoyed immensely and the presentations almost always produced positive results of one kind or another. The research and preparation required added greatly to one's knowledge and fund of experience.

What were these addresses like? Some were sermons. Nearly all were biblically based. As the years passed in my case they became of necessity more theologically sophisticated. One's travels and mission field visitations, contact and correspondence with national leaders all contributed to the richness of what one could present. Some of my addresses were published in periodicals and annual reports or included in books.

During the course of my fourteen years I spoke in forty-six of the then forty-eight states. It was exciting, and it greatly enlarged my circle of acquaintances among a host of fine people. It gave me also an almost unequaled opportunity to observe our great Church at work across the world. I would take nothing in exchange for this experience. An analysis of my time use during this period showed that about one-fourth was spent in such field-work. One naturally had to carry some paperwork along on these trips so that such duties were not neglected.

Some experiences of mission cultivation were interdenominational, particularly one in Florida. It was my privilege to be a part of the Florida Chain of Missions during three different years. It was also an honor highly prized by missionaries. It afforded us an opportunity to "tell our story" to receptive and appreciative audiences all over Florida. As I write there come to my mind the large congregations who gathered to hear the messages. We always felt that our efforts resulted in large dividends for the kingdom. We were especially fortunate to get to know Louise Woodford, the organizer of the effort. She was a tremendous spirit, a regular generalissima! She possessed enormous organizing and management skills and was the real heart and secret of the success of the enterprise. It was always an inspiration to see her at work. Though she drove hard the "Chain Gang," for so we called ourselves, she was also always very considerate and saw to it that we had occasional relief and the chance to see some of the sights of Florida. One cannot praise her too highly, and she is a person of most happy memory.

Then, we had a good team spirit. We made acquaintances with our colleagues that endured. There were really some great and outstanding persons on the Chain: Martin Niemoeller and Helen Kim among them. It was delightful too to stay as guests in the homes of people in so many places. Their hospitality is well and gratefully remembered. Above all we who spoke on the Chain of Missions are grateful to God for the privilege of serving him in witnessing to his Son in a significant way. The pastors also proved very cooperative; this was practical ecumenism before the term became popular. I wish there were some contemporary counterpart to this undertaking.

Hardly had I arrived in New York in June 1946 until one day there came to my office a man who had himself been a missionary to India but with whom I was only slightly acquainted. He was a professor at Drew University and a thoroughgoing scholar. His name was Dr. George W. Briggs. I can remember as if it were yesterday his sitting across from me at my desk and saying, "You can either waste your time here merely as a secretary of this board, or you can equip yourself better for your work in the future." He encouraged me to enroll in a doctoral program at Columbia University. He was so earnest about this that I did enroll.

Then I found that under the GI Bill of Rights I could get my tuition paid, so I had no excuse. For the next three years I worked on my Ph.D. while I was carrying on a full-time job at the board. Here I am writing about this just fifty years after the GI Bill was enacted by Congress. It has been called "the best deal ever made by Uncle Sam." Together with millions of others who benefited by it I am deeply grateful. Most of all, our country benefited, for the result was a more highly trained citizenry than any other nation could boast. Incidentally, at the time of my enrollment in Columbia University tuition cost was fifteen dollars an hour!

Finally I did complete my Ph.D. in the field of History of Religion. I did it the hard way by taking night courses, Saturday courses, and studies in summer school sessions. Then I discovered that they had a six-week summer school at Columbia University that went for half a day. One could take either morning or afternoon classes. I found that I could earn nine hours of credit during the summer school, which sounded pretty good to my ears. I went to the morning classes for six weeks and then I would go to work in my office in the afternoon and I would study in the evening. I was due a month's vacation, but I used up three weeks of my vacation with classes. That left me a week to recover. By that time I would be exhausted. I did that for three summers.

Then I took evening courses. I would have to dash away from my office and catch subways to get up to Columbia University. If I hit it just right, I could make my classes on time. The evening class was always a very important seminar. Afterward I would go home for supper. Fortunately we lived nearby, just a block away on Morningside Drive. After supper I would hasten back for night classes. Happily, I was able to bring the sixteen hours of credit from Boston University (1937–38). By 1949, in three years I had finished the sixty required hours. Later I satisfied the language requirements, both French and German, and then I passed the comprehensive exam. I vividly remember how exhausting that exercise was, writing exam papers for twelve hours, producing about fifty typewritten pages of material. But I was accepted for the doctorate. Soon after this we moved to Upper Montclair, New Jersey.

I was into so many things at that time and engaged in work all over the church that it was not until 1957 that I actually received the degree, having by then finished the dissertation. For my doctoral work on Mahatma Gandhi I think I read everything he ever wrote, and he wrote a lot because he was a journalist for most of his life, in South Africa and then in India. The dissertation at last came together. It was published in India years later (1989).

An earlier reference was made to the fact that throughout my educational work prior to going to India I was obliged to work long hours to support myself while a student. The price for this I have already noted: failure to gain full mastery of my subjects, though I did succeed in getting good grades. How I longed for an opportunity of unhampered study! That time never really came for me.

Nevertheless, I was thrilled at the opportunity to be back in an academic atmosphere. It was like a breath of fresh air and seemed to release new energies—too long dormant within me.

My professors were able persons and it was a delight to be their student. Among them was Professor Horace L. Friess, who was my adviser for my dissertation. He and his colleague Professor Herbert W. Schneider, a Methodist, led the study of religion at Columbia. Their work in the survey course in History of Religions was undergirded by visiting professors, specialists in one or another of the religions. Among these were Professor George W. Briggs in Hinduism, Professor Samuel N. Kramer for the ancient religion of Sumeria, Professor Elder for Islam, and D. T. Suzuki for Buddhism. I greatly enjoyed the classes in psychology conducted by Professor R. S. Woodworth. One summer course was conducted by the dean of American anthropologists, Alfred L. Kroeber, in which field also we had lectures by Ruth F. Benedict and Margaret Mead.

To return to my work-study program: it was not easy, particularly in light of my heavy travel program. Throughout my years at the board I was traveling no fewer than 50,000 miles a year, most of it by train. When use of planes became more common, I traveled even more miles. This meant that sometimes I had to send Eunice to my classes, which meant that she had to arrange for baby-sitters. She took lecture notes in shorthand and then typed them. They were the best notes I had; otherwise, they appeared in my almost indecipherable scrawl. On a few occasions, when my sister Alice was visiting us, she was recruited as my substitute. Columbia was generous in this respect; such times were rather few overall, and besides I kept up the reading and writing assignments.

Having just mentioned train travel perhaps I should relate one notable instance. It happened that I and one other person were the only travelers on an entire Pullman car. I instantly recognized my fellow-traveler and said: "You are Dr. Albert Einstein, are you not?" The gentleman replied with a twinkle in his eyes, "No, but I'm a good friend of his." This was his gentle way of reminding me that he would rather be left to his own deep reflections.

I delighted in our little family. It gave me great pleasure particularly during spring or summer evenings to take Anne out for a walk on Morningside Drive. Sometimes I would carry her "saddled" on my shoulders; in this she was especially delighted. On one such journey we met General Eisenhower. He showed a friendly interest in our two-year-old and somewhere we have a picture of her standing beside him. On occasion we would chance upon some of my fellow students, to whom I was pleased to show her off.

Our second child was Janice, or Jan. She was born early on a Sunday morning, November 9, 1947, at nearby Women's Hospital on West 109th Street. Anne had been deposited for the event with my sister Elizabeth in Montclair, New Jersey. Our neighbor Miss Laycock insisted that we awaken her—as it turned out it was at four in the morning. She drove us to the hospital in her ancient Ford, for at the time we had no car. In due course Jan arrived.

This was long before the practice of the husband being in the delivery room. What goes on there is still something of a mystery to me.

Jan is a redhead. This was a puzzle to us, for we knew of no ancestors on either side who were so colored. The puzzle was soon solved. Shortly after the new arrival Eunice's father came to visit. He told us that his mother's hair had been red, the same shade as Jan's.

We were snug in our little apartment. Public transportation was near at hand. So were the necessary shops. New York's entertainment—theater, music, sports—was available, as were baby-sitters. Tickets were phenomenally cheap when compared to standards prevailing half a century later. The cultural advantages of being near a great university were evident. I recall hearing lectures by Arnold Toynbee, Emil Brunner, Paul Tillich, Reinhold Niebuhr, and hosts of others. We were within walking distance of Riverside Church and frequently heard Harry Emerson Fosdick preach. On one visit there we chanced to enter at the same time as did John D. Rockefeller, Jr. He kindly invited us to sit with him. The reader will forgive us for recalling that we noticed he placed a one hundred-dollar bill in the offering plate; so my one dollar was not disproportionate. Close by also was the Cathedral of St. John the Divine—unfinished then and unfinished now. One Sunday we worshiped there at the final service in the United States of the newly elected Ecumenical Patriarch, Athenagoras. He proceeded directly from there to LaGuardia Airport to board a plane offered by President Truman, which carried him to Constantinople to assume his duties. Athenagoras was a tall, stately man; when he was wearing his crown he seemed about seven feet tall. Later, I was to visit him in the Phanar in Constantinople in 1963 and again in 1968.

At about the time my course work and comprehensive exams at Columbia were completed (1949) we moved from the city. We had no trouble selling our cooperative apartment. With our growing family we needed more room. We were able to purchase a four-bedroom, two-and-a-half bathroom Dutch Colonial house in Montclair, New Jersey, costing $13,000. We were also finally able to purchase a car, a new Chevrolet for $1,200. Since there was really no place to park it in the city, this gave us added reason to depart for the suburbs. Montclair was a fine community and was to be our home throughout the 1950s. There our children started their schooling and formed their first friendships. There too we developed a circle of close friends who have remained dear to us through the years.

There was a succession of interdenominational gatherings during the post–World War II period. A notable one, held in Columbus, Ohio, in October 1948, was sponsored by the Foreign Missions Conference of North America, which represented 108 Protestant foreign mission boards in the United States and Canada. Hundreds of missionaries and missionary executives came together for this occasion. Dr. Ralph Diffendorfer and his associate secretaries and their counterpart officers in the Women's Division of the Board were all present. Plenary sessions were interspersed with regional and "functional"—educational, medical, agricultural, audiovisual—meetings.

My notes record that addresses were given by Diffendorfer and by Bishop G. Bromley Oxnam, one of the newly designated presidents of the World Council of Churches, which was organized the previous summer. Other speakers were Dr. Henry Sloane Coffin, former president of Union Theological Seminary; Dr. Vera M. Dean, advocate of the United Nations; Congressman and longtime medical missionary to China, Dr. Walter H. Judd; and Harold E. Stassen, at that time president of the University of Pennsylvania. Greetings were sent by President Harry S. Truman, President Syghman Rhee, General Douglas MacArthur, then in Tokyo, and other notables. All these dignitaries gave ringing affirmation of the positive contributions of the Christian missionary movement. Then there were messages given by "younger church" leaders from various countries. One was from Chief Albert Luthuli of South Africa, later Nobel peace laureate. Another was by Dr. Hilda M. Lazaras, the new principal of Vellore Christian Medical College in South India. Her strong evangelical witness, her passion for the ailing, and her ardent advocacy for the dispossessed had a tremendous effect on the whole meeting.

Two speakers from Japan were also impressive. One was the Reverend Michio Kozaki, a leader of Japan's National Christian Council and moderator of Kyodan. He was one of the few church leaders who had been able to leave Japan so soon after the war. The hearers hung on his words as he told of Christians worshiping in railroad and police stations, in schools or any facility available due to the loss of bombed-out churches. He spoke of Japan's new constitution, which gave unaccustomed religious freedom and a new opportunity for the church. Even more telling was the presence of the Reverend Takyo Matsumoto, principal of Hiroshima Girl's School, which had been established in the 1880s. He electrified his audience as he told of the 18 teachers and 350 girl students killed when the school was in an instant leveled to the ground. Matsumoto's wife had been severely injured in the bombing. The speaker dwelt on a new future for the church in Hiroshima, a sentiment echoed in the response of Dr. Diffendorfer when he voiced the hope that "we may create a world in which atomic bombing will have no part whatsoever." He helped to fulfill this hope as after retirement he became a founder of Japan International Christian University. When I read in 1999 of a generous couple on Long Island having given millions of dollars to this fine university, I recalled how "Diff" had struggled to raise funds for it.

The meeting was troubled about developments in China, which were to become worse; about the threat of communism, which was stated strongly by Walter Judd and others. Western and American responsibility for replacing autocratic with democratic principles in economic life was stressed by Bishop Oxnam:

> The church must recognize that hunger has been a fact for centuries and that it is not a task of relief but a problem of reordering our economic life so that every man has enough to eat, decent clothing and a place to live.
>
> The church must reach into the mind of our economists, engineers, and educators in such fashion that the moral ideal is translated by them into the realities of the common life. The problem is finding the means to give life to the ideal . . . the whole church should set itself to the total task of winning the whole world to Christ. . . . That's the mission of the church in our world.

This meeting released tremendous new energies for the worldwide mission of the church. Missionaries and missionary agencies had suffered sorely from the ravages of war, but though beaten down, they were not destroyed. Such events as this one helped to redirect the churches in their worldwide mission. Dr. Diffendorfer expressed it well:

> We missionary people must demonstrate to the world that we can adjust ourselves to new conditions and to new challenges just as thousands of people have done in the conduct of the recent war. . . .
>
> Either we are going to rise to the opportunities that are before us today or we are going to be moved increasingly upon the sidelines and other forces and agencies are coming forward with positive programs to meet the world's needs. . . .
>
> Humanity stands at the parting of the ways. In one road stands the universal Christ—His road leads to peace within a world community of brothers. In the other road stands black Chaos—His road is the way to war and to the suicide of civilization. For the world-minded Christian the choice ought to be perfectly clear, and the cost of the choice, the cross, to be paid with singleness of mind and gladness of heart."

This conference was not all rhetoric, for the heart of it was in the practical. For instance, the conference announced a new Protestant radio station for Asia, based at Silliman University in the Philippines. This was under the creative leadership of Dr. S. Franklin Mack and the Reverend Everett C. Parker, who were to continue for years to make great contributions in this field. Other fields of missionary endeavor also were given a boost:

rural and urban training centers, literacy, literature, youth and student work, home and family life, medical and other ministries of compassion, adult and technical training, relief and rehabilitation, all empowered and undergirded with evangelism. The Christian mission is nothing if not comprehensive.

The "Threes"

In the summer of 1948 our board embarked on an ambitious program of emphasizing short-term missionaries alongside career missionaries. Now I was myself originally a short-term missionary to India. But the new element was the idea of a *group* of young short-terms, recruited, trained, and sent out together to some area of the world, another creative strategy of Dr. Ralph Diffendorfer.

The first was a body of approximately fifty young Christians who were sent to Japan and Korea, known as "J3s" and "K3s." There was a ready response, for many young people at the time were highly motivated to serve. The same energy that manifested itself a few years later in the Peace Corps was tapped earlier in programs of "threes." Indeed the Peace Corps is said to have been inspired in part by the "threes" missionary undertaking. Individually and collectively they made a great difference and a lasting impression in East Asia.

Then came southern Asia's turn. During the summer of 1949 about fifty young persons were recruited for India and Pakistan, to be known as the I3s and P3s. I was asked to be the dean for the training of this group. Mildred Drescher, who served a long time in Bombay, was dean of women. The course was housed at Hartford Seminary and lasted for six weeks. Our daughters Anne, three years old, and Jan, age two, were with us and were "adopted" by fifty aunts and uncles.

A great deal was compressed into this experience. In an effort to encourage disciplined living there was early rising, morning and evening devotions, and a great deal of intellectual and practical emphasis. The faculty was a strong one: Dr. Malcolm Pitt taught Indian religions and drew on his considerable knowledge of southern Asian art and music. Professor Matthew Spinka gave a course on Christianity and Communism. Dr. Harold DeWolf of Boston University taught theology. Professor Eddy Asirvatham, Indian faculty member also of Boston University, lectured on Indian Christianity. Dr. Henry Scholberg, retired missionary from India and a fine linguist, presented an introduction of Hindi and Urdu. Dorothy Clarke Wilson also took this training as a prelude to her own visit to southern Asia, resulting in a number of fine books. Eunice's father, E. Stanley Jones, also spent some days with this group, an experience they recall with joy.

The trainees were introduced to Indian food, dress, and culture. Visiting lecturers enriched the experience in many ways. We visited the United Nations in New York and were briefed by Admiral Chester Nimitz on the Kashmir Question. The training was comprehensive and by the account of the young people themselves and those who observed their work in Asia they were as well trained as possible in a short course. If they were not "ninety-day-wonders," they were "forty-five-day wonders."

Dr. Diffendorfer thoroughly approved of the I3 program

and gave it his full and enthusiastic support. My own evaluation of this experience is altogether positive. Almost all of these young people did serve well in a variety of posts. A number became career missionaries. Others discovered their vocations during their time of service and later served in a wide variety of ways in church and society. Most continued active in the church and "leavened" church and community when they returned to their homeland.

So it was that I served as associate secretary for India and Pakistan and Burma for three and a half years before I was actually to visit the field again. Meanwhile, Dr. Ralph E. Diffendorfer retired at the end of 1948. Dr. Eugene L. Smith, a pastor from Brooklyn, New York had been elected as his successor and I was to serve with him for the next decade. Gene had neither the missionary experience of Diffendorfer nor his pronounced passion for the church—at least to begin with. He did, however, have a pastoral heart and a gift of impassioned speech. Gradually he became an informed and articulate spokesman for the mission of the Church. It was a privilege to be able to work with him and to count him and his wife, Idalene, as friends.

For the first six months of 1950 I undertook an extended field trip to India where I visited these short-term missionaries, as well as full-term ones, and our Indian associates as well. Of this I will speak later in a chapter devoted to my travels. Though I undertook a series of journeys to southern Asia, my orbit soon began to expand: to Africa, to Europe, to South America. All this was a necessary part of my enlarged role as coordinator of various mission fields.

Let me share one incident that occurred in Cochabamba, Bolivia. This city is located at an altitude of over 8,500 feet. Though not as trying as the even higher city of La Paz, still the air is very thin. We were conducting a baptism in a chapel located on the fourth floor of a high school. It was discovered as the service proceeded that there was no water in the baptismal font. As the youngest clergyperson present I volunteered to get some. Going down four floors was simple, but carrying the water up four flights was one of the hardest jobs I can remember. I had no idea that baptizing could be such a breathtaking experience.

A year later I was present at the World Methodist Council in Oxford. I had missed the first post–World War II session held in Springfield, Massachusetts. Here I got a fresh sense of the global nature of the Wesleyan family. We were housed in the various colleges of Oxford University. In my case it was in Christ Church College, a college that had been particularly associated with the Wesleys. It was a memorable experience to take meals in the great hall of that venerable establishment. At the sessions proper I heard addresses from the renowned leaders of our fellowship.

To me 1952 was a kind of banner year. For example, on February 6, 1952, Princess Elizabeth became Queen Elizabeth II. On February 17 our third child, James Stanley, was born. He was another redhead and a most welcome addition to our family. Later that year Sir Edmund Hillary and the Sherpa Tensing Norkay first conquered Mt. Everest. That year, too, President Eisenhower began his first term. And I was elected associate general secretary of the

Board of Missions. In that role I continued to be a strategic planner and coordinator of work in some forty countries—this in addition to administering southern Asia until 1956.

During this period there was a considerable shift of staff membership, due to retirements and in two instances to the fact that secretaries had been elected bishop in Central Conferences. Tracey K. Jones, Jr., succeeded Dr. Cartwright for the China work. Ralph E. Dodge followed Raymond Archer for Africa and then later Melvin Blake succeeded Dodge. James E. Ellis was successor to Dr. Wasson, while Roland W. Scott assumed my southern Asia portfolio. Meanwhile Burnham Kirkland was made treasurer and Dr. Harold Brewster, a former medical missionary in China, became medical secretary. I can testify to what a capable group they were, without exception committed to Christ's mission and to teamwork with one another.

Dr. Clarence T. Craig, dean of Drew Theological Seminary, invited me to teach a course on southern Asia during that spring. Dr. Craig was a New Testament scholar for whom I had the greatest respect. I had come to know the president of Drew, Fred G. Holloway, and his predecessor, Dr. Arlo Ayres Brown, who were both members of the Crusade Scholarship Committee. It was exciting to me also to become associated with other faculty members: Ralph A. Felton, professor of rural sociology; Nolan B. Harmon, later bishop, but then lecturer on the Methodist *Discipline* and book editor; Frederick A. Shippey, scholarly lecturer in urban work; Henry L. Lambdin, homiletics; and especially Dr. Carl D. Michalson, professor of systematic theology and until his tragic death a theological adviser and trusted friend. With the encouragement of my "chief" I gladly accepted this assignment.

I had always enjoyed teaching and believed that I had at least some skill in it. Accordingly I worked out a careful syllabus for a weekly two-hour course. Its range: "survey of various aspects of the cultures of India and Pakistan—historical, religious, social, political; the relevance of the Christian undertaking in these lands; the development and role of the Christian church there." Some fifty students enrolled for the course and we all appeared to enjoy engaging in learning together. I have had pleasure in keeping in touch with some of them through the years and encountering others from time to time. This is a part of the bond that teacher and students forge as I came to know its joys. I recall too the demand that this discipline placed upon me. In 1956 I was asked to repeat this course substantially at Drew, by which time Bernhard Anderson had become dean.

Then during April-May 1952 the General Conference met in San Francisco. The Bombay Annual Conference, of which I was then a member, honored me by electing me as its ministerial delegate. This was the one time that I was a member of a General Conference, although, as an associate general secretary, I was seated with voice but not vote at the sessions in Minneapolis in 1956 and Denver in 1960. It is a great deliberative body, and to observe or participate in its sessions is as thrilling as it is significant. As a visitor I attended the 1948 meeting in Boston and had been introduced to its procedures then. Incidentally, my wife and I hosted the southern Asia delegates and friends at an Indian dinner in Boston. We continued this practice through the General Conference of 1980 in Indianapolis when some three hundred persons attended at Roberts Park Church in that city. People began to like chicken curry and rice!

San Francisco proved to be an excellent site for the session, and our California hosts were superb. A number of matters linger in my memory. One was the very long episcopal address delivered by Bishop Paul B. Kern. It was brilliantly written and delivered but went on for nearly three hours. Another recollection is of the then Governor Earl Warren addressing the gathering. Dr. Walter VanKirk, specialist on matters of church and society, broadcasted daily news of the conference over some one hundred stations. I was impressed by the parliamentary skill of the bishops who presided. They included J. Waskom Pickett, the first Central Conference bishop to occupy the chair.

The main business of 1952 was reorganizing the structure of the local church, which was ably and successfully shepherded through the session by Dr. Alexander B. Smith of Philadelphia. Not so successful was the famous Survey Report arising out of the 1948 General Conference, which ordered a study of the general structure of the Church, a perennial passion among us it seems. We had more of this in 1972 and again in 1996. I may interject here that if restructuring would do it, it would have been done long ago! The report did propose a rather drastic overhaul of our ecclesiastical machinery. It was presented by Boston University president Harold C. Case, chairman. Immediately it hit headwinds and was challenged by New Jersey layman and lawyer Charles C. Parlin. Finally a committee of six—three from the sponsors and three from those who opposed the report—was raised to negotiate a greatly watered-down version, which was passed. I was not impressed much by the proposals nor by the final outcome.

Several times I spoke from the floor about overseas matters. Twice I made points of order that prevailed. Once I spoke in opposition to a motion that would have done away with the Week of Dedication offering, which funded the Crusade Scholarship program. As chairman of the scholarship committee I was in command of information that helped sway the vote; hence, the proposal was voted down. About $2 million was at stake. I was delighted that the vote went my way. Bishop Oxnam commended me for my speech, which helped save an important program. Altogether I agreed with Bishop Welch's evaluation of the session: it was inclusive, independent, characterized by high idealism and fraternal spirit.

The 1956 General Conference was held in Minneapolis at which time the Centenary of Indian Methodism was celebrated. The centerpiece of this was a pageant written by Dorothy Clarke Wilson, a pastor's wife from Maine. It was graced by a Centenary Choir from India led by a talented musician, Victor Sherring.

Returning more specifically to the board years, both Eugene Smith and I attended a meeting of the International Missionary Council in West Germany in 1952. This session, which I shall describe in more detail in another chapter, greatly stimulated attention to the theology of missions. As time passed it became more and more clear to me that we needed to encourage a discussion group of Methodist missionary leaders with theologians. I suggested this to Dr. Eugene L. Smith, who immediately proposed its implementation. There followed from the mid-fifties until the mid-sixties a series of such consultations. Most of them were held at a delightful spot on Glen Lake, Michigan, near the summer home of Bishop Richard C. Raines. Among the theologians who came were: Walter G. Muelder of Boston University School of Theology, Carl Michalson of Drew, Harvey H. Potthoff of Iliff, Harold DeWolf, J. Robert Nelson, Paul Schilling, John Godsey, Richey Hogg, J. Creighton Lacy, and Edward Carothers. Later we reached out to include British missionary secretaries Basil Clutterbuck and Donald B. Child as well as theologians Rupert Davies and A. Raymond George. Special mention should be made of John Foster, a former British Methodist missionary to China and later professor at Glasgow University. His little book *After the Apostles* is a rare gem as indeed was his whole contribution to our discussion.

Intellectual stimulation regarding the mission of the church came from other quarters as well. As early as 1947 Ralph Diffendorfer proposed my name for membership in a venerable discussion group of missiologists called "Lux Mundi." I was honored to have been accepted and its discussions were of tremendous value to me. Its organization had been prompted by the famous mission leader J. H. Oldham, who had organized a similar group in London. Dr. A. L. Warnshuis, the Dutch Reformed Church leader, brought it to the United States, where it began in

1926. The gatherings were held over weekends three or four times a year, and in my time they generally met at Seabury House in Greenwich, Connecticut. The members took terms presenting papers that were discussed by the group and then very often published in the *International Review of Missions*.

The group had no constitution or bylaws and no minutes were kept. It was not attached to any parent organization. It had two foci: to promote fellowship and to stimulate the interchange of ideas in connection with the world mission of the Church. Chairmanship was rotated. No one was quoted outside the meeting. I was active in this group for fifteen years and have the most pleasant memories of my time with it, for its roster of under forty members reads like a Who's Who in the missionary, ecumenical, and theological education world. Latterly and happily Roman Catholic leaders were brought into the fellowship. It was interesting that they were dealing with the very same issues and problems as the rest of us.

During the period of the 1950s I was also a part of another group of younger mission leaders. We met under the aegis of our friend Dr. Charles W. Ranson, general secretary of the International Missionary Council. We met several times a year at Drew University, whence we dubbed ourselves with the rather inelegant sobriquet, the "Drewps." In addition to Ranson its members included Eugene L. Smith, Tracey K. Jones, Jr., and me of the Methodist board; E. H. "Ted" Johnson of the Student Volunteer Movement; Russell Stevenson and Edwin Espy of the National Council of Churches; Charles Long, Episcopal missionary; John Deschner of the Student Christian

Movement; and Bruce Copeland, a Canadian missionary to China. At the same time our wives met regularly for devotion and fellowship and dubbed themselves the "Bible women." We engaged in theological and biblical study and addressed the more pragmatic elements of the church's mission. This I will say: people in the mission vocation need to be nourished by such support groups.

In late 1954 the Board of Missions approved a policy of sabbatical leave for elected staff members. This was of course common practice in universities but the need was no less urgent for church executives. The practice has since spread to all of the general agencies, and later to the Council of Bishops of The United Methodist Church.

At the end of the summer of 1955 I was due for a much-needed vacation. I applied and was approved for a three-months' sabbatical, which I used for travel in the United States and study at Cambridge University. The whole family sailed for England on the SS *United States*. On the Sunday aboard I preached at the services and recall that Senator Russell of Georgia was present together with other members of a congressional delegation to Europe. He spoke kindly of my effort. This journey was followed by a month of travel around the British Isles; this was our vacation month. We hired a small Hillman "Husky" into which our family of three children, ages nine, seven, and three, and our baggage would just fit. The three would remind me from the backseat: "Keep to the left; keep to the left!"

It was a wonderful tour in which we visited friends, many from India days, and saw the sights and monuments with which the country abounds. The travel was marred in part by one of our daughters, Jan, getting sick. Through the kindness of Charles and Grace Ranson we left her with them for nearly two weeks and were able to continue. We came across the Mathews roots in England, the MacDonalds in Scotland, the Treffrys in Cornwall, and naturally the Joneses in Wales. Looking up the family tree is somewhat hazardous, but I will not pursue that now. Then we settled down for study.

We were fortunate enough to be able to get a marvelous place to live. It was the Old Vicarage in Grantchester, out a couple of miles from Cambridge. This was the home of Rupert Brooke, the English poet. It was a fifteenth-century house, celebrated in one of Brooke's poems, a charming place along the River Cam. Our English friends, whom we had gathered through the years, especially in India, said, "Oh, we want to come and visit you." They all wanted to see the Old Vicarage and they did. We rode bicycles back and forth to Cambridge, two miles away, and we bought an old Vauxhall car for one hundred pounds and used that for adventures farther afield. When we were ready to leave, we sold the car for one hundred pounds, so that was not a bad deal! The vehicle served us well, taking us to London and more than once to Stratford to see Shakespearean plays. We particularly enjoyed *Macbeth* with Sir Laurence Olivier and Vivien Leigh.

The fall of 1955 in England was beautiful; crisp autumn days, the sky was blue nearly all the time, the larks in full throat. They said it was one of the best seasons they had had for many, many years. It was one of the happiest periods of our life. We enrolled one of our children in boarding school, where she quickly acquired a broad British accent; the other two were in small private day schools. As Christmas approached, a children's party was organized by Lord and Lady Grantchester. Gifts were provided for all the village children, including our three. When our son, aged three and a half was announced—"Stanley Mathews"—the whole house erupted with applause. How were mere Americans to know that *Sir* Stanley Matthews was the leading English cricket player of the time.

While in Grantchester we enrolled all three of our children in riding school at a reasonable price. They were assigned horses or ponies appropriate to their size. Then it occurred to me that, erstwhile cowboy that I aspired to be, I did not know how to ride, so I enrolled also. I actually learned to post. My equine partner was a huge mare, twenty-nine years old, named Chocolate Bun. Our mutually gentle dispositions were made for each other. We were indeed an excellent match.

Once again I reveled in my studies. As a courtesy, I was charged no tuition. Yet I enjoyed studies under New Testament and theological greats Charles Moule, H. H. Farmer, the Chadwick brothers, Owen and Henry, and Gordon Rupp. Local Methodists were very kind and hospitable to us. I was privileged to join a Wednesday afternoon seminar on the liturgical dimension in New Testament study. There were some really notable scholars present and I was clearly beyond my depth.

I read in the Cambridge University library, going frequently to London to view microfilms in the British Museum of Gandhi's earlier writings. I finally began to write my doctoral thesis. I "broke the back" of the thesis at that time.

As I write this it is forty years later. When I reread the rather full letters I wrote home at the time I am thrilled all over again. We enjoyed Guy Fawkes Day firsthand—a kind of Fourth of July celebrated on the fifth of November. Then there were marvelous dinners at the "high table," one special one in Peterhouse, Cambridge's first college, then presided over by scholarly Methodist historian Dr. Herbert Butterfield. That autumn Billy Graham preached a series of meetings at St. Mary's Church—a bit of Jerusalem in the Athens of Cambridge University. I also recall the lines from Rupert Brooke's poem:

> Stands the clock at ten to three.
> And is there honey yet for tea?

The answer was "yes," for we frequently enjoyed honey-sweetened tea in the little café next to the Old Vicarage. As our family made our way home on the SS *America* just before Christmas 1955 we all showed benefit from this sabbatical. Some years later we were invited to buy the Old Vicarage, but we could not manage it. Incidentally, the house in the early 1990s was purchased by British novelist Lord Jeffrey Archer, who on one visit allowed us to look around the premises again.

At the risk of becoming wearisome I have written at length about my Board years. More than enough has been recorded to indicate that they were full ones—filled with endless variety and rich association with all manner of men and women.

One important thing I haven't yet mentioned was the writing. I was required to write lengthy annual reports, the details of which still amaze me. For example, in 1947, the year of independence for India and Pakistan, my report was a detailed outline of the missionary personnel needs of these two countries as well as of the nonrecurring (capital) and recurring needs of all of our annual conferences. The total was such that I called it "a $2 million vote of confidence in two newly independent nations." Our Methodist people were interested in nation-building in the name of Christ and nearly all these needs were met at the time. They made all the difference.

In addition, I wrote several articles. My first published article was addressed to world hunger and was entitled "Food: America's Arsenal for Freedom." Many other articles and tracts followed, mostly on missions and international concerns.

In 1955 I finished my first book, *South of the Himalayas*. It was a mission study book on India and Pakistan. It was simply written but fairly comprehensive and enjoyed a widespread circulation. A second effort was more of a pamphlet than a book. It dealt with social issues and was called *Eternal Values in a World of Change*. I finished a third book in 1959, called *To the End of the Earth*. It was a study of Luke–Acts on the life and mission of the church written for the National Methodist Student Movement. It took a month to write but was also the fruit of years of study and reflection. Many readers seem to have liked it. More was to be written later, and I regret that I did not do more writing and perhaps less speaking.

Although I was never a firebrand, I was involved in considerable social and political actions. Ordinarily my mode was to do this in a quiet way and as a part of group activity. Upon India/Pakistan independence I sent congratulations to Prime Minister Nehru and persuaded the Foreign Missions Conference of North America to do the same. I have worked on the Kashmir issue for years and became acquainted with Sheikh Abdullah, the so-called "lion of Kashmir." He was a fine man and once joined Eunice and me in an effort to rebuild a church in Gulmarg, Kashmir. Even though he was a Muslim he gave ten thousand rupees for this purpose. We also came to know his son, Dr. Farooq Abdullah, who was more than once Chief Minister of Kashmir.

On July 27, 1953, an editorial in *The Christian Century* appeared, entitled "Will India Be Next?" It took for granted that as China and much of Southeast Asia had succumbed to Communism, so inevitably must India. This was a notion altogether too widespread at the time. Under the date of July 30, 1959, I wrote a lengthy and closely argued retort to the editorial. As I write these words forty years later I take some pride in the fact that such a calamity did not befall the Indian people and that despite all the forces and odds to the contrary, India still stands solidly for democracy.

I was also active during the early 1950s in pressing for a two-million-ton loan of wheat by the United States to India, which was shipped and prevented widespread famine there. In September 1956 I addressed a strong letter to President Eisenhower regarding the Suez Canal crisis, urging that opinions of the nations of southern Asia, the Colombo Powers, be sought on the matter. I joined with others in efforts to dissuade our country from arming Pakistan, which I have always considered a great mistake. During the Eisenhower administration I accompanied

Dr. Fred Nolde and Bishop G. Bromley Oxnam on a visit with Secretary of State John Foster Dulles. We discussed a broad agenda, but I noticed that when I was asked to express concerns about India and Pakistan, Mr. Dulles turned on a recording machine, so somewhere in the files of the State Department there must be some record of the wisdom to which I gave utterance that day.

On another occasion a group of church leaders waited upon President Eisenhower at the White House. When I was introduced to him as a "specialist" on India, he said, "Tell me in *one sentence* what you have to say about India." Quite a challenge, but when the commander in chief of all the armed might of the United States makes such a challenge, you do your best! With unaccustomed brevity I replied, "Mr. President, in Asia today there are two gigantic nations: China on the north side of the Himalayas and India to the south. Both are confronted with essentially the same problems; the one is attempting to solve them by the compulsive methods of communism, the other, India, by the voluntary methods of democracy. Our national interest and the welfare of our world points to our support for India!" I believed that then and still do. When Ike finally visited India in December 1959, he received an ovation as six million people in New Delhi sought his *darshan* (the supposed virtue attached to seeing an illustrious person.)

Meanwhile my extensive travels continued both in the homeland and abroad. Every year saw me traveling out of the country, one might almost say, in all directions. This was a part of my responsibility as associate general secretary.

During my period of service Nepal was opened up for missionary work for the first time, due to the efforts of Methodist missionaries from India, Dr. Robert and Dr. Bethel Fleming, and the faithful witness of a Methodist layman—a Point IV representative working in the country who had started a Sunday school in Kathmandu. It was my joy to visit this mountain kingdom at that time and during a later church meeting in Lucknow to make the motion that there be a *united* mission to Nepal. This it has been—one of the great stories of modern missions.

In early November of 1956 there was a notable celebration in Lucknow: the centenary of Indian Methodism. This is not the place to tell the story of that one hundred years. It is told all too briefly in my book, *South of the Himalayas,* and in more detail elsewhere and by others. It was a story of great achievements often against desperate odds. The occasion well and truly remembered the achievements of very much by very few for very many. It deserves to be recalled that Indian Methodism raised a lakh of rupees, that is, one hundred thousand rupees, toward the establishing of a chair of southern Asia studies at American University in Washington, D.C. This recalls to my mind the New Testament account of Paul's taking to the "Mother Church" in Jerusalem a similar offering from "daughter churches" he had planted in the Mediterranean world.

This celebration was followed by meeting of the Central Conference of Southern Asia, also convened in Lucknow. Both Bishop Pickett and Bishop Rockey were retired at this session and replacements were to be elected. On the second ballot, *I* was elected! So for twenty-four hours I was a bishop—although not yet consecrated. Telephone calls from India to the United States were very difficult in those days. I had to sleep fitfully by a telephone that night. In the wee hours of the morning I finally reached Eunice in Montclair, New Jersey, and told her of our predicament. She was not really very helpful. She responded as Ruth did to Naomi: "Where you go, I will go." After prayer and after employing my method of considering pros and cons, I decided against acceptance. It seemed to me that at age one hundred Indian Methodism was mature enough to elect its own bishops. So it did: Mangal Singh and Gabriel Sundaram were chosen, and I continued a Board secretary. In 1958 my membership in the Bombay Conference was transferred back to the New York Conference, from whence I had come.

I still have in my possession a considerable file about this event, of which I have written a little. Friends were supportive and perhaps I may be forgiven for dipping into this file occasionally: to enjoy a little nostalgia and to be recalled to Christian humility!

Other alternative tasks had preceded this one and others still would follow. Among them was an offer to become executive secretary of the Division of Foreign Missions of the National Council of Churches. Another was to be executive of the Council of Churches of Greater New York. Later came the offer of general secretary of the National Council of Churches and later still to be the secretary of the missions division of the World Council of Churches. After my Ph.D. came openings for teaching in the field of history of religion, and explorations from two colleges and a newly organized theological seminary about presidencies. Yet another invitation came to the deanship of a newly organized School of International Affairs at one of our universities. None of these seemed right, and I was content for the time being to remain involved in missionary administration where my heart was.

Too little has been said here about our growing family in whom I took great delight. Nor have I spoken much about my parents, in-laws, or siblings. All these relationships have meant much to me and I did what I could to cultivate them. Finally, an alternative form of my Christian vocation did come to me—unsought and unexpected. To this I did respond affirmatively. But that is another story—or a continuation of this one.

8

THE BOSTON YEARS

As they say, lightning does not strike twice in the same place. Well, in my case it did strike twice, though not in exactly the same place. As it happened, I have been elected bishop twice. After the first time in Lucknow, November 1956, there was a second time, in Washington, D.C., June 1960. In the earlier instance I declined the office in favor of nationals and was not inducted or consecrated. The second time I accepted.

The practice in our denomination is that bishops are elected by what we call Jurisdictional or Central Conferences, which convene every four years some weeks after the General Conference. There were five geographical jurisdictions and one based on race in the United States at that time. The Central Jurisdiction has since been eliminated and merged into the geographical entities. Outside the United States the counterpart of the Jurisdictional Conference is called the Central Conference.

That summer the Northeastern Jurisdictional Conference met in Washington. There were four vacancies to be filled due to the retirement of four bishops. The conference is made up of equal numbers of lay and ministerial delegates representing the some twenty annual conferences within the jurisdiction. A vote of three-fifths effects election, the votes taken in a series of ballots until the necessary vacancies are filled. Then the bishops so elected are consecrated and assigned to their areas of administration.

I was not a delegate to this session that convened at Metropolitan Memorial Methodist Church immediately adjacent to the campus of the American University. It so happened, however, that I *was* present at the university when the conference was opened, having come there from the Furloughed Missionary Conference in Greencastle, Indiana, for an important meeting. My purpose was to meet with a committee that was planning a university for the Belgian Congo to be located in Stanleyville (now Kisangani) on the Congo River. This technical university was actually established, prospered for some years, and then was absorbed into the government's educational system so that it no longer has a church connection.

The next morning I was returning from breakfast to my dormitory room just before departing for the airport. I was overtaken on the campus by Charles Parlin, a Methodist lay leader and a distinguished lawyer. He asked me to address the conference on a rather delicate matter that was related to the election of bishops. When I explained that I was soon to catch a plane for Des Moines to speak at an annual conference, he took responsibility for booking me on a later flight so that I could speak.

When the Jurisdictional Conference assembled I was on the docket to address the body. It had to do with whether or not Bishop Newell S. Booth, elected in 1944 specifically for assignment to the Africa Central Conference, should continue there or be reassigned in the United States. He had already served Africa for a long time as missionary, and then sixteen years as bishop. He was a fine linguist and possessed a profound knowledge of Africa and the work of the church there. It was my view and the view of many that at a time of the most sweeping changes in that continent a person of his background ought to continue to be at the helm. My understanding was based on information that came to me regularly as associate general secretary of the Board directly from our missionaries and also through the Reverend Melvin Blake, Africa secretary. Clearly opinion in Africa favored his continuing there. Another Board secretary also had this same information at his disposal but was reluctant to voice it for he expected to receive votes for bishop, and to speak to this issue was judged to hazard his election. Since I had no such expectation, I could speak directly and did so for ten minutes on this subject. Then I left for my meeting in Iowa.

That evening I attended the session of the North Iowa Conference, held in Marshalltown, Iowa, and spoke on the world mission of the Church. After the address I was driven to Cedar Rapids, where I spent the night. The next morning I flew by stages on an old C-47 (DC-3) plane back to Newark, New Jersey, and proceeded to our home in Montclair. Then a strange thing occurred.

When I arrived our younger daughter was crying and our son seemed miffed and didn't speak to me. Then I asked my wife, "What's wrong?" "What's wrong?" she replied. "They've elected you bishop!" They had tried to reach me with the news but could only get through to Eunice.

Thus I learned that while I was making a missionary tour in the Midwest all this had taken place. Hardly the conventional way! At any rate I was spared any anxiety that might have attended my presence throughout the voting process. I was the fourth bishop elected, on the twelfth ballot, following the election of Fred G. Holloway, G. Vernon Middleton, and W. Ralph Ward, Jr. I was not a shoo-in but I did receive 201 out of 229 votes cast, with 175 required for election.

I was asked to report to Washington as soon as possible. Hastily we informed the other family members, packed, and took a midnight plane to Washington, arriving at our hotel at 3:00 A.M. Saturday morning. Later that morning Eunice and I were introduced to the conference. Bishops-elect sat with the other bishops in a special section on the platform. It had already been determined that my assignment was to the Boston Area.

On Sunday, June 19, 1960, the consecration service was held with senior Bishop Herbert Welch preaching. Bishops G. Bromley Oxnam and John Wesley Lord laid hands on my head, joined by two elders, James V. Claypool, longtime friend from the New England Southern Conference, and Dr. Eugene L. Smith, general secretary of the Board of Missions. I was pleased that my mother and three of my sisters were present but regretted that my father and two brothers could not be there. At the close of the service I was bishop of the Boston Area and in something of a state of shock.

It has never been a secret that in some respects I was not well qualified and prepared for the office. For example, I had had minimal experience as a pastor of a local church and had certainly not served what was called a "high steeple" church. On the other hand, I had churchwide experience, had been a missionary and administrator, was acquainted with the leadership cadre of our church, and had been a constant participant in the church at the local level. However aware we may be of inadequacies, by the grace of God who calls us, we must try. Let me say that this new responsibility did evoke all the humility and energy I had, for the full weight of the task rested heavily upon me.

After the conference we returned to Montclair and to my New York office, where my colleagues gave me a very touching farewell. My counterpart, Lucile Colony, stated on that occasion that we had worked together for fourteen years in complete harmony and that during those years no program innovation was instituted except that I had originated it or had given it my immediate support. Undoubtedly this was an exaggeration—a forgivable hyperbole—which nevertheless sounded good in my ears.

Hundreds of letters and telegrams poured in, so many that I had to resort to a brief printed acknowledgment. I recall that a reporter from the *Boston Globe*, Stanley Eames, came to New Jersey to interview me. He gave a lovely rendition of the story. It chanced that our son, Stanley, then eight years old, came in during the interview. The reporter mentioned to him that the State of Maine was a part of the Boston Area. When asked if he knew where Maine was, young Stan replied, "I'm not quite sure, but I think it's somewhere off the coast of Kansas."

It was painful to our children to leave Montclair, where they had a host of friends. They also greatly missed the ready access they enjoyed to a neighbor's swimming pool. As for Eunice, she was torn by having to leave a circle of close friends, a lovely new home, and a cherished rose garden. We did sell our home and bought another one in Newtonville, Massachusetts. By early September we had settled in there.

The Boston Area was made up of four annual conferences—New England, New England Southern, Maine, and New Hampshire. It incorporated most of New England: all of Massachusetts, Rhode Island, Maine, New Hampshire, the eastern half of Connecticut, and four churches in Vermont. There were 755 congregations in twelve districts, with a total constituency of 262,000 persons. Each district was presided over by a district superintendent. In each conference the bishop and the district superintendents made up what we call a Cabinet. In some other polities district superintendents would be known as assistant or auxiliary bishops.

My office was in the Wesleyan Building on Copley Square in Boston, opposite Trinity Episcopal Church, where I had received my call to India in 1937. In twenty-three years I had come full circle! It was a modest office but of adequate size for my secretary and myself. My secretary was Ida L. Moody. She was experienced: she knew everything and everybody. She was precise to a fault, and had been a secretary to my two immediate predecessors. Before that she had worked with Dr. (later Bishop) Lewis O. Hartman, who had for years been editor of *Zion's Herald*, a really distinguished journal of New England Methodism. It is said that during the years she was assistant editor of the periodical no printing errors escaped her sharp eye as a proofreader. I am inclined to believe this. It was her intention to retire at the close of Bishop Lord's term. But I tried to persuade her to continue to work with me. Her response was that we would give it a try and then decide. I knew then that *I* was the one on trial, but I must have passed muster for she stayed with me for six years. In those days I dictated correspondence and was inclined to long letters. She had arthritic hands and taught me the virtue of shorter communications! She was immensely helpful and I cannot praise her enough.

At this point I should pay tribute to another person to whom I am indebted. He was Warren Carberg, editor of *Zion's Herald*. He was a real professional as a journalist and kept New England Methodism before the public. He was a World War I veteran and a fine person in every way. He used to urge me to attend Red Sox games. One I recall was the last one in which Ted Williams played. Believe it or not, I *saw* him hit that last home run!

My predecessor was a man who was greatly gifted as a pastor and loved as a bishop. He did everything he could to facilitate my takeover. Twelve years later I was also to succeed him in the Washington (D.C.) Area. One could scarcely be more favored than to follow in office John Wesley Lord. Margaret Lord was a choice person too. Years later I delivered eulogies for both of them at the Council of Bishops.

In 1960 twenty new bishops were elected in our church, nearly half of the active total. It is the practice now to have some orientation for the new bishops soon after their election. In our case this was not actually held until November 1960, by which time we had already plunged into the task—"sink or swim." During a later period there was a considerable comradeship among the bishops elected in the same year. This was not the case with the "Class of 1960." Some of us did, however, determine to do what we could to change the mode of the Council. That seems to be the intention of every new class.

There were other tasks of orientation. In my case I arranged a series of lengthy interviews with experienced bishops. I still have handwritten notes of the long talks I had with some of my most respected brethren: Bishops Frederick B. Newell, Lloyd Wicke, Richard Raines, William C. Martin, G. Bromley Oxnam, and of course John Wesley Lord. Moreover it was possible to telephone any of the bishops at any time if one needed counsel, which was often the case. I even had a chance to exchange notes with an Anglican, R. S. Deane, Bishop of Caribou in Canada, and later assistant to the Archbishop of Canterbury. He particularly stressed the importance of a life of devotion for a bishop.

I also learned from the district superintendents, the ministers, and the lay leaders as well. On my first visit to Boston I met with all the twelve district superintendents from the four conferences. We met in Copley Methodist Church, near my office. We assembled "in choir" and began with Holy Communion. Only later did I learn that the committed clergy historically met "in choir" within the chancel, so I had stumbled onto the right procedure. We also cared for the most urgent business and set important dates for the autumn, for many were on holiday during August. Then, I recall that I embraced each of the superintendents and told them that although they had been appointed by Bishop Lord, from that day on they were my appointees. They were a splendid body of men indeed, including the wise and experienced Reverend Guy H. Wayne, the scholarly Reverend Clarence F. Avey, the Reverend C. Homer Ginns, all of Massachusetts; the Reverend J. Manley Shaw of Connecticut; the Reverend Roy H. Cowen of New Hampshire; the Reverend Lester A. Boobar and the Reverend Elwin L. Wilson of Maine— the latter a typical Yankee from "down East." I learned to love these men and their able comrades. Our areas are so large that a Methodist bishop could not function without them.

Meanwhile my family and I were also much in need of some vacation. For some years we had planned to go on a camping trip to the West Coast, visiting national parks along the way. We had chosen 1960 as the best year so that our youngest child would not be too restless from the tedium of travel and our two daughters not too sophisticated for camping. This turned out to be the case and, encouraged by my new staff and our own common sense, we ventured out on this memorable journey despite my new role. The trip was combined with speaking responsibilities to which I had been already committed in Cleveland, Denver, Los Angeles, and Tacoma, Washington.

Camping was a real adventure. We became quite proficient in breaking and striking camp and roughing it in general. A few times we stayed with relatives and occasionally stayed in motels to get clean and rested. Our children still remember this family odyssey fondly. It took us to the replica of the Alamo in Brackettsville, Texas, where the famous film was shot. Then there was Langtree, Texas, seat of Judge Roy Bean, "the law west of the

Pecos." White Sands, New Mexico, was next, followed by Carlsbad Caverns, the Grand Canyon, Los Angeles and Disneyland, and Yosemite and Sequoyah National Parks in California. A two-day visit to a lumber town, Chester, California, was particularly memorable, as we were guests of Truman and Marybeth Collins—delightful people. The Collins Company practiced sound forest management and sound Christian stewardship. Next we visited the unforgettable Pacific Northwest, with its peaks, forests, and rivers. Then it was on to Yellowstone, the Grand Tetons, and the site of Custer's last stand, to the lovely Black Hills and the unbelievable Badlands. Such places I had always wanted to see, and actually to do so with my family was especially full of meaning and made us very proud of our national heritage. Frequent telephone calls to Boston kept me informed about affairs at my new "home base."

Back in Boston by Labor Day, the following week was filled with a meeting of the Boston Area Pastors' School at Geneva Point, Lake Winnepesaukee in New Hampshire. The majority of the pastors from all the area were there to "size up" their new bishop, and vice versa. This annual gathering contributed much to us all, intellectually and spiritually. It was a reinforcement of morale for everyone and an effective generator of team spirit and solidarity. All of this was undergirded by the lovely lake and mountain scenery, surely as fair as anywhere on God's green earth. It was for me a helpful beginning. I liked my many new comrades in Christian ministry and was determined to serve them as well as I could.

In Boston I learned of the heavy demands of administration, personal consultation, and endless meetings. Locally this included membership on the boards of Deaconess Hospital, Boston University Board of Trustees, and its Executive Committee. I became a trustee of Boston University in 1960. When I left the area I resigned, but the university would not accept this. So it was that I continued to serve until 1982, at which time I became an honorary trustee. It was a privilege to have had as friends a succession of presidents of the university: Daniel Marsh, Harold C. Case, John Silber, John Westling. Under Silber's leadership the university advanced greatly. Then I was ex officio a member of the Massachusetts Council of Churches and other ecumenical bodies in Massachusetts and in the other states of the area. In each annual conference I had to attend many meetings. Naturally I was a member of the Council of Bishops; chairman of MCOR (Methodist Committee for Overseas Relief) and of the Coordinating Council; a member of the Board of Education of the general church; and held membership on the governing board of the National Council of Churches. All of this, together with local travel across New England, required journeying of nearly 100,000 miles a year. According to Methodist tradition the bishop is supposed to travel "throughout the connection" and I did!

During the fall of 1960 I was well advised to give major attention to the local churches. I spent three or four days on each district to visit them all. The average district had from sixty to seventy congregations. The superintendent would arrange a schedule and escort me. We would visit as many as twenty churches a day. The pastor and one or more lay representatives would meet us at the church and conduct us around the premises. Ordinarily I would ask questions about the church, its size, its makeup, its problems and challenges, its relations with the community, its vision or prospect, and so on. One could learn a great deal by such a process and by the direct observations one made. Sometimes the pastor's spouse was present, though many had outside jobs; and sometimes we visited the parsonages also. On occasion we would gather for lunch with the pastors and lay representatives of a district or subdistrict. By such a process, over a period of weeks, a collective picture began to come into focus. This method had been used by other bishops—especially by Bishop Oxnam—and I found it an invaluable experience. By Christmas I had covered the whole area, missing very few churches. Twelve years later, during my last year in the Boston Area, I repeated such a visitation—a very different experience from a far broader base of understanding.

Again and again I had reason to rejoice in the beauty of the New England countryside. There is endless variety, great contrasts between the urban and rural scene; mountains, lakes, rivers, the ocean—New England has it all. Each section had its own peculiar character. The annual autumnal display of the changing colors of leaves is nothing short of spectacular. An elderly English friend taken by Eunice to New Hampshire to observe this remarkable display said, "My dear, don't you think this is a bit overdone?" I learned to love the area and learned too that the great reserve that is supposed to define the character of New England people was not always warranted, for I found the folk of the region to be open and friendly.

One learned that not all Yankees were alike. A resident

of Maine was different from the Cape Codder; the Connecticutian from the New Hampshireite. Moreover, there was considerable variety within a given state: the southerner of Maine, for example, contrasting with those who dwelt in the northern reaches of the state, "the county," Aroostook. This potato-growing county is larger than some states. I could observe and finally revel in the rich sense of humor so many possessed, just as I learned that people seem much to prefer telling jokes about *themselves*—a privilege not readily yielded to the outsider; that is, one who is "from away."

It always seemed to me that to be a Methodist in New England during my time there required something of a plus quality. By that I mean they had to have a considerable degree of commitment and conviction because it was so easy to be something else. Sometimes we were called "a minority of a minority"; that is, the Roman Catholics were in the majority, and the United Church of Christ (UCC) were the largest Protestant community, except in Maine where Methodists had the largest Protestant constituency. The fact is that we had a solid community, a small body of intellectuals. We were middle class, and we had a laboring group including many union leaders.

At the same time it did not seem to me that New England Methodists were adequately aware of their strength and potential, and their self-esteem was not in keeping with what they really were. Therefore, in the autumn of 1960 the Area Cabinet determined to conduct a survey of the Area. This was officially approved by the four annual conferences the next spring. All of this had been authorized by the General Conference of 1960, which advocated just such an approach.

An organization was created with the Reverend Ralph T. Mirse, a pastor in Worcester, Massachusetts, as the Area director. Associated with him were annual conference directors and district directors for each of the twelve districts. Dr. Wayne Artis, director of Church Surveys of Boston University School of Theology, was in charge of the technical aspects of the study. We looked toward a reappraisal and renewal of our church.

Five major areas of concern were explored in detail: church extension, the local church, the ministry, Methodist beliefs, and annual conference boundaries and personnel. Each congregation was examined and a profile made of it. An enormous accumulation of data was analyzed. All concerned cooperated in this process.

By June 1963 the survey was complete and a six hundred page compilation was the result. The volume in size resembled nothing so much as a Sears-Roebuck catalogue. It was an impressive work and was titled *The Changing Face of New England Methodism*. The front cover displayed a profile of New Hampshire's "Old Man of the Mountain"—the Great Stone Face. Incidentally, a New Hampshire Methodist pastor had "saved" this profile. He discovered that its massive granite forehead, which gave character to the face, was gradually slipping away due to freezing and thawing. As a result of his crusade it was anchored by cables—a real "face-lift."

Then in the fall of 1963 I toured the area, district by district, interpreting the survey and recruiting a thousand laymen as "minutemen" who pledged ten dollars a quarter in response to calls to help the building of new churches. Real enthusiasm was generated in this process.

How I wish I could report that all the dreams this endeavor engendered were realized! This was not true, but much was accomplished: (1) we knew who we were and our pride increased; (2) a new fervor for evangelism was generated; (3) property improvement was effected in hundreds of our local churches, making it more attractive to be a Methodist; (4) the program—educational, preaching, social service—improved. Then one discovered that between 1900 and 1960 only three new congregations had been established in New England. At least from 1960 to 1972 seven new ones were brought together, three of them with Ralph T. Mirse as organizing pastor; not impressive nationwide but worth noting in New England. It helped us along the way.

Almost every Sunday the bishop was expected to preach at one or more churches in the area. This required careful planning and what I would call "balanced scheduling" so that one is seen as being present throughout the area. The visit of the bishop was usually seen as an event, and my wife and I were constantly the recipients of unmerited hospitality for which we are still deeply grateful.

Each Christmas I would send some kind of greeting to each parsonage. Some years I would send a book to every pastor. Thrice a year we held what was called an Area Cabinet meeting; that is, the district superintendents from all over the episcopal area would gather for two or three days of sharing and overall planning and spiritual renewal. During the course of these meetings Eunice would provide a dinner for the whole group, especially at the one which gathered just before Christmas. These were great and joyful occasions, to be savored through the ensuing years. Twice during the summer season we held clambakes, that unique New England feast.

During the fall of the year district superintendents would hold quarterly conferences or charge conferences in each church or circuit of churches. This was a way for the general Church to be present in the local churches, an avenue of communication and interchange. We are what is called a "connectional church"; we are not made up of so many independent congregations. We are all related and the district superintendent is the chief connecting agent. Thus, when we met as a cabinet or area cabinet, in a real sense the whole district or conference or area was present. During their local church visitations the superintendents assessed the needs of local churches, their pastoral needs, and also the needs and goals of individual pastors.

Then early in each calendar year the cabinets met regularly with the bishop to consider appointment needs. This is one of the prime duties of a bishop and one for which he or she must finally assume full responsibility. Methodists have an appointive rather than a "call" system for ministers. Persons in denominations that follow the latter approach find it difficult to grasp the Methodist method. It does work, and the fact is that the responsibility and authority of stationing preachers is the focal point of the Methodist conception of episcopacy. This method of matching pastors with churches has been much criticized and much misunderstood. Without question instances of abuse can be cited; certainly instances of faulty judgment can be found. Yet appointment-making is not a role assumed by an arbitrary autocrat. Bishops are elected to the office and remain accountable at many levels. They are under the authority of the *Discipline,* as well as being themselves subject to appointment periodically.

Beginning in the fall of 1961 I began a practice that was to continue to be a hallmark of my episcopacy for all the remaining years I continued in that office. It was what, for lack of a better designation, I called Study Days. Both in autumn and spring I would visit each of the districts for a day devoted to common study. The time span was from 9:00 A.M. to 3:00 P.M. We began informally with coffee and conversation while the pastors gathered. Though it was not a "command performance," nearly all attended. The district superintendent or some pastor designated by the superintendent led in an act of worship. The day closed with Holy Communion or, alternatively, with a Wesley Covenant Service.

In between these acts of worship I always taught a selection from the Bible. Then I would hand out a study piece—an article or chapter by some theologian, a chapter of a contemporary theological work, a sermon, say, by Wesley or a modern one by Tillich or one of the Niebuhrs or some other preacher. This had not been sent to them earlier, for I found that when they saw it by surprise, as it were, it was a great "leveler" and it would get everyone's attention. This document was studied privately for an hour. Then we had open discussion of the paper, using chalkboards or other aids. Brown-bag lunches were the rule. Sometimes when some had forgotten food, others shared, so fulfilling a New Testament model. As we ate we engaged in the lost art of Christian conversation. Afternoon sessions either continued the morning discussion or launched out on a creative direction; for example, group sermon preparation.

In the eyes of most participants and in my own view this was an almost entirely positive experience. To this day I meet many of the pastors who felt this was the single most important venture that I undertook. It was, I believe, good for morale. The fellowship was free and open. It was surely a bit of a risk for me, for in a teaching-learning relation there are doubtless hazards. For my part, I was willing, though, to exchange an authority or father image for a brother image. I learned to know the preachers and they learned to know me. I could observe how they thought and could assess their particular gifts and abilities. Above I have observed how I came to know the local churches and their needs by my systematic travel about the area. Now I came to know the pastors well, knew them by name, and in the appointment-making in our Cabinet I was able to participate in a manner rooted in genuine knowledge.

This required immense energy and long hours of preparation, but it was an important part of my own ongoing study as well as a significant part of in-service training for the pastors. Once I made a serious scheduling error. One day I led a Study Day in Northern Maine. My plane out of Bangor was cancelled that night and I was forced to hire a car and drive through the night to meet my 9:00 A.M. schedule at New London, Connecticut, the next morning! This exacted a toll from me, but it was a price worth paying.

Let me insert an important "news bulletin," as it were, at this point. It is said that all American adults at the time of President John F. Kennedy's assassination know exactly where they were at the time that tragic event occurred, Friday, November 22, 1963. In my case it was a Study Day session with pastors held at Belmont Methodist Church near Boston. We had just had a brief recess during which the unhappy news came over the radio. We immediately adjourned our meeting, for it was clear that in such a national emergency it would be wise for the pastors to be at their posts. Some of us did return to Belmont Church that evening for a previously announced service with laity, which turned out to be an occasion of prayer and mourning.

Meanwhile I already had long been announced as the preacher of the National Cathedral in Washington for a telecast service on the afternoon of November 24, 1963. It was to have been a National Service of Thanksgiving and was sponsored by the local Council of Churches, the National Capital Area Churches, Church World Service, and the National Council of Churches. The following Thursday, November 28, was Thanksgiving Day. I had been chosen as preacher because of my role as chairman of Agricultural Missions, Inc., and as a member of the governing board of the National Council of Churches. Under the circumstances I immediately telephoned the Reverend Francis B. Sayre, dean of the Cathedral, offering to withdraw as preacher. He insisted that I continue for plans had been made. The Harvard Glee Club and the Radcliffe Choral Society were to be present as the choir, but he acknowledged that the theme would have to center on the loss of our young president.

This meant that I had to start all over again to prepare my sermon. This took all day on Saturday, November 23, and well into the following morning. On Saturday night I flew to Washington in a driving rain. The gentleman seated next to me appeared interested in my concentration on the manuscript. I let him read it, which he did critically. He turned out to be the writer Gore Vidal, half-brother of Jacqueline Kennedy. A White House limousine met him, and he was good enough to drop me off at my hotel. During the following weeks I had some correspondence with him.

Meanwhile, by Sunday morning, I had a telephone call from home. Our two daughters wanted to come down to Washington, for they sensed that this would be a significant event in their lives. By noon my brother and I met their plane. They were then present for the service at the Cathedral and the following day witnessed the funeral procession in which notables from all over the world walked behind the coffin borne on a horse-drawn caisson.

The Cathedral service itself was duly televised; the choirs performed in elegant fashion singing in Latin and presenting a Johann Sebastian Bach cantata in German. An undersecretary of Agriculture, the Honorable Charles S. Murphy, read the Old Testament lesson and Senator George McGovern read the Gospel. The congregation, which filled the edifice, listened with quiet reflection to my sermon, entitled "The Gift of a Man."

Some citations will give the tone of the address:

Today, Americans can have but one thought; for we have been present at a new crucifixion. A people who could endure the villainous murder of Medgar Evers without undue remorse; who could observe the slaughter of the innocents by a bomb in a Birmingham church and not really cry out for justice, have called for a yet more costly sacrifice—that of the President of their country. Truly, then, Americans are weeping not only for him but for themselves. . . .

To take seriously the death of a martyr is to take the meaning of that death upon ourselves. For in his mortal wound is our own hurt and the hurt of all mankind.

We are a proud, and even arrogant, people who have told ourselves that this sort of thing could not happen here. In more primitive periods of our history, yes. Among more primitive peoples even today. But not here! What could *not* happen *has* happened and it has happened to us all. . . .

Our Lord says: "Every one to whom much is given, of him will much be required." This word of God is a summons to accountability, just as the events of these days are a summons to accountability. For all too long now we have not been called to account; either to one another; or to the world; or to God. We have been ready to *receive* abundantly of God's grace, but it is when the *demands* of that grace are upon us that we fail to measure up. . . .

Yes, we have been seized by forgetfulness. No wonder we debate about our national purpose! No wonder we worry about what other nations shall think of us as a people! Is it not here that we have lost our way? We have forgotten who we are. We have forgotten whose we are. We have forgotten whence we have come. Therefore we do not know where we are going. . . .

This effort was well received, the sermon widely distributed. The Honorable Thomas Cocoran, Franklin Roosevelt's friend, was present and spoke with apprecia-

Back row (left to right): *Elizabeth, Margaret, Don; front row* (left to right): *Joe, James K. (Ken) Mathews, 1915.* Semple Studio, Wellsville, Ohio

James K. Mathews on far right with Marathi language teachers in Bombay, 1939

The wedding party of James K. Mathews and Eunice Jones, Naini Tal, India, June 1, 1940

Eunice Jones Mathews, circa 1942

James K. Mathews, circa 1942-43

James D. and Laura M. Mathews, parents of James K. Mathews

Rayappa, former owner of the site of Holston Hospital, Yadgiri, Dn., S. India

Anne, Stanley, and Janice Mathews

From left to right: *Janice, Eunice, Jim, Stanley, Anne Mathews, circa 1961*

With Martin Niemoeller (l.), circa 1961

James K. Mathews (age 50) and Bishop Herbert Welch (age 100), *1963*

From left to right: *Dr. Harold Dewolf, Billy Graham, James K. Mathews, Stan Mathews, Trinity Church, Boston, 1964*

With Bishop Charles Golden (center), *and the Reverend Wendell Taylor* (right), *Easter 1964. Religious News Service*

◀ With Eunice and Pope Paul VI, Castel Gandolfo, 1966. *Pontificia Fotografia, Felici*

➡ Leading the World Council of Churches delegation to Pope Paul VI

From left to right: *Dr. Lee Tuttle, General Secretary of the World Methodist Council; Charles Parlin; James K. Mathews; Bishop Roy Short; Bishop Reuben H. Mueller at World Council of Churches headquarters in Geneva, Switzerland, 1966.* John Taylor, World Council of Churches, Geneva

Anne, Eunice, and James K. Mathews with Indira Gandhi, New Delhi

From left to right: *James K. Mathews, Dr. Ralph David Abernathy, Morjari Desai, deputy prime minister, and Homer Jack, New Delhi, 1968.*
Capital News Photo, New Delhi

With George McGovern (center) *and Professor J. Robert Nelson* (left), *Uppsala, 1968*

From left
to right: *John
Brademas, James
K. Mathews, Carl
Albert, Chaplain
Edward J. Latch,
1976.* Dev O'Neill

🔺 *With Walter Mondale, 1978*

🔻 *Presenting John Wesley's* **Letter to a
Roman Catholic** *to Pope John Paul II
in Washington, DC*

With speaker Thomas P. O'Neill and Chaplain Ford, 1980.
K. Jewell

With Eunice and President George Bush at the dedication of Camp David Chapel

With President Clinton aboard Air Force One, 1995

tion of what I had said. So did the *New York Times'* columnist James Reston. The Kennedy family also seemed grateful and wrote to me about the service, inviting me to various events that ensued. This experience did involve me rather directly in a tragic bit of history.

Among the pastoral appointments a bishop has to make none are more important than the district pastors and superintendents. This I found an onerous task. There were always more able candidates than there were openings; thus some are inevitably disappointed. Some particularly deserved and even sought the role, a lesser number were not interested, and some declined. For my part, I liked to have variety on the Cabinet. Rather than appointing only men who had attained a certain number of years of experience, though they remained the largest category, I also sought a range in age, experience, theological perspective, ethnicity, and finally gender. This meant that there was an element of representation and inclusiveness in my cabinets. Sometimes observers remarked that this could not succeed, but I believe it did and we worked well together. Doubtless I made some mistakes in my choice, and to the degree that this may have been true, I express regret.

In 1967 I was able to take a brand-new step. I appointed the first woman as district superintendent in this country, though I believe there was an earlier instance in the autonomous Methodist Church in Korea. My appointee was Dr. Margaret K. Henrichsen, a member of the Maine Annual Conference. Of course, the cabinet members knew my intention, but it was a well-kept secret. I can still hear the collective gasp that was sounded at the conference session in Bangor when I read out this assignment.

At the time, Margaret had been a widow for twenty-four years, her husband, an electrical engineer, having died in 1943. An active layperson, she completed the necessary studies and was appointed to serve in Maine. She was ordained deacon in 1947 and elder in 1949. There were nearly a dozen women serving in pastorates in Maine, and there was an increasing reason that women should be represented in a cabinet. Henrichsen, who had an honorary degree from Colby College, served a circuit of seven churches based in North Sullivan. Many distinguished clergymen vacationed on the Maine coast, among them Dr. Henry P. Van Dusen, president of Union Theological Seminary in New York. He regarded her a superb preacher and pastor. In 1953 she published a widely read book about her circuit, entitled *Seven Steeples*.

With her new appointment I told her she would have to write a sequel to be called *Seventy-Seven Steeples*. Actually there were ninety-one churches on her district, most of them small. She did well in this office. Her cabinet work was cooperative and constructive; she won her way. I was particularly impressed by her regular district newsletters to the pastors—real gems they were. Though a bit hesitant at first, the young pastors finally sought her out for her wise and kindly counsel. She loved classical music, was an avid birder, and was a great reader. She liked also to drive and unfortunately met with a serious automobile accident. This shortened her term as a district superintendent but she pioneered the field well, opening up the way for the large number of her sisters who have followed her in the office, some of whom have gone on to the episcopal office.

I have been speaking of what bishops *do* by actually describing their work as I tried to do it. The story is told that an African was ushered in for an audience with the pope. With naive and disarming candor he is reported to have asked the pontiff, "What is Your Holiness *for*?"—a good question. Likewise is the query, "What are bishops *for*?" One would like to reply as Victor Hugo does in *Les Miserables*, "a bishop is only to bless." Surely the New Testament standard, as set forth in the Pastoral Epistles, is very high indeed. Bishops are inducted in a service of consecration, which states that bishops are "set apart to serve," so, ideally, the servant-mode has described bishops.

It may be illuminating to state what United Methodist bishops do *not* do:

- They do not speak (unless specifically invited to do so) nor vote at General and Jurisdictional Conferences. They may speak at annual conferences but have no vote there even to break a tie.
- They do not choose other ministers for the episcopal office.
- They do not determine constitutional amendments nor do they legislate.
- They do not have veto power over legislation.
- They do not make any rules governing annual conferences.
- They do not determine who shall be ordained.
- They do not confer orders but rather *confirm* and convey orders authorized by the ministerial members of the annual conference.

- They do not exclude ministers or laypersons from membership.
- They do not give final determination on matters of church law, but their rulings are subject to review by the Judicial Council and are either sustained or reversed.

One of our bishops early in the twentieth century stated that Methodism is not governed *by* bishops but *with* bishops. Another observed, "I have many duties but no prerogatives." The late Bishop Roy H. Short said, "The only real power that any United Methodist bishop has is that which flows out of the example of his/her life and character as well as demonstrated qualities of church leadership." All of this should be enough to keep us more humble than we often are.

In sum, a bishop, among United Methodists at least, is a preacher-evangelist; in some measure a social prophet; an administrator; an appointing officer who "stations the preachers"; a teacher, as I have been at pains to show; a scholar; a liturgical leader; an ecumenical liaison agent; a guide to spiritual formation; and a presiding officer. We do the necessary deed—what comes to one to be done—and we must do it.

A United Methodist bishop, I suppose, has no greater anxiety at the beginning of the task than presiding over annual conferences. This hangs over one's head during the whole first year. One seeks help wherever it may be found. Over and over again I turned to Robert's *Rules of Order*. Then I sought the aid of the Reverend Edgar Skillington of the Central Pennsylvania Annual Conference, for whose parliamentary skills I had the highest admiration. At the meetings of the Council of Bishops during the first year of each quadrennium we were coached for this task. "Keep stating the question" that is before the conference at any given time. "Be impartial." "Let everyone be heard." "Finally bring the question to a vote and care not at all what the result may be"—or words to that effect. The very first responsibility assigned bishops in the 1798 *Discipline* stated the bishop's duty: "To preside in our conferences."

Finally the day arrives when one actually has to do this job. For me it was at the 1961 session of the New Hampshire Annual Conference held in Lebanon, New Hampshire. No insuperable problems arose and somehow I acquitted myself adequately but not triumphantly. In those days there were four conferences in the area over which I had to preside, so one gained lots of experience.

Our bishops have to preside not only at annual conferences but at numerous other gatherings, and then in rotation with the other bishops at the Jurisdictional Conference. In addition, when requested to do so, the bishop may preside in rotation at a General Conference, for one of the bishops *must* do so. This is a most demanding role, for a General Conference is a great assembly. One bishop likened it to mounting the saddle of a bucking bronco! Usually the body is courteous and, with the backup of a colleague, it can be a pleasant and invigorating experience. Relaxed freedom on the part of the one presiding is communicated to the whole body and makes for an orderly assembly that discharges its work promptly.

It was my privilege to preside at a session of the General Conference every quadrennium while I was an active bishop. The first time was at Pittsburgh in 1964, where I felt I did not cover myself with honors. In 1968, however, at Dallas I was called without warning to preside on the last night of the conference, when a great glut of business has to be completed. A colleague had unfortunately allowed the meeting to get out of hand and into a hopeless parliamentary tangle and asked to be relieved of the chair.

When I took the chair it was with a measure of fear and trembling. I did entertain a motion of thanks for my predecessor's work, which must have reassured him a little. Then I asked for unanimous consent to "clear the deck" of all business. This was done and we started afresh. My notes recorded at the time stated:

> I knew that I could not take over that conference with its pending motions and amendments intact, or I would simply flounder in the same complex procedural problems of my predecessor. I knew that I must somehow get things started over procedurally. Thus, I asked common consent of the conference to dispense with all pending motions and amendments. The participants graciously accepted my request, and that acceptance left us open for a new proposal in which a proper order of priority of business could be ensured; thus we would not spend time on the lesser items of business until after we completed the most important items.

We did complete all the business in good order, and the conference adjourned promptly. I had supposed that the method used was a unique instance, but in his autobiography Bishop Francis J. McConnell records that in a similar situation years before Bishop Charles C. McCabe likewise proposed: "Let's wipe out all those motions and start afresh." At any rate my reputation as a presiding officer was enhanced, and I was thereafter called to the chair when a difficult session was anticipated.

It may seem that since I was traveling a great deal, I must never have been at home base. Who kept the store? As already indicated, ours is an itinerant ministry. This is a specialized term with Methodists. A full conference member, fully ordained as an elder, is called a "traveling minister." He or she is subject to reevaluation every year with the question being raised as to whether a pastor shall continue in the present assignment or be moved to another. A bishop is an itinerant too, in the sense of visitation of the local churches and traveling throughout the connection as well. I certainly did a great deal of this.

Yet statistically I was within the area at least three-fourths of the time. Moreover, when I was there I was "on call" seven days a week. When I was out of the area I kept in touch with the home office and, when on a lengthy tour, asked another bishop or one of the district superintendents to cover for me. Ongoing administration continued under my direction by the office administrative secretary. My door was "open" and pastors could see me or make an appointment to see me at a mutually agreeable time. Usually they saw me alone, for privacy was taken for granted, or if there was an ongoing issue involving the superintendent, he or she might also be present.

In 1961 two important international meetings demanded my attendance. The first one was the tenth session of the World Methodist Conference, which met in Oslo, Norway that year from August 17 to 25. This was followed some months by the Third Assembly of the World Council of Churches, held in November 1961. I was a delegate to both of these meetings.

We wanted Eunice to be present at these meetings, and it took careful arrangements to make this possible. First of all we had long planned for our children to have some of their schooling overseas—this in keeping with their missionary heritage and our desire, at first dimly felt, to prepare them for an increasingly global society. Arrangements were made for the two girls to be enrolled in College Cevenol in the Cevenne mountains near Le Puy in south-central France. This was a fine Huguenot school, closely related to the French Resistance Movement during World War II and a haven for French Jews in that period. During previous years close friends had enrolled their children there, and they had greatly profited from the experience. In addition, my brother Joe in Austin, Texas and his wife, Lyn, wanted their son, of similar age to our daughters, to study in Cevenol. Eunice was to take all three to Europe, and our son, Stan, was to spend a term in school in Austin while living with his aunt and uncle.

In July, Eunice escorted the three teenagers to Europe by ship and enrolled them in a language school in Switzerland for them to be introduced to French and then to their Huguenot school later. I may say this was an adventure for all concerned. Our children have never complained about this arrangement. They did master French and profited immensely by the intercultural experience.

After holding the fort at home for a month I joined Eunice in Geneva a week before the Oslo meeting. We drove across Europe in a car she had hired in Paris. Our trip took us across Germany, through Denmark, and into Sweden, our first exposure to Scandinavia. We have learned the virtue of staying at bed-and-breakfast establishments, adequate but not plush accommodations. Fortunately, we were able to glimpse some of the fjords of Norway, fell in love with the city of Bergen, and were no less entranced by Oslo as we had been by both Copenhagen and Stockholm.

As I shall note in detail later on, I attended the World Methodist Conference in Oxford in 1951 and then the next session at Lake Junaluska, North Carolina, in 1956. Already I had a fair acquaintance with brother and sister Methodists from around the world, and I must say that I had profited by this. The conference in Oslo itself went off well under the skillful eye of its president, Dr. Harold Roberts, a top leader and educator of British Methodism. At the first session we were honored by the presence of His Majesty King Olav V of Norway and other dignitaries.

The theme of the meeting was "New Life in the Spirit." My own part in the program was being paired with Sir Hugh Foote (later Lord Caradon) in presenting a paper, "Reconciling Races and Nations." One amusing aspect of my address was that I had written it out by hand and had taken it with me to Switzerland for Eunice to type. She could only borrow a Swiss typewriter, which apparently "spoke German and not English"—the letters were in a different order. The result was a typescript nearly as indecipherable as my scrawl. We did enjoy the fellowship and Scandinavian hospitality, which lasted throughout the long Nordic day.

After Oslo we drove together with Board of Missions colleagues of mine, Lucile Colony and Margaret Billingsley, to Copenhagen, whence I returned to Boston. Eunice and our two friends had a hilarious journey as she drove them on to Paris and returned the rental car. After a short visit to the girls in Cevenol she was off to India, where I was to join her later. She had not visited the land of her birth for sixteen years and was anxious to do so.

After some busy and very long and lonesome weeks back home, during which I moved (with the help of my sister Elizabeth) from Newtonville to Wellesley, Massachusetts, I left for India in early November. We met in New Delhi. It was a week before the Assembly so we made good use of our time and some accrued vacation by going to Kashmir, where we had spent our honeymoon. This was our first experience of seeing the Vale of Kashmir in autumn dress. It is beautiful for the trees change color as in New England and in contrast to the plains. The flowers had a burnished hue and the Moghul gardens could not have been more beautiful. The few days sped by and almost immediately we boarded a converted DC-3, World War II surplus airplane for Delhi. It added greatly to our interest that also aboard was mystery writer Agatha Christie. We speculated that perhaps from *her* journey might come another thriller, *Murder on a Houseboat,* but as far as I am aware she did not write it.

The Third Assembly of the World Council of Churches had as its theme "Jesus Christ, the Light of the World," significant because it gathered in the Diwali season, the Hindu festival of lights. The site was Vigyan Bhavan (House of Learning), a new and spacious auditorium, to which was attached a huge *shamiana* or tent. Our Indian hosts were generous and attentive, from the Prime Minister Jawaharlal Nehru to the humblest citizen. It was a proud hour for Indian Christians.

Two events made New Delhi a notable meeting. One was the joining together of the International Missionary Council (IMC) and the World Council of Churches (WCC) in a new and altered unity. I had come to Delhi representing the IMC. The second remarkable event was the joining of the WCC by the Russian Orthodox Church and some other Orthodox bodies of Eastern Europe. Naturally, the enemies of the Council lost no time in alleging that this was a Communist takeover of the Council. Undoubtedly Moscow would have had such aspirations, but it did not happen. The stifled, oppressed faithful Christians in the Soviet Union, starving for a wider Christian fellowship, which in the final analysis transcends all boundary walls, finally had a window open to the world. Actually this was cause for rejoicing. The whole session— my first assembly—was a tremendous experience. The detailed account of this gathering is readily available in the official record, and I shall return later to a discussion of the World Council of Churches.

During the WCC Assembly a cable came to me announcing that my father had died in Connecticut at age ninety-two. At the time I was forty-eight, and this was the first death in my immediate family. The decade of the 1960s was not so kind to us, for before its close my brother

Don, my mother, and my sister Elizabeth would die. We were a close-knit family and we felt these losses deeply. I could not go home for my father's funeral. It was conducted by my brother Joe, whose sermon "The Time My Father Died" has been widely published and quoted. Since I have always thought of myself primarily as a missionary it was not unfitting that I should not have been at home at the time, for this has been the regular experience of multitudes of missionaries. I was grateful for the touching letters I received from friends, not the least those from clergy and laity of the Boston Area.

Thanks be to God that life's shades are not always somber. We did get together as an extended family throughout these crowded years and they were happy days and as precious as they were few. As to our small nuclear family, we tended to be scattered a lot but when we were together, we spent what was later to be called "quality time." We liked to travel together and although we never had a summer place—they seemed always to slip out of our grasp—we did use rental places for vacations, especially at Silver Bay, New York, which became a very important place to us all. Through the busy years when we went on holiday I usually took a lot of work with me. Then after a few days I found that the work was left undone. I was "unwinding," as they say, but that is what vacations are for, so holidays become *holy* days!

As I write I realize that I keep getting ahead of myself, sometimes years ahead. Nevertheless, the passing years *are* rather circular in the actual living of them. The basic routines are much the same but ever-changing in emphasis, and all are punctuated by special events that lend shades and lights to the whole. For Methodists, we live not just by yearly leaps but by quadrennial ones, for our General Conferences meet every four years and an immense amount of energy flows into these meetings and then flows out as well.

During my Boston years I was sustained in part by an external fellowship that I enjoyed immensely. It was the Minister's Club of Boston. It was founded by no less a person than Phillips Brooks and some of his contemporaries. It was made up of a truly distinguished group of clergymen, including some Roman Catholics, and met from time to time for dinner "at seven o'clock, *precisely*." Then one of the members would present a paper, which became the center for lively discussion. Among the members were the deans of Harvard Divinity School, together with the deans of Andover Newton and Boston University School of Theology. Ted Ferris, rector of Trinity Episcopal Church, the Reverend Frederick Meek, pastor of Old South Church, and Professor Amos Wilder of Harvard were among the members. Naturally I was pleased to be invited to be a part, as had my predecessor bishops in Boston. Together with *Lux Mundi*, already alluded to, this proved to be one of the most intellectually stimulating groups of which I have ever been a part.

At about this time a small support group emerged within the Council of Bishops. Bishop Fred Holloway was our mentor and the group included the following bishops: Dwight Loder, McFerrin (Mac) Stowe, Marvin Stuart, James Thomas, and myself. Bishop Holloway was a scholar, a poet, and a prophet. The whole church owes much to him.

In this context I mention the fact that I was invited to deliver the Lowell Lectures at King's Chapel in Boston in the spring of 1964. My topic had to do with Church Renewal, a theme much favored at that period. This was a series of six lectures titled "Prophetic Cadre: Image for the Church in the World." I had earlier delivered the Fondren Lectures on Missions at Southern Methodist University in 1962, and in 1967 the Gray Lectures at Duke on Ecumenism. The Lowell Lectures were later transferred to Boston University School of Theology.

Early in our Boston years, my father-in-law, E. Stanley Jones, was visiting us. We invited to dinner President and Mrs. Nathan Pusey of Harvard; Bishop and Mrs. Henry Knox Sherrill; Professor and Mrs. John Goodenough of M. I. T. and Lincoln Laboratory. The conversation was most stimulating as we inquired of what of special significance was going on in their lives. Dr. Goodenough, a solid-state physicist, reported that his laboratory was working on a new development that did not yet have any practical application. "We are calling it *laser*," he said.

Mention must be made of the bishop as social prophet. One is naturally more than a little sensitive about claiming too much with respect to this exalted role. Nevertheless, it is expected of the bishop as chief pastor of an area. New England had had a proud history in this respect; one need only to mention combating the evils of slavery or advocacy of meeting the educational needs of all the people. The New England periodical *Zion's Herald* was often in the forefront in its advocacy role in the struggle for social justice. Several of its bishops have been on the front line in this respect: Gilbert Haven and Edwin Holt Hughes of an earlier period, and Herbert W. Welch, G. Bromley Oxnam, Lewis O. Hartman, and John Wesley Lord more recently.

For example, Bishop Oxnam pioneered in establishing a ministry to labor, called the Boston Area Social and Industrial Relations Committee, which his successors continued. The Reverend Luther Tyson and the Reverend John C. Bryan gave distinguished leadership as industrial chaplains. Moreover, Boston University School of Theology was quite literally a "school of the prophets," blessed with bold and informed professors in the field of social ethics; preeminently Walter G. Muelder, dean of American social ethicists as well as valued friend and colleague. I could scarcely overstate how helpful he was to me.

All I can say is at least I *tried* in this difficult field. The issues were clear and inescapable: peace and international understanding, racial equality, economic justice, and plain humanity. It is not for me to engage in a self-serving effort of claiming to have dealt effectively with them all or to pretend that I was always on the right side of every conflict. As I review my record, I was not always unwavering in my opposition to the Vietnam War, but I did speak out against it and its excesses in addresses to annual conferences, in preaching, in study days with pastors, in articles, and in direct involvement in public protest. Most bishops write columns in area periodicals; I certainly sounded notes with respect to nuclear armament. I often gave voice to church–state issues, emphasizing that the so-called Separation Doctrine was in large part intended to release the religious sector for its rightful prophetic role and to be a constructive critic of the body politic. In 1965 I spoke to a Jurisdictional meeting at Boiling Springs, Pennsylvania, on the topic "Who Speaks for the Church?" and at Buck Hills Falls, Pennsylvania, on "Some Theological Guidelines for the Churches' Involvement in International Affairs."

Of involvement in the struggle for racial justice I shall speak in a moment, but I want to say a word about what I call the "fan mail," which everyone in a leadership role receives in abundance. Anonymous letters can, of course, be discarded, usually without reading. One such missive I recall. After complaining about my misguided thinking and reflecting adversely on my ancestry as well, it concluded: "Many people feel the same way I do but are not bold enough to say so." It was left unsigned. That was not as bad as the experience of Bishop McConnell, who in a letter was called a "skunk." *It* was signed, "Your brother in Christ." When I would return home often late at night I would tell my Eunice that if any letters of that type had come, please let me see them the next morning. I did not want to lose a night's sleep. On the other hand, there were often letters of support. Usually I did not reply to letters of mean criticism. My father-in-law usually did reply and called his critics the "unpaid guardians of my soul." My brother Joe *never* replied, and he was the recipient of a superabundance of such communications. This must be said: let no one be the keeper of your conscience!

On racial justice I can claim to have written and spoken out incessantly. It could scarcely be otherwise. I am a veteran of the 1960s and as such have some scars to show for it. My notes and documents show the following partial listing:

- Meetings with Jackie Robinson and other prominent Negroes (the terminology then) in 1960 in which "early warnings" were sounded.

- Invited with church leaders to White House by President Kennedy on June 17, 1963, to discuss civil rights.
- Participation in the March on Washington for Jobs and Freedom, August 28, 1963. (Occasion of Dr. Martin Luther King's "I Have a Dream" speech!)
- Proposed ringing of church bells all over the country in protest against the murder of Medgar Evers. This was approved by the president of the National Council of Churches, J. Irwin Miller.
- Sponsor and participant in Boston Conference on Religion and Race, January 13, 1964, at which Mr. Whitney Young, Rabbi Abraham Joshua Heschel and others spoke.
- Easter Sunday (1964). Witness with Bishop Charles F. Golden at Galloway Memorial Methodist Church in Jackson, Mississippi.
- Launching of the Bishop's Housing Corporation in Boston's South End, January 1965.
- Spring of 1966. Member of Committee of the NCC to negotiate with James Forman on Black Manifesto.
- Explored at Harvard Business School with the Reverend John Bryan the possibility of organizing a National Black Development Bank. This was an intriguing prospect, studied carefully, but it never matured.

Particularly I want to refer to the incident at Galloway Church. Bishop Golden and I were turned away when we attempted to worship together there on Easter Sunday 1964. I should mention that I had known Bishop Golden for years. We were at Boston University together in 1937–38. We had been colleagues on the staff of the Board of Missions, he for

National Missions and I for Foreign Missions. We had been elected bishops the same year, 1960. It had been clear to both of us for some time that such a joint witness should be made by bishops. We explored as early as the previous December 1963 the possibility of others joining us but none was prepared to do so. When he abruptly suggested a visit that Easter, I could do no other than agree. The district superintendents agreed to cover for me at Easter services.

We arrived in Jackson on Saturday and registered in a nearby motel. There we planned for the next day, including the preparing of two papers: one to be left if we were admitted, the other if we were not. Later I wrote:

> Easter 1964 dawned bright and sunny in Jackson, Mississippi. It was a beautiful day—well suited to flowery Easter bonnets and other seasonal finery. People flocked to the city's many churches whose doors were open to all worshippers who wished to share in the ever new experience of relating themselves to their Risen Lord.
>
> Well, not quite *all*, for some were turned aside from this intent as I can testify personally. For at twenty-five minutes to eleven, Bishop Charles F. Golden, a Negro, and I presented ourselves to worship at Galloway Memorial Methodist Church. Our passage was blocked on the front steps and entrance denied to us. . . .
>
> We do not regret having participated together in this symbolic act. . . . There are dimensions of the incident which have particular significance to Methodists. Methodist bishops are *general superintendents*; that is, bishops of the whole church. . . . They are, in a real sense, pastors of each church. . . .
>
> But what of the compelling, contemporary issue of continuing racial injustice? Can we, as a church, possibly rest any longer in regard to this present issue, particularly as

it intrudes into the very sanctuary of worship, to say nothing of the way it infects our whole society?

To their credit some of the white worshipers did indeed welcome us. Later also the pastor, the Reverend W. T. Cunningham, expressed his humiliation and regret about the incident, for had he known he would have insisted on our being seated. As it was, we walked to a nearby Black Methodist Church for Easter worship. Years later, April 1991, I was invited to preach in Galloway Church during a session of the Council of Bishops in Jackson. It was a deeply moving event for me.

The message we left with the church I quote, a part of a full statement of the incident which was published in *The Christian Century*:

A Christian's desire to participate in public worship—especially on Easter—should neither occasion surprise nor require explanation. This would appear to be an undeniable right both from the standpoint of our national heritage and common Methodist practice.

At a deeper level, the very nature and meaning of the Christian faith supports this desire and right. Indeed, we are assured that our God and Father *seeks* man to worship Him in Spirit and in Truth. Moreover, the New Testament faith assures us that this God-given privilege is open to *all* people, without regard to their race or color.

It is because we are prompted by such encouragement of faith that we have come to worship at Galloway Memorial Methodist Church today. We are aware, of course, that some members of this congregation, though surely not all the members, do not desire to have other than white people attend services of worship here. We are aware, too, that some Negroes and others have been turned away. We stand united with such ones and regard that in some sense we represent them. This is true partly because we are Methodist bishops, responsible to the whole church for the whole church. But in a larger sense there cannot, in fact, be any true Christian worship at all which is not an intercession in behalf of all mankind, for Jesus Christ died and rose for us *all*.

We trust that our presence will not provoke you to wrath but to good works. We are hopeful that we shall be admitted for worship, despite contrary attitudes which may have been expressed here in times past. The meaning of these acts may now be altered—from the Christian perspective. For this is Easter Sunday, which offers not only victory over death, but infinite possibility for renewal of individuals and of churches and of society. Easter is an occasion for entirely new attitudes and fresh beginnings. We believe that the Feast of the Resurrection affirms life for *all* men. All Christians together believe that Jesus, the Christ, is the Living Lord of *all*. Furthermore, for Christians every Sunday is a commemoration of Easter and its meaning.

If we are not admitted, we shall harbor no ill-will toward those who may feel compelled to turn us away. We shall naturally be disappointed. We shall be deeply concerned for the witness of the whole church before the world. We shall also wonder at those who presume to speak and act for God in turning worshippers away from *His* House. We shall remain unshaken in the conviction that we share with Christians everywhere that God has chosen to work in our day to bring into operation that reconciliation of all men of which the Cross-Resurrection is both the symbol and the reality. And we shall pray for the forgiveness of us all and hope that we might all come fully to know Christ and the power of His resurrection and the fellowship of His suffering."

Signed:

Charles F. Golden
James K. Mathews
Bishops of The Methodist Church

The next matter to which I shall make brief reference arose out of the above incident and more particularly out of the whole atmosphere of racism that prevailed during the decade of the 1960s. It closely involved the work of my new secretary, for Ida Moody had to retire due to ill health in the spring of 1967. During that summer Eunice served as secretary. Just after Labor Day 1967, Faith Richardson, wife of Dr. Neil Richardson, a professor of Old Testament at Boston University School of Theology, became my administrative and executive secretary. We remained in association and worked with each other (with interruptions) for nearly twenty-five years in all. She was extremely able and blended deep Christian commitment and social conscience with boundless energy. Quite the contrary to complaining of her heavy workload, she would ask that even more be loaded on her.

At the Council of Bishops in the fall of 1967 at Miami Beach, Florida, as chairman of the Coordinating Council, I presented a detailed draft for a quadrennial program for the 1968–72 quadrennium. It took into account the merger of The Methodist Church and The Evangelical United Brethren Church at the forthcoming General Conference. The program was to be designated "A New Church for a New World," but its focus was sharply on the fact of racism in Church and nation. I was to present a further draft of this program in Chicago early in January. I had my draft, extensive notes, and supporting material, but had not had the time to prepare a more complete statement. This was a Friday night before it was due. On our way down on the elevator when we were headed home I mentioned this to Mrs. Richardson. She volunteered to help. We returned to the office and picked up the material. Meanwhile I proceeded with a weekend of preaching in Maine. On Monday morning Faith came to the office with a revised draft, which was substantially that approved by the General Conference in the following April. This was typical of her work.

A major part of this program was a Fund for Reconciliation, with a goal set for $20 million, half to be used within the annual conference that raised it and half for the general Church to combat racism and to effect reconciliation in our world. The goal was not entirely reached, but much of the fund was used to stimulate "matching funds" from other sources. The result was that we achieved about $50 million in all. Some fourteen hundred reconciliation projects were established at home and abroad. Whitney Young said of the program that United Methodists had done more to combat racism than any other denomination. More than that, it stimulated other churches to embark on similar programs, especially the Roman Catholic Church, which specifically used our model in raising its Fund for Justice, which continued for years. Its first in-gathering was larger than any other fund they had hitherto raised. It was my task to present the Quadrennial Program—the Fund for Reconciliation—to the General Conference, where it passed with only six negative votes, and then to chair the resulting committee through the next quadrennium.

Through this fund we were also able to undergird the Commission on Religion and Race, Black Methodists for Church Renewal, and the United Methodist Volunteer Service, which was similar in conception and appeal to the Peace Corps. It also afforded emergency relief and reconciliation programs in Vietnam. For example, when an amputee project was established there for civilians maimed by land mines, the United Methodists were able to respond immediately with $700,000 for this purpose. Likewise, when the World Council of Churches in 1969 established a Fund to Combat Racism, we were ready immediately to contribute our rightful share, the first member church to do so.

I am delighted to recall that New England Methodists gave a total of more than a million dollars to the Fund for Reconciliation. Had the whole church responded proportionally more than $200 million would have been received.

One other incident I record. There was a rare special session of the General Conference held in St. Louis in April 1970 in order to refine certain elements of the merger of the two churches welded into one to form The United Methodist Church in 1968; and further to address the racial issues continuing in our Church.

I was to preside at one of the sessions—this on very short notice. It was projected to be unruly, so I was anxious. About midnight I had a telephone call from the Reverend James Lawson, an African-American pastor from Memphis. We had been friends for years, for he had been a short-term missionary to India. There I had shepherded him, saw to it that he became acquainted with Gandhian methods, and arranged for him to return to the United States via Africa. At the Christmas season of 1964 I received a call stating that Jim, Ralph Abernathy, and others were in the Shelby City jail in Memphis. Would I preach for him? I was able to do this, for once again the Boston Area church where I was to preach allowed me to postpone my engagement and go to Memphis instead. I called on the prisoners in jail, and had Communion with them and the jailers. The next morning I preached in Lawson's church.

All this came to mind when I had Jim's midnight call. He told me that he owed it to me to tell me of the demonstration planned for the morning session of the General Conference. I asked whether it would be orderly. He said it would be and asked me to secure permission of the conference to hold it. I inquired what would happen if the conference refused. He said that he did not know. Even yet I recall reading Psalm 55 before I retired: "Cast your burden on the Lord, and he will sustain you" (NRSV). That night I slept like a baby. The conference did give consent for a peaceful demonstration—a show of solidarity by Blacks, Hispanics, and Asians, with White brothers and sisters entirely surrounding the area of the conference. The whole assembly was entranced by the short address of Rosa Parks. All went off peaceably. It was a triumphant service in which once again it was demonstrated what the Spirit of God is able to do when God's people act out their faith through love.

What I have written will afford a glimpse of my Boston Area years. They were very full, demanding, and exciting. They saw our family grow, ourselves mature, and the church and its members rise to the demands of challenging times. They were years of almost constant travel—a part of which I will sketch in a later chapter. They were from my standpoint productive years in planning and executing programs, in articles written, books penned or edited, sermons preached, years of social service engagement, and of intense ecumenical involvement. As I think of the period this rich variety comes to mind. For example, Bishop Roy Nichols and I were interviewed on May 1, 1972, by Frank McGee on the *Today* program. I recall the faces and names and stories of a multitude of pastors, laypersons, and a host of friends and associates worldwide who allowed me the honor to be their associate and colleague through one of the most exciting periods of history. For this I am grateful. The summer of 1972 came all too quickly when the demands of the calendar placed me in a new setting and a new ministry.

9

THE WASHINGTON YEARS

According to the practice of our church at the time, there was a limit of twelve years for assignment of a bishop to any one area. Thus I knew full well that I would be moved in 1972. The question was, where to?

Conceivably it could have been to any other area in the Northeastern Jurisdiction—or any other area in the church. It was not my intention or practice to seek a particular area. I was, as I have observed, not even consulted when I went to Boston and that was satisfactory to me. In 1964, when there was the possibility of many episcopal transfers, all the areas of the jurisdiction expressed their readiness to receive me. I am not certain that that happy attitude still prevailed in 1972.

With me it was a matter of principle that a bishop should not seek a particular assignment. Perhaps it is better for the area to seek the bishop. After all, we United Methodists have an appointive, itinerant plan of ministry. Theoretically, a minister is to go where sent. It seemed to me, therefore, that the same process ought to apply to bishops themselves. They are appointed by the Jurisdictional Conferences of which they are a part. It is possible that one may be appointed across jurisdictional lines, but so far this has not happened.

I was informed only hours before assignments were

proposed by the Jurisdictional Committee on Episcopacy that I was recommended for Washington. This was then affirmed by action of the Jurisdictional Conference as a whole.

Upon my arrival in the Washington office, I found a considerable accumulation of mail addressed to a bishop from the Midwest who was expected by some to be assigned to the nation's capital. Although I was greatly astonished by this, I quietly directed my secretary to forward this mail to its rightful destination.

The Washington Area was generally regarded as an important assignment. Some giants in the past had served there, among them Bishop Matthew Simpson, friend of Abraham Lincoln. Though there was, strictly speaking, no *resident* bishop in Washington in those days, he was a frequent visitor. Then there was Bishop John Fletcher Hurst, book lover and collector, founder of the American University. Bishop Earl Cranston followed Hurst. The practice of assigning a bishop to a particular area began only in 1912. Serving as bishop in Washington from 1916 to 1932 was William Fraser McDowell, saintly and eloquent preacher of the gospel. The deep impression he made upon me the one time I heard him when I was about ten years old lingers with me to this very day. He was followed (1932–46) by Edwin Holt Hughes, likewise a giant pulpiteer, who was together with Southern Methodist Bishop John M. Moore, and Bishop James H. Straughn, Methodist Protestant, one of the principal architects of Methodist Reunion in 1939. Regrettably I never heard Hughes preach except for a recorded sermon, which preserved his eloquence. After Hughes came

Bishop Adna W. Leonard, precise in speech and administration, who lost his life in a military plane crash in Iceland during a mission to U.S. troops in Europe, where he was sent by President Franklin D. Roosevelt. He served from 1940 until his death in 1943. Following Leonard as resident bishop was Charles Wesley Flint, formerly chancellor of Syracuse University, a man of great good humor endowed with a quaint and unique gift of expression.

Bishop G. Bromley Oxnam was resident bishop from 1952 until his retirement in 1960. He was, of course, a towering figure, aptly designated "Paladin of Liberal Protestantism" in his biography by Robert Moats Miller. Finally, there was my immediate predecessor with the wonderful name of John Wesley Lord, whom I had also succeeded in Boston, a greatly admired episcopal leader. Both Bishop Oxnam and Bishop Lord laid hands on me, as I have said, when I was consecrated bishop in 1960. All these predecessors were a remarkable succession and I scarcely merited following them.

It is hardly proper to dwell on such feelings of unworthiness, for a task is to be performed and I had been chosen to do it to the best of my ability. After all, by 1972 I had had thirty-five years experience as an ordained minister. Though short on conventional pastoral experience, I had been a pastor and district superintendent in India, as well as administrator in a large general agency.

The Washington Area was in 1972 made up of two annual conferences. The Peninsula Annual Conference consisted of about five hundred congregations in the State of Delaware and Maryland's Eastern Shore. In this region our church was strong with approximately 10 percent of the people United Methodists. This conference was linked with the larger Baltimore Conference, also strong, with some nine hundred congregations in the rest of Maryland, the District of Columbia, and the eastern panhandle of West Virginia. I was soon to become intimately acquainted with this beautiful and varied region; it was far more compact than the Boston Area.

I say it is varied and so it is: mountains, foothills, lowlands, shoreline, lakes, rivers, bays, inlets—it's all there. It included the nation's capital, two state capitals, two large cities—Baltimore and Washington—numerous smaller cities and towns, and a considerable range of farmlands, studded with churches that serve the rural communities. The region is rich with history and in touch, through Washington, D.C., with the whole world. Though not a major industrial region neither is it entirely lacking in this respect. Baltimore is a great manufacturing and shipping center that can also boast of an impressive and rather unique cultural heritage.

Sometimes citizens from other parts of the country speak disparagingly of Washington, which is in fact no mean city, but a capital in which every American should take pride. Although we who live there have in more recent years been able to cast our votes for president, we have no voting representative in Congress. Sometimes I have said to our critics, "We do the best we can with those you send here," and I am not entirely joking! Government is, of course, our chief business, but secondly Washington's chief business is higher education. In fact, of Greater Washington it can be said that it is peopled by those who possess the highest average educational attainment of any city in the world and of any city in history.

From the standpoint of Methodist history, the Washington Area could claim to be at the very heart of it. Within the Peninsula Conference in Frederica, Delaware, still stands Barratt's Chapel, where Thomas Coke met Francis Asbury in 1784. Nearby was Judge White's house, hideout for Asbury during a part of the American Revolution when he was wrongfully suspected of being a Tory. A few weeks later the famous 1784 Christmas Conference convened in Baltimore in Lovely Lane Chapel to establish the Methodist Episcopal Church. The original building is no longer standing, the spot marked by a bronze plaque, but the congregation continues Lovely Lane Church, termed "the mother church of American Methodism." The present structure itself is now a historical monument designed by the famous architect Stanford White. Not far from Baltimore is the home of Robert Strawbridge, notable early local preacher. Near Baltimore's Inner Harbor stands Old Otterbein Church, so significant for the Evangelical-United Brethren branch of our tradition. Bishop Otterbein came to Baltimore as pastor in 1774, remaining there until his death in 1813.

In Baltimore also is to be found Mount Olivet Cemetery, burial place of many Methodist leaders: Francis Asbury, John Emory, E. Stanley Jones, Mabel Lossing Jones, and others. The whole region is replete with reminders of Asbury's travels but also of a host of others—laity and ministers who are rightfully remembered and honored in our heritage.

In addition to the many worshiping congregations (about fourteen hundred), the Washington Area has been a center for higher education with the American University in Washington and Wesley College in Dover, Delaware. Goucher College in Baltimore and Western Maryland College in Westminster, Maryland, were established by Methodists but are no longer so affiliated. Then there is Wesley Theological Seminary, formerly in Westminster but now in Washington, Sibley Hospital in the nation's capital, in addition to a number of camps and retirement homes. Finally, the Board of Church and Society has for decades been located opposite the Capitol. Altogether it is a fascinating, exciting, and challenging area.

One reason that it may be termed demanding is the very diversity of its makeup. Here are to be found all three of the Wesleyan strands, which became one in 1939; namely, those who had been affiliated with The Methodist Episcopal Church, The Methodist Episcopal Church, South, and The Methodist Protestant Church. Then several hundred of the congregations were African American, formerly a part of the segregated Central Jurisdiction established by the 1939 reunion as a way of solving the "problem" of Black Methodists. Happily, this came to an end in 1972. The former Delaware and Washington Conferences had proud traditions that we endeavored to honor. Moreover, a considerable number of the congregations were of Evangelical or United Brethren origin, together forming the Evangelical-United Brethren from 1946 to 1968. The fact of the matter was that even when I came to Washington in 1972 all those strands had not become thoroughly amalgamated. It required constant care, fairness, and ingenuity to further the process of their effective union. Part of this involved impartial pastoral appointments and attention in the appointment of district superintendents to a just representation from these various backgrounds.

The Baltimore Conference was also the mother conference of American Methodism. Its members took great pride in this fact. They often betrayed a kind of superiority that proved to be a problem rather than an advantage to them. The reality was that there was a high degree of self-satisfaction and a consequent resistance to change.

The area was made up of thirteen districts, four in the Peninsula Conference and nine in the Baltimore Conference. All the superintendents were in place. No women were a part of these cabinets, although that would change under my administration. Peninsula had one Black superintendent while Baltimore had two. For a period we would vary from this formula, but on the whole the effort was to maintain such a balance. During my first few days in the area I met separately with the two cabinets. As I had done in New England, we began with a Communion service. Then I embraced each one and, as in the Boston Area, I affirmed that although they had been appointed by my predecessor, they were now *my* appointees.

Each conference had separate headquarters, one at Dover, Delaware, and the other in Baltimore. Both had small staffs. Each one had a program director, one of whom was a layman and the other a minister, a treasurer, a missions secretary, another for Christian education.

My own office was separate and in downtown Washington. It was in The United Methodist Building, built in 1922 by the old Board of Temperance, Prohibition, and Public

Morals, now the Board of Church and Society under the guidance of a strong leader named Clarence True Wilson. Up to that time the plot was an eyesore, a kind of trash heap marked by large billboards. Under Wilson's visionary leadership it was rescued from this condition and somehow paid for. I have met people who in their youth in the early 1900s sold peanuts on the streets of cities in the Northeast for the building. Its address, 100 Maryland Avenue, was to be my home office for eight years. To my mind it was the best location in the country. For example, I could sit at my desk and see to my left the Supreme Court building and to the right the Capitol. Or I could look out other windows and see the office buildings of the Senate and of the House of Representatives. What a setting!

It had one drawback: lack of adequate parking space. But this was not insurmountable. Pastors and people could come to see me. Or I could go to them for I considered myself a field bishop and would from time to time hold office hours in Baltimore or Dover or at other spots around the area.

Upon arrival in Washington I found that the office secretary who had served my predecessor well wanted to retire. For a brief period my wife, Eunice, served as my secretary, then our daughter Jan helped me out until she had to take up her teaching position. To my delight I discovered that my longtime secretary in Boston, Faith Richardson, was just waiting to be asked to come to Washington. So it was that for eight years she commuted almost weekly from Boston. Her husband, Neil, was a busy professor at Boston University School of Theology, so that she really only saw him on weekends anyway.

They always claimed that this arrangement improved their marriage because it afforded them quality time together on weekends.

Housing too was a problem for us because the area did not own an episcopal residence. To our dismay we discovered that housing costs in Washington were nearly twice those prevailing in Boston at the time. Nevertheless, we finally found and purchased a satisfactory residence within the District of Columbia, in which we continue to dwell twenty-seven years later.

Already I have spoken of the excellent relations between President Lincoln and Bishop Matthew Simpson. The president delighted to hear Simpson preach. In fact, he often invited the bishop to come to Washington to "brief" him, as we might say nowadays. Simpson was renowned for his sagacity and moreover traveled constantly all over the country. He had his fingers on the pulse of the nation in a rare way and was in a position to know the temper of the populace. More than a hundred years later there are far more effective means for the chief executive to be informed than by a bishop of any communion. Some other bishops have found the door to the Oval Office more or less open to them, but not in our day.

This is not to say that a United Methodist bishop is unaware of the special responsibilities that rest upon one assigned to the nation's capital. Personally, it seemed to me that I should keep a rather low profile in this respect. Moreover, I soon discovered that no political leader wants to appear beholden to a religious leader. I was neither disposed toward being much of a news maker myself and certainly was disinclined toward name-dropping. Rather, it was my practice quietly to cultivate such avenues and access as might be helpful for the Church to both houses of Congress and to the White House itself. These channels too I used only sparingly but not infrequently. An example would be Congressman Robert W. Edgar of Pennsylvania, himself a United Methodist pastor, who often was available to speak to our meetings and to counsel us. Congressman John Brademas, a more experienced legislator and loyal Methodist, was also invariably helpful, as was Senator George McGovern.

During my years in Washington there was a breakfast held in the Capitol each month at which denominational leaders met with congressional leaders for fellowship and mutual exchange of information. In this way we were afforded the opportunity of some acquaintance with both senators and congressmen or members of their staff. I recall that arising from one of these associations I was able to render a small personal service to a then leader of the House of Representatives. He never forgot this as was shown by our subsequent meetings while he was president, Gerald Ford.

With President Richard M. Nixon I enjoyed no access whatever. Ever since Francis Asbury and Thomas Coke made a friendly call on President Washington, whenever Methodist Episcopal or Methodist bishops gathered in Washington there was some contact with the president. Also, United Methodist bishops had been regularly invited to inaugurations. When, however, I hosted the Council of Bishops gathered in Washington in April 1973, Nixon declined to receive us! We could only guess at the reason.

On occasion there were invitations to the White House; for example, when Greek Orthodox Archbishop Iakovos was awarded the Presidential Freedom Medal by President Carter. Another memorable event was a dinner given by President and Mrs. Carter and at which the well-known English actor Alec McCowen recited from memory the whole of the Gospel of Mark in a most meaningful way.

There were opportunities in abundance for other contacts. Among these was the occasional privilege of opening one or the other house of Congress with prayer. These appeared in the Congressional Record together with the courtesy remarks from a United Methodist member. Or one had a picture taken with the Speaker of the House or the vice president. Or there was testimony before one of the congressional committees. Or there were repeatedly calls on members in respect to some pending legislation vital to the religious or moral interests of the country. Times without number letters were directed to congressmen and senators or to the president. Likewise there were times when communications with ambassadors were helpful. Of course, there were various ceremonial occasions when a church leader was invited to be present, especially during the Bicentennial year, 1976. Then too I served my turn at leading worship at the Pentagon. During the late 1970s Elliot Richardson, a longtime friend, worked with the United Nations on the Law of the Sea program. He sought through the Washington episcopal office cooperation of United Methodists and was grateful for the help. Through the years, when I have met with leaders, almost always we concluded our meeting with prayer together.

On the whole I would have to conclude that my contributions at this level were modest. This would certainly be true when compared with Bishop G. Bromley Oxnam. He was always quite visible and vocal in the public arena. This was particularly so in his testimony before the House Committee on Un-American Activities. There he struck a blow for justice and freedom that placed the whole nation in his debt.

My moving to the Washington Area almost exactly coincided with the breaking of the Watergate scandal. It was, of course, a highly complicated matter, the truth only gradually emerging—the whole truth not entirely revealed a quarter of a century later. At the same time it had strong partisan overtones. I did, of course, speak of it in small meetings, in conversations and made references to it in sermons. The fact remains that I personally did not speak out as forthrightly as I should have done. In retrospect, Watergate confronted us with a clear constitutional issue that challenged deeply fundamental liberty and our very identity as an American people. Furthermore, it was an abuse of power that jeopardized the moral purpose and values of our society, dedicated as it must be to openness and justice for all. In spite of all this, I feel that I failed in my errand, which was precisely to focus on these very matters and address them with clarity. Possibly the Church as a whole gave forth only an uncertain sound at the time.

During the 1960s and 1970s the issues were indeed clear as I have already observed. With respect to peace and justice I think I can say that I was deeply and consistently involved. A number of military leaders, for example, General Eisenhower and General Matthew Ridge-way, warned against a land-war in Southeast Asia and they proved to be correct. Too much credence was given to the inevitable operation of the so-called domino theory, which showed a lack of common sense as well as lack of confidence in ourselves and the real powers of democracy. We are still paying a heavy price for our Vietnam adventure. I did advocate nuclear disarmament and stood for racial justice—never alone because multitudes of our citizens spoke out for it and marched for liberty and justice for all. Most of all and behind all the specific social issues of this period was the manifestation of a deep search for human dignity, which intense search generated immense propulsive energy toward its fulfillment. It was a great time to be around and to be involved. To this I shall be returning.

In more recent years it has become our practice that a bishop begins service on September 1 following election or assignment by the Jurisdictional Conference. In 1972 the newly assigned bishops assumed responsibility immediately; in my case on July 16. In the weeks that ensued we were welcomed to the area at separate services in the two conferences. In Washington the Baltimore Conference held this meeting in Metropolitan Memorial United Methodist Church, where I had been elected bishop in 1960. The counterpart meeting for the Peninsula Conference was held in Salisbury, Maryland. We were welcomed heartily and made to feel at home. In both gatherings I delivered an address on "What May You Expect of Your Bishop?"—a kind of inaugural intended to set the tone of my administration. I then turned the question to, "What may we expect of the Church?" In essence my response was as follows:

> I would expect the future to involve harnessing the hidden resources of the church . . . If the people of God fail to reformulate society, to whom shall this task be entrusted?
>
> I would expect the church to address secularized men and women and to teach them that they are not merely secular but holy.
>
> I would expect the church to be about the business of humanizing society.
>
> I would expect a new emphasis on ecumenism to emerge. It would be local; it would be personal. It would be less organizational.
>
> I would expect the church to reclaim a sense of discipline . . . to take up the cross and to follow its Lord.
>
> I would expect the church to be found seeking and following the will of God.

There is a great difference in starting out as a new bishop, as I was in Boston, and being translated to a new area. Already I had hit my stride as it were; nevertheless, I found that one never ceases to learn from the new circumstances that confront a person in charge. The very process of being a bishop is an exercise in continuing education. Each area has its own personality and in some degree it is necessary to conform to this and honor well-set tradition, but not to be bound by it. A program is developed by regard for the basic mission mandate of the gospel, the traditions that have emerged in the past, the specific demands of the time and place we find ourselves, and the determination of laity and clergy to respond to all these factors.

One thing I was determined to do in the Washington Area, as I had done in the Boston Area, was to visit *all* the churches. This had to be done over a period of months, a not inconsiderable task, for there were fourteen hundred churches in the area. This was done district by district with each of the thirteen district superintendents who assisted me. We would do about fifty per week. My record shows that by December 1972 I had gone to about five hundred churches: "that's nine hundred to go." As I had experienced before, this process gave one a good sense of the church under my supervision, and it enabled me to see and be seen by those I was assigned to serve. Since my role was to appoint pastors to the churches, then it was my job to become acquainted with them. Sometimes pastors' children were home for my visit. I recall one five-year-old who asked, "Who's the bishop—Jesus' boss?" The father replied, "No, Jesus is the bishop's boss."

On later tours of the districts I requested the district superintendents to help me understand the wider community. Consequently they arranged for me to meet with the governors of Maryland and of Delaware and the mayors of Washington, D.C., and of some of the larger cities. We visited industrial plants and schools, historical sites, hospitals, and homes. During my eight-year tenure there was a continual updating of this kind of experience and this too proved of great value.

From time to time I was afforded the privilege of meeting with representative laity. Sometimes these gatherings were termed "Listening to the Laity." They proved to be mostly constructive in nature but were also forums for complaints. This practice helped to balance somewhat my far more frequent meetings with the pastors in various settings. For example, each year we held an Area retreat for pastors and spouses at some attractive place, with a strong and provocative faculty. This did much for esprit de corps and morale.

Earlier I described at some length my practice of having Study or Teaching Days with the clergy. These were held in each of the districts in both the autumn and the spring. The informal fellowship was mingled with worship in an atmosphere of addressing together the intellectual demands of our common tasks. The endeavor was not to assert my fatherly and supervisory role, but rather the brotherly role, to be a bishop *with* the people.

We continued invariably to do some study of the Bible on each Study Day. The central focus, however, was our study and discussion together of some solid theological document. This procedure was for most an interesting and stimulating process. It was a new experience for many to engage with their bishop in the scholarly dimension of our common task. As I have observed before this was an exercise that drove me to study. It proved to be a powerful stimulus also for pastors to enhance their qualifications for ministry. In all districts some were prompted by this experience in corporate study to work for advanced degrees; in one district alone thirty pastors enrolled in the doctor of ministry programs of various seminaries. A by-product too was that these days proved to be useful for their preaching, for they were a rich source of sermon material, a constant need of a preacher. In a word, this methodology furthered an astonishing degree of profound corporateness in our exercise of ministry that was entirely in accord with the nature of the Christian faith.

Our most elaborate venture in corporate study was carried on twice a year from autumn 1973 through the spring of 1975. It had to do with the Holy Life. Toward the end of the 1970s spirituality was widely emphasized across Protestant churches, but we began the effort rather early. Since the Washington Area had thirteen districts we chose one religious classic for each district that all pastors were to study intensively. These ranged from *Confessions* of St. Augustine to Dag Hammarskjöld's *Markings.*

It was my practice then to lead each district in the study, which ranged over four sessions. They began with worship, followed by the study of a paper; for example, an essay by H. Richard Niebuhr, "Toward a New Other-Worldliness" or a chapter from Karl Rahner's *Shape of the Church to Come* titled "A Church of Real Spirituality." Discussion of the essay was followed by an in-depth consideration of the given classic. Sometimes various pastors would write papers on the volume they were studying. Before me as I write I have one of these: "An Evaluation of Pascal's *Pensees.*" This was a carefully crafted essay, worthy of doctoral level study. This particular pastor "came alive" in the process, and the Holy Life emphasis literally transformed his ministry as well as contributing mightily to his own self-esteem. This is one example out of scores, for it must be recalled that about seven hundred ministers were involved in this process—a real demon-stration of what we United Methodists mean by our being a connectional church.

More than this, the collective undertaking resulted in the compiling and printing of a devotional book, a daily office. It was given the title *Deeper Furrows*. At first blush that may seem a peculiarly inappropriate title for a con-temporary aid to Christian daily devotion. Nevertheless, the Scriptures and Christian tradition are replete with agricultural imagery—the sower, the harvest, the vine-yards, the plow—and we are not altogether removed from the soil. The plain fact is that we are not likely to advance farther in the spiritual life without digging deeper.

This volume contained various orders of worship for daily devotional use. Included also was an impressive array of suggestions for cultivating the life of prayer and for extending the inner life to outer expression in social action. Then there was a lectionary, which guided the reader through the Psalms quarterly, the New Testament annually, and the whole Bible every two years. Selected prayers from every century of Christian history as well as contemporary prayers were provided. Finally, for daily reading of "homily" the pastors had chosen selections from the thirteen classics they had studied.

We had a vision of these books being used in the churches to contribute to spiritual renewal. Where this was seriously undertaken, exactly that occurred. Yet it must be noted that in too many instances the pastors did not pursue this avenue with sufficient vigor. It has seemed to me that the ministers somehow did not have enough confidence in their own abilities, despite the fact that they had produced a very helpful spiritual guidebook. That, it was too readily conceded, was something someone else did for us! Meanwhile, I found that calls came from all over the country and indeed from other countries for copies of this book of which they had heard. To this day such calls still come.

Between 1976 and 1980 our attention was turned toward evangelism: that task of effective Christian witness for lay and clergy alike, but as difficult as it is essential. Our generation will not be seen as one of the great periods for evangelism. Paul Tillich told me in personal conversation, "Ours is a waiting time before God." Nevertheless, we must work on it. We followed Key-73—a Churchwide, interdenominational effort at evangelism. It was only moderately successful. We made evangelism a theme in our Area retreats. Toward the end of the decade of the seventies we sponsored the preaching of Dr. (now Sir) Alan Walker of Australia, director of World Evangelism of the World Methodist Council. His work elicited a positive response in spite of a dreadful unseasonable snowstorm that marred the last night. My point is that we did not desert the field, leaving it only to the fundamentalist and charismatic churches.

We studied evangelism on each district by all pastors twice a year for four years. We developed a collection of helpful readings on the subject. One was a chapter from Tillich's *Shaking of the Foundations* in which he emphasizes that effective evangelism must "make men aware of their predicament," as a prelude to healing. He continued, observing that the preacher's predicament is the same.

We *all* need healing. Then he reassures the messenger that there is no greater vocation than theirs; therefore, they rejoice that they are God's messengers.

Another article from Karl Rahner stressed that evangelism or the apostolate was the layman's task as well as the clergy's. Still another article by H. Richard Niebuhr saw that the church is itself *apostle* as well as pastor and pioneer and social prophet. Our group study of the evangelistic task was carried on with theological depth, steeped in biblical insights, especially as afforded in the New Testament and even more particularly in the Gospels. All this was prelude to a careful endeavor to explore how a Christian congregation might responsibly engage itself in witnessing to the good news in Jesus Christ.

Our studies resulted in the production of a pamphlet or guidebook entitled "Showing and Telling the Good News." The title was deliberately couched in the form of present participle that happens to be the most frequent form of the verb in the Greek New Testament. It implies *present participation.* Moreover the word "Showing" was intentionally placed preceding "Telling." As a rule the evangelist is so anxious to verbalize the gospel that he or she may actually be answering questions nobody is asking. A careful examination of the Gospels reveals that the *deed* of the gospel precedes the *word*. It is at once a *necessary* deed and a *provocative* deed—one that evokes a life-question that requires an affirmative answer: for us Christians that answer is Jesus Christ.

Once again our corporate research resulted in a carefully crafted essay of our understanding of what evangelism is for our day:

Evangelism in today's complex world implies that Christians need to speak about Christ and obey him wherever humanity is to be found and in terms which all can understand: "We who have been grasped by Christ the Lord are obliged to commend him to all." "In a word evangelism aims at changed lives and changed communities—a changed world." "We may witness but it is God who calls forth the response."

These are brief extracts from a tightly written essay—the distillation of the insights and wisdom of some fifteen hundred pastors and laity who were engaged in the common study. We then examined with great care the reasons why our clear understanding of evangelism seems to be hindered from fulfillment. What were the inherent contradictions and roadblocks involved? This was followed by the formulation of proposals for removing these barriers. In turn, we understood that proposals may in themselves be just "bright ideas" and remain so until they are translated into doable tasks or tactics, which tasks are further assigned to specific teams of witnesses who acted along a specific time line. What emerged was a holistic conception of evangelism well within the capacity of any local church to execute. The resulting instrument was made available to all the congregations.

Furthermore, groups of laypersons district by district were assigned the task of paraphrasing the Letter of James in colloquial English or Spanish. After all, evangelism is in large part a "translation" of scriptural truth into understandable acts or words. *James* was chosen because of its brevity, for its emphasis upon the needs of the poor, for its correlation of works and faith. The book was divided into thirteen parts to correspond to the thirteen districts. Their resulting paraphrases were brought together as a whole. It was a job well done and thoroughly enjoyable to the participants. The laity discovered that they too could interpret the gospel.

Wherever the pamphlet "Showing and Telling the Good News" was taken seriously and put into use, the method was effective for local church evangelism. I was myself involved in introducing this process to a number of congregations and observed its power as an instrument for effective witness. But sadly, it was once again true that pastors and people did not show sufficient confidence in their own work, leaving the matter largely unimplemented. But at least we tried and tried hard!

As in the Boston Area, I continued to find that visitation of all the churches and my fairly deep acquaintance with the pastors in my Teaching Days was of great help in matching the skills of a pastor with the needs of the congregation. Since the 1976 General Conference a greatly expanded consultative process—with pastors and congregations—has been mandated churchwide. This has not served to make the appointive process more easy, but it has corrected some of its shortcomings. My journal reveals how meticulously we endeavored to follow consultation guidelines in the Washington Area.

One of the most important aspects of appointments of pastors during the 1970s was our immense effort to make them inclusive. The whole struggle against racism was not as intense during this period as it was during the previous decade at end of which we saw the murder of Dr. Martin Luther King, Jr. The reason for this decline in intensity was due in some part to the great progress made during the 1960s and the premature conclusion that the problem had largely been brought under control. This proved to be illusory, and in spite of ground gained, the plague of racism has proved more persistent and virulent than some of us had supposed. Indeed a leading professor of sociology of religion observed that white Protestant churches had become the last hiding places of segregationists.

The Washington Area was far more of a testing ground than New England because of the greater presence of African Americans in the Middle Atlantic States and due also to the higher concentration of black United Methodists in this area from the formerly segregated Delaware and Philadelphia Conferences of the Central Jurisdiction.

Tremendous effort went into the strengthening of the black churches. Resources and programs were concentrated on these churches. We chose ten central city churches for particular reinforcement. We established a "Black Think Tank" devoted to survey and programming. The bishops and cabinets committed themselves to open itinerancy. We implemented as far as possible the 1976 General Conference's emphasis on Ethnic Minority Local Church Development. A manual was devised for such development following the sound methodology we had used on the Holy Life Study and Evangelism, already described. During the late 1970s the General Commission on Religion and Race reported that there were seventeen inclusive appointments across the whole denomination; that is, black pastors appointed to white congregations.

Nine of these were in the Washington Area. The bishop had to be deeply involved personally in this effort. Special training programs were mounted for these pastors in an endeavor to help them succeed.

Meanwhile we kept pace with the rapid increase in women pastors and received them in much greater proportion than prevailed in the church as a whole. Inclusivity also related to Hispanic and Asian Americans, where some progress could be reported. A special word must be said of Native Americans.

During the spring and summer of 1978 there was a most interesting development among Native Americans. They organized what was called "The Longest Walk," starting in California and ending in Washington, D.C. The numbers actually walking at any given time were never very large, but some walked the whole distance. The symbolic act called considerable attention to the plight of Native Americans.

John Adams of the General Board of Church and Society, and crisis intervention specialist at Wounded Knee and Kent State, kept me informed of this movement and the area became deeply involved. Altogether we raised some $75,000 toward the walk. We arranged for the walkers to stay in churches at many places along the route. We became acquainted with its leaders, such as: Bill Wakanepah, a Kickapoo; Clyde Bellecourt, Oujibwa; Wally Feather, Yankton Sioux; Philip Deere, famous Creek medicine man and others. I accompanied them to the White House to visit Vice President Walter Mondale, who was friendly to their cause. When the walkers arrived in Washington a number of United Methodists joined me in marching with them. We interceded for them with the FBI and National Parks Service to allow pitching of tepees on the Mall. We attended press conferences in their interest with Mohammed Ali, Dick Gregory, and "Buffy" St. Marie. We joined them in a celebration at the Kennedy Center, where Marlon Brando spoke. He was always friendly to the cause of Native Americans. Our churches collected food for hundreds camped in Green Belt. Altogether this made for improved relations and furthered the course of justice for Native Americans.

In my office files is a precious letter to my secretary from Russell Means, leader among the Oglala Sioux, dated August 15, 1978, which reads in part: "Suffice it to say that your office led by the beautiful Bishop Mathews extended the Longest Walk the hand of spiritual brotherhood and resources unmatched in the sordid history of American Indian people."

What I have reported so far about my work as United Methodist bishop in Washington surely suggests that the tasks were many and varied; my schedule was extremely full. Years later as I review my journal and scan my timetables for the period I am appalled at what was demanded and undertaken. The days were long, and more often than not my schedule required seven-day workweeks.

Now I mention in outline some of the specific projects that required my attention during the Washington years.

The American University

Already I have referred to the fact that the American University was established in 1893 by The Methodist

Episcopal Church. This was largely due to the vision of Bishop John Fletcher Hurst. Our denomination has in fact founded more institutions of higher learning than any other body in American history. Hurst was determined that one should adorn the nation's capital city. It was to be supported by the whole church, and its student body was to have been recruited from every state. Bishop Hurst had received his own graduate training at the University of Halle in Germany and deeply desired to follow the German model of liberal education. So it was that he acquired ninety acres of choice land that is the university's site today.

The bishop of the Washington Area has long been an ex officio member of the board of trustees of the university. This role I filled during my tenure and beyond. In 1976 a group from the trustees invited me to become chairman of the board. I continued in this office for six years, during which I worked closely with the administration in a period of growth and development, while at the same time doing all I could to encourage the most constructive relationship between the university and the Church. In this latter endeavor I believe I was at least partially successful.

THE INTER-FAITH CONFERENCE

Soon after I was assigned to Washington, Archbishop (later Cardinal) William Baum was appointed to the Roman Catholic Archdiocese of Washington. We had been friends for a number of years. Almost immediately in 1974 we agreed that we must jointly undertake an ecumenical initiative particularly addressed to the quality of life in our capital city. We were soon joined by others: the Rt. Reverend John T. Walker, newly elected as Episcopal bishop of the diocese of Washington; Rabbi Eugene J. Lipman; as well as leaders of the Greek Orthodox Church and additional representatives from across the whole spectrum of religious life in the city. Later on Muslims, Hindus, Sikhs, and Buddhists were involved. Initially our basic concerns were housing, criminal justice, world and local hunger, and education. What emerged was an Inter-Faith Conference of Washington, the most widely representative such body in the country. It continues vigorously nearly a quarter of a century later under the direction of the Reverend Clark Lobenstine.

THE METHODIST CORPORATION

During the late 1960s the Board of Church and Society and the Washington Area formulated a vision for a national denominational headquarters or center to be established in Washington, D.C. Consequently a plot of land of about twelve acres located on Nebraska Avenue between Massachusetts and New Mexico Avenues, and directly opposite the American University was acquired. The General Conference authorized a representative churchwide committee as a holding body: The Methodist Corporation, of which the resident bishop in Washington was chairperson. The property was acquired partly from funds advanced by the Board of Church and Society and partly by contributions made by annual conferences across the denomination. Elaborate plans were drawn for the development of the center.

Within a decade, however, it became clear that the funds for full development would not be readily forthcoming. A nearby national Presbyterian center was having difficulty, and it was almost as if denominational centers had "gone out of style." As chairman of the Corporation I had the unenviable job of winding down the operation and disposing of the property. This was not done lightly nor without thoroughly considering a number of other options. Among these was to *give* the plot of land for the President Kennedy Library, which would also be the working library of the American University. This was considered carefully by the Kennedy family, but was finally declined. The Board of Church and Society desired to withdraw as joint owners, and about a third of the land was sold through that body to a housing developer. The remainder was finally disposed of by the Corporation by selling it to the American University. The original property had cost about $1 million. It was sold in 1976 for $4 million. From this amount all monies provided by annual conferences were repaid to them with interest. A sum of $2,000,000 went to the Board of Higher Education and Ministry for a scholarship endowment fund benefiting the whole church.

THE CHURCHES' CENTER FOR THEOLOGY AND PUBLIC POLICY

The remaining $1 million was held by the General Council of Finance and Administration with the interest to be used for the Churches' Center for Theology and Public Policy. This was approved by the 1976 General Conference, and altogether this outcome seemed in accord with the original vision of a denominational center; that is to say, the whole church benefited and continues to do so.

Other mainline Protestant churches and the Roman Catholic Church in 1976 joined together to establish this body. It had originally been envisioned by Dr. Paul Minus, a United Methodist minister, and Professor Paul Minear of Yale. It was not to be a lobbying group or a partisan body but a center for objective research and an informed resource or think tank for the use of the churches in relation to public policy issues. The first director was Dr. Alan Geyer, who after some years was followed by Dr. James Nash. It is a base for both resident and visiting scholars who need to be in Washington. It holds seminars and conferences; produces books and pamphlets on a wide range of public concerns: peace, urban policy, health and tax policy, world hunger, and much more; issues a quarterly bulletin; holds an annual lecture forum and dinner named for one of its early leaders, Dr. Cynthia Wedel; and offers a research service to the churches on social issues. Of particular note was the great help director Alan Geyer rendered through the Council of Bishops on the nuclear arms control project "In Defense of Creation," clearly a major contribution to this debate, as later acknowledged by even a number of leaders in the Pentagon. This is something we have done right.

OLD OTTERBEIN CHURCH, BALTIMORE

Earlier, allusion was made to the Evangelical United Brethren Church, which in 1968 united with The

Methodist Church to form The United Methodist Church. The EUBs, as they were familiarly called, were a union of the Evangelical and United Brethren denominations in 1946. Within the Baltimore Conference there were nearly one hundred congregations that had in their earlier history been United Brethren in Christ, their formal name.

The most outstanding of these congregations, indeed the Mother Church, was Old Otterbein in Baltimore. It stemmed from the German Reformed Church. A small chapel was built in 1771 on Howard's Hill near Baltimore harbor. In 1774 Philip William Otterbein was called to be their pastor and remained there until his death in 1813. A new church building, the present-day one, was built on the original site in 1785, a considerable part of the cost being borne by Otterbein himself. His role as one of the clergy who participated in Francis Asbury's ordination is well known. Bricks for the church building's construction came from England as ballast on merchant ships at the nearby dockside. It had a notable ministry, and the simple beauty of the structure made it a landmark in the city. At the same time a huge city grew up around it, and by the middle of the twentieth century only a handful of loyal members were on its rolls.

By 1976 serious structural defects appeared and services had to be suspended until extensive repairs could be made to the very old oak beams supporting the roof. The costs to do this were far beyond the ability of the tiny congregation to bear alone. They did succeed in raising $25,000. This was matched by funds from Mayor William Donald Schaefer designated for Inner Harbor restorations. It was again matched by various Maryland historical societies, for it was a national historic shrine, and from several foundations of businesses in Baltimore. Let me record here that Mayor Schaefer made Eunice an honorary citizen of Baltimore, her father's hometown, for she had no American hometown, having been born in India.

The remainder was met by gifts from across the denomination, from many episcopal areas. We addressed special letters to the several hundred local churches that bear the Otterbein name and nearly all of them helped out. Finally, the total amount was raised, no minor achievement for a small church. The repairs and renovations were completed and the church was rededicated on November 20, 1977. The preacher was Bishop Paul W. Milhouse, as former EUB and at the time president of the Council of Bishops of The United Methodist Church. The old edifice continues to add character to the city and in its own way even outshines one of its new neighbors, the stadium of the Baltimore Orioles.

GENERAL ASSIGNMENTS

Every United Methodist bishop is assigned to membership on one or more general boards or agencies of the church, an assignment beyond one's episcopal area. In 1968 I was designated to be a member of the Board of Global Ministries. During the ensuing quadrennium I was very much involved with the black revolution, as I have already recounted.

Then in 1972, the year I was transferred to Washington, I was again assigned to the Board of Global Ministries. This time I had expected to be made president of that board and must record frankly that I was disappointed that I was asked instead to be a vice president for Christian Unity. Although I was interested in Christian Unity and ecumenism, my real passion was missions. For this work I was well equipped since for more than twenty years I had been engaged in this work both as a missionary in India and a mission administrator. Nevertheless, I wasted no time brooding over the matter and tried as well as I could to fulfill my other responsibilities. Since I shall later be writing a chapter on my wide-ranging ecumenical involvement, I shall not speak more of it here.

My other principal general Church responsibility from 1976 to 1980 followed my election as secretary of the Council of Bishops. This occurred at the Council's meeting at Lincoln City, Oregon, just prior to the Portland General Conference. This was a heavy task that I undertook in succession to Bishop Ralph Alton, whose predecessors had been Bishop Roy H. Short and Bishop G. Bromley Oxnam—stalwarts all. Since we do not have a presiding bishop, much of the interim business of the Council and the Church as a whole falls to the lot of the secretary in consultation with the president of the Council of Bishops, who changes every year. One of the chief tasks of the secretary is to prepare the agenda for the semiannual meeting of the Council. The agenda is then approved by the Executive Committee.

I should not have wanted to act as secretary without the very great supporting role of my administrative secretary and assistant, Faith Richardson. Elsewhere I have paid tribute to her—a creative and tireless worker. Together we systematized a lot of the work. For example, we devised a method of enumerating each separate action of the Council as a whole and of its Executive and Standing Committees. Hitherto it had been very difficult to index the minutes. Now it became simplicity itself. We noted also that some prominent and vocal bishops were repeatedly given responsibilities to lead in worship or special assignments abroad, while others were never asked to do anything special. We therefore compiled a list for the past ten years of all such assignments so that thereafter there were more participants and equalization.

We also believed in prompt minutes. I would write up the minutes as business proceeded at our meetings and gave my handwritten copy to Mrs. Richardson at every break in the meeting. By the close of the session the minutes were also completed. The following Monday morning we would write all letters arising out of the minutes and then dispatch the full text immediately to the printer. This is typical of the pace of work of which Mrs. Richardson was capable. We were able to carry the secretary-ship of the Council of Bishops without having to employ any other assistance. It is not surprising that in 1980 Faith Richardson was chosen for a term as secretary of the General Conference, the first woman to fill that important role. Before I retired I sought for her an honorary doctor's degree. Columbia College in South Carolina immediately saw her worthiness and granted it to her.

The meetings of the Council shifted about the United States from one episcopal area to another. Our gathering in November 1976 was held in Philadelphia, with one session held in Independence Hall. We worshiped in the historic Old St. George's church and at Tindley Temple.

The following spring we assembled in Williamsburg, Virginia, where we were addressed by Virginia's governor. Still other meetings were held in Milwaukee, Oklahoma City, Colorado Springs, Boston, and Albuquerque. The mere listings of these cities indicates how the Council over a period of years was able to gain a sense of the whole Church.

Mention should be made of several memorable events that occurred while I was Council secretary. One was that at our Boston meeting the Council was addressed by the Speaker of the House of Commons, the Right Honorable George Thomas, a British Methodist layman, later awarded a peerage as Lord Tonypandy. Another session authorized the Council to meet jointly with the bishops of the African Methodist Episcopal Church, the African Methodist Episcopal Zion Church, and the Christian Methodist Episcopal Church. This was done first in Atlanta in March 1979 and several times since as a Pan-Methodist Council, later to explore some form of union for these four denominations.

Another episode, and this a sad one, was the Pacific Homes crisis in southern California during the late 1970s and early 1980s in which homes for the aging underwent a severe legal battle that shook the whole church. Pacific Homes was a system of retirement homes sponsored by the Pacific Southwest Annual Conference. A small segment of its residents brought a class action suit involving nearly $500 million against the annual conference and its officers, which later extended to various general agencies of The United Methodist Church, to the Council of Bishops, and to the whole United Methodist Church. Naturally this was of great concern to our whole denomination and for other churches as well. An immense amount of litigation followed. The details of it are a matter of record and need not be elaborated here.

The story itself is really not mine, but as secretary of the Council of Bishops I was obliged to inform myself about it and did write a considerable article on it for circulation to the bishops and to keep them on the alert. The matter directly involved Bishop Charles Golden, bishop of that area, and his successor, Bishop Jack M. Tuell. Fortunately for the whole church Bishop Tuell was trained in both law and theology. He was able to effect a settlement of the litigation and a reorganization of Pacific Homes. The cost of this undertaking came to more than $20 million but much less than the colossal sums at stake in the suits. By heroic efforts under the bishop's leadership and with the cooperation of the whole church, the funds needed were raised. The funds were in the nature of a loan to stabilize the operation of the homes, and are being paid back with interest.

Great credit also must be given to Bishop Edward L. Tullis, an officer of our General Council on Finance and Administration and an administrator of wide experience. He was of great help to Bishop Tuell in the raising of the funds. Moreover, he equipped himself as an expert witness, spending endless hours in legal depositions and testimony. We are greatly indebted to these bishops and those who supported them. Disaster was averted and the whole Church awakened to the importance of sound administration and strict fiscal accountability.

Frequently the issue of homosexuality came before the

Council of Bishops, especially as it related to the ordained ministry. The Council was often criticized for not speaking forthrightly on this. The definition of "forthrightly" seemed to mean different things to different people; that is, that the hope was the bishops would issue a statement that would dispose of the matter on the side of one or the other partisan view. Actually, the bishops did issue a statement at their meeting in Milwaukee in November 1977, but it was generally thought not to be decisive enough. Personally I never "specialized" on this subject, considering that it was better dealt with in a pastoral way rather than juridically. In my own view we should approach this issue with great compassion to all concerned, informed by Scripture and tradition as well as by clinical and scientific data. To the best of my information the latter are not yet decisive.

During the autumn of 1976 I was invited by the Korean Methodist Church to help launch an evangelistic program. This church had since 1930 enjoyed a relationship with The United Methodist Church as an affiliated autonomous denomination. The first modern Protestant missionaries to Korea had arrived in 1885—Presbyterians and Methodists arriving at Inchon on the same ship. The Koreans were found to be most receptive to the gospel, and the churches were an important factor in helping the people survive under thirty-five years of oppressive Japanese rule. By 1976 Korean Methodists numbered about 350,000, worshiping in some 1700 congregations. In 1976 their vision was that by the time of the centenary of Korean Methodism—nine years later—they would have grown to one million members and five thousand churches. It was for the launching of this program that I was invited to Seoul by all four of the Korean Methodist bishops. Having great evangelistic interest and missionary experience, I readily accepted in spite of heavy burdens at home.

During my years with the Board of Missions I was deeply involved in the rebuilding of Korean Methodism after the devastation of the Korean War, 1950–53, for I had proposed the Korea Appeal, which made this possible. I had been there only once, in 1956. What a surprising experience it was to return and find that the capital city was a burgeoning metropolis of more than seven million inhabitants, complete with emerging industry of all types, skyscrapers and all; and a modern economy, yet bristling with problems.

My schedule was more than crowded during the short five days I was in the country. While there I averaged only four hours sleep at night. Twice I gave addresses to audiences of five or six thousand people. The program of evangelism was accepted. As I met with their leaders I helped them devise a plan of reaching their goal by stages: three three-year steps in the nine years remaining. They called this the "Three-Three Plan." They did indeed reach their goal of a million members and increased their total number of congregations to about 3,500. That growth has continued to the present, more than twenty years later. There have been some critics of this rapid expansion and there were some difficulties, but given a choice I would opt every time for the problems related to growth rather than decline. Korean Methodism has shown the kind of fervor and power that characterized American Methodism during the nineteenth century.

During this very period there was considerable disunity in the Korean church over human rights issues. Two
parties emerged: the Headquarters or Constitutional
Group and a smaller Renewal Group, although there
were various factions within both of them. Happily there
had been established a Reunification Committee. I was
able to meet separately not only with the two parties but
also with the reconciling body and believe that I was able
to encourage the move toward preserving unity, which
eventually prevailed. Naturally I was pleased to have
played a small role in this process.

The government of South Korea was indeed authori-
tarian, a carefully managed society. The recent conflict
and the constant threat of its renewal contributed to a
considerable degree of suppression, but surely the South
Korean government is not to be compared with the total-
itarian regime of North Korea, as some have alleged. I did
visit some of the oppressed and families of those who
were imprisoned. Then I visited with the prime minister,
advising restraint while acknowledging the pressures he
felt. He appeared to hear me respectfully. Back in Washington I reported to the State Department, pleading on
behalf of those whose human rights had been denied
them.

Meanwhile I found a very tense relationship between
the Korean Methodist Church and our Board of Global
Missions. The matter was complicated and partly occasioned by the political atmosphere in the country. The
Board was often perceived as trying to exercise undue
influence upon the internal affairs of the church. The tensions were reflected within the missionary community.

Here again I tried to play a mediating role both in Seoul and back in the United States.

As Council secretary I had constant tasks to perform at the borders of church and state. The Korean experience demonstrated this. In the autumn of 1977 I was asked to be involved in Liberia. On October 31, 1977, United Methodist Bishop Bennie D. Warner of Liberia was inducted as vice president of Liberia at impressive cere-monies in Monrovia. Once again, I was invited to be pres-ent and was entertained very well indeed, as well as having some role in the inaugural activities. Bishop Warner had been nominated by his political group, the National True Whig Party and also had been President William R. Tolbert's choice. He was duly elected. I had known Bishop Warner for years and had appointed him to a student pastoral role while he was studying at Boston University School of Theology.

Some would severely criticize a bishop accepting such an office that he held while continuing his episcopal duties. His political work was not very time-consuming, but he would have had to surrender his church office in the event of his elevation to the presidency. President Tol-bert was himself a Baptist preacher and his predecessor, President William V. S. Tubman, was a Methodist local preacher. About the same time Bishop Abel Muzorewa had been inducted as interim prime minister of Rhodesia (later Zimbabwe). In neither case was the outcome as pos-itive as many hoped. I can say the induction of Bennie Warner, with his wife strongly helping him, gave a new burst of energy to the nation. One wonders what the future of Liberia might have been if a person of Bishop

Warner's ability, training, and experience were president of Liberia today.

In the General Conference of 1976 in Portland a renewal leave of up to three months—a kind of sabbatical—was approved for bishops. Incidentally, in both Boston and Washington Areas I had initiated such a provision for district superintendents during the sixth and final year of their tenure in order to reequip them for return to a conventional pastoral appointment. This proved helpful to them and also encouraged a periodic sabbatical leave for pastors, also subsequently approved in our *Discipline*. In any event, from mid-August till mid-November of 1978 I was able to have such a renewal leave in Israel. Though I had visited the Holy Land before, this afforded an unhurried possibility of getting fairly well acquainted with Israel, ancient and modern.

We stayed at the Albright Archeological Institute in East Jerusalem. This proved a splendid and comfortable place, with good food and stimulating company every day. We also had access to a fine library and, most of all, to the land itself. It was a great delight to have breakfast each day and to converse with biblical scholar Father Raymond Brown. Although I was not formally enrolled in academic study, I did engage—and Eunice too—in some directed reading in Bible and archeology. What a privilege to read about some ancient biblical site one day and then to be able to visit it under proper scholarly guidance the next day.

Every day possible we walked about the city of Jerusalem and got to know its sacred places well, more often than not, humming the spiritual, "walking around

Jerusalem, just like John!" More than that we met Israeli and Palestinian scholars and leaders. We toured the whole country, quite literally from Dan to Beersheba. Then there was a remarkable side tour to Cyprus, where we were guided by an American archeologist, Anita Walker. We visited with Cyprus's president and with Archbishop Chrysostomos, who had succeeded Archbishop Makarios to the see of Barnabas. We were afforded a visit to the late president-archbishop's apartment, kept just as the way he left it but with his *heart* displayed in his bedroom in a hermetically sealed plastic container!

Another trip from Jerusalem took us to the southern seaport of Eilat and then on to St. Catherine's Monastery at Mt. Sinai. It is reported that at Sinai it rains only one day a year. We chose such a day, and there was a deluge! This latter journey we made with our daughter Anne accompanying us, for she had come to Jerusalem for a fortnight's visit. We were treated most kindly by Jewish friends everywhere and beyond that obtained a sympathetic view of the plight of Palestinians in Israel. A renewal leave it was indeed!

Returning from Israel we had another exceptional privilege. It was to be present for the reopening of John Wesley's Chapel on City Road, London, in the presence of Queen Elizabeth II and Prince Philip, whom we were privileged to meet that day. Back in 1972 I had been a delegate to the British Methodist Conference in Harrogate, Yorkshire, where the proposal for this restoration of the chapel was presented. In speaking to it, I made the most-welcome proposal that The United Methodist Church should have a part in this. The proposal was approved by the Council of

Bishops but later on it was sidetracked by Hurricane Relief on the Gulf Coast. When this occurred the British Conference planned at its 1975 session to abandon the restoration. As it happened, just prior to the conference some three hundred Methodists from the Washington and Baltimore Areas were on a Wesley Heritage Tour of the United Kingdom under the direction of Dr. Frank Wanek of the Baltimore Conference. When the word came to us that Wesley's Chapel was to be leveled, I again took the floor and pleaded for another chance. We raised $1,500 on the spot and pledged another $10,000. Later, Wanek's group raised more than $100,000. This helped ignite another effort—a successful one—in which, of course, many participated, whereby the chapel was saved. Therefore All Saints Day, November 1, 1978, when the chapel was rededicated, will always carry a special significance for us.

One other deep concern I must mention. It has to do with the hostages taken by Iranian students at the American Embassy in Teheran in November 1979, a serious crisis. I am not an expert on Iran, although my wife, Eunice, and I were there as visitors for the celebration of the 2,500th anniversary of Cyrus the Great. We did at that time sense that beneath the surface of an apparently joyful occasion there was a sullenness and seething on the part of students. Having noticed and even reported this we had no idea of the depth of resentment of the Shah's regime. Now the seething became an eruption; the Shah was gone and replaced by the fanatical regime of Ayatollah Khomeini.

Soon afterward, on December 11, I was asked by the National Council of Churches to consider becoming a part of a delegation of church representatives to Iran in the interest of the hostages, particularly out of pastoral concern for them. My journal records almost daily references to this impending visit. Finally on December 22 the trip was called off. Another delegation, including a fellow bishop, did go over at the Christmas period 1979. This was not the end of it.

Meanwhile during January, a very busy time, I spent a good deal of time with John P. Adams, the community-police relations officer of the United Methodist Board of Church and Society, concerning the Iran crisis and the churches' possible role in it. As already mentioned John had performed yeoman service in behalf of the church, both at Wounded Knee and at Kent State. He was as devoted and skillful as he was fearless. During late January Adams went to Teheran and for several weeks stayed in a hotel there. He was accompanied by John Thomas, a Sioux Indian from South Dakota, who enjoyed a certain credibility with the Iranian students who were holding the hostages.

For many days following I received repeated calls from John Adams in Teheran, sometimes several calls a day and at any hour of the day or night. My international telephone bill for a month was over five hundred dollars. It was difficult to evaluate what he told me, but I followed through on every request he made of me. Dr. Alan Geyer, director of the Churches Center for Theology and Public Policy, was also deeply involved in this episode. This involved relaying telephone calls to many other people, keeping the National Council of Churches informed, telephoning and visiting the State Department, conferring with Congressional leaders and top staff at the United Nations, considering going to Iran myself, seeking needed funds, and so on. I even traveled to Strasbourg, France, to a meeting of the Executive Committee of the World Council of Churches, seeking their help. At the same time there was the possibility of my going on to Iran from there. This did not happen.

Then Adams and Thomas returned to the United States. They brought with them a huge quantity of mail from the hostages—the first that had come through. This was distributed by the two directly to family members, whose representatives met at certain airports as the emissaries crisscrossed the country, a condition imposed by the Iranian students. Later the two returned to Iran with letters and packages from families to the hostages. This was no small service. Much more significantly I am convinced, as are some others who were close to developments at the time, that they very nearly secured the release of the hostages! As events transpired, this did not happen until President Reagan's inauguration day, January 20, 1981. The whole episode was indeed dismal and its effects still linger with us.

When I was transferred to Washington during the summer of 1972 I began for the first time systematically to keep a journal. How I wish I had started the practice earlier. Mine reveals neither literary gift nor very much reflection upon my inner state of being. Nevertheless, I can account for every day of my life for the next twenty-five years and more. As I have reread my account of my eight years as bishop in Washington, I get tired all over again and am appalled to be reminded of the relentless pace I chose (perhaps I should say, *presumed*) to undertake.

It may seem that my family receded to the background during these years. Certainly I exacted a toll from my wife and children. They have all displayed tolerant and forgiving attitudes.

Life did go on. Our son married during this period. Our first grandchildren were born. Eunice's father died on January 25, 1973, in India. During the months that followed we prepared his very imperfect final book, *The Divine Yes,* for posthumous publication. It addressed effectively those who must undergo the limitations and ailments of aging and those to whom life seems to have said "No," that they may hear God's "Yes!" October 16, 1977, brought death to my close colleague and brother Joe, who meant and continues to mean much to me and to many, especially the many who are his sons and daughters in the gospel. Then on June 23, 1978, death claimed Eunice's mother, Mabel Lossing Jones, full of years—one hundred of them—and a lifetime of service and friendship to others all around the world. So life comes and goes, while for the believing Christian, life is perceived as eternal.

Let me add a further word here in tribute to my late brother Joe. Through his entire life we were exceedingly close. I could always turn to him for counsel in times of uncertainty. There were periods in which we were in touch almost daily and without exception he was available and helpful. To him I could unburden myself without any reserve. I miss him sorely and daily. It is a blessing to me that my sister, Alice Mathews Neill, continues to be for me a wise counselor—and on the same terms.

On August 31, 1980, I retired—for the first time! When I was elected bishop in 1960, I was to have served until

1984, but new church law shortened the term. I was disappointed for I was still full of energy and plans, but our times are in the hands of the Lord and are best left there.

As I look back over what I have written, I may seem to have spoken as if all were sweetness and light. This is not entirely true, of course; for I am all too aware of shortcomings and failures. A side of me can be petty and mean. I can lose my temper—but not for long. I have had an abundance of harsh critics who have given me many grounds for being more humble than I am.

Upon our retirement a purse of about $15,000 was collected for us by the Washington Area. We contributed this entirely toward a professorship, which was to be called the James K. and Eunice Jones Mathews Chair of World Christianity at Wesley Theological Seminary in Washington, D.C. Any compensation due me for teaching at the seminary was also assigned to this. It finally took the shape of a million dollar insurance policy upon Eunice's life—she was the better risk—so that upon her death the chair will be inaugurated. The money we contributed as did others paid up the premiums. We are somewhat amused by the fact that the seminary president often inquires as to Eunice's state of health. He may be just a little disheartened that she springs from a long heritage of longevity!

In a farewell service at the Baltimore Conference addresses were made by Supreme Court Justice Harry Blackmun and Congressman John Brademas, Majority Leader of the House of Representatives. These appeared later in the Congressional Record. So we were sent upon our way.

10

"ON JOURNEYINGS OFT"

The title of this chapter derives from 2 Corinthians 11:26. It stands out among the many *arpeggios* that characterize this remarkable letter of Paul. The phrase "on journeyings oft" has been borrowed frequently, and I do not hesitate to borrow it here in an account of some of my own travels.

Journeying is one of the things missionaries do: they are *sent* and they go. Sometimes I have defined a missionary as "an evangelist without boundaries," for they are inveterate boundary-crossers. This is what I have been for the past six decades. Then as a Methodist minister I have also been an itinerant. Indeed, "itinerancy" is one of the peculiar descriptions of our calling; it is a part of our idiom. Bishops, in their turn, are also a part of this itinerant ministry.

The other name for bishop is "general superintendent," meaning a person with responsibility for our whole denomination or "connection." This is another word from the Methodist vocabulary, for a congregation is not an independent entity but each is related to every other congregation. We regard this as theologically appropriate. Our bishops enjoy a real collegiality, with one of their number chosen each year to preside over the semiannual sessions of our Council of Bishops. We have no overall presiding bishop.

One of the unique requirements of bishops of The United Methodist Church is that they are to "travel throughout the connection." This we continue to do as needs arise and as we may be assigned by the Council. This I have done, at the time of this writing, for nearly forty years. In the course of bishops' "journeyings oft," they are consumed by another burden Paul mentions in 2 Corinthians 11; namely, "I am under daily pressure because of my anxiety for all the churches."

This is familiar enough, historically, for the apostolic role of bishops. Paul himself is a model for this concern for he was himself a belated member of the original circle of apostles of an itinerant Lord. John Wesley traveled incessantly about Britain, including twenty-one trips to Ireland alone, for more than fifty years. He did this on horseback (or near the end of his life in a specially fitted coach or carriage) for a total of about one quarter of a million miles—an incredible record for his day.

It was similar in the case of Francis Asbury, who over a period of about forty years traveled throughout the emerging American nation. His *Journal* tells the story—itself a valuable historical document. In all he tallied about the same mileage as Wesley, and in the course of his itineration he saw more of America and had been seen by more Americans than any other person of the day. The roads traversed by this extraordinary ecclesiastic were mainly of two kinds: abominable or nonexistent. Very often he had to blaze his own pioneer trails through the wilderness. It is commonly said that he drew the map of his country by the hoofprints of his horses. Interestingly enough, he even records the names of some of these faithful beasts—Jane, Foxx, and Spark, a rather touching note from the pen of this apostolic man. His successors have followed in this tradition, though their means of conveyance have changed drastically.

Most bishops have kept rather careful records of their travel. Bishop Francis J. McConnell, for example, noted that while he was on his first assignment to the Denver Area he journeyed about 42,000 miles a year. Much of this was by railway, and it was commonly the courtesy of railroads to issue free passes for Methodist bishops to travel on their trains. Bishop Joseph C. Hartzell of Africa computed that he had traveled a million and a half miles while he was assigned to Africa. John W. Robinson, a longtime episcopal leader in India, traveled more than a million miles during a very full career.

Altogether by 1997 I find that I have covered nearly four and a half million miles. This has involved twelve trips around the world. My records reveal 220 one-way trips across the Atlantic; 55 trips to India; some 28 journeys to Africa and 16 to Latin America; a dozen trips to Japan and Korea, and so on.

No effort can be made to detail all this but a sampling may make clear my extensive involvement. For example, just before Christmas (1949) I returned to India for the first time. On this occasion I flew out in a very noisy Canadian version of the DC-4. It was a demanding journey indeed. My departure date was such that I missed Christmas with my family. Somehow I had allowed myself to be persuaded to get to India in time for some meeting at that very period. This I now know was a mistake and is one of many illustrations of how I did not always put family considerations first.

Since I had last visited southern Asia in 1946, Mother India had had twins—India and Pakistan, the latter itself oddly divided into East Pakistan and West Pakistan, the two parts separated by a thousand miles of India. Independence had come in August 1947. I recall having sent greetings to Jawaharlal Nehru at the time. There followed weeks and months of chaos on both sides of the border with West Pakistan. Tens of thousands were slaughtered and other millions fled both ways across the border. Many of them for some years camped on a road just outside Bishop Pickett's residence in Delhi. When I traveled into Pakistan—once part of India—I was sharply reminded that I was *not* in India. This took getting used to and I came to a very changed situation where the Church was challenged to be a part of nation-building.

The visit also afforded opportunity to further one's acquaintance with the bishops. Bishop J. R. Chitambar, the first Indian Methodist bishop, had died in 1940, leaving behind a saintly wife and a wonderful family that included two daughters, one of whom became a professor in Isabella Thoburn College, and three sons: a senior pilot of Indian Airlines, another a heart surgeon, and a third who was principal of Allahabad Agricultural Institute. Bishop Chitambar usually wore a clerical shirt and a fancy turban of a style characteristic of India's Northwest Frontier. It was quite a sight. Once on a visit to the United States an American approached him inquiring of his identity. When he replied that he was from India, the man commented, "Well, I knew you must be from somewhere!"

Then in 1947 Bishop John W. Robinson died. He was a missionary of broad experience and a bishop as indefatigable as he was able administrator, and a uniquely gifted preacher as well. The year 1949 saw the death of Bishop Brenton T. Badley, a skilled linguist, born in India and a specialist on the Indian culture. All of these men are of most happy memory.

Other bishops followed these stalwarts. The first was J. Waskom Pickett, who had been elected in 1935. At one time or another he had administered all four episcopal areas in India and in 1950 headed the Delhi Area. He had served as professor, pastor, district missionary, and editor. From 1930 until his election as bishop he had served as secretary of the National Christian Council of India. During this time he engaged in the study of the Christian mass movement of India upon which monumental study he established his reputation. He possessed such varied gifts that, as a colleague stated of him, "All the things a bishop is supposed to do, Pickett did well." His wife, Ruth, daughter of Bishop John W. Robinson, was a beautiful person and charming hostess skilled in human relations. It was a delight to be in their home as I was frequently during this visit. He was a man of vision and of action. We continued to work well together during the years to come.

Another was Bishop Shot K. Mondol to whom reference has already been made. Elected in 1941, the second Indian national bishop, he served in the Hyderabad Area for sixteen years and for another eight years in Delhi, all this with unusual grace and dignity. He saw to it that he came to know India's leaders personally.

Bishop Clement D. Rockey was resident in the Lucknow Area, which included Burma for a time, and later presided in West Pakistan. Clement had been born and bred in India, was a master of languages, an able administrator, and a theological professor. He was a little rough-hewn, but few persons knew and loved the land and the people more than he did. He in turn was beloved by all. For some years he presided over expanding industrial areas in the states of Bihar and West Bengal and planted many churches. He was full of Indian lore that he delighted to relate to children or anyone else who would listen.

The fourth bishop was John A. Subhan, who presided at the time over the Bombay Area, which included the Bombay and Gujarat Conferences. He was born a Muslim but was converted and baptized at an early age, becoming an Anglican. He studied for a time for the Roman Catholic priesthood but finally became a Methodist. Subhan was an accomplished linguist, at home in half a dozen languages. Along the way he was a theological professor and the author of a number of books, as well as a recognized scholar of Islam. Born in a Muslim mystic (Sufi) family, his autobiography is entitled *How a Sufi Found His Lord*. He was a fine man, a committed evangelist, and a passionate and sensitive soul.

These four leaders are mentioned not only for the important leadership roles they played but because it was of the utmost importance to relate effectively to them if one were to administer southern Asia for the Board of Missions. Moreover, all of them helped to shape my ministry. I found them all congenial and cooperative. In meeting them one naturally became acquainted with their associates and with leaders of other denominations, both national men and women as well as Methodist foreign missionaries of whom there were more than three hundred at the time. Later I hope I can mention a little more about some of these people, many of whom were so devoted to their work that it could be said that the world was not worthy of them.

Bishop Pickett used to say that I had probably seen more of the work of Methodism in southern Asia than any other person. This may seem an exaggeration, but whereas the bishops I have just mentioned worked largely within their areas, I traveled over the whole country. In 1950 there were about 550,000 Methodists in India and 35,000 in West Pakistan. There were in southern Asia eleven annual conferences spanning at least twelve language areas and divided into sixty-four districts. There were hundreds of churches and preaching points. To this must be added about five hundred village schools and 120 primary, secondary, and high schools attended by more than 30,000 students. We were involved in what became higher secondary schools (junior colleges), two degree-granting colleges founded by Methodists, plus cooperation in several others. Then there were fourteen hospitals and twenty-seven dispensaries—and on and on and on. My visits led me to many of these institutions, my means of transportation ranging all the way from camelback, oxcarts, horse-drawn vehicles, and bicycles to trains and planes—sometimes I even walked!

While on this journey I also spent a week in Burma, where most of our work was concentrated around Rangoon. Methodists had been in this predominantly Buddhist country since 1879. The small annual conference there was linked with the Central Conference of southern Asia. The land was long under British rule. The Baptists had a large following, especially among the non-Burman subnational groups such as the Karens, the Kachins, and the Shans. Christians in all made up only 3 percent of the total population of about twenty million. There were three thousand Methodists and we had twelve missionaries. These were able ones and cannot be too highly praised for reestablishing their work after the devastating war. Several of them had made their way by foot on the long trek to India just ahead of the invading Japanese. We had nineteen schools of good quality in Burma. One was at Kolaw some 200 miles north of Rangoon. I recall a flying trip there in a tiny plane, called a Dove. Kolaw grew the most gorgeous sweet peas I have ever seen. Indeed, as I returned to the capital city, I was entrusted with a huge basket of these flowers and two Pekinese dogs to deliver to friends in Rangoon. This service was not a part of my job description. Work among Chinese in Burma was also notable. I left Burma with high hopes for the future, though later developments did not justify these hopes.

The year 1950 marked the end of Burma's relation to Indian Methodism and its new linkage with Southeast Asia. Bishop James M. Thoburn had inaugurated our work both in Burma (1879) and Malaya (1885) and later still in the Philippines (1890); so I proceeded to Singapore for my first visit there to attend the organizing session of the Southeast Asia Central Conference, which was to encompass Burma, Malaya, Sumatra, and Sarawak (Borneo). In the course of this visit there was a huge youth meeting that I was privileged to address. While there I stayed at the famous Raffles' Hotel for one night (rates were cheap then) and then found accommodations with missionaries. Singapore was a delightful city then with a distinct Chinese flavor, but with few hints of its becoming the teeming metropolis and independent state that it was to become later. At this conference, my colleague at the Board of Missions, Dr. Raymond T. Archer, was elected bishop, the wise choice of a quiet, able, and scholarly man. I laugh as I recall that I too received two votes for bishop on one of the ballots. This did not really set a trend.

It was a great joy for me to rejoin my family after the longest absence (six months) I had ever subjected them and myself to. My faithful secretary, Marjorie Koller, and my colleagues had carried my administrative load during my lengthy absence. We were indeed a team. I discovered that when one returned from such a journey one was expected to tour intensively across the country and tell the story. This I did.

What I have just recounted about a 1950 missionary tour of southern Asia is, of course, only one of scores of similar though briefer journeys. Again and again through the years I (or often Eunice and I) have returned to that subcontinent—several times to the newly opened (1954) land of Nepal. Many of the pioneer missionaries there were our personal friends.

My introduction to Africa in 1954 deserves a chapter in itself. My itinerary included Nigeria, the Gold Coast (Ghana), where I stayed with friends formerly resident in

India; the Belgian Congo, later Zaire (1960) and again Congo (1997); Northern Rhodesia (now Zambia); Southern Rhodesia (now Zimbabwe); Portuguese East Africa (now Mozambique); South Africa and Kenya. A whole new world hitherto hidden from my eyes was opened to me. Little did I suppose that through the years I would return to this vast continent—nearly thirty times in all—and that I would visit more than half of its fifty-one nations. Even less did I imagine that I would thirty years later serve as bishop in Africa (Zimbabwe). In 1954 only two countries were independent (I would hesitate to say free). By 1997 *all* of Africa's countries were self-governing.

Then in 1956 I ventured for the first time into East Asia. This journey led to Japan, Korea, Okinawa, Taiwan, Hong Kong, Philippines, Sarawak, Singapore, Sumatra, Malaya, Burma, as well as India. By this time my global awareness was expanding at a phenomenal rate. My colleagues who administered these regions for the Board of Missions constantly reminded me that I must go to the territories they had learned to love. They helped me immensely in opening doors for me and I certainly found their enthusiasm to be well-grounded.

Then came my visits to Hispanic America, beginning in the mid-1950s and continuing for a total of some twenty journeys to the present. Later still Australia, New Zealand, and the islands of the Pacific were added to these experiences. Firsthand, I could observe how missionary obedience had literally led to the ends of the earth. Yet never did I go to a place that outreached God's love or find a people I did not love. Though I never ceased to engage in missionary visitation, I gradually moved into travel that was related to the Ecumenical Movement as such.

WILLINGEN, 1952

My first experience of a significant ecumenical meeting was at the session of the International Missionary Council held in the village of Willingen in West Germany for two weeks in July 1952. Willingen was located in the beautiful hills of Waldecke about 80 miles east of Cologne. I recall visiting in Cologne on my way to the meeting and I was deeply impressed with the colossal cathedral there surrounded by blocks of destruction, a legacy of World War II.

The some two hundred delegates were quartered in the homes of local Christians. My own hosts were hospitable folk, apologetic about Germany's role in the war. They did their best to make us at home and went out of their way to make amends for the past.

A host of missionary "greats" were at the meeting; among them John Mackay, the chairman, a Latin-American specialist and president of Princeton Seminary; Lesslie Newbigin, bishop of the Church of South India; Charles Ranson, general secretary, International Missionary Council (IMC); M. A. C. (Max) Warren, head of the Church Missionary Society; Hendrik Kraemer; W. A. Visser't Hooft, the WCC's general secretary; and Professor Walter Freytag—to mention only a few. Of no less significance were the "younger" churchmen: J. Russell Chandran and Rajah B. Manikam of India, W. T. Huang of Formosa, G. Baez-Camargo of Mexico, John Wesley

Shungu of Congo, and many others representing some fifty countries in all.

The meeting was of special meaning to our German hosts. This was voiced by Professor Walter Freytag and Dr. Karl Hartenstein, German missionary leaders; Dr. Reinhold von Thadden, founder of *Kirchentag*; and by Bishop Otto Dibelius and Bishop Hans Lilje, both of whom preached at the conference. Especially notable too were the outstanding Bible lessons that Hendrik Kraemer gave on 1 Corinthians. Even more interesting was an informal presentation he gave on the launching of the church on the island of Bali. One session was held at the University of Marburg, where delegate Kenneth Scott Latourette of Yale was given an honorary degree.

The basic theme of the consultation was "The Missionary Obligation of the Church." Intense preparation for the meeting had been made over a period of two years. It took the form of a study conference in which all participants engaged through the medium of five discussion groups. The theme was explored from every conceivable angle. Plenary sessions were marked by outstanding lectures on such subjects as "The Covenant and the Great Commission" and "The Church Under the Cross." In many respects the tone of discussion was sobering. It stressed the testing time the Christian mission had been through, and the even more testing period that was ahead. The absence of representatives from China was particularly noted and lamented.

There was the frankest dialogue between representatives of the so-called Older and Younger Churches, a terminology already outmoded though very appropriate for

Madras in 1938. American participants had to endure a certain *hauteur* on behalf of some of those from Britain and the Continent.

As a neophyte I did participate with a certain sense of awe, stimulated by the exalted nature of the discussions and the standing of its leaders. The theological level of discourse enforced ever thereafter the need to think and speak of missions in a more theological way. Willingen was a ringing affirmation of the missionary summons. It was an awakening to a brand-new missionary situation. It was a call to action and a call to prayer. It became a watchword after Willingen that "the church exists for mission as fire exists for burning." But most of all for me I carried away from this meeting new and renewed friendships, which have continued until broken by deaths. For example, I recall long conversations with Carl Michalson on the hills of Waldecke as together we struck the walking pace from which comradeship is generated.

On all continents there was a follow-up of Willingen—such was its stimulus to the missionary movement. This was certainly true in the United States and Canada. For a number of questions had been raised; for example: What does it mean theologically and practically to fulfill the Christian mission in an ecumenical era? What of the tensions between an *Inter-Church Aid* (relief) and *Missionary* prospectives in addressing the world? This was a surprisingly divisive issue that tended to align the International Missionary Council opposite the World Council of Churches. What is the relation of the missionary imperative to the kingdom of God? We have continued to wrestle with such questions. I did a series of five lectures on these topics and delivered them on three occasions.

My ecumenical involvement increased after Willingen. Nearly every summer thereafter there were follow-up sessions in Europe. Travel costs in Europe during the 1950s were still moderate as was the expense of food and lodging. Therefore I was able to visit in turn such places as Herrenalb in Germany, Davos in Switzerland, Spittal in Austria, Thessaloniki, Greece, and East London for a wonderful session in St. Katharine's. Other gatherings were held at Oxford University and finally at University College at Accra, Ghana. The mere mention of these places calls to my mind wonderful experiences that they afforded. At Herrenalb I first met our great friends Robert and Patricia Nelson. In Thessaloniki I formed friendship with Count Klaus von Bismarck, who displayed a deep missionary commitment. He was a grand-nephew of the great German chancellor. Following the same meeting I traveled on a memorable journey into Macedonia with Anglican clergyman A. W. Blaxall of South Africa. He knew Jan Smuts and indeed closely resembled him in appearance. He had served Britain in Serbia during the first World War and knew the Serbian language. He proved to be a very agreeable traveling companion.

St. Katharine's was renowned for its social programs in East London. I asked its very high church rector how it was that the church's program was addressed to the very poor. His enlightening response was that where high value is placed on the Holy Sacraments there was an accompanying great regard for the needs of marginalized people who were also a part of Christ's Body—the church.

Not infrequently through the years my foreign travel has been cast in a trouble-shooting mode. Though I have had no inclination to rejoice in the situations that occasioned these ventures, I always was pleased to be a part of attempting to ameliorate them. To my surprise, I found that I apparently had considerable aptitude for this sort of thing. Various demands have led me to Korea, Chile, to various parts of Africa, the Philippines and, of course, to India, as well as to Mexico. Among these I choose two for brief elaboration. The fact was that in late 1958 a serious split arose in the Methodist Church of Mexico, which had become autonomous in 1930.

During the session of the General Conference of the Methodist Church of Mexico meeting in Monterrey, September 1958, Dr. Eleazar Guerra was elected bishop, succeeding Bishop Zapata in that office. Since Bishop Guerra had already been bishop for four terms prior to Bishop Zapata's term, he did not have hands laid on him in consecration to that office for the new term. Already within the Methodist Church of Mexico there was a group, mostly of young ministers and laymen, who were dissatisfied with Bishop Guerra's administration and who were desperately opposed to his reelection. They had established in the summer of 1958 a Wesley Group, for the purpose of purifying the church. As time went on it became more of a political group aimed at opposing Bishop Guerra's election and assuming office again. They were a fine group of Methodists, though undoubtedly unwise in some of their approaches to their very real problem. When, however, Bishop Guerra did not have hands laid on him in consecration, they seized upon this technicality to repudiate him as bishop. They took the position that there *was* no bishop of the church of Mexico. Tension rose in the church during the fall of 1958, and when the Central Mexico Conference met in Mexico City in January 1959, there was a split in the body. The Wesley Group met in the historic Gante Street Church and elected its own president while Bishop Guerra and the rest of the conference met in another church. This came to a head while the General Board of Missions was in session at Buck Hill Falls, Pennsylvania.

The matter became so serious that the Board of Missions determined that, even though we had not been invited, a delegation should be sent to Mexico City in order to try to effect a reconciliation. Therefore, Bishop Richard C. Raines, Dr. James E. Ellis, and I left the annual meeting at Buck Hill Falls to proceed immediately to Mexico City.

My two colleagues asked me to take a lead in the proceeding. Dr. Ellis, who administered the Mexican work, felt too close to the work, and Bishop Raines felt he was too remote. As one familiar with the details and as Dr. Ellis's superior, the burden fell on me. This I was pleased to undertake, partly because Dr. William Butler, who pioneered American Methodism in India, had also launched our work in Mexico.

In order to make clear the reason for our coming, we three emissaries prepared a statement of purpose while on the plane. It was read to representatives of both parties who met us at the airport in Mexico City. This served to clear the air both in our own minds and in that of the brothers and sisters in Mexico; and it gave us a point of reference throughout the whole discussion. This statement was followed in every respect.

We had dinner with three young missionaries of the Division of World Missions upon arrival. This enabled us to get a fairly objective picture of the situation, though it must be said that the missionaries were personally more sympathetic to the Wesley Group. They had at the same time bent every effort toward trying to reconcile the two factions. Bishop Guerra mentioned several times his appreciation of these sincere efforts.

On Friday morning, January 23, Bishop Guerra came to our hotel with a party of eighteen ministers and laymen. The meeting lasted eight hours, during which they had every opportunity to state their position frankly and fully. Everything was put both in Spanish and English. The Board representatives made no effort to comment on their statement and only asked questions that would elucidate their presentation. The meetings opened and closed with worship. In general, the line of questioning was as follows:

1. What is the current state of the Church in Mexico?
2. How did this come about?
3. What is the opponents' position?
4. What, if anything, can be done about it?

On Saturday, January 24, the Wesley Group, with ten representatives led by the Reverend Maurillo Olivera, presented a well-documented case for their side of the dispute during the following seven hours. The procedure was precisely the same as with the other body. At the close of each session we made it clear that neither group could expect to gain all of its points if a settlement were to be arrived at.

An excerpt from the statement will afford a sense of what we undertook:

Dear Brothers and Sisters of the Methodist Church of Mexico:

The Board of Missions of the Methodist Church has learned with deep distress of the misunderstandings and tensions which threaten the unity of our sister communion—the autonomous Methodist Church of Mexico.

The Board's interest, of course, is rooted in long historic, as well as present, mutual relationships. It has seemed to the Board of Missions that if several of its representatives were sent to Mexico City, they might be in a position not only to be acquainted first-hand with the situation itself as it directly affects the Board's activities in relation to the work in Mexico, but might also be of service to our Methodist brethren in Mexico in their present circumstances.

We come, therefore, to hear and learn from those who may desire to see us. Our minds and hearts are open. We have no plans nor commitments, except to express brotherly, Christian concern for the unity and welfare of the Church. Though we do not come in response to an invitation, we dare to believe we will be welcome, for we believe our fellow-Methodists in Mexico share these very same concerns.

The line of settlement became fairly clear to the Board representatives by the time we were through with the second delegation. Indeed, each of the three of us wrote down the gist of a possible solution and they coincided in remarkable degree. We then united them into one document and presented our proposals for solution to the three missionaries with whom we had contact on the first night. They were entirely in agreement with them. The proposals were then put to Bishop Guerra, who was in agreement. They were not put to Mr. Olivera because he had stated that he was ready to accept any solution we proposed.

We then called together representatives of both groups to meet with us on Saturday evening, January 24. We determined to present the proposed solution in two parts. First of all, a preamble that summarized our discussion and six propositions were presented. If these were agreed to, then the detailed solution was to be presented to them. They did agree to the propositions that rather generously set forth basic views of both parties. The group then assembled at 9:00 P.M. Saturday and continued until 2:30 A.M. Sunday. At first they had some difficulty facing a proposed solution. They then met separately for two hours and came back together in a much more agreeable and considerate attitude.

The next afternoon both parties met again and signed an agreement written both in English and in Spanish. At that meeting also, Bishop Guerra signed in the presence of all a declaration that he would accept the laying on of hands and that he would neither seek nor accept the office of bishop following his present four-year term.

On the evening of January 25, Bishop Raines preached in the Gante Church and afterward consecrated Bishop Guerra according to the *Discipline* of the Methodist

Church of Mexico. There seemed to be a genuine spirit of reconciliation at the conference that unanimously ratified the agreement. Two district superintendents were elected from the Guerra party and one from the Wesley Group. Mr. Olivera of the Wesley party was given cabinet-status, thus giving equal representation to both parties in the cabinet.

Neither the mediators nor the contestants were under any illusions about the difficulty of *abiding* by this agreement, but we felt that a genuine reconciliation had been brought about. This reconciliation has continued as has a friendly and cooperative relationship between our two churches. A few years later the Council of Bishops met in Mexico City, the only time it has assembled outside the United States. Later still a concordat relation was reached between these two sister denominations, which continues nearly forty years later.

Among my treasured letters is one from Dr. G. Baez-Camargo, revered theological professor, who thanked me profusely for my role as mediator and reconciling agent in "the most critical period" in Mexican Methodism. I am proud to have had a part in this effort, which had enduring results.

Another venture in trouble-shooting was my involvement in a special session of the Philippine Central Conference in November-December 1968. The task was to elect two bishops for that Central Conference. An earlier session had failed in election of any bishop after many ballots. I was determined to do my best to help them succeed this time.

First of all, I concentrated very hard and learned the names of all the delegates. Whenever there were those who sought the floor, I called upon them by name. Of course, this could not be done at larger conferences, but in this instance the effort led to confidence in the chair.

Moreover, I knew that both laity and ministers in the Philippines prided themselves in their knowledge of the *Discipline* and wished it to be adhered to with great strictness. Many of the lay delegates were lawyers. Before leaving the United States, I tried to get a copy of the newest *Discipline* that the 1968 General Conference had enacted earlier that year. The best the book editor, my good friend Emory Bucke, could do was to supply me with the galley proofs. Thus I was the only one present who had the most up-to-date copy. Whenever a question was raised concerning a legal matter, I would hold up the relevant page of galley proof. This seemed to carry with it something of the authority of Moses lifting up the tablets of the law.

In addition, more calls for episcopal rulings at law arise in Philippine Methodism than from any other quarter in our Church. A formal request for ruling must be made in writing and responded to in writing by the bishop in the chair—usually following due notice. Two such requests were made of me on two successive days. A friendly missionary advised me of this in advance in both instances. Rising very early in the morning to do my research and writing, I was prepared both times to respond immediately. In accordance with our practice, such rulings must then be submitted to the Judicial Council to be affirmed or denied. Both of mine were in due course affirmed. No more such rulings were requested at that session.

By such means and by pleading with the conference to be at its best, they overcame rivalries and in fact did elect two bishops: Paul Granadosin and Jose Ferrer. Both succeeded admirably in the office, and I was pleased to have had a part in their consecration. A little footnote is warranted. Bishop Valencia, my host, and I made a courtesy call on the presiding bishop of the Aglapayan Church, an offshoot from Rome, whose bishops carried "apostolic succession." I suggested he join us in the consecration service. Bishop Valencia, who would have had to live with the consequences, thought better of this and the invitation was not given. If it had been, what consternation it might have caused—two United Methodist bishops in the apostolic succession!

Other special overseas assignments by the Council of Bishops took me to Central Conferences in India on several occasions. In 1980 the General Conference gave authority for the India Central Conference to sever ties to The United Methodist Church to join in church union with the Church of North India. Subsequently the Central Conference in India voted *not* to consummate this union. This left our church in India in limbo. I negotiated successfully for it to rejoin The United Methodist Church temporarily until steps could be taken for it to become an autonomous Methodist Church in India, which in due course came into being.

There was another dimension of travel related to family. We as parents have always felt under obligation to make it possible for our children to become acquainted with as much as possible of our wonderful world. So it was that in the spring of 1959 I took our eldest daughter, Anne, for a month of visitation on the west coast of South America. Our collie had seven puppies at about this time. The sale of six of them paid for Anne's trip! The following year came the "turn" for our second daughter, Janice, to accompany her father around the entire South American continent, beginning in Brazil and proceeding to Uruguay and Argentina. There followed a marvelous portage by lake and bus over the southern Andes to Chile and thence north along the west coast. Our girls have always regarded these trips as highly significant for their young lives, and they have continued a similar tradition with their own families.

By the end of 1962 our son, Stanley, approached his eleventh birthday. Mindful of his sisters' experience, he complained, "I never get to go anywhere!" That inequity was soon remedied for I took him around the world with me—on half-fare, which the airlines still offered to those under twelve years of age. His ticket cost $669.73.

This particular journey was in fulfillment of the quad-rennial plan of episcopal visitation. In this instance it was longer than usual because the intention was to refresh missionary contacts in Africa and Asia, which had been established in the previous decade. I also asked my brother Joe to accompany me, for I was anxious to intro-duce him into the global orbit since his emphasis and work were tending more and more in that direction. His presence was welcome as a good companion and an insightful observer. The tour extended from February 23 till April 12, 1963.

We began by flying from New York City to Lisbon. Our short stay there afforded a reminder of the role the Portuguese had played in exploration and colonization in South America, Africa, and Asia. It was good to see something of their home base and to taste briefly of their culture.

We proceeded to Liberia for a short trip inland and to participate in the Liberia Annual Conference under the leadership of my colleague Bishop Prince A. Taylor. He enjoyed good relations with President William V. S. Tubman. Contacts we made served well for further relationships with Liberia that were to follow.

At this point we were to experience a bitter disappointment. We had been invited for a visit with Dr. Albert Schweitzer at Lambarene. A change of plane schedules made it necessary to cancel this portion of our itinerary. We discovered that in the Africa of that day you could not always "get there from here," particularly at the time you intended.

Therefore we proceeded to the Congo. The country was still trying to find itself after its independence, which had come with surprising rapidity in 1960. When I had been there in 1954 the Belgian governor-general had said, "Independence? Come back in a hundred years and we'll talk about it." That was according to the colonialists' calendar no doubt; may we say that God's timetable was different? Independence came six years later, ready or not! In the light of subsequent developments in the Congo or Zaire, it may be as well to put the situation in some perspective. Due to my India connection I was quick to realize that Congo had almost exactly the same geographical size of India; that is, the equivalent of the eastern half of the United States. Yet when India became independent in 1947 it had a population of some 390 million; Zaire had only 13 million, one-thirtieth of the size of India. In 1947 India had had nearly two hundred years of British rule and could boast hundreds of thousands of college graduates. Congo in 1960 had just *thirteen*! The odds against early development were exceedingly poor, and it is small wonder that Zaire's early years have been so chaotic.

We had the experience of being flown for more than a week in a single-motored plane over much of central and southern Congo. This was in a mission plane piloted by Paul Anderson, a missionary aviator from Texas. He was competent but something of a cowboy, we thought. Flying over miles and miles of trackless equatorial rain forest with few emergency-landing places is not an experience for the faint of heart. Yet God took care of us as did our many African and missionary hosts who offered us their hospitality along the way. My son many years later revealed to me that he was terrified as we traveled in that tiny plane. But he and his uncle were introduced to the many facets of missionary work, which always leaves a lasting and often life-changing impression on one.

African culture impressed us deeply. For example, we encountered the word *Muntu*. Literally, it means man, and it is a word found in one form or another in the Bantu languages. Yet it means far more than man—it speaks of humanity, humanness, humanism. It rings of humanity related to all things; to nature, to music, to dance. As one young African woman said, "This is a very precious word to us." This carries over, I think, into African American culture, with its deep sense of humanity. It is notable that two basic forms of American music, jazz and the spiritual, show this quality to a marked degree. We proceeded to northern Rhodesia (Zambia), visited the ecumenical center near Ndola, and entered southern Rhodesia (Zimbabwe) at Victoria Falls. It has been my privilege to glimpse this natural wonder a number of times since, and it always seems to me that to describe it as awe-inspiring is an understatement. Imagine how it must have appeared to a boy who had been born and reared in New Jersey. Meanwhile my brother Joe was inspired with a kind of ecstasy as, Zorba-like, he danced on the rim of the chasm.

Those were momentous days for the Church in southern Africa. Independence was not to come to southern Rhodesia until 1980, but with unerring vision Bishop Ralph Dodge was blazing a pioneer trail in his insistence upon higher education for as many Africans as possible. The church owes much to his leadership as of course to that of his colleague, Bishop Newell S. Booth, and those who preceded them. The stirrings for freedom were very evident at the time of our visit, and many people questioned me about India's struggle for freedom. I was pleased to commend to them Gandhi's nonviolence methods. A prescient American consul-general in Salisbury (Harare) estimated that freedom was about fifteen years in the future and his guess was very near the mark. Our very brief stay in Johannesburg gave me occasion to observe how strong the grip of *apartheid* was upon South Africa, and I did not like what I saw.

Our trail led to India, where during a week's stay I was delighted to introduce our son, Stan, and Joe to what had become my second homeland. Young Stan is the proud owner of a book autographed by Prime Minister Jawaharlal Nehru during our visit with him on March 22, 1963. During one nocturnal journey to Sat Tal Christian Ashram, established in the lower Himalayas by Stan's grandfather, we were fortunate in seeing a tiger with his kill and a black leopard—rare indeed. We completed our circumnavigation of the globe by proceeding to Hong Kong, where we stayed at the charming Hotel of the August Moon; to Taiwan, and then Tokyo, where we stayed in an ancient Japanese inn while we observed the contemporary scene in that rapidly recovering country; to Honolulu, and then directly home.

My son kept a careful diary, which he presented with pictures to his school classmates. It made for exciting reading. This journal he concluded with these words, which seemed to me to justify taking him along:

> I think this trip has been very worthwhile. I think this trip was taken just at the time the world is at its height in politics and in beauty for this decade. This trip has shown me the hate in Leopoldville, the refugees and the homeless in India and Hong Kong, and the good job missionaries are doing all over the world. I will remember this trip all my life, and it will help me in my later years because you can't face the world until you know what the world is facing.

Stan, not yet twelve, also tried his hand at a little poetry. I share two samples:

Victoria Falls

Listen to the sound of its roaring calls
It comes from the deep, wide waterfalls.
And from its mountainous clouds of spray;
You get rain even on the sunniest day.
And the name of the falls that makes the sound
Comes from the queen who long ago was crowned.
The Zambesi river looks easy to swim
But the currents are strong and the chances are slim.
My short little verses must come to an end
But the Falls will remain for me a very dear friend.

On Indian Trains

Piles of cinders, clouds of smoke
Making people cough and choke.
Filled with noise and eerie sights.
Coaches swaying
Muslims praying
Children screaming
People teeming.
Thundering down the narrow rail:
Here comes the roaring Indian Mail.

As I have said, whenever possible my wife, Eunice, accompanied me: this, of course, enriched the travel experience in every way. For instance, in late August of 1970 I had to attend an ecumenical meeting in Geneva. We linked the trip with our vacation. So it was that we were able to attend a performance of the Passion Play at Oberammergau. This charming Bavarian village is worthy of a visit in its own right, but the experience was enhanced by the lovely inn where we stayed. The son of the proprietor appeared in the drama as did many of the villagers.

To this we added a journey by car through the Austrian Dolomites and into Yugoslavia. We fondly recall our short stay in Plitvice National Park. This gem affords a superb view on a mountainside of a series of small mineral-laden lakes of various shades of blue and green water, each feeding into another which constitute a landscape of surpassing beauty. It is said that Julius Caesar journeyed from Rome to see this great sight and it is not surprising that he did. Add to this the unique attraction of the Dalmatian coast and the scores of towns and cities that made up this now troubled land. Add to that the desperate experience of locking the keys of our hired Volkswagen in the car. And add to that the fact that there was on hand an auto mechanic who opened the door. He chanced to be the boyhood chum of the only person we knew from Yugoslavia, now Professor Paul Mojzes, son of a Methodist pastor near Belgrade.

Another vacation period enabled us to have our children with us. One daughter Jan was a translator in French for the well-known Church and Society Conference of the World Council of Churches in Geneva, 1966; our other daughter was doing graduate work in France. Our son spent the summer with a French-Swiss family and began to master French. Our whole family was afforded a fresh opportunity to experience solidarity by traveling together across France and Spain. This has been the more precious to us because it was the last time we could have such a privilege as a complete family.

If I may hold memory's door open for a moment longer, I would refer to the fall of 1971, when Eunice and I went to India for a special session of the Central Conference of Indian Methodism. We had not counted upon flying through a cyclonic disturbance in the Bay of Bengal, but we did. We had counted on visiting refugees from a war in East Pakistan, which resulted in Bangladesh's independence from West Pakistan; and we did indeed see some of the 280,000 Bangladeshi refugees settled on the salt flats near Calcutta. There we saw the outstanding service of UMCOR as it helped to feed and clothe people who had lost everything. Many of them had found shelter in huge sewer pipes waiting to be installed.

Then suddenly, out of the blue as it were, came an invitation from the Shah of Iran to attend, with other religious leaders, the celebration of the 2,500th anniversary of Cyrus the Great. We did indeed proceed to Teheran to be feted for a week as we visited Shiraj, drove down highways and through villages over Persian carpets spread across the road. We toured the nation's treasure trove of piles of precious gems and glimpsed the Peacock Throne, pillaged from Moghul emperors in Delhi's fort centuries before. We visited the tomb of Cyrus, observed the Shah and his family at Persepolis, and witnessed an astounding parade portraying twenty-five centuries of history. The star of the show proved to be an American Indian chief who was a member of our party. He was in full regalia, complete with a long and elaborate white feather headdress. Incidentally, as I have already mentioned, on this tour we became aware of student unrest in Teheran and the first stirrings of the movement, which within a short time came to topple the Shah's regime and led to the hostage crisis and the ensuing events that still trouble the world scene.

Another facet of our travel has been as a part of special tours with which many bishops have been related. It seems to me that our church has been greatly enriched during recent years by the increased opportunity for travel that has been possible for pastors and laity. This is especially true with regard to the Holy Land; but Wesley Heritage tours in Great Britain, and Reformation tours to Germany and Rome have expanded the horizons of thousands.

When we went to the Washington Area, we found that one of the ministers, Dr. Frank Wanek, had been appointed by my predecessor, Bishop John Wesley Lord, to a special travel ministry. He pioneered as far as Methodism was concerned in Wesleyan Heritage Tours in Great Britain, as well as Israel and Jordan. He then extended this to Germany and other parts of Europe. To begin with, Dr. James Ridgway was associated with Frank. Later Ridgway branched off and organized a much larger enterprise called Educational Opportunity Tours. Eunice and I have traveled with both organizations on several occasions. After retirement we also participated with Dr. and Mrs. Wanek on educational and church-related tours in Mexico, the Caribbean, and South America. For years I taught Bible with these groups.

On three different occasions (1982, 1985, 1988) Dr. Wanek helped us organize tours to India, Nepal, and Sri Lanka (Ceylon). The emphasis was upon acquainting the party with the work of the Church in the regions visited. Eunice delighted in introducing these friends to the land of her birth and I in sharing with others the land and its people where I had proudly served as a missionary.

India is in some respects a difficult country to visit, such is its variety and even more its abysmal poverty. For the newcomer the culture shock can be considerable. We used to begin our tours by advising, "You are either going to love India, or hate it. You must decide which." Thus forewarned, they determined to open their eyes to what the country and its citizens had to offer of the most appealing quality. We are glad to report that without exception these friends left southern Asia with positive attitudes. Their interest in and support of the work of the church there has continued.

In 1970 still another dimension was added to our itinerant ministry. In 1930 my father-in-law, Dr. E. Stanley Jones, had founded a Christian ashram or religious retreat in the lower Himalaya Mountains, about 250 miles northeast of New Delhi. It was called the Sat Tal Ashram (Sat Tal means Seven Lakes.) He had purchased, with what he called his "book money" or royalties, some 450 acres of lovely forest land, complete with a large house and several cottages, at a height of about 5,000 feet. Later he gave it to the Methodist Church in India. How he loved this place! How he delighted in sharing it with others! So the starting of a

Christian ashram was the fulfillment of a dream he had long cherished.

Each May Christians and non-Christians alike would gather there for a period of reflection, Bible study, preaching, and hard labor. The program was conducted in English and in June a similar experience was available in Hindi. For the rest of the year a much more modest program continued.

After years of evangelistic work in India and throughout the world, he had concluded that Christians greatly needed the corporate dimension of Christian living together. He called this a miniature kingdom of God—or "vacation with God." It was a mode of evangelism, yet it was not high pressure. Non-Christians were invited to participate, but conversion was not thrust upon them. Many did indeed seek and find new life in Christ.

For forty years this program had continued, and in addition a Christian ashram movement had been established in the United States, in some countries in Europe and in Japan, and even in Africa and Latin America. Dr. Jones led the movement in addition to his regular evangelistic preaching in various parts of the world. Meanwhile age had crept up on him.

For this reason he invited me to go with him to the Sat Tal Ashram in May 1970. He wanted me to be there even for a very short time, which was all I could afford because of a very busy episcopal assignment in Boston. In 1971 he asked me to do the same. I recall that that year I was asked to preside at the last session of the India annual conference of which he was a retired member. I led the session where the annual appointments of pastors were read out. When I came to his name I announced that he was appointed "Ambassador extraordinary and minister-plenipotentiary of the kingdom of God." He was greatly touched by this gesture.

Later, in November 1971, he suffered a brain-stem stroke, which all but incapacitated him for his strenuous work. He did recover enough to be able to preach again and, in fact, preached some thirty times during his last year of life. With the help of his grandson, Stan, and his granddaughter, Anne, I took him back to India in May 1972. Together, we taught him to walk again. There he died in January 1973. That final year is another story.

Virtually on his deathbed he asked Eunice and me to take responsibility for the continuation of Sat Tal and the ashram movement, plus other programs he had started in India. To the assuming of these heavy responsibilities we were in no position to say no. He had provided also some means to travel to and from India as might be required. This we have continued to do, even after our own retirement to the present.

Well, enough of our peregrinations! They seem to have taken me nearly everywhere: repeated times around this round orb we call Earth; from the northern reaches of Finland where I could experience a twenty-four-hour day of sunlight to Punta Arenas, the world's southernmost city, and beyond that to Tierra del Fuego and the little village of Porvenir. Porvenir means "future" but this was hard to believe. It might well be a place God has forgotten. But not quite, for there one can visit a tiny school-orphanage where dedicated Chilean deaconesses are striving to share a future with deserted children. One can glimpse southward from there and know that a two-hour flight would bring one to a northern spur of Antarctica. *That* continent I have not had occasion to visit!

Any tendency to see a resemblance between one's own travel and those of Asbury or Wesley or St. Paul's is doomed from the start. Only reread 2 Corinthians 11:23–27 and one's own record pales into insignificance. Flying through cyclones and typhoons is not a pleasant experience; nor is picking up a severe case of malaria in Africa; nor is a severed Achilles tendon in the Himalayas; nor is being stranded for a week on Guadalcanal. But travel in our age is a luxury compared to any earlier period in history. In our day we all travel like kings!

Nevertheless, the recollection of our journeying affords one the sheer ecstasy of moments long past: the smell of a daily rain in Singapore, a blowhole in Tonga or Hawaii, a dawn over the Sahara, a sunset in Alice Springs, an aurora borealis display over the North Atlantic, a magnificent nocturnal display of lightning while flying over Central Africa, towering cumulus clouds there in the daytime. Traveling in the Lord's work should enhance rather than diminish the astonishing variety and beauty of this small planet, this celestial ball we share together. The splendor of this "blue marble" we appear to be from outer space does not diminish in close-ups. The golden sands of Sahara, the kaleidoscopic colors of tropical seas, the towering Himalayas with 360 peaks all taller than their closest rivals in other parts of the globe, the fjords of Norway and Alaska, the tundra and tiaga of Russia, Table Mountain at the Cape of Good Hope, the matchless falls of the Zambesi—the tens of thousands of eye-feasts that display the endless marvels of earth. Beyond this are the myriad creatures both great and small, all with their rightful claim on the bounty of their common Mother Earth. All this climaxes in an eternal anthem in praise of the Maker.

Then, how many of our contemporaries who ride upon our globe floating through trackless space do we see in a lifetime of travel? They must number in the tens of millions. We are under mandate to love them all. But how can we fulfill this impossible and unending obligation? One way surely is to be found striving for justice throughout our world, for "justice" is the plural of "love."

Somewhere Santayana has written that before he sets out, the traveler must possess fixed interests and faculties, to be served by travel and not go nosing about like a peddler for profit, but rather should be an artist recomposing what he sees.

This is what I have in mind. People and places rub off on us. So I have tried not simply to be a sightseer, but to reach beyond that. I have found that where I have been has affected the way I view almost everything, that is, from a global perspective. At the same time I have come to feel at home everywhere. The Latin poet Horace wrote: "They change their sky but not their soul who cross the ocean." This I have not found to be true, for I have rather been profoundly changed by my journeys. One comes to agree with Descartes, who once observed that traveling was almost like conversing with people of other centuries.

11

THE ECUMENICAL DIMENSION

It has been a surprise to me to discover how indelibly my life and ministry have been stamped by the Ecumenical Movement. Assuredly I did not plan it that way nor did I intend to be seen in that way. Many of my friends and acquaintances see me as social activist and ecumenist, whereas I see myself primarily as missionary and evangelist.

The fact is that the latter emphases lead to the former, or such has been my experience. Missionary endeavor is transferred and transformed into ecumenical endeavor. Many of our contemporaries have emphasized this: the linkage of mission and unity. They ever cite Scripture in support of this, such as Jesus' prayer in John 17:21 "that they may all be *one*" (unity) . . . "that the world may believe" (mission). So it is that typical missionary experience is that one who walks the missionary road finds others walking the same road in obedience to the same Lord: "Why not then walk *together*?" "Why not *be* together?"

Within days of my arrival in India, very much a neophyte missionary I found myself in a circle of dialogue among both Protestant and Roman Catholic missionaries on our common responsibility in relation to Hindus and Muslims. Shortly afterward I was in dialogue with these non-Christian neighbors, ill-equipped as I was for such an encounter. Ecumenical involvement even on this simple scale was inescapable. I repeat: the missionary road for me became the ecumenical road. It followed that when I became involved in the International Missionary Council, or the Theological Education Fund, I was on the way to the wider ecumenical involvement that the World Council of Churches represented.

It has been of interest to me that *oikoumene,* the Greek root of ecumenical, is found only infrequently in the New Testament. One instance is in Luke 4:5, one of the Temptation episodes, in which Jesus was shown "all the kingdoms of the world." He was not enticed into grasping this as the occasion for his own self-aggrandizement. Rather, it was the arena for God's action and God's glorification: "the earth is the Lord's."

The word *oikoumene* literally means "the whole inhabited world." In a more derivative sense it means "the whole church throughout the whole world." Still further derivatively it refers to "the whole task of the whole church throughout the whole world"; that is, its mission. The twentieth century has been a struggle toward the visible unity of the church, toward the recovery of what it literally means and is.

The symbol of the World Council of Churches (WCC) is a little ship surmounted by a cross. Above the cross is the inscription: *OIKOUMENE*. This tiny barque is in the midst of the sea, often storm tossed, but the small vessel has touched on every shore. It's all right there!

For my part, I have found The United Methodist Church (and its predecessor denominations) to be a congenial setting to participate in this global undertaking.

Our current and historical position is entirely in accord with affirming Christian unity and this has been stated clearly and affirmed repeatedly in our Constitution, our *Discipline,* and in official statements by our General Conference. This is also the perspective of John Wesley's famous sermon "A Catholic Spirit." Moreover, we have afforded generous financial support to the enterprise (during the early years, 25 percent of the WCC budget), just as many of our laity and clergy have been towering advocates of ecumenism.

THE WESLEYAN FAMILY

This account mainly concerns my own involvement in the work of Christian unity. It may as well begin close to home, within the Methodist household. Just as our history is one of divisions, some very sad indeed, it also tells of our reunions. In 1939, after nearly a century of separation, The Methodist Episcopal Church, The Methodist Episcopal Church, South, and The Methodist Protestant Church reunited to form The Methodist Church. In 1946 the United Brethren Church and The Evangelical Church joined to form The Evangelical United Brethren Church. Then in 1968 these two communions merged to form The United Methodist Church. All this must be seen as considerable progress. Earlier, in 1931, three branches of Methodism in the United Kingdom became one.

In 1881 the Ecumenical Methodist Conference was organized in London as a consultative arena for the various branches of the Wesleyan family around the world. Its name was said to be the first use by a modern organization of the long-neglected term "ecumenical." At first it met every ten years and later at five-year intervals, although interrupted by World War II.

My own first exposure to it was at the Eighth Session, which met in England at Oxford, August 28–September 7, 1951. I was a delegate from Indian Methodists and not from the United States. We were accommodated in the various colleges, in my case Christ Church College. We were cared for very well and the food was good. My friend Charles Wesley Ranson took me around Lincoln College for a visit to John Wesley's rooms kept in eighteenth-century fashion. Fittingly there was in those quarters a globe map of earth as known in his day—he whose parish was the world! Ranson also kindly drove me in his sporty MG to visit the hinterland of Oxfordshire, especially the quaint Cotswold villages. It has always been my delight that I came to know this towering ecumenist in a close personal way.

At the Oxford Conference I naturally met leaders from all over the world and from every part of the Wesleyan family. The Americans I mostly knew already. But from Britain there were Eric Baker, Newton Flew, Rupert Davies, Benson Perkins, Gordon Rupp, W. E. Sangster, Harold Roberts, Donald Soper, Maldwyn Edwards, and a host of others. In addition to these clergy I recall laypersons too, such as Dorothy Farrar and Professor C. A. Coulson, a distinguished scientist and mathematician. President W. V. S. Tubman of Liberia was among the delegates, as were the Reverend J. B. Webb of South Africa, the Reverend Alan Walker of Australia, and many more.

It was particularly impressive to meet one evening in the ancient University Church of St. Mary the Virgin, where both John and Charles Wesley had preached. That evening the preacher was Dr. J. Scott Lidgett, C.H., who had reached his ninety-seventh year. The "C.H." following his name stands for Companion of Honor, a very distinguished royal recognition for a British subject. He had been one of the "Legal Hundred," the "collective successors" to John Wesley. Indeed Lidgett had been called "the greatest Methodist since John Wesley," and among his mentors were those who were taught by Wesley himself. There we were, two steps removed from our father in the faith. I once heard Professor Gordon Rupp quote from a Lidgett sermon: "God has given us length and breadth. May he also give us depth."

I found this experience to be enriching in every way. This was true of the successor conferences I attended in Lake Junaluska (1956) and Oslo (1961), at both of which I was a speaker—teamed once with Sir Hugh Foote (later Lord Caradon)—and in London (1966), Denver (1971), Dublin (1976), and Nairobi (1986). It is pleasant to recall what a generous host Bishop Odd Hagen was at Oslo. These family gatherings are a legitimate form of confessional ecumenism just as are those of counterpart world bodies in the other communions. At the Oxford meeting the name of our association was changed to World Methodist Conference, dropping the word ecumenical, which seemed more properly reserved for interdenominational affiliations of a broader nature.

A Concordat with British Methodism

During the early days of The Methodist Episcopal Church, established in 1784, there was intermittent relationship with the "Mother Conference" in England and occasional interchange of fraternal delegates. For the most part, however, the linkage was not particularly close throughout the nineteenth century, partly due to disunity at both poles and, of course, to distance. The establishment of the Ecumenical Methodist Conference in 1881 afforded an arena in which all branches of Methodism could meet on common ground. It became a powerful engine to stimulate reunion in both the United States and the United Kingdom. Moreover, it prompted a fresh venture in fraternal interchange.

By the time of the London session of the World Methodist Council (1966) a bilateral commission of representatives of British Methodists and The Methodist Church had been established to determine what new form the relation would have. It was my privilege to be a member of this commission. We had a series of meetings in London, Bermuda, and Boston. As a result of these deliberations a recommendation went to the 1968 General Conference, which by constitutional amendment established a Concordat relation between the two Methodisms. This was in due course ratified by our annual conferences and by the British Conference. This provided for two ministerial delegates and two lay delegates from each church to sit in the governing body of the other. They were with full voting rights, thus establishing a vital connection between the two: a brand new conception of relationship.

This same concordat device was utilized later between our church and the Methodist Church of Mexico as well as with the Methodist churches of the Caribbean. In my view this pattern should have been followed for a strong continuing relationship with the increasing number of autonomous Methodist churches, which were formerly a part of our own. This would have afforded a viable way for The United Methodist Church to be a world body. Then hesitation seemed to overtake us. It should still be done, I think.

The first exchange of delegates under the Concordat took place at our 1972 General Conference in Atlanta. This firm acknowledgment of the heritage has greatly linked us and has enriched both parties immensely. A year earlier, that is, June 23–July 1, 1971, the first United Methodist Council reciprocal delegates attended the British Conference in Harrogate, Yorkshire. It was my privilege to be one of the clergy delegates. According to their custom I stayed in the home of a Methodist family named Burns, and they proved to be delightful folk. With their two daughters they saw that I was afforded all the comforts of home. Every evening they sang for me a folk song, "On Ilkla Moor Baht'at" ("without a hat"), which I dubbed the "Yorkshire National Anthem." During the session I was asked to preach at a great service in Lidgett Park Church in Leeds, an experience I enjoyed immensely.

As a guest of the Methodist Conference I had attended one of their earlier sessions held in Birmingham, in the Black Country, as the coal and manufacturing section was called. There I became acquainted with some of their unique practices: having a ministerial session that dealt solely with clergy items and the representative session, which cared for general business. In contrast to our way of doing things, they do not allow instruments to accompany the singing of hymns at conference, which are led by a designated precentor, beginning with the singing of the *Te Deum,* which is rendered in a superbly beautiful way. The president of the Conference is considered a "successor to John Wesley" and is seated in his chair and at one session wears his preaching gown while preaching. Then those who speak to a question are recognized by the chair and mount a small platform called a *tribune* to make their remarks. At the Harrogate meeting I spoke in support of help from The United Methodist Church for the rebuilding of Wesley's Chapel.

Yet a third time Eunice and I attended a Conference session at Westminster Hall in London in June 1979. This time we were hosted by a fine couple in Wimbledon. An outstanding feature of the conference was an ecumenical service in Westminster Abbey attended by the Lord Mayor of London. Short addresses were delivered by Cardinal Basil Hume, Roman Catholic Archbishop of Westminster, and by Donald Coggan, Archbishop of Canterbury. The ceremony was marked by the singing of Wesley hymns, while the Conference president placed a garland on the Abbey Memorial tablet to both of the Wesley brothers. Upon the tablet are the familiar inscriptions: "The best of all is, God is with us." "I look upon all the world as my parish." "God buries his workmen, but carries on his work."

Our acquaintance with world Methodism has extended to six continents through the years. Especially notable was a visit to Australia, where my missionary friend

Frank Gribble was our host. We were much impressed by the outstanding and unique central city missions that are found in all the major cities that must rank as among the best Christian service to be found anywhere. The same may be said for central missions in New Zealand. The work of the late Reverend Ted Noffs among hippie-types at King's Cross, Sydney, was most effective. We observed the work among Aborigines at Alice Springs, located in Australia's outback.

Mention must be made of a visit to two former Crusade scholars, both of whom studied at Drew, and who became leaders in the Pacific Islands. One was Setereki Tuilavoni of Fiji, a tall handsome islander. He took us to a small island, Bau, where in a church he showed us a large rock where in pagan days children's heads were smashed in infanticide rituals. It had been transformed into a baptismal font!

Then John Havea, who was to become a Conference president, welcomed us to the islands of Tonga, where 90 percent of the people are Methodists. This included the King, Taufaahau Tupou IV, a giant of a man with an intellect to match his stature and a mathematician of some repute. He hosted us to a gigantic feast, featuring roast pig. The king, son of the famous Queen Salote, worshiped with us on Sunday. We had heard that they sang very well and requested the "Hallelujah Chorus." We had expected the choir to render this but, behold, the whole congregation lifted their voices as one in singing, which surely must have reached the ramparts of heaven! It was magnificent!

PAN-METHODIST COOPERATION

I round off this tour of the Wesleyan Family by referring to Pan-Methodist cooperation. This refers to the four
largest Methodist denominations in the United States,
whose bishops were fairly well acquainted with one
another. The World Methodist Council in Denver, 1971,
stimulated their fuller expression of mutuality. A little
later I was in conversation with Bishop Frederick O. Jordan of The African Methodist Episcopal Church, Bishop
Herbert Bell Shaw of The African Methodist Episcopal
Zion Church, and Bishop Bertram W. Doyle of the Christian Methodist Episcopal Church. We all determined to
press cooperation further by recommending concurrent
action by our several General Conferences to this end.

By 1976 this had been accomplished by all four bodies
and their representative bishops gathered in Atlanta on
March 11, 1978. It was decided that a consultation of
Methodist bishops be established. A steering committee
was formed with officers representing the four communions. The consultation met in 1979 and periodically
thereafter. Then the consultation expanded to include not
only bishops but other clergy and laity too. A good deal
of cooperative programming was initiated: publishing,
missions, education, mutual laying on of hands at ordinations, and so on.

At present the four General Conferences have sanc-
tioned a joint commission on church union, which is
engaged in deliberations. Where this will lead it is too
early to tell. Each of the four churches is proud of its heritage. Speaking personally, I would advise exploring a

Federal Union, which my late father-in-law, E. Stanley Jones, advocated in season and out. In a word, it would allow both maximum unity without uniformity and maximum liberty with diversity. Not a bad combination!

CONCILIAR ECUMENISM

My view of world Methodism and similar bodies in other communions is that they are manifestations of confessional ecumenism. I turn now to conciliar ecumenism. Again, my understanding is that conciliarity is one of the essential marks of the church universal. This is suggested in Matthew 18 and even more specifically in Acts 15. Being the Church is in some sense the association of each body of Christians with other Christians, and to be reciprocally subject to their help, their criticism, and their counsel.

It continues to be an astonishment to me that I have been so involved in the ecumenical venture and in its many councils. At one time or another the involvement has been at every level: local, urban, state, regional, confessional, national, and international.

It has always been a disappointment to me that I was not present at the formation of the World Council of Churches in Amsterdam in 1948. A kind of "interim" World Council of Churches was launched in 1937, but was interrupted by World War II. Of course, I was involved in the Foreign Missionary Conference of North America which, in turn, was related to the International Missionary Council, itself a fountainhead of the ecumenical movement and finally in 1961 a part of the World

Council of Churches. It so happened that I was privileged to make the motion that the Foreign Missionary Conference of North America become a constituent part of the proposed National Council of Churches.

I was a member of the Methodist delegation at the creation of the National Council in Cleveland in 1950. Though the ecumenical climate was good, the weather was not, for a blizzard blanketed the city. Nevertheless, it was a really great occasion and built upon the broad foundations of the predecessor Federal Council of Churches and seven other cooperative interdenominational organizations covering a wide sweep of interchurch cooperation. At Cleveland, delegates came into touch almost immediately with the very able leaders of every communion and could in some sense claim them for one's own. Bishop G. Bromley Oxnam, of course, was there; so were Bishop William C. Martin, Henry Knox Sherrill, presiding bishop of the Protestant Episcopal Church, Edwin Dahlberg of the American Baptists, Herman Morse of the Presbyterians, a highly skilled parliamentarian, Franklin Fry of the Lutherans, and many more gifted women and men. President Truman could not be there but sent Dean Acheson as his substitute to address the Assembly. In all, twenty-nine denominations were represented, from Orthodox to Quakers and the Salvation Army. But one could not help noting the absence of others: the Roman Catholics, the Southern Baptists, and most of the conservative evangelicals. They were and are sorely missed. Bishop Sherrill was elected the first president of the National Council of Churches and gave it outstanding leadership.

For half of the life of the NCC I have served on its governing body and have twice been one of its vice presidents. Together with a host of others I can claim to have invested an enormous amount of energy in its undertakings. Although it is frequently viewed as a social issue forum, this is only a small part of its purpose. Basically it is the expression of the common faith of its member churches that in affirming their unity in Christ strive toward the oneness of the whole human family. Together in the Council we make our common witness to Jesus Christ as Lord, help meet an array of basic human needs, work for justice and peace, safeguard the environment, encourage Christian education and evangelism, and not least unite in translation, publication, and distribution of Bibles. This broad mandate has almost always been ignored by the Council's many critics. As to Methodist involvement, our leaders in the old Federal Council of Churches virtually bequeathed our Social Creed to that body.

My first direct involvement with the World Council was in August 1960, about two months after I was elected bishop. My revered colleague Bishop William C. Martin, already a friend for many years, was a member of the Council's Central Committee, which met that year in St. Andrews, Scotland. Since he had a scheduling conflict at that time, he designated me to attend as his proxy.

Fortunately, I was able to get a room in a hotel adjacent to the Royal and Ancient Golf Links. I even ventured to play a little golf there with Dean Liston Pope of Yale Divinity School. The course looks easy, but it is deceptively difficult. Within about four holes we both managed to roll up enough points that would have looked good for nine. The course was a real challenge, even though we could claim no bragging rights except for the fact that we had actually played there at all.

Another grateful memory lingers. On the first morning, Episcopal Bishop Henry Knox Sherrill invited me to have breakfast with him and Mrs. Sherrill and with Geoffrey Fisher, Archbishop of Canterbury and Mrs. Fisher. I was made to feel at home, fledgling bishop that I was. These two men were among my heroes. Both bishops had shown an unusual openness to the ecumenical venture. Both possessed a great sense of humor. Neither of these men took themselves very seriously and that in itself was a lesson well worth learning.

In the American press the Archbishop of Canterbury was often confused with the *Dean* of Canterbury, the somewhat notorious Dr. Hewlett Johnson, called the "Red Dean" because of his pronounced leftist views. When Archbishop Fisher arrived in New York on one occasion the reporters thought he was Johnson. He shouted in a microphone, "I'm not the Red Dean! I'm not the Red Dean!" Incidentally, one of our close friends "Ted" Johnson, a missionary, a mission executive, and a staunch Canadian Presbyterian, was a nephew of this same "Red Dean" and used to delight in references to "Uncle Hewlett."

The St. Andrews session gave me a taste of my Scottish heritage. It afforded a glimpse of both Edinburgh and Glasgow as well as of the famous cathedral at Dunblane, where we held an ecumenical service. It allowed me to become acquainted with the unique way the World Coun-

cil discharged its business. Then I recall meeting churchmen from Central Europe, from behind the Iron Curtain.
The fear and restraint under which they had to operate
was sad to see.

At St. Andrews final preparation was made for the next
assembly, which was to convene in India only a little over
a year later. I was pleased to have heard the discussion
and to have voted for a recommendation to that meeting,
which I have sometimes termed the most important sentence to come out of the Ecumenical Movement:

"We believe that the unity which is both God's will and
his gift to his Church is being made visible as all in each
place who are baptized into Jesus Christ and confess him
as Lord and Saviour are brought by the Holy Spirit into
one fully committed fellowship, holding the one apostolic
faith, preaching the one Gospel, breaking the one bread,
joining in common prayer, and having a corporate life
reaching out in witness and service to all and who at the
same time are united with the whole Christian fellowship
in all places and all ages in such wise that ministry and
members are accepted by all, and that all can act and
speak together as occasion requires for the tasks to which
God calls his people."

Here was a magnificently stated goal that I have kept
before me through the years. The fact was that I was to
encounter these very same words again in New Delhi and
again lend them my support as they were adopted there
by the whole council.

Mine was a missionary road to the Third Assembly of

the World Council of Churches in New Delhi, November 19–December 5, 1961. Ten percent of the delegates were named by the International Missionary Council and I was among them. The modern Ecumenical Movement, as we have seen, began in 1910 in Edinburgh's great missionary conference. This gathering had spawned three worldwide movements: Faith and Order, Life and Work, and the IMC. The first two came together at Amsterdam in 1948, and the latter joined with them at New Delhi for an enlarged World Council of Churches.

This union was the first great accomplishment of New Delhi. How fitting it was that it should have occurred in Asia, home continent of the Christian Faith; and in India, one of the great modern missionary lands, traditional scene of the apostle Thomas's missionary labors and possibly St. Bartholomew's too. It must be said that the Indian people were most hospitable, from Prime Minister Nehru, who addressed the assembly, and President Radhakrishnan to the humblest citizen who helped us. The Assembly met during the Hindu Diwali season, the festival of lights when cities throughout India are bedecked with lamps. All this was not out of keeping with the Assembly's theme: "Jesus Christ, the Light of the World."

In Delhi I became acquainted with a very broad spectrum of Christian leaders throughout the world. I had first met the General Secretary, Dr. Willem A. Visser't Hooft, when in the mid-1930s he visited New York City as a young leader of the World Student Christian Federation. He was a brilliant man, a competent theologian, a talented linguist, and certainly a gift to the ecumenical movement. He seemed to have been everywhere and known everyone in church circles. He possessed a profound knowledge of Christian unity stemming from service as a steward at Archbishop Soderblom's Life and Work Conference in Stockholm in 1925 through hundreds of international conferences. He was a winsome, stubborn, and persuasive man, as well as a humble and obedient Christian servant. Joseph Hromadka described him as one who "identified himself with the weaknesses as well as the strengths of the churches."

Wim, as he was called, went to great lengths to bring the Russian Orthodox into the World Council of Churches. The story is that he sat with them at a breakfast table and drafted on the back of a menu a new wording for the basis of membership of the WCC in a trinitarian statement more congenial to the Orthodox view: "The World Council of Churches is a fellowship of churches which confess the Lord Jesus Christ as God and Saviour according to the Scriptures and therefore seek to fulfil together their common calling to the glory of the one God, Father, Son and Holy Spirit."

This basis was adopted and opened the door for the Russian Orthodox Church to join the Council. This admission was another accomplishment of New Delhi, though a highly controversial action. Critics of the Council have been insistent that the step was tantamount to giving the communists of the USSR entree and control of the body. This is to ignore the fact that oppressed Christians of that country finally were given some opportunity to breathe a fresher air from time to time. It would not be too much to say that this was a part of an opening wedge through which the shackles of atheistic communism were thrown off in Eastern Europe three decades later.

Through the years I came to know many of the Russian delegates quite well. I know all too well how they and their families suffered under their regime and the price they paid to exercise their faith. The least other Christians could do was to welcome them as Christian brothers and sisters.

Of course, the animosity toward their representatives was often sharply focused particularly upon Archbishop Nikodim, metropolitan of Leningrad and Novgorod. This bishop was thirty-two years old when he led his delegation to New Delhi. He was often accused of being a member of the KGB. He always denied this and it was never proved otherwise. Without doubt all delegates were questioned by the KGB as they returned from church meetings outside the Soviet Union, and their answers were doubtless checked carefully, but I have never felt that the World Council was justifiably under condemnation for admitting Russian churches into its membership. As to Nikodim, his health deteriorated through the years and at age forty-eight in the Vatican he died literally in the arms of Pope John Paul I, who himself was to die only a few days later.

As things transpired, New Delhi was to prove only the first of four Assemblies of the World Council in which I was to participate. I do not deem this to be the place to enlarge on these gatherings, whose work has been well recorded elsewhere. A few references must suffice.

It is a long way, in every respect, from a New Delhi autumn to mid-summer in the ancient university town of

Uppsala. It was daylight about twenty-four hours a day when the Fourth Assembly convened July 4–19, 1968. The Biafra War was being waged at the time. Representatives from more than two hundred denominations were present among a total of nearly two thousand. I was proud that our United Methodist delegation included Senator George McGovern of South Dakota and Congressman John Brademas of Indiana. This later helped to accent the growing number of laypersons who participated. The number of women and blacks had swelled greatly as compared to earlier assemblies.

The King of Sweden graced one of the sessions by his presence. Greetings from Ecumenical Patriarch Athenagoras and from Pope Paul VI and Cardinal Bea were all most welcome. Notable addresses were given by President Kenneth Kaunda of Zambia and Lady Jackson (Barbara Ward), who spoke eloquently on "Rich and Poor Nations." Lord Caradon and novelist James Baldwin spoke against racism. "Pete" Seeger entertained the delegates at night with his music. Roman Catholic presence and participation was noteworthy. Martin Luther King, Jr., had been asked to deliver the principal sermon. His tragic assassination in April 1968 cast something of a pall over the occasion. Sri Lankan Methodist D. T. Niles acquitted himself well as he substituted in the high pulpit as preacher. Quite appropriately the worldwide scourge of racism was placed in a sharp focus. The Assembly's theme was "All Things New"—and not a moment too soon!

Such meetings are not always serious in an unrelieved sense. Perhaps I may be allowed to recall one small incident in one of the saunas that abounded in Uppsala. I was seated in a sauna with friends when our meditations were interrupted by the entrance of an archbishop with whom I was acquainted. I took it for granted that protocol ends in one of the saunas. Besides he was armed only with a tiny hand towel and clothed only in his archiepiscopal ring. I felt prompted to say, "Have a seat, your Grace. Don't stand on ceremony!" He sat.

It was my privilege to have been a member of the committee that planned the Fifth Assembly of the World Council. We met repeatedly to lay out every detail. The theme adopted for 1975 was "Jesus Christ Frees and Unites." I wrote a paper on this subject, taking my lead from Mark 5, the passage about the man possessed of demons, "Legion." This name described his shattered inner state: there were six thousand soldiers in a Roman Legion. When he met with Jesus, he was indeed *freed* and the scattered fragments of his personality *united* into one new man. The application of this story to the situation current at that time was clear and apt. "Frees" and "unites" fit in neatly also with the two Swahili equivalents that everyone knew at the time : *uhuru* (freedom*)* and *harambee* (togetherness).

As matters developed it also applied well to the situation then prevailing in Indonesia. For the meeting had been intended for Jakarta. Unrest, oppression, and disunity that developed there necessitated cancellation. Within a year's time a quick shift had to be made to Nairobi. One could not praise our Kenyan and African hosts too much for their resiliency. This assembly went off without a hitch. The Kenyatta Conference Center in the heart of the city proved ideal as a meeting place. It was the first assembly to be held in Africa—the cradle of the human race—and something of the flavor of that continent was imparted to the proceedings just as its two immediate predecessors had been touched by Europe and Asia.

The assemblies have always been not only experiences of deliberation for the designated delegates from the member churches, but also festive gatherings of the people of the host and neighboring lands as well as visitors and guests from afar. Once again, the color, the music, the dance, the vitality of Africa made the Fifth Assembly notable.

Through the years a characteristic format for WCC meetings has emerged. Central to all else is worship and prayer, enriched by elements from many traditions and from all over the globe. Then there is invariably Bible study related to the theme and led by gifted scholars from many lands. This attention to the biblical text extends to multiple small groups, partly determined by language. Then larger groups or sections reflect upon the subthemes and upon the concrete issues before the various constituent administrative units of the Council. The fruit of these discussions and their recommendations find their way to plenary sessions where they are debated and appropriate action taken. All this culminated in a celebratory dimension that was pervasive throughout the session. This was particularly noticeable at Nairobi. Not surprisingly the assembly ended with its participants— from village laity to bishops and archbishops—dancing in the aisles and singing:

"Break down the walls of separation,
And unite us in a single body."

It did indeed suggest that Jesus Christ *frees* and unites.

Incidentally, one day while at Nairobi a friend, Bishop Charles Golden, and I took a little time off. We spent the night at Treetops where Princess Elizabeth and Prince Philip had gone some years earlier: the night she went to sleep as a princess and awoke Queen of England. Nothing so astonishing happened to us. It was, however, a pleasant retreat where we enjoyed a fine dinner and feasted our eyes on some of Africa's great wild animals, including a fine rhinoceros.

One way in which these forces were at work was through the broad new acknowledgment of those who suffered disability. This was another first for the Council, which had long ago taken a stand against racism and discrimination against women. Ruth Elizabeth Knapp of New York City, cofounder of the Committee on Church Unity and the Disabled, was particularly ardent and effective in her advocacy at Nairobi in behalf of these millions. She wrote a poem titled "Who Am I?" which has haunted me through the years, for she sang of overcoming her handicaps through triumphant affirmation of life. Another American woman who made an impression at both Uppsala and Nairobi was Margaret Mead, whom I had seen earlier at a WCC meeting at the University of Paris and at many subsequent gatherings. She was a kind of scientific adviser on racism, nuclear policy, and much more. I think she, an active Episcopalian, delighted in this work, and I came to know her quite well. You could always find her in a crowd, for she constantly carried a forked staff that she had acquired somewhere in her wide-ranging anthropological studies.

One day during the assembly I said to Dr. Mead, "Margaret, I'd like to take you to lunch." She accepted and we went to the nearby Hilton Hotel, where she discovered that there is no such thing as a free lunch. For I had been assigned to proceed from Nairobi to Papua-New Guinea to visit newly opened United Methodist work there. She was an expert on that part of the world and proceeded to give me a short course in anthropology of the South Pacific. She shared with me advice as to where to go and where not to go, what to do and what not to do in a region still emerging from almost the Stone Age. She told how its hundreds of languages developed, and of the strong taboos that shape life and culture there. I was treated to a feast of knowledge that served me in good stead during the days that lay ahead.

At first blush, when confronted with the problem of going from Kenya to Papua-New Guinea, one might conclude: "You cannot get there from here." For much of history that would have been virtually true, but not nowadays. You can make the trip in about forty-eight hours flying from Nairobi to Johannesburg, to Perth, Australia, via the Island of Mauritius in the Indian Ocean; continue from Perth to Sydney and then to Port Moresby, the capital of Papua-New Guinea, which had only gained its independence a few months before my visit.

Once New Guinea was very much a mystery island, large to the point of subcontinental proportions and thought to be of very small population. Actually it is peopled rather extensively, though its regions are separated by almost impenetrable mountain ranges, readily accessible only by plane. New Guinea is divided into two almost equal parts: the western portion, West Irian, a part of Indonesia; the eastern portion is Papua-New Guinea. Once the region was ruled under a mandate assigned to Australia and the coastal areas were fought over between the Japanese forces and Western Allies during World War II. During recent decades it has become partly Christianized and has both a Protestant and a Roman Catholic presence. United Methodists play a relatively small supportive role there but enough to warrant my visit.

It is not my purpose to give a travelogue but I found the region fascinating. A visit to Goroka in the Eastern Highlands was of special interest, particularly the Melanesian Institute, where a high grade of scholarship in cultural studies is being carried out. As I write I look up from my desk at an ironwood crucifix crafted by Sepak carvers nearby. I met with leaders and missionaries of the various churches. Leslie Boseto, moderator of the United Church, later a president of the WCC, I had known for several years and had just seen in Nairobi the previous week! There were visits to schools, small hospitals, and church services in Pidgin English, a kind of *lingua franca*. Several flights in single-engine planes across trackless mountains rising to 15,000 feet over thick forests made life interesting and precarious, while reminding me of similar flights in Central Africa years before. On one leg of a flight I shared the cramped plane with a man straight out of the Stone Age who sat next to me while holding a live pig in his lap. At another extreme, I visited a surprisingly modern university that had just been established. Everyone was kind and hospitable. Moreover, I saw genuinely good promise in this newly emerging democracy. Pleasant and vivid memories of this unique visit still linger with me.

After a week it was time to head home, for Christmas was near at hand. So it was that we took off in a two-motored Fokker and headed east over the Solomon Islands and on to Guadalcanal. And there we sat for several interminable days. We found that the jet that was to carry us on to Fiji was grounded. Fortunately we were put up in the newly built hotel Medana, named after a Portuguese explorer. The accommodations and food were good and the passengers became well acquainted.

There is not too much to do in Guadalcanal, but the setting was historic enough. One could look out on the shark-laden waters of Iron Bottom Bay, where a famous naval battle was fought during the late war. Sunken Japanese and American naval vessels give the bay its name. We visited the battlefield where for months American Marines had been pinned down at Heartbreak Ridge and other bloody struggles. There was a small museum that preserved something of South Pacific culture. Every day we could even hear spontaneous explosions in the ammunition dump, sequestered with their tens of thousands of tons of ordinance abandoned after the war. I visited an Anglican archbishop who was a Solomon Islander. All of this was interesting but time moved slowly.

Christmas Eve came. An Australian missionary couple—Methodists they were—kindly invited me to share Christmas dinner with them, and a splendid repast it was. The next day our relief plane finally came. It transported us to Fiji, pausing on the way at Brisbane and at New Caledonia, both very hot at that season of the year. We were also served a Christmas dinner en route. At Nadi we caught a flight to Honolulu. Since it was Christmas Day, we had another mammoth feast. Meanwhile, we had crossed the International Date Line and it was again Christmas Day, so between Honolulu and Los Angeles another Christmas dinner was offered. From Los Angeles I telephoned Eunice saying I would be home on December 26. She reassured me by saying that she was postponing our family Christmas dinner until I arrived! Five Christmas dinners: such is God's overflowing and sometimes overwhelming goodness!

For the Sixth Assembly held at Vancouver, British Columbia, July 24–August 10, 1983, I was not actually a voting delegate. As a retiring member of the Central Committee, of which I had been a part for twenty-three years, I was entitled to attend the session. The theme was, as in the past, christological: "Jesus Christ—the Life of the World." Its points of biblical reference were all life-related—Invitation to Life: Ways, Birth, a Loving Home, Bread, Treasure, Water, Crown of Life. The whole experience was built around these images.

This was the first assembly to be held in North America since Evanston in 1954. Appropriate to its setting in Western Canada, the grounds were marked by the raising of a giant totem pole carved with Christian symbols. This now has found a permanent lodging at the WCC headquarters in Geneva. Moreover, a mark of Vancouver was that much of the meeting took place in a gigantic tent of white and golden stripes. This might suggest a circus or a county fair of global proportions. It was neither and it was both and much more: a revival meeting, a university of life, but mostly a vivid and vital gathering of representatives of God's people in worship, praise, and devotion. It was a people's meeting, more so than earlier assemblies were.

Women were a greater presence than in any predecessor assembly. For the first time children had a real part, and the many posters they had prepared for the occasion were deeply moving. Conservative Evangelicals were present in large numbers and expressed their gratitude for being there. They proved a positive factor. Though there had been a few observers from other religions at Nairobi, in Vancouver they were accorded greater visibility and fraternal status; a new day and a largely unexplored field lay ahead.

One further recollection: *apartheid* was still in full force in South Africa, and it lay heavily on the consciences of participants. Thus the arrival of Archbishop Desmond Tutu for a major address was a high moment at Vancouver—almost ecstatic in its pitch. His own opening remarks speak for themselves:

"When one looks at the state of the world today, one says with relief, 'Thank God I'm not God!' When you stand in this place where so many of God's children are gathered together, you say, 'Thank you, God, that you are God!' It is one of the most wonderful things to belong to the church of God."

COMMITTEES OF THE WORLD COUNCIL

Since the assemblies of the World Council convened only once every seven years or so, a great deal of their planning and governing fell to committees. The principal ones were the Central Committee, meeting about five times between assemblies, and the smaller Executive Committee, which gathered at six-month intervals.

From 1961, following New Delhi when I was first appointed, I served on the Central Committee without interruption until 1983. In the course of this service members naturally become well acquainted with their counterparts throughout the world. Sometimes I have observed, only half-jokingly, that a delegate to a WCC Assembly, equipped with a list of fellow delegates, could be parachuted to almost any part of the inhabited globe and be within a local telephone call of some ecumenical acquaintance.

Already I have described the flow of business at an assembly. On a somewhat lesser scale this is followed at Central Committee meetings; that is, a gathering of the whole community for worship, followed by small group or unit committees to consider items carefully and in turn make recommendations to plenary sessions for action. Usually also a solid theological paper is presented to the whole committee on a weighty topic such as "The Ecclesiological Significance of a Council of Churches." This is then subjected to discussion by the members who in succession made speeches or "interventions" in a quite formal manner until all who desired have spoken. The atmosphere was pretty much as must have prevailed at the great Councils through the centuries. Proceedings were simultaneously translated into various languages, according to the needs of participants. Sometimes discussion became heated, and sometimes it was lightened by humor. Invariably, however, goodwill and a Christian spirit prevailed. So the business—financial, theological, issue-oriented matters, and programs addressed to the topics of the day—as analyzed, formulated, and approved for administrative action. Through the years the topics have been very wide-ranging.

The Central Committee has met mostly in Europe or Geneva, but through the years in many other countries as well—from Crete to Jamaica, from Berlin to Addis Ababa, from Buenos Aires to Delhi, from Enugu, Nigeria, to Canterbury, and occasionally in the United States. This made it possible for the host countries to offer their particular forms of hospitality, and stories are attached to all these places.

Allow me to recall one or two of these. One meeting was held in 1963 at Rochester, New York on the campus of Colgate-Rochester Seminary. Dinner was served cafeteria-style and the members moved to tables of their choice. Here was Michael Ramsey, Archbishop of Canterbury, a marvelous man but a bit forbidding and notably taciturn on occasion. Seated next to him in almost terrified silence was a Methodist woman, a longtime friend and colleague of mine. Her eyes pleaded with me almost audibly to come and share her table. Since she was seated at the archbishop's left, I took a seat at his right. It so happened that I had recently read one of Dr. Ramsey's books. Then I said to him, "Your Grace, do I understand in your book *The*

Gospel and the Catholic Church that what you are essentially arguing is that the liturgy itself is a powerful declaration of the gospel?" The response was immediate, affirmative, and abundant. My query seemed to open up the flood-gates. It was as if he had mounted his professorial chair to instruct us in the meaning of Christian worship from the standpoint of a High Churchman: that the Blessed Sacrament itself is a preaching! That sort of encounter was always happening in World Council circles.

How pleasant it is also to remember a Central Committee meeting in Dresden, East Germany, in August 1981. Our son, his wife, and their infant daughter journeyed with us. We saw the Sistine Madonna and other art treasures of that city. There I saw for the last time my longtime friend Bishop Samuel of Egypt, who only a few weeks later was to be assassinated in Cairo together with President Anwar Sadat. From Dresden we took a side trip, as every good Methodist should do, to Herrenhut, the Moravian center. The whole WCC delegation made a trip down the Elbe River, whose banks were lined with Christians lifting sheets painted with the cross in testimony to their faithful, though suppressed, discipleship.

Aside from serving on the Central Committee as such, members were often assigned to special committees or task forces. I mention two in which I was involved. The first was to serve on a committee that was to choose a general secretary who was to succeed Dr. Visser't Hooft— not an easy task, partly due to the fact that Wim had grown up with the Council since 1937 and was virtually identified with it.

At the Central Committee session in Enugu, Eastern

Nigeria, in 1965 a nominee was brought forward by the Executive Committee. The recommendation was defeated. It was not so much of a rejection of him as a person, for he was well-trained and in many respects remarkably equipped. Rather it was a kind of rebellion against the very fact that the powerful Executive Committee should arrogate the nomination to itself. The failure to accept their nomination precipitated something of a crisis. To resolve it a committee from among the Central Committee members was appointed to engage in a fresh search, and I was named to it. Bishop John Sadiq of India was its able chairman. Following two meetings we nominated the Reverend Eugene Carson Blake, a minister of The United Presbyterian Church in the United States of America, who was installed in 1967 and served until 1972, when he was succeeded by a Methodist from the Caribbean, Dr. Philip A. Potter.

Even earlier, at the Rochester session in 1963, I was designated chairman of a committee to examine the structure of the World Council and to make recommendations for changes. We were a committee of sixteen members, widely representative of the council in every respect: communion, region, age, gender, clergy-laity balance, and so on. Restructuring was called for on several reasons: the passage of time (Peter Drucker has observed that any organization needs to reconsider its organizational plan every twenty or twenty-five years), a growing dissatisfaction with the existing format, and the necessity of change to accommodate to the new situation occasioned by the merger of the International Missionary Council (IMC) and the World Council of Churches (WCC) at New Delhi.

This writing does not call for a detailed account of our procedures. It may suffice to mention that we took our assignment seriously. We did consult frequently with the staff and with scores of people of ecumenical experience or specialized knowledge. We met repeatedly in Geneva, Germany, Norway, Sweden, England, the United States, and Africa. Moreover, we made progress reports at every Central Committee meeting and to the Executive Committee from time to time.

One report to the Executive Committee was made at Windsor Castle. The group gathered in St. George's Chapel, there surrounded by the symbols of the Royal Order of the Garter, which had met there for centuries. The dean of the Chapel was one of the Queen's chaplains. At this 1967 meeting it was arranged for the participants to be received by Her Majesty, Queen Elizabeth II. At the appointed time we were assembled, clad in our best ecclesiastical attire, in a huge drawing room, not as a cluster but individually scattered around, each of us in the company of one of the queen's aides. In my case the aide was Field Marshal Sir William Slim of the Burma Campaign, part of the China-Burma-India (CBI) theater of World War II where I had served. The reason for this arrangement was so that every guest could meet the queen individually and then for all time tell the story as I am now doing. She was, of course, all graciousness as sovereign ladies are supposed to be, and we were all immensely impressed. What she may have said to others, I have no idea, but what she said to me was simply this: "Nowadays no nation may conduct its affairs as if other nations did not exist." I totally agreed and rather wished that some of her predecessors had been aware of this: George III, for instance.

Serving on the Structure Committee was not, however, "all tea and crumpets" as they say. It required a great deal of hard work as discussions proceeded. We made a detailed interim report at Uppsala (1968), after which we received a fresh mandate including the request to reconsider the role and composition of the Assembly, the organization of the Secretariat and the committee structures. After four more meetings we presented a final report to the Central Committee at Addis Ababa in 1971. It was adopted and constitutional changes subsequently ratified. The structure was fixed for the next twenty years.

These are some elements of our report:

> The Structure Committee was guided by two basic considerations. First, the structures of the churches and ecumenical organizations clearly need to change as the context and challenges posed by society and by the churches themselves change. And secondly, there is no "right" structure and no such thing as a theology of structure. Any decisions about a new structure of the World Council of Churches must therefore be pragmatic ones.
>
> In assessing the functions of an Assembly in the present complex ecumenical situation, the Structure Committee suggested that the Assembly must "be the occasion for a celebration which will include the conducting of business of the World Council of Churches; for worship and study; and an occasion for common Christian commitment. In its composition it will have to be both a representative body and an occasion for participation of a wider circle among the people of God." . . .
>
> Member Churches should be obliged to observe certain rules in selecting their delegates to assure a balance of

church officials, parish ministers, laymen, women and young people. In addition, it was proposed that 15% of all delegates should be chosen by the Central Committee upon nomination by the churches in order to provide additional opportunities for achieving the necessary balance. . . .

In its recommendations concerning the administration of the World Council, the Structure Committee departed from the former Divisional structure in favour of three more flexible Programme Units, each grouping a number of sub-units. The titles of the three Programme Units ("Faith and Witness," "Justice and Service," "Education and Communication") were chosen to reflect the major functions of the World Council of Churches as laid down in the Constitution.

What I have reported about some of my involvement in the National Council of Churches and the World Council of Churches should more than suffice. When I survey the record of these organizations over almost half a century, I find their achievements to be astounding and extremely positive. In a world in which centrifugal forces seem often to outstrip centripetal forces, these effective cohesive movements should be most welcome. To most fair-minded persons who have troubled themselves to be informed objectively about their programs, I believe they are welcome. The whole world has been healed and enriched by their contributions and the church enhanced by their loyalty to Jesus Christ, whom they acknowledge as Lord. Sometimes I say to myself that if either the National Council of Churches or the World Council of Churches was to cease to exist today, we should busy ourselves in creating their successor councils tomorrow.

Indeed they are constantly changing while remaining true to their original intentions. If they were to be reconstituted I would hope they could be reconceptualized and reconstructed to be even more inclusive of the Christian family. This would not be easy.

Both the NCC and WCC have had their severe critics. Moving as they often have on the cutting edge of the great issues that confront human society, they have had to take risks and invite criticism. For example, the World Council Assembly at Uppsala (1968), as we have seen, took seriously the plague of racism, just as the National Council of Churches grappled with this at the same time. At the Canterbury (1969) session the Central Committee began implementation of an authorized Program to Combat Racism. I was among those who spoke in favor of this and voted for it. Incidentally, in my speech from the floor I made friendly reference to Caesar Chavez's work among farmworkers in America, and he later on wrote to me a warm letter of appreciation. The United Methodist Church from its Fund for Reconciliation made available the first large grants for the racism program.

A little later the first grants from the World Council's Fund to Combat Racism were announced for specific projects in various parts of the world, including the United States. With each announcement of support, the swell of opposition increased. I myself occasionally felt that some grants were of dubious worth, yet taken as a whole they amounted to a tremendous assault on institutional racism. In my view this is exactly the kind of witness the church should have been making. Without a doubt this contributed to the considerable progress that has been made on the issue. More than that it was a principal force leading to the dismantling of *apartheid* in South Africa.

But the volume of mail that was received by members of the Council, including myself, was overwhelming. It did not make for pleasant reading nor was it conducive to restful sleep at night. Sometimes these letters extended to personal attacks. Our denominational office for Christian Unity for months averaged about a hundred letters a day, mostly against the program. Yet the Councils have stood their ground.

The critics have been many. The *Reader's Digest* was especially persistent. In October 1971, not a digest, but an original article entitled "Must Our Churches Finance Revolution?" appeared. This was followed the next month by "Which Way the World Council of Churches?" A decade later this periodical was still at it, for in August 1982 another attack against the Councils was published: "Karl Marx or Jesus Christ?" In December of the same year came: "Do You Know Where Your Church Offerings Go?" Altogether these were not directed only against the Councils but at the churches themselves and their leaders. These biased attacks were answered point by point and their false accusations systematically refuted, although this periodical did not admit this nor confess its own wrongdoing. In fairness, it did in April 1972 publish a reply by industrialist J. Irwin Miller, once president of the NCC and a WCC Central Committee member, an earnest layman of the Disciples church whose daily practice was to read from the Greek New Testament. He called his article "Should Churches Play It Safe?" He strongly argued

the churches' rightful and essential prophetic role, assert-
ing that we all suffer if the church does not resist evil.
Coming as it did from a layman who had been president
of the National Association of Manufacturers it was a
powerful affirmation of conciliar Christianity.

In my files I have extensive notes on a meeting I hosted
at the Copley-Plaza Hotel in Boston on June 11, 1970. So
far as I know it was never reported publicly. The then
general secretary of the National Council of Churches, Dr.
Edwin Espy, was greatly discouraged and asked me to
convene the group. So it was that nearly all the past presidents of the National Council gathered for an extended
lunch: Henry K. Sherrill, William C. Martin, Edwin
Dahlberg, Eugene Carson Blake, J. Irwin Miller, Arthur
Flemming, and Cynthia Wedel. Ed Espy, W. David
Hunter, the deputy general secretary, and I were also
present. We all shared in a round table discussion. All
present united in a somber assessment of the current
scene. (It was at the period of the Vietnam debate, racial
tension, unrest among youth.) People had lost their sense
of humor, their sense of balance, and their perspective.
There was much anger on every hand in the United
States. There was a moral crisis. Much of our society
seemed united in their disapproval of what was going on
in our country. Behavior of the young was evidence of
moral degradation, yet youth were taking super-moral
positions. Many institutions appeared ungovernable. It
was reported variously: "Erosion of the foundations in
our society," "Pastors feel alone," "We are not part of a
melodrama (there was no villain) but a Greek Tragedy,"
"Loss of faith in our instututions, and in one another."

This gives the tenor of the discussion. Yet at the same time there was a reaching for the basics of the Christian faith, a plea for sympathy, a yearning for an articulation of the gospel for this moment, a need for a structure of permanence, a call to give power to the real constituencies, to recover evangelism. All this may seem a bit jumbled but light shone through. I believe Dr. Espy left the meeting with a sense of reassurance.

I am now convinced as I was then that as separate denominations we cannot "go it alone." We need one another. We belong to one another because Jesus Christ is brother of us all. In the minds of some, while the body politic and the social order can appropriately come under critical appraisal by every other institution in our society, this privilege is denied the church. Yet the church cannot keep silent. It is the keeper of the nation's conscience. It is a guardian of society. It is a prophetic voice for God.

ROMAN CATHOLIC RELATIONS

Since my election as bishop in 1960 I have made hundreds of addresses on ecumenism, including the sermon I preached at the 1976 General Conference in Portland, Oregon. In 1969, my book _A Church Truly Catholic_ was published. This material had been delivered as the Gray Lectures at Duke University Divinity School. Moreover, I gave addresses before the general assemblies of both The United Presbyterian Church and The United Church of Christ. I must say that all this speaking was rooted in such an array of ecumenical involvement that, as I look back, I marvel at where my energy came from. There were some surprises along the way. What amazed me most was the tremendous change of atmosphere vis-à-vis the Roman Catholic Church. For this I was almost totally unprepared.

When I was assigned to Boston, I found my Roman Catholic counterpart was Cardinal Richard Cushing, the very colorful and hard-bitten Roman Catholic Archbishop of Boston. Not much religious news was reported in which he was not somehow involved. Somewhat naively I supposed that other denominational leaders, including the Roman Catholics, would take the initiative to welcome the "new boy in town." This did not happen, so I took the initiative and introduced myself to the leaders. All were very friendly. When I called on the cardinal, he received me as a brother—almost a father—and our relations continued on a cordial level up to the time I stood beside his bier at his cathedral. This warm cordiality continued with his successor, Cardinal Medeiros. That this should have happened, not just to me of course but generally, should not have been such a surprise to us, for we all are very much alike. The factors that unite us far exceed the things that divide us. I am reminded of what my Cambridge University teacher, Professor Gordon Rupp, told one of his Roman Catholic friends: "Very roughly, I mean by 'Protestant' what you mean by 'Catholic.' "

Methodists from several parts of the world represented our Wesleyan tradition very ably at Vatican II. Among the observers were such scholars as Albert C. Outler, Robert Cushman, Walter G. Muelder, William R. Cannon, and Professor Rupp. Although he laid no claim to the scholarly standing of these academics, my colleague Bishop Fred P. Corson was also an observer, who by his dignity and episcopal role made an acknowledged contribution, greatly appreciated by Roman Catholic leaders.

I did not myself enjoy observer status but for a time during the fourth and final year of the Vatican Council I was present as an invited guest and accorded the same courtesies as the official observers. It happened that I had to be in both London and Geneva for World Council of Churches committee meetings, already alluded to, so that it did not take much persuasion for me to include Rome in my itinerary. So it was that I could witness some of the proceedings of the greatest ecumenical gathering of our time. My brother Joe was in Rome at the same time and saw even more of Vatican II than I did. We both recalled with gratitude a midnight tour of the fountains of Rome guided by Professor Nikos Nissiotis. How he loved the Eternal City!

We stayed at the *pensione* near Vatican City, which had served as the residence of Professor Outler for the four sessions he and Mrs. Outler lived in Rome. Indeed, he made all my arrangements and within a short time "showed me the ropes" of this great event. The plenary sessions were held in St. Peters, and the large nave was transformed into a kind of football field with bleachers on either side to accommodate the more than two thousand bishops who took part. At the crossing near the famous statue of St. Peter and facing the Bernini altar was a section for observers and guests where they could take in the whole of the proceedings. Just opposite were similar seats for the cardinals. In front of the altar was a throne for the pope, from which he presided when present; in front of him were six seats from which one of a presidium of cardinals presided in turn during the pontiff's absence. Each day's business began with mass, the pope presiding on one of the days I was there. Proceedings were in Latin. Since my own high school level of the language was not adequate, either Professor Outler or a young American priest would translate for me. It was all very interesting. The fact that I had access to the refreshment area of the hierarchs added to the interest and allowed me to mingle with Roman Catholic bishops from many lands, and in some cases to meet old friends from India and elsewhere.

It chanced that while I was at the Council the subject came up concerning the ninety-five theses which Martin Luther, on October 31, 1517, had nailed to the church door in Wittenberg. The very delicate question of indulgences was discussed. This was not officially one of the *schemata*, and I recall the acute embarrassment that prevailed during this discussion. It was reflected accurately to me by my interpreter. One of the bishops was frank enough to acknowledge on the floor of St. Peter's that this was the focal issue that had triggered the Reformation and that the very basilica in which they were meeting had been built largely from the sale of indulgences. No action was taken by the Council, but elaborate measures were taken to explain this subject to the press and visitors. Monsignor Gregory Baum acknowledged that indulgences symbolized all that Protestants feel about Rome. Responsible intercession by the whole church for its wayward members is what indulgences mean, so said the monsignor.

This is precisely an illustration of why Vatican II was

necessary. As Cardinal Cushing once told me, "We simply *had* to have the Council." Its aim was *aggiornamento*— updating of the church in the face of the modern world. In sum, Vatican II was a modern miracle—the impossible had happened, the immobile had moved. It was a venture in international adult education par excellence. Just imagine what it meant for twenty-five hundred of the top leaders of a great institution to go aside for fourteen weeks, four years in a row, to come to know one another and to sit at the feet of the greatest minds that institution affords. In Rome a new morale was released, a new momentum generated. A new openness characterized the Roman church, and a new opportunity confronted her.

Still, it was not so much what Vatican II accomplished that was significant, but what it made possible. To many persons, the Council that was so exciting a generation ago has receded, and for them its aims have not been realized. Theological students today seem strangely unmoved by it, but those of us who experienced it, whether from near or far, knew that it was one of the truly significant happenings of all church history: our generation had seen God manifestly working his will in history with and through his people in an unprecedented way.

One of the things the Council enabled was dialogue in a new key between Rome and other churches and confessional families. For The United Methodist Church this has been going on ever since at the international level through the World Methodist Council. At the national level since June 1966 a series of bilaterals, as they are called, have been going on between our church and the Roman Catholics. At present (1997) these talks with

United Methodists are in their fifth phase. The discussions have moved from laying groundwork to a number of specific themes: "Shared Convictions on Education," "Holiness and Spirituality of the Ordained Ministry," "Eucharistic Celebration: Converging Theology . . . Diverging Practice," "Holy Living and Dying," and a fifth focus not yet defined. I was engaged in the first three. A Roman Catholic and a United Methodist bishop were co-chairs of the conversations. To begin with they were Bishop Joseph B. Brunini of Jackson, Mississippi, and Bishop F. Gerald Ensley of Columbus. Later on I shared the chair with Bishop Brunini, and later still with Bishop James Malone of Youngstown.

Some of the values arising from these dialogues are those experienced by the participants themselves. Thus Roman Catholics came to know their Methodist or United Methodist counterparts, persons such as Albert C. Outler, J. Robert Nelson, Harold Bosley, Robert Huston, our ecumenical officer, Harry Richardson, Dorothy McConnell, John Deschner, Charles Parlin, Paul Minus, Gerald Moede, Donald Saliers, Susan Morrison, Sharon Brown-Christopher, and many others. For their part the Methodists would meet and debate with Roman Catholic scholars and leaders: Barnabas Ahern, John F. Cronin, Georges Tavard, Bernard Law, and William Baum (both later cardinals), Richard McCormick, Sister Rose Eileen, Gerald Sloyan, John Hotchkin, and more. The colloquies were, of course, far more than personal encounters. There is much evidence that the substantive findings and agreements were productive in and of themselves. They became foundations upon which the future could build.

To my mind the most significant gathering was at the Methodist Theological School in Ohio, at Delaware, October 9-11, 1969. Robert Huston remarked, "An optimistic mood concerning the future importance and creativity of our dialogue was apparent." Professor James A. Doyle, S.J., of Georgetown presented an insightful, provocative paper entitled, "Christ, Salvation, Sacrament and Ministry," which launched a stimulating discussion on ministry. There are no minutes to vouch for this, but United Methodists who were present recall that the Roman Catholic theologians by the end of the session expressed this conviction: "That although they understood that it was for the hierarchy to conclude this, they saw no *theological* reason why Methodist orders should not be regarded as valid." They went further to state that from the Roman Catholic standpoint Methodist orders may be *irregular*, but they were not *invalid*. In my view this is progress in dialogue!

Vatican II also paved the way for national councils of churches to relate to Rome in a fuller way. On March 17 and 18, 1969, in my role as vice president for Christian Unity of the National Council of Churches, I led a delegation to Rome to confer with Bishop J. G. M . Willebrands of the Netherlands, who was in charge of the Secretariat for Promoting Christian Unity. Our delegation consisted of the Rt. Rev. John E. Hines, Presiding Bishop of the Episcopal Church; Dr. Robert J. Marshall, President of the Lutheran Church of America; Dr. John W. Williams, African-American Baptist leader; Dr. R. H. Edwin Espy and Dr. Robert Dodds both of the National Council of Churches. We were joined by Professor J. Robert Nelson, then teaching in Gregorian University, as well as Bishop Ernest L. Unterkoefler, bishop of Charleston, South Carolina, and also secretary of the National Conference of Catholic Bishops, and Monsignor Bernard Law, director of the U.S. Bishops' Committee for Ecumenical and Interreligious Affairs.

In the ensuing two days of meeting, Bishop Willebrands and I served as co-chairs and alternated in presiding. We discussed a number of items with the Secretariat for Christian Unity and other Vatican Officers. The list of these persons read like a Who's Who (I name some of them without their rank or designations, which have changed through the years, some becoming archbishops and cardinals): Jerome Hamer, Pierre Duprey, Thomas Stransky, John Long, William A. Purdy, Sergio Pignedoli, Joseph Gremilion, and Charles Moeller. Some of the topics were simply reports of the programs of the National Council of Churches and various ecumenical developments in the United States, such as the Consultation on Church Union, local and regional councils of churches, and unofficial or spontaneous interchurch developments. The Secretariat made similar reports for information from their side. Then, with an eye to the future, other matters were touched upon: possible Roman Catholic relationship to the National Council, Christian-Jewish relations, collaboration on programs of justice and peace, joint seminary training, and mixed marriages—all occasioned by the new situation brought about by Vatican II. Then, about an hour before our scheduled meeting with the pope, our proceedings were interrupted by a sudden summons of Bishop Willebrands to the papal office. More of that later.

The high point of our visit was naturally our audience with Pope Paul VI. It took place in his private library and lasted for forty-five minutes, while an impatient archbishop from the Holy Office waited outside to see His Holiness. The twelve of us gathered around a table. We were greeted individually by the pope as he welcomed us in an informal manner: "We welcome you to our home." The pope sat at one end of a table on a slightly elevated dais flanked by Bishop Willebrands on his right and me on his left. I then introduced Dr. Robert Marshall, president of The Lutheran Church in America, who read our prepared formal statement, stressing the religiously pluralistic nature of American culture. To this His Holiness gave careful attention. I may say that he looked much frailer than when I had last seen him in 1966, for he had recently undergone surgery, but he seemed to gain strength as we proceeded. Then he read a formal reply in clear, somewhat accented English. He emphasized his great pleasure at the new day of collaboration. There was no sense of hurry, and we almost felt that he did not want the meeting to end. Finally, he led us in prayer and invited us to join the Lord's Prayer. Calling to his side the two Roman Catholic bishops who were present—in collegial gesture—together they gave the benediction.

At this point I remarked on his numerous papal visits to various parts of the world as being of symbolic importance in a jet age: to Jerusalem to meet the ecumenical patriarch in the interest of Christian Unity, to New York City for peace, to Latin America in pastoral concern, to India and Africa in the interest of missions. To this he responded: "Not just symbol—reality!"

We then presented gifts: the new Bible published by the National Council of Churches, pictures, and books. As the current chairman of Consultation on Church Union, I handed him several books produced by that consultation. "I see you want me to read a lot!" he remarked. Then he gave each one of us papal medals but, above all, a marvelous set of the two volumes of the Decrees of Vatican II—in Latin. As he hefted this weighty gift, weighing 14 pounds, he said: "I am afraid you will find this a little heavy for your baggage." To this I felt prompted to respond: "Your Holiness, when a gift is given in love, it takes on wings!" The group picture taken at the time reflects the great pleasure all of us felt. As we left we passed the new and now well-known sculpture of John XXIII at prayer. His faithfulness to the heavenly vision had made this visit possible.

We returned to our rooms at the Hotel Columbus and to lunch with our host—now *Cardinal* Willebrands, for he had been called out of our meeting earlier to learn from Pope Paul that he was to be elevated to this new rank. It was the pleasure of this United Methodist bishop to toast our host, who had become the guest of honor at his own luncheon. I even recall my words emphasizing the stages in hierarchic advancement: "We toast one who already displayed *excellence, grace, and eminence* before these designations were *bestowed* upon him." The honoree seemed pleased and we all enjoyed a splendid meal.

Vatican II, as already suggested, made the pope more accessible to his own people but also more human and approachable by other Christians. For example, when Paul VI came to New York City October 4, 1965, to address the United Nations on Peace, Protestant leaders were invited to meet with him at nearby Holy Family Church. So it was that we gathered together for an ecumenical service near the United Nations. Then the next year when Cardinal Cushing learned that Eunice and I were to be in Rome, he kindly arranged that we should be received in private audience by Paul VI. During August 1966 we proceeded to the papal summer residence at Castel Gondolfo near Rome. It was a lovely lakeside villa resplendent with gardens. The Swiss guards snapped to attention as we entered. We had about five minutes with the Holy Father. He presented us with medals: he gave Eunice one of *gold*—a medallion of Peter and Paul, while mine was of *silver*, a commemorative piece recalling his visit to Bombay in 1964. On the obverse was the "Gateway to India," and I told him my little church in Bombay years ago was about a hundred yards from that monument. This sparked his interest as did the fact that Eunice had been born in India of missionary parents, for he had considerable interest in missions. His parting word to us was intended to be reassuring: "Though we may not be one in this life, we shall be one in heaven!"

The final time I saw Pope Paul VI was in Rome on Sunday, September 14, 1975. The occasion was the canonization of Elizabeth Ann Bayley Seton, a Sister of Charity, and the first native-born American so to be distinguished. Since I was at the time president of the United Methodist Ecumenical agency and since Mother Seton's labors had been within the bounds of the Washington Area, I was invited to be present for the occasion. I was not the only American there by any means, for some fifteen thousand of our citizens had made the pilgrimage to Rome for the event. A total of one hundred thousand crowded St. Peter's Square for an outdoors service on a very sunny day. The service itself was deeply impressive and strongly moving as well as rich in symbolism. For example, five gifts were offered: bread, wine, candles, a bird and flowers. These gifts symbolized the three essentials for life, food, drink, and light, as well as beauty and animate nature. It was as if to suggest that all creation was involved in this celebration of humanness. The Gospel lesson, Luke 10:38-42, the story of Mary and Martha, was read by women in both Latin and Greek. The pope's short homily referred to sainthood as implying not merely moral perfection, but also as being an expression of the image of Christ. This Elizabeth Seton did, and here she was being remembered during International Women's Year.

Our Roman Catholic hosts welcomed heartily the Protestant representatives, including the Episcopal bishop of Baltimore, David Leighton, for Mother Seton had been an Episcopalian in early life. Cardinal Dearden of Detroit, speaking to the Protestants present, was gracious enough to say, "You cannot know how much your presence means to us." I wrote an article about this experience entitled "For All the Saints," emphasizing that God makes saints; the church merely acknowledges them and we all—Catholics, Orthodox, and Protestants—have our own ways of doing this. If churches do not identify exemplary human beings, then secular forces—the sports world or the movies—will do so. At the suggestion of Professor Albert Outler this article was sent to every

Roman Catholic bishop in the United States. I have a thick file from the replies of scores of them, without exception, expressing deep appreciation.

Three years after the canonization, Paul VI had died and was succeeded by John Paul I, who served for only a month, and then by John Paul II. He was, of course, to become a pope who extended global itineration far beyond even what his predecessor had done. He came to Washington in October 1979 and Cardinal William Baum invited Protestant leaders to meet him. I was among those so honored, and at an Ecumenical Service of Prayer I presented him with a leather-bound copy of John Wesley's *Letter to a Roman Catholic*. This was subsequently acknowledged with thanks by the Holy See. Meanwhile I was under some heavy criticism from some Protestants for doing this on the grounds that the new pope's inter-church credentials were not considered good. Little did my critics know that several Roman Catholic theologians had urged me to do this as a means of possibly arousing greater affirmation of ecumenism. I do not know if this gift was a factor, but the fact is that in John Paul's volume *Crossing the Threshold of Hope* (1994) he did indeed make a strong plea for Christian unity. Encouraged by this note, I was bold enough to write him a letter urging him from his very extensive royalties to gift the Archbishop Iakovos Fund for Faith and Order with $1 million. The response from the Vatican was that His Holiness preferred that such gifts be through regular channels. At any rate the Vatican did not seem offended by my boldness. Meanwhile it was applauded by close Roman Catholic friends in the United States. When I met John Paul II in New York

City, October 1996, he remembered me from our previous meetings.

This section has been longer than intended, but perhaps it is forgivable in the light of the unexpected and unprecedented advances in Christian oneness that have taken place as a result of Vatican II. At all costs we must not allow the strides toward unity to become eroded. Rather we must "make fast with bonds of peace the unity which the Spirit gives" (Eph. 4:3 NEB), regardless of the risks. Nearly a century ago a British layman said that we "must be daring if we want reconciliation. After all, God took the risk of incarnation."

ORTHODOX CONNECTIONS

We of the Methodist family have rather special links with our Orthodox brothers and sisters. John Wesley himself saw to that, and for many of our doctrinal emphases we are indebted to that tradition. Therefore, it is not my intention to go into detail with these relations. Indeed, the various Orthodox autocephalous churches are already deeply committed to the ecumenical movement. The rest of us have not made the road easy for them, and at times they have wavered in their commitment.

It so happens that from my brief presence in 1964 at Vatican II I proceeded to Istanbul, or as the Orthodox prefer, Constantinople. In fact, I carried on my person a message from Orthodox observers to the ecumenical patriarch, Athenagoras I. I have already mentioned his departure from the United States to assume this elevated office. He received me with the warmest welcome to the Phanar.

His humble quarters stood out in sharpest contrast to the grandeur of the Vatican. Thanks to the generosity of many and the intervention of President Jimmy Carter with the Turkish government the headquarters have been greatly improved during the recent past.

His All Holiness was delighted to hear my report fresh from the Council and to receive the special message I carried. He entertained me at his table with a marvelous meal featuring lamb cooked with quinces. This feast was followed by his inviting me to ride with him along the Sea of Marmora to the Black Sea, an outing for both of us. Four years later there was an occasion that brought me back to the Phanar. This time Eunice was along and our daughter Anne, just graduated from college, was also with us. The patriarch took a liking to her and treated her with special kindness, a memory she has treasured ever since.

Then in 1991 I called on his successor, Patriarch Dimitrios I. He was a quiet, reserved man who did not speak English. His interpreter was New Testament Professor Vasil Istavridis who together with Archbishop Makarios had trained for his Ph.D. on a Methodist Crusade scholarship at Boston University. He was very grateful and proved friendly as, of course, did the patriarch.

I came to know the current Ecumenical Patriarch Bartholomew when we served together on the Central Committee of the World Council of Churches. He was most brotherly when I called on him at the newly built Phanar in 1995, this time the visit was with Dr. Joan Brown Campbell, general secretary of the NCC, and her associate Dr. Albert M. Penneybacker. In my ecumenical service I became acquainted with the Orthodox patriarchs of Antioch, Alexandria, and Jerusalem. Similarly my path led to the leaders of the pre-Chalcedonian churches—Armenian, Coptic, Ethiopian, and Syrian Orthodox. It is pleasant to recall two meetings with Pope Shenouda of the Coptic Orthodox Church, now one of the presidents of the WCC, and Vasken, Armenian Catholicos of Etchmiadzin, a most gracious man of superb bearing, as well as is his successor, Catholicos Khariken—friend of many years.

Special mention must be made of Archbishop Iakovos, the longtime Orthodox archbishop of North and South America, with the additional designation of Exarch. We first met in the 1950s in Geneva while he was serving as representative of the ecumenical patriarch at the WCC. We became even better acquainted at the Accra meeting of the International Missionary Council in 1958. After his assignment as archbishop of North and South America our paths crossed frequently, as when he received from President Carter the Freedom Medal, and at the Iranian visit celebrating the 2,500th anniversary of Cyrus the Great, at meetings with the pope, and so on. On one occasion I took our grandson Nicholas with me to meet him. This seemed to please His Eminence no end, particularly, I think, because the boy had a Greek name. This reminds me that I once encountered Iakovos during a six-month stint I was enduring on crutches. He was solicitous about my problem and inquired about it. He seemed startled when I replied that I was suffering from a well-known Greek ailment—I had severed Achilles tendon! I do not recommend this particular experience to others.

To conclude this Orthodox reference, I mention a trip to the USSR August 16 to September 18, 1974. This was the third such visitation from the National Council of Churches. On the first one in 1956 Charles Parlin was the Methodist representative; on the second in 1962 Bishop Richard C. Raines took part. For the third visitation Dr. Robert Marshall, president of The Lutheran Church of America, led the representative group. I was a United Methodist representative. It was greatly in our favor that we were given orientation for our journey by Dr. Paul Anderson, Dr. Bruce Rigdon, and Dr. Charles West, all of whom were experts on Russian history and the Soviet Union. Throughout our visit Moscow was our base. The whole delegation went from there to Zagorsk, 50 miles to the north, to the famous monastery of St. Sergius. There we were personal guests of the patriarch and were present for the elaborate ceremonies related to the Dormition of the Virgin.

His Holiness Patriarch Pimen proved to be a kindly host. This man, together with some other bishops, has often been a target of intense criticism by persons of Russian origin now living outside the former USSR. How is one really to evaluate such matters? How were they to conduct themselves as spiritual leaders in a well-nigh impossible situation? Here was a man—a monk—of great faith and prayer. He was a great authority on Russian church music and an expert in its liturgy. For fifteen years after his ordination in 1930 he was denied the right of exercising his priesthood and for a decade dropped out of sight altogether, a prisoner in exile. From firsthand experience, then, he learned what oppression and repression are. He was certainly an impressive person, acceptable to his people.

St. Sergius Monastery is the heart of Russian Orthodoxy. We were enabled to see a great deal of its periphery as well. For our total delegation broke up into four teams and on three separate tours spread out into twelve parts of the vast country. Thus we had a representative view, despite the fact that nearly 80 percent of the USSR was not open to outsiders. My own peregrinations led me to Siberia and to the Caucasus as well as to Vladimir and Suzdal, ancient political and religious centers well to the east of Moscow.

Siberia is vast beyond one's most extravagant imagination and is incredibly rich in natural resources. The diocese of Eastern Siberia is surely the largest in the world. One could stand on one part of it and on a clear day look across the Bering Straits to the USA—Alaska. Indeed, Alaska and California were, a little over a century ago, a part of that diocese! Within its borders too is to be found Lake Baikal, in which I swam *briefly*. It is the largest lake in the world, vastly deep containing 20 percent of all the fresh water on earth! In a word, the USSR was impressive in whatever way one looked at it!

But now, a look more directly at the life of the churches in the USSR. One way to look at it is this: just imagine a situation in which the church was allowed no missionary work, no evangelism, no church extension, no Christian education, no welfare programs, no access to mass media, no colleges, no involvement in public, social, or political witness, no hospitals or healing ministry, and no societies for youth or women. The list is not complete! Within such limitations the church had to work. And they did. About 70 percent were baptized in spite of repression. Possibly half of all Soviet citizens were believers. This included up to twenty million Muslims, over two million ethnic Jews, an indeterminate number of Buddhists, and perhaps sixty million Christians. This after more than half a century of Communist rule, by a party that has never enrolled more than about fifteen million members. This under a regime that was officially atheist—periodically militantly so. Church leaders were understandably shy of statistics; they did not wish to invite excessive attention to their flock. Were there fifty million Orthodox? Or eighty million? The Baptists generally admitted to half a million. Except in the Baltic region and the Ukraine, Roman Catholics were few.

One can understand what a Russian Christian meant when he told a visitor that fellow Christians in other parts of the world ought to thank God for the Russian church. The great miracle is that it has survived at all! In fact, it has survived with considerable strength. Officially, religion was viewed as a kind of cancer or tumor, dangerous to remove by radical surgery, but expected to "go away" if treated drastically. Yet years ago a leader of the Militant League of the Godless, an organization that is now defunct, observed that "Religion is like a nail. The harder you hit it on the head, the deeper it goes into the wood."

How has the church survived? By the grace of God? By the deep commitment of multitudes of faithful men and women? By the vitality of its corporate worship? By all of these and more. As a recent British report puts it—in

Shakespearian language—it has survived *by discretion and valour!*

In Siberia we visited a flower show; yes, a *flower* show in Siberia! The blooms were rich and lovely. I was given a beautiful yellow rose. I knew its name, for they grow in our little rose garden at home: the "peace" rose. But my Russian rose bore a label. I had learned enough of the Cyrillic alphabet to make out the letters. These atheistic people had a better name for my rose: *Gloria Deo.* Then it dawned on me that the two belong together, for God put them together. The angels' song links them: "*glory to God* in the highest, and on earth *peace* to people of goodwill." To which we can only say, Amen. I told this story at a final banquet in Moscow. I think most of my audience breathed an amen too.

The whole journey was filled with sights and insights of the most soul-searching kind. As guests we were treated with an extravagance of hospitality, which was humbling to us all. I like to think that our presence with our hosts was also a sign of hope to them, a hope that some fifteen years later was realized in fullest degree with the collapse of the Communist order.

The following spring (1975) a return delegation visited the United States. It was our turn to be hosts, though in this we fell far short of their achievements for us. It fell to my lot and privilege to perform this role in Washington, during which time we filled the National Cathedral to celebrate their visit. As always the meeting was picketed by the Reverend Carl McIntire and other so-called Christians carrying insulting placards—the kind of people who seem to rejoice in despising their fellowmen, the very opposite of ecumenical spirit. Whenever I see mean-spiritedness I am convinced that those who persistently demonstrate this attitude know none of Christ. In fairness, I am pleased to report that years later McIntire repented of some of his excesses.

THE CONSULTATION ON CHURCH UNION

Dialogue has not been restricted to talks with Roman Catholics and Orthodox but also has taken a multilateral cast. The fact is that the different branches of the Christian family are *talking* with one another and they are listening to one another. For more than thirty-five years earnest conversation has been going on in the Consultation on Church Union. This continues among the nine denominations that participate at present, and it is being overheard by others.

The genesis of the Consultation stems from a sermon preached by Presbyterian Dr. Eugene Carson Blake in Grace Episcopal Cathedral in San Francisco, December 4, 1960. The proposals were seconded, as it were, by Episcopal Bishop James A. Pike, and suggestions were for a time called the Blake/Pike proposals. Within two years the first meetings of participants took place, and by 1964 ten denominations had officially approved their engaging in these discussions. They were:

The African Methodist Episcopal Church
The African Methodist Episcopal Zion Church
The Christian Church (Disciples of Christ)
The Christian Methodist Episcopal Church

The Evangelical United Brethren Church
The Episcopal Church
The Presbyterian Church in the U.S.
The United Church of Christ
The Methodist Church
The United Presbyterian Church in the U.S.A.

My own involvement as an observer began in 1962 when the meetings were held in Washington. Methodists officially entered the talks in 1964 after approval by the General Conference of that year. Within a short time an administrative office was started in Princeton, New Jersey. Chairpersons were elected for two-year terms, and I was chosen to serve in this office from 1968 to 1970. Earlier sessions dealt with various items of prolegomena, but in time a restlessness manifested itself for the Consultation to move beyond being a mere polite debating society toward formulating a plan that might give some idea as to what a united church would look like. So on my watch *A Plan of Union* was carefully formulated, and at our St. Louis meeting this was tentatively approved and commended to the churches for study in 1970. This was a necessary step but proved provocative of much discussion. It was astonishing how much we readily agreed upon: matters of faith, sacrament, and worship, even ministry. Structure and governance were more formidable barriers than many of us had supposed would be the case. But no longer could any of us say to the other, "We have no need of you." We had discovered a family likeness. To quote Archbishop Geoffrey Fisher again, "We may not like each other but we are strangely alike." I confess, however, to disappointment that the plan was not taken more seriously; it seemed quickly to drop from sight.

Two other special events marked my term. One was when Bishop Jon G. M. Willebrands of the Secretariat for Christian Unity spoke at our Atlanta meeting in March 1969. The other was to preside over a nationally televised Christmas Eucharist service of the National Cathedral in 1969. This was well received and stimulated some countrywide interest in COCU, as it was called.

By custom, when one's turn had ended the president dropped out of active involvement in the Consultation, but I have kept a watchful eye on its proceedings. I believe the Consultation on Church Union has been justified. It has been a forum for theological discussion and much of that need not be repeated. For example, it has been an umbrella under which bilateral unions have taken place. Both The United Methodist Church and The United Presbyterian Church, as they are now constituted, are the result of unions that have taken place between members of COCU. It has encouraged discussions between The Christian Church, Disciples of Christ, and The United Church of Christ, which have not yet resulted in full union. It has furthered the current talks among the four Methodist members of COCU, already alluded to. It has stimulated efforts toward mutual recognition on the part of various churches. I do not look for any monolithic form of united church to emerge, but movement toward unity at the local levels, progress toward consensus "Churches in Covenant Communion," toward affirming baptism and recognizing each other's ministries—all those prospects are most promising. Something like Federal Union could then possibly develop from these initiatives, much as I have earlier suggested could be an outcome of Pan-Methodist discussions.

ECUMENICAL MISCELLANY

To round off this chapter brief reference should be made to other ecumenical involvement that has characterized my ministry. In some instances this reaches beyond the Christian family to other religions. As far as Jewish relations are concerned they were proper and cordial in every place I have served, though I tended to leave the deeper ties to my colleagues who had special interest or competence in this area. My experience as a missionary in India and my academic specialty in the history of religions pointed to interfaith involvement in the larger sense, which I have customarily referred to as "the larger ecumenism." Our shrunken world, the increasing trend toward international travel, and the large influx of immigrants during the last half century have all contributed to the meetings of the faiths, an encounter for which few are well prepared and for which fewer still are equipped to be involved in interreligious dialogue.

Some would readily adopt an inclusive view and conclude that all religions are at heart the same, thus making dialogue unnecessary, a view that among other things cuts the very nerve of missionary endeavor. Others would move to the pole of exclusivism; that is, that Christianity alone is true, so that no dialogue is possible. Some other religions readily conclude that they are the only true faith. It has seemed to me that a navigable channel must be found between the Scylla of universalism and the Charybdis of exclusivism. This way is what I would call confessionalism: adherents to each faith are expected to take a stand within their tradition as dialogue proceeds with those of another position of integrity. Then perhaps God in God's time will show the way forward. In my view, dialogue should not be seen as a debate in which one party or another must entirely prevail. Meanwhile there are tasks in our world—peace, justice, and hunger, among others—in which there can be interreligious common action. As we work together, purely dogmatic differences can gradually be addressed in a new spirit. Archbishop Nathan Soderblom was correct in his insight that doctrine divides but service unites.

WORLD CONFERENCE ON RELIGION AND PEACE

A prime example of this latter trend is the World Conference on Religion and Peace (WCRP). This movement emerged in the 1960s when Homer Jack and Dana McLean Greeley, both Unitarian-Universalist ministers, met with Rabbi Maurice Eisendrath over a common concern for world peace, especially in the light of the nuclear threat. The circle of concern was gradually broadened to involve Roman Catholics, such as Bishop (later Cardinal) John J. Wright of Pittsburgh, and Protestants, including Methodists Herman Will and Bishop John Wesley Lord. The group expanded further, until Muslims, Hindus, Buddhists, Sikhs, Jains, and representatives of the other principal religions of the world were included.

Very soon I too was recruited. In January 1968 Eunice

and I, along with the above-named persons, were joined by others: Episcopalian Herschel Halbert, Monsignor Edward Murray, Bishop (later Cardinal) Joseph Bernardin, Dr. and Mrs. Ralph Abernathy, Bishop John Burt, and the Honorable Harold Stassen, to name a few. We traveled as a group in the interest of WCRP. Our itinerary took us to Geneva to see World Council of Churches leaders, including Charles Malik, who was particularly interesting, then to Rome where we called on Vatican leaders, and to Constantinople as guests of the ecumenical patriarch. Then it was on to Jerusalem for cordial greetings by Israeli leaders, especially Abba Eban. At New Delhi we had a longer stay for a Peace Symposium at the Gandhi Peace Foundation. Present at parts of this meeting were the president of India, Dr. Zakir Hussain, Prime Minister Indira Gandhi, and her deputy Morarji Desai, Sheikh Abdullah of Kashmir, socialist leader Jai Prakash Narayan, Pyarelal secretary to Mahatma Gandhi. There were also representatives of the nine major religions of the world that are present in India. More important, we were joined by such personages as Archbishop Angelo Fernandes of New Delhi, who was later to become the world president of the WCRP. Another outstanding participant was Princess Poon Pismai Diskul, a Buddhist from Thailand and a descendant of the king known to us in *Anna and the King of Siam* or *The King and I.* Altogether it was a mind and soul-stretching experience for us all.

I should report here our delight that our daughter Anne could be with us on this trip as far as India. She had recently been graduated from Earlham College and was to join her grandfather, E. Stanley Jones, in Delhi to tour India as his secretary, just as her mother had once done. Later still our second daughter, Jan, served her grandfather in this role traveling through Australasia and around the world.

The group proceeded to Saigon, after which Eunice and I went on to Australia while the main body continued to Kyoto. In Saigon we visited Vietnamese leaders as well as the American Ambassador Ellsworth Bunker and General William C. Westmoreland. On a Sunday I preached to the U.S. Army headquarters staff and troops, an experience I have never forgotten. Nor can I fail to remember getting a haircut the next day. As I arose from the chair, the barber wished me "Happy *Tet!*" Within an hour or two the Tet offensive began!

In a way, the purpose of this pilgrimage was to lay the foundation for the first World Conference for Religion and Peace, which convened in Kyoto, Japan, October 16-21, 1970. The official delegates numbered more than two hundred and represented every continent and every major religion from many countries. It was a period of nuclear threat, so what more appropriate setting to praying and pleading for peace than the only country in the world that had experienced nuclear bombing. This assembly and its four successors held under the auspices of the WCRP have done much to raise the consciousness of humankind with respect to finding alternatives to violent conflict. A united universal religious voice against war was raised, a splendid model of what religions should be doing together.

Of great significance for peace also were two meetings in 1978 and 1980 between representative church leaders of the United States and of the USSR. Their contacts arose out of the Conference on Church and Society called in 1966 by the World Council of Churches and led to important bilateral sessions in Geneva. These gatherings were marked by the most frank interchange of views, often in a tense atmosphere but without exception one in which mutual respect prevailed. The participants from the USSR were, of course, unwavering in their condemnation of U.S. involvement in Vietnam, but when it came to Soviet intrusion into Afghanistan it was another story. I recall asking them, "Do you remember what the attitude in your country was in regard to the U.S. and Vietnam?" They did. Then I remarked, "Well, that's how Americans feel about your country's intrusion in the Afghan war." They seemed nonplussed by this.

During the rather short period in which this bilateral was in conversation, we were briefed by leading experts on the nuclear issue and disarmament so that ours was an educational experience. Two major reports resulted, the most notable one entitled "Choose Life"; a clarion call for nuclear disarmament. It was published in its entirety in periodicals in the Soviet Union—a first of its kind. The principal authors of this document were Dr. Arie Brouwer and Dr. Alan Geyer, who was later the principal adviser to United Methodist bishops in their study of disarmament, which has the title *In Defense of Creation*. Another result of these meetings was that they laid the foundation for a series of visits of American Christians to the USSR and Christian institutions there. Hundreds were involved in these tours, which contributed vastly to understanding and *rapprochement*.

Yet another ecumenical venture over which I presided from 1980 to 1992 was the International Christian Federation for the Prevention of Alcoholism and Drug Addiction. It was a modest venture but was able to exercise considerable influence, particularly in the Third World. The leadership teams included the Reverend J. Kenneth Lawton, a Methodist from the U.K.; the Reverend Frank Gibson of Scotland; Dr. Jonathan Gnanadoson and Metropolitan Alexander Mar Thoma of India; Bishop Lawi Imathiu and Dr. John Gato of Kenya; the Reverend Bengt Taranger of Sweden; and Salvation Army officers from several continents. We held consultations and study conferences in India, Kenya, the Netherlands, Italy, Sweden, and the U.K. and became an effective part of a global network in the fight against substance abuse.

Much earlier while in Boston I chaired the board of North Conway Institute, founded by Dr. David Works. The institute did a tremendous job in the field of chemical dependency.

My relationship with the Taizé community was not extensive but nevertheless very precious to me. It was, of course, a part of the extensive quest for church renewal that arose following World War II and was prompted in some measure by the devastation which that struggle visited upon much of Europe. Taizé is named for what had been a deserted village in southeast France, a region of very sparse Protestant presence. It is a Protestant monastic community founded by a Swiss Reformed pastor, Roger Schutz. Though he was himself the son of a pastor, as a youth he was an agnostic who after a profound conversion felt strongly prompted to help Jews escape occupied France. He stayed on to develop a dedicated Christian community. A little later Roger's sister established a sister order for women at Grandchamps, near Neuchatel, Switzerland.

Gradually other young men of similar disposition and search joined Roger, Frere Max Thurian among them, who became the most reflective theologian of the group. Both ministerial and lay members were added, bringing with them a wide range of talents. A Taizé Rule emerged and a characteristic liturgical practice after the mode of historic orders. It was self-supporting and gradually engaged in missionary outreach in Europe, Britain, Africa, and the United States. They place emphasis upon a "mission of the presence," which takes seriously Jesus' word that "where two or three are gathered in his name" he is in their midst. The community places central emphasis on "burning zeal for the unity of the Body of Christ." Naturally, the Roman Catholics were interested, and popes since Pius XII have given the work their blessing. The ecumenical patriarch also showed a friendly interest, but Taizé has continued its Protestant character.

Through the World Council of Churches I became aware of this development and on two occasions have visited Taizé. One time was during the summer of 1962 when I was invited there to participate in the dedication of the magnificent Church of the Reconciliation. This splendid and modern edifice is so named because it was made possible by gifts from German Christians as an act of contrition and reconciliation after the war. At that time I became acquainted with Taizé's leaders and many of the brothers. In August of 1980 I returned to Taizé with members of the family to take part in the great gatherings of tens of thousands of youth who have made it a place of pilgrimage. This emphasis is possibly the richest contribution of this effort at Christian renewal. I personally have been deeply influenced by this experiment in contemporary monasticism and liturgical recovery.

Speaking of Christian renewal, soon after the war I became aware of a unique venture in Germany called *Kirchentag*. At Willingen (1952) I met for the first time the very gifted founder of the enterprise, Count Reinhold von Thadden. In a word, this man was acutely aware that postwar Europe, particularly Germany, was not suffering merely from physical hunger and deprivation, but from a hunger for peace, justice, and community—for the Spirit. *Kirchentag* addressed these needs at a deep level of Bible study, worship, sacrament, and fellowship in an atmosphere of a rally, a fair in celebration of being Christian. To this was added music, concerts, art, theater, exhibitions, and revival of culture in general.

For a long time I had wanted to attend such a session but not until the fourteenth *Kirchentag*, meeting in Stuttgart July 16-20, 1969, was I able to be present. Accompanying me was my brother Joe and a young pastor from Maine, the Reverend Peter Misner, and Father Robert Quinn, a Paulist priest from Boston. More than thirty thousand persons attended, including a thousand visitors from overseas. A certain amount of turmoil was evident at the sessions occasioned by a quite vocal youth presence. In 1969 Richard von Weizsäcker, later West Germany's president, presided over the *Kirchentag* and observed that the younger generation did not want to leave the church in the hands of the older generation, but "claims its own place in the church." All four of our small company were deeply addressed by the spirit and thrust of *Kirchentag*, and Peter Misner found that it greatly empowered his future ministry. We also discovered that a visit to Hans Küng in his chalet at nearby Tübigen was a lasting benefit to us.

The postwar period was clearly characterized by a renewal of religious interest and a growth of churches in the 1940s and 1950s. By the following decade this upsurge began to erode. This was accompanied by unparalleled ecumenical development, which I have touched upon at some length. There is more often a suggestion that all religious bodies discerned that they required more cohesive relations as they faced problems common to all. Ecumenical ties were multiplied to help meet this sensed need. Let me illustrate two of these.

One was a gathering near Minneapolis, October 6–8, 1969. Its theme was "Relevancy of Organized Religion: Agenda for the Future." The gathering was supported financially by the George D. Dayton Foundation. Dayton was a concerned layman and department-store executive. He enabled fifty representative religious leaders, clergy and lay—Roman Catholics, Protestant, and Jewish—men and women to discuss this broad topic. Among participants were those long familiar to the conciliar movement: Eugene Carson Blake, William Thompson, John Hines, Arthur Flemming, Cynthia Wedel, and Andrew Young. Others who were well known but not ordinarily seen at NCC/WCC gatherings were former Archbishop James P. Shannon of Minneapolis, Father Andrew M. Greeley,

Father Charles Davis, Sister Mary Luke Tobin, and Sister Martin de Porres Grecy; and Jewish leaders Rabbis Marc Tanenbaum and Jacob P. Rudin. Father Greeley delivered the most telling address in which he stressed that religion in the future would have to do the following: address the question of personal meaning, encourage self-fulfillment in community, recognize sexuality as the paradigm of all human relations, help humanity to recover a sense of oneness with the universe—a fresh sense of the sacred, and reflect these goals and aims in a humanized organization. This was a sociologist speaking. Others added: taking the race issue more seriously, turning toward the poor, and bringing the sacred into the public domain. One follow-up meeting of this group was held, but its original intention did not come to full fruit.

At the beginning of the modern ecumenical exploration Christians often found themselves separated from some of their sisters and brothers by an enormous chasm. Then voices seemed to be raised from either side. As they began truly to listen to one another, they found that both sides were lifting the same cry: "Brother!" "Sister!" The gap has narrowed and has in fact been bridged at many points.

We ought not to stumble by concluding that this movement toward one another is merely the work of men and women. We would conclude this at our peril. Nor is the movement merely horizontal. It is vertical. Ecumenism is the work of God: God graciously invites his people to unite with him to make his work our own. Father Ives Congar used to liken the church to water in a lake. Whence comes the water? From the evangelical standpoint it comes down vertically as rain; from the catholic viewpoint it comes horizontally by rivers and canals. We might extend the metaphor and say that from the reformed point of view God controls both the rain and the floodgates.

Speaking personally, my own participation in the ecumenical venture has enlarged my horizons immensely. I have been enabled to *be there* in witness, service, relief, and mission. Professor H. Richard Niebuhr has said that "to believe is to be united with both the One in whom one believes and with all those who believe in him." The same note was sounded at Amsterdam in 1948 when the World Council of Churches was inaugurated and where it was insisted that the unity we seek arises out of the love of God in Jesus Christ, which binds the churches to him and binds them to one another. This is indeed the work of God.

We United Methodists are a part of the catholic tradition. Our line can be traced through the Anglicans to the Western church and to the church universal. Therefore, strictly speaking, our separation was not based on doctrinal quarrels, but on a kind of "piety quarrel" that resisted religious formalism and sought the recovery of vital religion through turning our faces toward the poor, the neglected, and the dispossessed. We were thus freed for mission. When we are true to our heritage, we unite with others in mission. For with others we are restless until we can all partake at one table, then arise from the table to be propelled in witness and service to all humankind as a part of the mission of Christ.

12

Is There Life After Retirement?

At the stroke of midnight on August 31, 1980, I retired—for the first time! A little earlier that same evening I received a telephone call from one of my episcopal colleagues who was also retiring. He commiserated with me, for he did not particularly want to retire and neither did I. The fact is that we had no choice in the matter because the law of our Church decreed that if a bishop reached the age of sixty-seven by the time of a General Conference—as I had done the previous February—retirement was mandatory.

Why then did I not welcome retirement? Many people look forward to it with increasing eagerness. For one thing, I was in good health and quite able to continue. For another, according to the rules in force at the time of my election in 1960, I would have continued until 1984 and felt that a "grandfather clause" should have been attached to the change in legislation. My plans had been laid for retirement in 1984. Besides, the Church had invested a great deal in me and was entitled to a further return on the investment as I saw it. At the same time there is something to be said for stepping down and making room for younger hands and minds.

While I have spoken of retirement, traditionally that has not been a typical term used in Methodist parlance.

Rather, bishops were relieved from the necessity "to travel" and, rather like generals and admirals, they are put on the inactive list (though in my experience "inactive" was not an accurate description of my situation) with the possibility at any time of being recalled to active duty. In my view there is no real retirement for the Christian. As long as strength of health in body and mind continues one is on duty all the time. As we are given our first breath by our Maker, so by God's pleasure we draw our last breath. Then we are truly retired.

Let me confess to a little naïveté in this matter. We have always liked Florida and its climate and knew that many friends had retired there. Consequently, we purchased a condominium in Ft. Myers and supposed that we would spend the rest of our days in that pleasant atmosphere. In fact, after nearly ten years had passed and we had spent no more than a month *in toto* in our new apartment, we finally sold it and continued living in our home in Washington, quite close to where our two daughters and their families live and not far from our son's family in Ohio.

This chapter I have captioned with the query: "Is There Life After Retirement?" By now it must be evident that the answer is yes. Life goes on, and goes on much as it had before. We did continue to travel much as I had. I continued to preach and teach and consult and generally tried to keep up with what was going on in our Church and the world. I used to greet somewhat skeptically the frequent claim of my retired friends that they were "busier than ever." Then I learned the truth. It is generally supposed that when you retire you have an infinite amount of time on your hands; hence, you are asked to volunteer for all manner of tasks. Soon your platter is full. One recalls Tennyson's Ulysses, who found it dull "to rest unburnished, not to shine in use."

Our denomination does have a plan that provides that if a bishop must retire before the mandatory age of retirement for ordained ministers, he or she may be assigned some special task on partial salary until the age of seventy is reached. The task assigned to me by the Council of Bishops was to write a book on episcopacy in the Wesleyan tradition. Such a comprehensive study had not been made for some decades and needed to be updated.

It was to this specific task that I turned my attention. What a joy it was to have a chance once again to immerse myself in the literature of this broad field! Not only did I peruse the literature on Methodism, but I went farther afield to examine the episcopal office in the experience of Orthodoxy, Roman Catholicism, and Anglicanism. I am in considerable debt to friends in these communions who gave some direction to my research. To these must be added my access to my colleagues' experiences. To my astonishment I found that although some three hundred ministers had held this office in the history of The United Methodist Church and its predecessor bodies, I had known or at least had met more than half of them personally! I asked my fellow bishops to complete a rather wide-ranging questionnaire, which revealed a great deal about the office. In addition, I had had two decades of experience in the office and had written a number of documents on various phases of the responsibility.

Finally, I wrote a volume titled *Set Apart to Serve*, a phrase appropriated from the Service of Consecration of

Bishops, and which in essence encompasses the episcopal role. It was of incalculable help to have several friends who read my drafts along the way. They were Bishops Roy Short and Nolan Harmon of the Southern Methodist tradition and Bishop John Warman, who had been a Methodist Protestant. Albert Outler as theologian and church historian helped me from his broad grasp of the field. The book certainly has helped me, and some of my colleagues have been kind enough to say that it has helped them as well. The volume has been made available to all bishops and presidents in the Wesleyan family throughout the world and has been translated into Korean. Though the book was not to become a best-seller, I learned from those who have read it and used it that the work had proved its worth.

Intermingled with this writing project was the opportunity to teach once again. Dean Philip Wogaman of Wesley Theological Seminary invited me to give a course in Missions and World Christianity. This I did for a number of semesters, twice as a part of the Washington Theological Consortium so that I taught some who were studying for the Roman Catholic priesthood. I enjoyed this opportunity and spent an enormous amount of time in preparing; as much, I think, for one course as I would have for a full teaching load.

As I reflect on my somewhat limited experience as a teacher, I realize that I could have been quite happy in that role had my more active years been devoted to it. Upon completion of my Ph.D. studies I did have an offer to teach at a college in Pennsylvania. I declined this opening as I did several other invitations to be a college or seminary president, though with some reluctance. It was gratifying to teach at Wesley Seminary, as I had done earlier, part-time, at Drew. I taught a summer course at Asbury Seminary as well. So I experienced some fulfillment in this appealing field. Together with my teaching ministry as bishop, it meant that I was not entirely a frustrated teacher.

Mention has already been made of the fact that Eunice and I were "commissioned" to carry on some of the work of her parents in India and elsewhere. In our efforts to do this we invested an enormous amount of time and energy. We have endeavored to be good stewards of the funds they left for work in India. They have made it possible for literally thousands of young people to receive an education at every level—hundreds in universities and professional schools. In addition we have raised many thousands of dollars for the maintenance and upbuilding of institutions they inaugurated.

So it was that the tiny school in Sitapur in North India, in the town where Eunice was born, has prospered. Similarly, the Nur Manzil Psychiatric Center in Lucknow, established by Eunice's father, also flourished. It was the first institution for family psychiatry in India and has always endeavored to link the best possible scientific service for mental health with the healing and caring ministry of the gospel. We have helped build up an endowment for the treatment of poor patients as well as cultivating funds for building improvement. The government of India is said to regard this institution very highly, and Third World medical visitors to India are often referred to it as a model of what can be done almost literally on a shoestring. In February 1999 we were immensely pleased when an entirely new and modern building was dedicated to house this ministry. "Nur Manzil" means "Palace of Light," aptly named for "Jesus, the Light of the World." He shines from there into minds darkened with fear and disease.

The other legacy of responsibility has to do with the Christian Ashram Movement, which as I have stated was started by Stanley Jones in India in 1930. Though modest in its scope, it has proved its worth in many settings. It has been my privilege to have chaired this effort since Dr. Jones's death in 1973. Some fifty ashrams (retreats) are held every year in various parts of the United States, plus scores of weekend Christian ashrams. These have contributed to new life in Christ and spiritual enrichment for a large number of people. Its work extends to Canada, to Scandinavia, and to Japan, as well as in India, where we travel almost every year to lend our energies to the enterprise. We have also endeavored to extend the movement to Korea, to Latin America, to Africa, and to the islands of the sea, such as Fiji and Hawaii. Twice, on the thirtieth and fortieth anniversary of Christian ashrams in Japan, Eunice and I were invited to that country to visit all the ashrams there. This took us to all four of the main islands, as well as to Okinawa in 1995, a most memorable experience among a delightful and devoted people.

This was my third visit to Okinawa. My brother Joe had served as chaplain there during World War II, and the brother of my colleague Bishop Dale White had been killed during the Battle of Okinawa. Just fifty years later, in June 1995, a striking peace monument was dedicated at the very spot of some of the worst fighting. Surrounding it were the graves of some 200,000 Japanese, Okinawans, Chinese, Americans, and Koreans. Inspired apparently by the black marble Vietnam War Memorial in Washington, hundreds of black granite markers are carved in appropriate languages the names of those interred nearby. Eunice observed a section in which there were a number of such black stones, only one of which had just five names carved in Korean; the rest were blank slabs. She inquired about these and was informed that they memorialized several hundred "comfort girls," Korean women forced into prostitution to serve the Japanese military. The families of most of the women had not approved the inscription of their names on the slabs. Eunice concluded that this was of significance, the bare stone untouched and uncontaminated, as it were, by the hands of men! On the spot I composed this little *haiku* to recall the event:

> Cold, black obelisks,
> Nameless amid thousands named:
> Pronounced chaste at last!

We have found it highly gratifying to be deeply involved in this mode of evangelism. It has led to other forms of retreat and renewal movements in many settings. It has afforded us association with outstanding Christians in other denominations: the Reverend John Oishi and Dr. Norimichi Ebisawa of Kyodan, Japan; the late Dr. Gordon Hunter of the United Church of Canada; and Dr. William E. Berg of the Evangelical Lutheran Church, a real saint of God.

Another facet of retirement living has been involvement in a great many "projects" both great and small for kingdom ends. In our experience possible projects simply emerge here and there: a need comes to your attention and must be met, and you as an individual, a couple, a group are obliged to do something about it. I recall, for example, a lovely young woman in Kenya. Her father and mother were ill and she was the sole support of a family of eight. She had been trained as a seamstress but had no sewing machine. The project was to see that she got the sewing machine. She did, and a family's welfare was cared for.

A second rather striking "project" warrants attention, and I shall recount it briefly. In 1985 Eunice and I were leading a group of United Methodists on a mission tour of India. We all worshiped on Sunday, February 24, in Immanuel Methodist Church in Madras (now Chennai), an outstanding congregation. After the service a physician approached me and shared an urgent concern. It so happened that one of his patients was a successful businessman who had become a lay evangelist, a man of considerable charisma. His name was D. G. S. Dhinakaran, who was regarded the most effective evangelist in the country. He had a radio program in the Tamil language that reached three million listeners. Unfortunately he was suffering from advanced kidney disease. If he did not secure a kidney transplant, he was given only three months to live. Since this operation was not available in India at the time, we were requested to secure a transplant for him in the United States. Though we had serious doubts that I could do this, I nevertheless felt compelled to do what I could.

Within a few days I returned home, arriving on February 28. The very next day I telephoned my colleague
Bishop Ben Oliphint in Houston, who responded immediately stating that the matter would be given his serious
and prompt attention—an attitude, which I might add,
has characterized his entire ministry. Brother Dhinakaran,
as he was called, was invited to come to the Methodist
Hospital in Houston. He arrived early in the summer at
the hospital where it was confirmed that he needed the
transplant. They promptly put him on dialysis while
waiting for a proper kidney.

A cousin in India was willing to be a donor and apparently was an appropriate match. However the American
consul general in Madras would not grant a visa to the
cousin. I appealed this both through Senator John Dan-
forth's and Senator Mark Hatfield's offices. Though both
of them were personally sympathetic, their efforts were
not fruitful.

Meanwhile, at the end of July 1985 a young man in
Houston was tragically killed in a motorcycle accident. It
turned out that his kidney was an exact match in every
way for Brother Dhinakaran—even to fitting precisely
into the cavity from which his own weakened organ had
been removed. Another person received the other kidney
so that two lives were saved through the tragic accident.
I visited Dhinakaran a week later, surprised to find him
walking around and well on his way to total recovery. As
I write these words years later he is still alive and well
and living in Madras. Moreover, he has established a
degree-granting engineering college in Coimbatore,
South India, which is named Karuna ("mercy") Institute

of Technology. Likewise he continues as a most effective agent of evangelism, bringing the light of the gospel to many, for "maker of daylight" is what the name Dhinakaran literally means.

Other projects were more complicated and demanding, requiring group effort. One of these has to do with Burma, with which I have been somewhat related for more than fifty years, both with respect to my military service during World War II and mission administration in the 1940s. To this must be added some acquaintance I have enjoyed with Burma's first prime minister, the late Honorable U Nu. The tragedy of modern Burma is accentuated by a number of factors. Its resources, both human and natural, are of such richness that the country should be one of the most prosperous in Asia. It has oil, minerals, abundant agricultural productive capacity, forests, waterways, and a highly talented people. It has also a strong Christian minority. After a good start with independence in 1948 it soon fell into internal strife and finally suffered a takeover by a harsh, leftist regime of military dictators. Quite contrary to being an asset to the family of nations, it has become a major source of illicit drugs; hence, a scourge among Asian countries. Its recently assumed designation as Myanmar does not cloak the realities of the situation.

Two persons have kept my conscience alive on the issue of Burma. One is U Kyaw Win, son of a prominent Burmese pastor in Rangoon. Dr. Win is now a professor in California. The other is Dr. Thomas B. Manton, a lawyer in the State of Washington and son of outstanding Methodist missionaries to Burma. Tom grew up in Burma and went to school with Aung San Suu Kyi, Nobel Peace laureate and rightfully elected head of government in Burma. Her longtime unlawful exclusion from office and house arrest in Rangoon is both a tragedy and travesty of the first magnitude. When a Committee for Restoration of Democracy in Burma was inaugurated in the 1980s, Eunice and I were delighted to accept the invitation to be a part of this effort together with friends and associates through the years, particularly Dr. William P. Thompson of the Presbyterians. The struggle has continued and in 1996 a kindred effort, the National Committee for a Democratic Burma, was established. We are pleased to be a part of this as well. This concern should rest solidly on the American conscience and deserves our very best national effort to bring about change and help establish freedom there.

Earlier on the India tour to which I have just alluded we visited Bombay (now Mumbai) and there something very interesting happened. I had learned that Arun Gandhi, grandson of the Mahatma, was living in the city. We invited him and his wife, Sunanda, to our hotel for dinner. He had met my plane in Durban thirty-one years before when I visited with his parents. Under his guidance I had my first introduction to the horror that was apartheid. I had not seen him since, although I had followed his career from afar.

Despite the long interval I easily recognized him, and it was as if we started out where we had left off nearly a third of a century earlier. He was by now a journalist related to the Bombay newspaper, *The Times of India*. I asked him about the intervening years. Where had he gone to school? To my astonishment he replied that he had never gone to school for a day in his life! Here he was, a refined and sophisticated person. Could this be true? Then he explained that his father had not wanted his son to go to school under the indignities of apartheid and undertook to teach him himself. Then I recalled that Manilal had been largely trained under the tutelage of his father. He further compressed his story by relating that he had gone to India to marry his bride, Sunanda, but the South African government would not grant her a visa, so he stayed in India for twenty-four years. In addition to journalism he had written several books, had with his wife engaged in significant village uplift work, and had for a time undertaken to study racism in the United States only to have his study grant terminated for economy's sake. So he was back in India—frustrated and in debt.

That very evening another project was born. Within a year, with the help of many interested friends, we were able to affect their transfer to the United States, where a new life opened up for them. They made the transition to our country rather readily. We saw to it that he was awarded a well-deserved honorary degree. Today he is the head of an Institute for the Study of Non-Violence at Brothers University in Memphis, and the couple is in demand as speakers in the United States and beyond.

At about this same period at a reception in Washington we met another member of the Gandhi family. There we observed a rather tall and impressive young Indian gentleman. We chanced to hear him respond to a query about his grandfather who was unnamed. He replied by saying that he had *two* grandfathers—as most of us do. It transpired that one of them was C. Rajagopalachari and the other Mohandas Gandhi. His maternal grandsire had been the first Indian governor general and successor to Lord Louis Mountbatten, the last viceroy of India. His father was Devadas Gandhi, youngest son of the Mahatma, an outstanding newspaper editor. That evening was the beginning of another warm friendship with this man, Rajmohan Gandhi, and his lovely wife, Usha. We think most highly of both of them and feel that they will serve India in an outstanding way during the years ahead. Rajmohan has been a leader of Moral Rearmament in India, and the two of them are persons of immense spiritual sensitivity. It is always a delight to visit in their home. We try to keep up with the Gandhis, and it has been my good fortune to have known five generations of this great family.

It has been a joy to work with Rajmohan Gandhi on several undertakings with respect to peace issues. Both he and I recall with pleasure a conversation we had with President Jimmy Carter at his center in Atlanta, a visit arranged by President James Laney of Emory University.

During separate visits of these two cousins in our home we discussed my doctoral dissertation on their grandfather. Both asked to read it and both insisted that it must be published. Finally, Rajmohan took the manuscript to Bombay, where in due course it was published in 1989 by the Bharata Vidya Bhavan Press in that city. It has enjoyed a modest readership in both India and the United States and will soon go into a second printing.

I was greatly surprised when in the summer of 1992 I received word from India that this book, entitled *The Matchless Weapon: Satyagraha*, had been awarded a prize from the Gandhi Peace Foundation as the best recent book on Gandhi! Naturally I was pleased and even more so when I found that some twenty-five books had been submitted by publishers for this recognition. Since I was traveling to India in connection with the Sat Tal Christian Ashram, I was able to collect the prize, which was presented by the Honorable K. R. Narayanan, vice president of India and longtime friend, later in 1997 to be elected president of India. An assembly of notables gathered on Gandhi's birthday, October 2, 1992, for the small ceremony. It consisted of a diploma and a cash grant of five thousand rupees. That is not a large sum in our economy, but I reflected that that was the equivalent of three years' salary when I first went to India fifty-five years before. I deposited the money in India, and when a severe earthquake was visited on my part of India—Maharashtra—I gave the prize money for relief work.

In passing, mention should be made of Mrs. Indira Gandhi. She has often been regarded as being related to Mahatma Gandhi. The fact is that Gandhi is a fairly common name in India and refers to "grocer," a vocational designation under the merchant caste. Indira was, of course, daughter of Jawaharlal Nehru. She married a Parsee named Gandhi. Stanley Jones formed close ties of friendship with her, and Eunice and I did too.

It so happened that around 1930 Dr. Jones had an extended visit with Mahatma Gandhi at his ashram in Sabarmati, near Ahmedabad. While there the postman delivered a letter and package from Mrs. Kamla Nehru, the wife of Jawaharlal. It had been dispatched from Switzerland, where Mrs. Nehru was under treatment for tuberculosis. The package contained a beautifully worked tea cloth made of fine homespun cotton cloth. The accompanying note from Kamla to Gandhi read: "I have spun the thread; I have woven the cloth and embroidered it for you." Gandhi appreciated this but felt that he had no use for a tea cloth in a spartanly equipped ashram. He therefore gave it to my father-in-law, saying, "Give it to Mrs. Jones with my love." She carefully labeled it and put it among her things, where Eunice discovered it after her mother's death.

Eunice took a picture of it and showed it to Mrs. Gandhi on her next visit to India. Mrs. Gandhi was excited and pleased to see it, saying, "I recall seeing my mother work on this and often wondered what had happened to it." Eunice promised to give it to her when she came to India again. In the meantime Mrs. Gandhi was assassinated. We subsequently gave it to her son, Rajiv, when he was prime minister. He received it pensively and shed a tear as he held this precious memento of a grandmother whom he had never seen. This memento may be seen nowadays on display in the Indira Gandhi Museum in New Delhi.

Another project took me into the Southern Hemisphere, specifically to Santiago College in Chile. In 1960 I had been elected chairman of a board in New York City, which gave the school a North America base since it was chartered by the Board of Regents of New York State. We were a kind of property-holding body that did not micromanage the school itself but did have a part in nominating its *directora* or principal and a veto power over any potentially disastrous actions proposed by the local board of directors in Santiago.

The school itself had been established in 1880 and was a part of the strategic vision of William Taylor for effective Protestant or Evangelical witness in South America, just as he had devised strategy earlier for Methodism in India and would later do in Africa. In this instance it was essentially to establish schools that featured instruction through the medium of English in cities in or near the coast around much of the continent. This met a felt need particularly for families of European origin. The founders were the Reverend Ira Haynes LaFetra, a recent graduate of Boston University, and his wife, Adelaide Whitefield LaFetra, both remarkable persons. The result was that it would become and remain what is possibly the best school in the country. It has attracted young women of some of the most prestigious families in the country. This fact was considered in earlier days one of the great strengths of the institution. Later, of course, it invited criticism on the ground that it was elitist. Following the LeFetras it was fortunate in having a succession of very able *directoras,* including Mary Sweeney Stuntz, Elizabeth Mason, Rebecca Donoso, and Elizabeth Grey Fox.

Although it was called a college, according to prevailing usage in Latin America it actually offered training from kindergarten through the high school level. With the passage of time it became more and more withdrawn from the minuscule Methodist Church of Chile, whose membership by 1960 was about twenty-five thousand, although a split-off group of Pentecostal Methodists dating from the early 1900s grew to more than a million and a half members. Meanwhile, the college prospered and was moved to a new and better location in the city, where a beautiful campus was developed from gifts by a generous wealthy alumna, matched dollar for dollar by the Methodist Board of Missions.

As already suggested the board of trustees in North America was for some years not very closely attached to the school. One action it took, however, was of great importance. During the 1970s the extreme leftist Allende regime came into power in Chile, attracting favorable attention from many of the "have-nots" of the country, including some church leaders. A committee of Methodists recommended that Santiago College be turned over to the Allende government. This would clearly have proved a disastrous course, and the institution would have been entirely lost by Methodism. This was more than the committee over which I presided was prepared to accept; consequently, according to our authority, we denied approval of such a step.

It became clearer that we must take a fuller role in the college. Therefore in August 1982, Dr. Joyce Hill, executive secretary of the Board of Missions for Latin America, and I proceeded to Santiago to help resolve a number of problems that had developed due to our inattention. Santiago is a beautiful city, though plagued by smog. It had grown rapidly since my last visit in 1959. Chile had suffered under an oppressive right-wing government which, after a violent coup, had replaced Allende. Then after yet another coup the rightist Pinochet regime took over. From August 21 to 28 we worked very hard toward putting affairs on a better footing. Our role was one of troubleshooting. Joyce had long served as a missionary in Latin America and had a good command of Spanish. Though I

could understand simple Spanish, she acted as interpreter. This was not only of inestimable help to me in
itself, but as I had learned through the years, the delay
occasioned by interpretation gave me more time to for-
mulate responses. The local control board was made predominantly of parents, ex-alumni, school administrators,
teachers, and even several maintenance employees; with
a distinct minority from the church. There was great tension between the church and the other representatives.
There was also an increasingly untenable situation
brought about by an unwieldy local governing body.

We undertook our task by becoming acquainted with
Methodist leaders and with those who considered us as
their adversaries. We met in turn with all the "communities" of or related to the school and listened to them
intently. No one could have complained that we did not
cover the whole terrain. I was asked to chair all the meetings and was a little surprised by the deference and
respect shown me. I had been for them a detached, somewhat mysterious figure, and in their minds of uncertain
authority. The mere meeting together of the various par-
tisans had the effect of breaking down walls of separation. We found that an effort had been made by the
ex-alumni and parents to purchase the school for $2 mil-
lion, though it was worth five times that amount. Then it
became clear that the church wanted to take over the
school and try to build a university. Gradually it emerged
that all parties wanted to see the school continue and
prosper; this was common ground.

After very complicated negotiations, we ended up by
reorganizing the governing body to become an organiza-

tion of sixteen members: the *directora*, three representatives of the ex-alumni, three from the parents, three Methodist clergy, three Methodist laypersons, with an additional three competent educators to be elected by the other twelve members. The teachers, administrator, students, and maintenance employees were left off the board. This proved to be a far more efficient and effective grouping. Then half the property was to be turned over by the New York Board to this newly constituted body and half to the Methodist church in Chile. The former was done almost immediately but the latter delayed till later so that the school could still be seen as a U.S.-related institution. This enabled it to receive a substantial grant from US-AID in order to construct an additional building and modernize the old.

More than a decade later Santiago College prospers. Eunice and I made a gift, which stimulated additional giving to acquire some thirty additional acres of land on the outskirts of the city for expansion and possible relocation of the school. This property suddenly increased in value to about $10 million, forty times its cost. Although not entirely free of problems, the school's future of usefulness to the church and the country seems assured. Meanwhile, between 1982 and 1997 Eunice and I have had occasion to visit Santiago College several times. Three times I have given commencement addresses there, and we have delighted in our association with this fine institution.

Another "project" reaches across to Japan and concerns the ministry of Dr. Toyohiko Kagawa, the remarkable Japanese evangelist and social prophet. Our paths crossed more than once through the years. He was a friend of Eunice's father and was a dinner guest in our home during his final trip to the United States. His daughter sent me a telegram announcing her father's death in 1960. A younger associate of Dr. Kagawa was the Reverend Masuo Kaneko, a graduate of Wesley Seminary. In the summer of 1985 Kaneko returned to the seminary and brought with him various memorabilia of Kagawa to add to the library's collection. Inspired by this event it almost spontaneously was proposed that there be a continuing connection with the Kagawa tradition and $1,300 was raised on the spot for this project. Within a few months we had raised more than ten thousand dollars—more than half of it from Japan—as an endowment to support a "Kagawa event" every three years. This means that periodically a lecture or panel or colloquy on Kagawa would be sponsored that would enable every seminary generation to become acquainted with this outstanding Asian churchman, a venture entirely appropriate to the global setting for contemporary ministry.

Yet another interesting involvement was the construction of a chapel at Camp David. This is the president's retreat located in the Catoctin Mountains about 70 miles northwest of Washington. This place was the "Shangri-la" established by President Franklin D. Roosevelt in 1942. It is really a naval installation used because of his naval connection. President Dwight Eisenhower renamed it Camp David after his grandson. Its place in history was established when President Carter invited Prime Minister Menachen Begin of Israel and President Anwar Sadat of Egypt there for the meetings that resulted in the Camp

David Peace Accords and finally led to the Israeli and Egyptian leaders sharing the Nobel Peace Prize.

Though Carter emphasized the religious basis of peace, the lack of a proper place of worship during the occasion exposed the need of an Interfaith chapel. Any worship services had then to be held in the mess hall. It was the dream of United Methodist layman Kenneth H. Plummer, Sr., that such a chapel should be built there. Plummer had been the contractor who had constructed a number of the buildings at Camp David and this project became a passion of his. The funds, however, would have to be raised privately without government involvement. It had the enthusiastic approval of both President Ronald Reagan and President George Bush. A committee was formed and I was invited to be a member. It was my privilege to recruit Cardinal James Hickey, Roman Catholic archbishop of Washington, Orthodox Archbishop Iakovos, and Rabbi A. James Rudin of the American Jewish Committee. These became the core of a representative committee, which also included Episcopal Bishop John T. Walker, D. Elton Trueblood, Bishop Felton E. May, United Methodist layman Wayne H. Smithey, Baptist Samuel D. Proctor, and others. We secured the Reverend Douglas G. Trout as professional executive director.

Within three years more than a million dollars had been raised and the lovely chapel was built. Unique windows were installed that captured symbols from all the major faiths. These windows, costing a hundred thousand dollars, were the gift of artist and designer Dr. Rudolph Sandon, a European immigrant, and were an expression of his gratitude to his adoptive land. On Sunday, April 21,

1991—a chilly and very rainy day—the chapel was dedicated and presented by Chairman Plummer to the people of the United States and received by President George Bush. Most of the committee members listed above participated with Cardinal Hickey, the preacher. Mrs. Bush read one of the lessons and pop religious singer Sandy Patti sang at the president's request. It was a beautiful service planned by Professor Lawrence Stookey of Wesley Seminary.

Afterward the President and Mrs. Bush invited those present to a Texas barbecue, which due to the stormy weather was held inside. Each one of us was photographed with the president, and Eunice and I were seated at Mrs. Bush's table. We noted that in contrast to our heaping plates, she was eating sparsely. She said, "It's a case of F.H.B. (*family hold back*)." She said that she had asked her husband how many would be there. He had estimated sixty. In the event, twice as many came, and reinforcements of food had to be brought in from the naval mess! This was the very sort of thing that can happen in the best-regulated families. The whole experience, of course, stands out in our memories. It is gratifying to note that the first international guests to worship with the Bushes in the chapel were the King and Queen of Spain. On that visit plans emerged for meetings in Madrid, and later in Oslo, leading to the present peace talks in Israel.

What I have recounted may more than suffice for the diverse undertakings with which for us retirement has been filled. One other role has been as bishop-in-residence at Metropolitan Memorial United Methodist Church in Washington, where Eunice is a member and where I had been elected bishop in 1960, a church served by colleagues of many years and outstanding preachers including the Reverend Dr. William A. Holmes and the Reverend Dr. William Lawrence. There were many more projects. The challenges have seemed unending, of great variety and interest. They continue to this moment— twenty years after retirement.

ONGOING TRAVELS

The travels continued, some optional and some obligatory. For example, we had always wanted to go to mainland China, but for most of my career it was behind the "bamboo curtain." When the opportunity finally came in 1984 we were indeed fortunate to travel in company of persons who knew China well. One was longtime friend and associate Dr. Tracey K. Jones, Jr., who spoke Chinese though his wife, Junia, did not. The leaders of our tour, Dr. Charles H. Long and his wife, Nancy, had been Episcopalian missionaries in China and were fluent in the language. Our whole company proved to be most congenial. It was nice to have another bishop along—the Rt. Rev. Ned Cole of the Episcopal diocese of Syracuse, with whom we had had a long acquaintance.

My purpose is not to give a travelogue, but we were of course struck by the sights of China: the palaces and temples of Beijing, the Great Wall, the terracotta soldiers of Xian. To travel by boat down the Yangtze through its magnificent gorges from Chungking to Nanking was to fulfill the dream of a lifetime. We had always supposed that the sharply pointed peaks seen so often in Chinese prints were simply products of poetic and artistic license, but, behold, in Quilon there they were! Most of all we were impressed by the people. To paraphrase Lincoln: God must love the Chinese for he made so many of them. To be aware of the oppression people had experienced and to observe how they had now been partially delivered was in reality an experience of deep religious significance. The church had suffered and endured, yet in spite of it all, it had grown. God is still on the throne. This was further confirmed as we returned to the United States via Korea, where we inaugurated several Christian ashrams with the help of Dr. Peter Sun and other Korea pastors. With Dr. Sun I also worked later toward the development of Pan-Pacific University in California.

During the spring of 1990 Eunice and I were privileged once again to travel with Tracey and Junia Jones. This time my sister and her husband, Alice and Alex Neill, were also in our little party, as we toured a bit of the USSR. As already recounted I had visited it twice before, but for the others it was a first. We are particularly glad to have visited Russia at the time, for within months the Soviet Union would be broken up and a new era in history would begin. There were already signs of impending change. Cracks in the system were evident and one could sense that the people were aware of this. The influence of Gorbachev was evident everywhere, but we were amazed that he was seen more favorably in the United States than the USSR. We were delighted to see Archpriest Vitaly Borovoy, a longtime friend and, as I believe, an authentic confessor of the faith who has carried marks on his body and spirit of the suffering he had undergone from Communist oppressors. Our trek was restricted to three cities and environs: Moscow, Kiev, site of the conversion of Russia to Christianity in A.D. 988, and Leningrad, soon to have its erstwhile name, St. Petersburg, restored—a kind of sampler, as it were, of the past of Russia's people on the very eve of an uncertain future.

I burst into song about it all and wrote a poem on each city. Shakespeare's and Pushkin's places remain secure, but for what it may be worth, here is my offering on Leningrad (now again St. Petersburg):

Sonnet on St. Petersburg, 1990

Venice of the north; Paris of the east,
Great Peter's dream fulfilled in brick and stone.
Two score of islands bound at last in one;
Canals that link with River Neva, least
Of streams; bridged a hundred times by art-decked spans
Graced by palaces, crowned by churches' spires,
Prospect pleasing, Phoenix-rising from fires
Of Nazi vandals, bent on Satan's plans.
Scarce can one grasp the magnitude of such
A city: culture, science, art, learning,
Industry, trade, music; all with human touch:
Fearing, loving, striving, writing, yearning.
Fired by dance, and most of all: Hermitage,
Palace marked by masterpiece of every age!

A kind musically inclined friend is undertaking to set the words of the three poems I wrote to music, to be called "The Russian Suite"!

On several occasions the Council of Bishops since 1980 gave me special assignments that involved travel. Sometimes these responsibilities had to do with India as a fraternal visitor to what had been called their Central Conference, but when they became the autonomous Methodist Church in India it was designated a General Conference. My India background made it natural that I should be chosen for this fraternal role and it has been a pleasure. In October 1989 their General Conference was convened in Jabalpur at Leonard Theological College. Its dates coincided with Divali, the Hindu festival of lights. Every town and city in the country is illumined by thousands of small oil lamps or electricity; but the celebration is also marked by fireworks day and night for several days at the same time beautiful and exceedingly annoying. The Conference itself proved something less than enlightening. There was much bickering and finally a failure to elect any bishops, which was the main business of the conference. Once again, the conference convened in Tambaram, near Madras (Chennai), site of the 1938 session of the International Missionary Council. Eunice accompanied me on this journey. Though the atmosphere had improved, once again it failed to elect bishops. This sort of thing is admittedly rather discouraging, but I have tried to keep the long view. Jesus, after all, reminded us that it is *his* church and the powers of evil will not finally prevail against it.

As a sign of this, bishops were ultimately elected a little later and in 1994 three more were elected on one ballot. In April 1995 I was asked to proceed to India to conduct an orientation and training session for the bishops. All the bishops, active and retired, and their wives were invited. An uplifting and successful gathering was held at the Sat Tal Christian Ashram in the Himalayas. This was the first meeting of this kind ever held in India, and for the bishops from South India it was the first time they had ever glimpsed the Himalayas. Theretofore new bishops were simply elected and assigned to an area without specific orientation. It is not surprising that some have found the task almost overwhelming. In this retreat we endeavored to mingle study, worship, reflection, fellowship, and relaxation in a way which would be helpful to all. For my part, I had carefully prepared a total program including lectures on *Knowing* (the history of the episcopal office), *Doing* (practices), and *Being* (the heart of the matter.) My colleagues have expressed hope that similar orientations will be available for them in the future.

In 1991 the Council of Bishops invited me to undertake a special tour of the Middle East. My itinerary took me from Constantinople to Cyprus, Egypt, Jordan, and Israel. Due to visa difficulties Syria had to be omitted. There were visits with the ecumenical patriarch, Dimitrios I, who died only a few weeks later and was succeeded by Bartholomew; Archbishop Chrysostomos of Cyprus, proud to be successor to St. Paul's colleague Barnabas in what is regarded as the oldest diocese in Christendom outside the Holy Land; Pope Shenouda III of the Coptic Orthodox Church; as well as leaders of many churches in Jordan and Israel. The midweek prayer meeting has gone out of fashion with us, but in Cairo Pope Shenouda's prayer service, where he teaches Bible, may attract as many as ten thousand people.

The Council of Bishops intends such a fraternal visit annually simply to keep informed about the region and as a gesture of continuing concern. The recent erosion of Christian presence in the Holy Land is a matter of proper concern for all Christians. We should pray for the peace of Jerusalem, for it relates to the welfare of the whole area and far beyond. Of particular moment is the treatment of the Palestinians, some of whom are Christian, and the continued building of Jewish settlements in occupied territory, which seem unconscionable to the observer and only exacerbates an already perilous situation. The eyes and conscience of the world must be kept focused on this issue.

Being Reactivated

It is clear that I have been trying to affirm that there is indeed life after retirement. Earlier it was observed that United Methodist bishops do not actually retire but are placed on a kind of inactive list. They can be reactivated. This has happened to me three times. Concerning these I have somewhat whimsically observed that being a bishop is a little like riding a bicycle or swimming. Once you have learned how to do it you do not forget. What I have done in these three additional opportunities was what I did in my Boston and Washington years, albeit in different times and places and among different people and traditions. Therefore, I feel no need to recount these experiences in detail.

In November 1985 the Council of Bishops met in Wichita, Kansas. It so happened that the session exactly coincided with the publication of my book on episcopacy,

Set Apart to Serve. Therefore, I gave an individually inscribed copy of this volume to each one of my colleagues. On the final day Eunice and I were in the lobby of our hotel, having just checked out, and were ready to proceed to California where at Claremont I was scheduled to give a lecture on her late father. At that very moment we were approached by Bishop Abel Muzorewa, who informed me that the Executive Committee had voted to ask me to proceed to Zimbabwe to take over the office of the bishop there for an as yet undetermined period. I could not have been more shocked and surprised. We did go on to California and returned immediately to Washington. A week later I was presiding at the session of the Zimbabwe Annual Conference in Old Mutare! It was just like that.

The second recall was five years later when a retired bishop was authorized to establish a tenth episcopal area in the Northeastern Jurisdiction; namely, by linking the Wyoming Conference and the Troy Conference to form the Albany Area. Though once again I had not expected to be activated, this time I rather wanted to do so. There were few alternative persons available at the time, but besides I liked the idea of completing the twenty-four years of active episcopacy for which I was originally elected, cut short by the lowering of the retirement age for bishops. This reassignment was done by the action of a special session of the Jurisdictional Conference meeting in Scranton-Kingston, Pennsylvania, on July 14, 1990, and confirmed by the Executive Committee of the Council of Bishops three days later, to be effective September 1.

This I will say, speaking scripturally again: "The

boundary lines have fallen for me in pleasant places." All of my assignments have been in beautiful places. Just think of them: New England, the Middle Atlantic states, the mountains of northeastern Pennsylvania, the Adirondacks, the Green Mountains of Vermont, the lower Hudson Valley and Long Island. All this is hard to beat. As to Zimbabwe, I have already sung the praises of Victoria Falls, but that is not all: add the rivers, the Eastern Highlands, the game reserves, the rock-piled high plateau. Once I told President Robert Mugabe that Zimbabwe was "Africa's best kept secret." It is a beautiful country with a beautiful climate—the best I have experienced year-round anywhere, with a beautiful people and, may I say, a beautiful future. Well, I cannot complain of dull and drab surroundings for my work, for wherever I have been assigned, just around every bend there always seemed to be a vista of splendor.

In these postretirement assignments I always tried to get to "know the territory." It has been my constant endeavor not to be desk-bound. As I have already emphasized, a bishop should be visible to the people who are to be served. So it was I moved about these areas and came to know and love the people. For they were without exception friendly and helpful. They seemed pleased that I did not plead advanced age as an excuse for inactivity but tried to set a pace that often challenged my younger associates.

My assignment was to be bishop of each one of these areas. Observers insisted on seeing me as acting or interim bishop. There is no such an office. I was the bishop and assumed full responsibility not in any exalted sense but because one cannot operate effectively if the role is seen as tentative or temporary.

In Zimbabwe I was to replace Bishop Abel Muzorewa, whose episcopal administration was seen as compromised by his political involvement. Of course, he was a patriot and partisan for freedom. After some fifteen years, war began to come to an end; he was designated as prime minister of the country until a settlement was completed. At that time he took leave of absence, during which time Bishop Ralph Dodge was reactivated to carry on. Muzorewa stood for office in the election of 1980. Since his party failed to receive the necessary number of seats in Parliament, he and some members of his minority party continued in the body and he resumed his church-work. In the 1985 elections he challenged his successor, Prime Minister Robert Mugabe, but with disappointing results. He was not even reelected to Parliament. Having opposed the party in power, it seemed to him wise to leave the country for a period. It was my role to carry on, to mind the church's administration and to help create an atmosphere in which he could possibly return. It was then my endeavor to lead in devising suitable programs, to raise funds, to pay debts, to stabilize the work of the conference. Fortunately, I had the cooperation of the district superintendents and staff, the clergy and laity in these efforts.

One undertaking was very close to my heart: an effort to build a comprehensive agricultural program for Methodism in the country. This seemed to me to be a highly strategic move. There were several incentives to do this. First of all, in the mid-1980s severe droughts in many parts of Africa had led to food shortages and famine, particularly in Ethiopia. Secondly, our denominational relief agency, UMCOR, had collected large sums for alleviation of hunger, even more than was strictly needed for direct food distribution. Why not use some of these funds for long-range purposes? Thirdly, our church in Zimbabwe had extensive land. At the beginning of the century Cecil Rhodes had given to Methodists through Bishop Hartzell some 14,000 acres of land at Old Umtali (Old Mutare). Parts of this huge plot had been traded for other land at three other locations; thus we had four large farms, none of which were fully productive. With the help of specialists in agriculture in the University of Zimbabwe and government as well as church leaders, we did produce a plan to make all four farms more fully productive. A young agronomist from California, Dr. Philip Northcroft, was of particular help in this respect. To launch and equip this program would have cost more than a million dollars, which we requested as a grant from UMCOR in whose coffers at that time were $7 million earmarked for Africa. For whatever reason, this help was not forthcoming.

While we were in our Africa assignment the proposal was made by Bishops Arthur Kulah and Emilio de Carvalho to establish a Methodist university in Africa. This conception I embraced with enthusiasm and wrote a memorandum outlining why I thought Zimbabwe was the best place for a university. This was grounded on climate, language, relative political stability, accessibility, a strong church base, and a good possible site: namely, Old Mutare. Moreover, I appointed a local committee chaired by Dr. John Kurewa, secretary to the Parliament, and later the first president or vice chancellor of the university, to foster this proposal. Naturally we were extremely gratified when the Zimbabwe location was accepted.

We spent just over a year in Zimbabwe in 1985 and 1986. By the very nature of our assignment, we worshiped and I preached in one or more churches—urban and rural—every Sunday, and often in between. We were deeply impressed by the powerful services of worship. Everybody participated in a wholehearted way; one could say they put their whole being in their glorifying of God. The music, the singing, the drums, the rattles, and the swaying of bodies in rhythm were all like nothing we had ever experienced elsewhere in this degree of intensity. We too were caught up in the Spirit of such worship and were totally involved. So it was that when we returned home to the more sedate and formal public worship with which we had been familiar, we found something lacking. It was dull and lifeless by comparison. Animated Christian worship in Africa is a great gift of God.

Or think of their all-night prayer and preaching services called *pungwe*. These meetings were introduced by Zimbabwe Methodism and have proved an effective means of evangelization and of deepening the faith of believers. It is a mode taken over by other denominations, including Anglicans. A *pungwe* is a kind of combination camp-meeting and watch-night service but with a peculiar African flavor. It is thoroughly indigenous, thoroughly Christian, thoroughly involving, and thoroughly effective.

One thing more: African Christians are not beggars. We are, from time to time, called upon to share with them in building churches, schools, providing vehicles for pastors and so on. All this is needed for effective building-up and extending the Church. Africans like to do for themselves. The Church is, for the most part, self-supporting. A notable example is the Harvest Offering taken once a year, after harvest, and in addition to their regular offerings from week to week. It is used to undergird the total program of the Church. If United Methodists in the United States were to share at the same rate, we would receive a total of about $50 million in one offering! Think of it! The Harvest Offering is a tremendous testimony of Christian devotion and effective stewardship. A former missionary, Charles Miller, had a great part in initiating this program.

We were acutely aware that in Harare we had a "grandstand seat" to observe what was going on in South Africa, particularly apartheid. It was an exceedingly troubled period and in most respects looked hopeless. Even as late as 1984 Margaret Thatcher made the offhand statement that "anyone who thinks that Mandela's African National Congress is going to run the government of South Africa is living on Cloud Cuckooland." But Eunice and I, after an extended tour in South Africa, shared with some others the notion that change was on the way, that a negotiated settlement could be made, and that a bloodbath could be avoided. More than once we raised this point of view to South Africa's ambassador in Washington. Indeed, in sermons I would remind the people of the fact that centuries ago God had performed a miracle in northern Africa, setting his people free—the Exodus—and that there was reason to hope that one day God would perform the miracle again at the southern reaches of the continent. This has by now happened, thank God.

We tried to learn a little bit of the Shona language. I think I developed a vocabulary of close to four hundred words and learned a number of idioms. Though I claim no special linguistic gift my last sermon was delivered in Mutare in Shona. I wrote it out in English. Then my secretary interlined it with the Shona translation. It is a fairly phonetic language, though there are some tricky tonal difficulties. Nevertheless, I plowed ahead and the kind and tolerant Africans claimed that they could understand what I said.

I will not elaborate on my assignment to establish the Albany Area. It extended from September 1, 1990, to August 31, 1992—exactly two years. They were pleasant years and the people most kind and considerate. We learned to love them. Although the two conferences, Troy and Wyoming, were of somewhat different character—each had its own ethos, as it were—they melded together in a fine way. It was gratifying to share in their heritage and history. So it was that we could rejoice in the Troy Conference's collective memory of such Methodist stalwarts as Philip Embury, whose earthly remains lie in Ashgrove, New York, and Freeborn Garretson, apostolic figure, whose footprints one often crossed. At the same time one could embrace the memory of Georgia Harkness, whose home church in Harkness, New York, we visited reverentially several times. As to the Wyoming Conference we learned that the very word in Indian languages means "broad valley." How appropriate to the mountainous basin through which the lovely Susquehana and its tributaries flow. The conference's story is replete with Indian lore, anthracite mines, and camp meetings. At the same time it reached to the voices of mighty preachers such as Henry Hitt Crane, who long served in Scranton. In passing it may be worth noting that it was this same Crane who introduced Joseph Kennedy to Rose Fitzgerald, from which meeting a lot of history has proceeded.

As always I continued my teaching ministry, visiting all the eight districts three times for daylong meetings with the pastors. In addition to regular Bible study I undertook to lead the pastors in a prolonged study of a book written by a longtime member of the Troy Conference, Dr. J. Edward Carothers, *The Paralysis of Mainline Protestantism.* Each pastor was presented a copy of this volume, which was a contemporary analysis of what ails the church. It also pointed the way to recovery—three themes we investigated in the three sessions just mentioned. For the church to be renewed one necessity was enlightened and obedient Bible study; a second necessity was the recovery of authentic and meaningful public and private worship; a third necessity was for the church "to turn its face toward the poor," an important part of effective evangelism in the Wesleyan tradition. As I survey the current scene it seems clear to me that such an approach is still valid and much-needed throughout the church. This is a sampling of the perspective from which I pursued the task. A new, viable, and working area was on September 1, 1992, turned over to my successor, Bishop William

Boyd Grove, and now is presided over by Bishop Susan Morrison.

The third reactivation—for the New York Area in May 1995—was neither anticipated nor very welcome. After all, I had reached my eighty-second year, well beyond the age that Scripture warrants even to the strong. Yet, once again, the possibilities were few among those who were considered. After two declinations by others, the responsibility fell to me. I accepted in spite of my age; indeed, I thought of myself as a representative of all older United Methodists, as a witness against ageism.

My predecessor, Bishop Forrest Stith, was well known to me, for I had given him his appointments over a period of eight years in the Washington Area. Nor was I a stranger to the New York Area. There I had been given my first appointment. There, sixty years before, I had been received into annual conference membership, as had my brother Joe. From that area I had been elected bishop in 1960. In New York City I had lived for six years and had studied or worked for a total of seventeen years. Within the conference borders both of my parents are buried. There was really more logic to the situation than may have appeared. I was at home. The Area was replete with history. It was moving to visit cemeteries, which are numerous in the region. Three graves I refer to: "Yankee Doodle's," Fanny Crosby's, and Teilhard de Chardin's.

Forrest Stith had been granted disability leave and subsequently early retirement. This created a profound trauma throughout the conference, a reality with which I wrestled quietly, persistently, and finally with some measure of success. The Stiths had been greatly admired and an ambitious program had been launched under his leadership. This I tried as fully as possible to honor and preserve while lending the work the accent that had developed in my experience. Of course the procedures and method I have already learned were applied to the new situation. In my effort I felt I was given the support of most of those with whom I was working. The New York Conference has long been beset with a host of problems. At the same time its resources of every kind are immense. When I completed my term at the end of August 1996, turning over the work to newly elected Bishop Ernest Lyght, Eunice and I were able to leave with a sense of deep gratification. After all, having joined the New York Conference in 1936 and laying down the burdens of office in 1996, I had come full circle—and I retired for the fourth time.

By now I have served in five areas and been resident bishop in ten annual conferences, and in parts of every state of the Northeast Jurisdiction, save New Jersey, where I was living at the time of election to the episcopacy. With my missionary background and commitment—my first love—it seems good to me that I finally served an area outside the United States. Though I had no profound knowledge and experience of Africa, I was not a stranger there either.

Allow me to add a brief footnote, so to speak, to this chapter. It is two-fold and has to do with my military service in World War II. The year 1995 marked the fiftieth anniversary of the end of that conflict. The Department of Defense arranged for commemorative visits of veterans to the various theaters of action. One was to the China-Burma-India (CBI) theater where I had served for four years. The U.S. Ambassador to India in 1995 was the Honorable Frank G. Wisner. He recommended me for this tour. In due course I received an invitation from the Department of Defense to be a member of the party that was to go to CBI. There were twenty of us in all; the list included representatives of all branches of the armed service who had served in the region. Among them were generals and colonels as well as those of lesser ranks. Some were pilots who had flown across the Hump—the Himalayas—and some were combat aces. Some had been wounded or were prisoners of war, nearly all decorated heroes. It occurred to me that I hardly belonged in such company. Nevertheless, I was well accepted; after all, it turned out that half of the group were Methodist-related, including one African American local preacher and one nurse, the only woman member of the party.

We were cared for well and honored beyond our expectation. The itinerary beginning at Andrews Air Force Base in Washington, D.C., on May 22, 1995, proceeded to Honolulu, Guam, New Delhi, Calcutta, Kunming, Beijing, Okinawa, again Honolulu and, after thirty thousand miles, back to Washington on June l, our fifty-fifth wedding anniversary. We were transported in military planes: the KC-10 tanker and later the C-17. The latter was a mammoth plane capable of carrying an incredible amount of cargo—the state of the art after its kind. Had just five of these craft been available during the war, they could have accomplished the entire supply operation over the Hump! We were greeted by military and civilian leaders in the countries we visited and met more "brass" than one could have imagined. Meanwhile, we formed friendships across the whole party. I found particularly congenial company in Major General Eugene Sterling of Florida and Major Frank Roth of Texas, both Hump pilots.

At each stop we had memorial services for fallen comrades in which we each in turn took some part. Our leader throughout was Lt. General Claude Kicklighter, likewise a United Methodist and a splendid man. As we were flying from Guam to New Delhi he advised me that Ambassador Wisner had invited five hundred guests to the American Embassy for a reception that evening. The speaker was to have been an undersecretary of the air force. Unfortunately he had been delayed in Washington in order to attend the funeral of Secretary of Defense Les Aspin. Would I make the speech? I could and would and did: more than half a century of India experience had equipped me. Since I was already on the printed program for the invocation, I had to do double duty. The invocation I gave in high Hindi, which was welcomed by the guests and my address, composed aboard the plane, was also well received and widely circulated in India. As a part of this speech I included the famous poem "High Flight" by pilot John Magee, whose parents I had known and who had given me a facsimile of the verse in his own handwriting.

Apparently this address established my reputation in the group and I was called upon for more such service. Later, General Kicklighter apprised me of the fact that he had to plan the final service of thanksgiving to be held in

Honolulu on September 3, 1995, the fiftieth anniversary of Japan's surrender and asked my help. I recruited Professor Lawrence Stookey of Wesley Theological Seminary, a specialist in this field. He proved of considerable help. Then in July the general asked me to have a part in the service and a little later still asked me to speak briefly for the veterans and to introduce President Clinton. I was surprised and, not surprisingly, I was pleased to accept. After another week or so a call from the Pentagon inquired as to whether Mrs. Mathews would like to go along? Answer: Affirmative. Shortly afterward another call came asking if we would like to fly to Honolulu aboard *Air Force One*? Again: Affirmative!

As it turned out, we actually flew on two presidential planes. *Air Force One* was at a base in Idaho near where President Clinton was vacationing in Wyoming. The backup plane, a Boeing 707, No. 26000, was the one used by previous presidents and had carried President Kennedy to Dallas. It was also on this plane that Lyndon B. Johnson was sworn in and John F. Kennedy's body conveyed back to Washington. We flew in this plane to Idaho Falls on the Snake River. The next day we boarded the current presidential plane, a Boeing 747. We were shown around it and found it well-appointed to say the least. We were seated in a special section of the plane reserved for special guests of the president. It was the same section about which Speaker Gingrich complained; for our part, we found no cause for complaint. Bill Clinton came around for a friendly chat and as it happened three of the other guests were close friends of his from Arkansas. Then young Chelsea Clinton came by to introduce herself and a girlfriend who was traveling with her. She proved quite the poised young lady as I remarked to her parents. Hillary Clinton also welcomed us aboard and was most gracious.

The flight to Hawaii was smooth, pleasant, and well-remembered. We were welcomed to the Golden Jubilee with genuine hospitality and spent three days among the great, the near great and those who were possibly aspiring to greatness.

As a part of a solemn religious service I did speak in behalf of veterans living and dead and then I introduced the Commander-in-Chief. Here is in part what I said:

"Many other World War veterans will share with me a childhood memory of Civil War veterans marching and commemorating together, both sides ... North and South.

Now *we* are the aging veterans—our ranks now thinning, but no less proud and patriotic as we recall victory fifty years ago.

Just as our forebears did, we women and men heeded duty's call from village and city; from farm and factory; from office and classroom; from every race and every religion.

We responded to our nation's summons to put our very lives where our professed loyalties and cherished values lay.

We all remember where we were when war began. I was a missionary in India. As soon as I could I volunteered and served for four years in the China-Burma-India theater.

We were molded into effective fighting units on land

and sea and air, supported by thousands of civilians on home fronts.

We did not do it alone, but were linked with allies who preceded us in the fight—for this very weekend marks the fifty-sixth anniversary of the outbreak of war in Europe.

We joined as one to oppose oppression and to strive for freedom. All this was long ago—yet, for us, not so long ago.

We remember: Our free, fair lands;

We remember: The infamy once visited upon this very place;

We remember: Those who in unsuspecting suddenness yielded their lives here—and made this soil sacred by their sacrifices.

We remember: The millions of others who likewise paid with their lives the price of justice and liberty; laying costly sacrifices on the altar of freedom in Lincoln's phrase.

We remember: Those who still rest in oceans deep, or jungles vast, or on hostile rock-strewn mountainside, or perhaps entombed forever in eternal Himalayan snows;

We remember that if there are ends worth living for, there are things worth dying for.

We are *grateful* also for the generous words of a fellow Veteran, President George Bush: 'I have no rancor in my heart toward Germany or Japan—not at all—World War II is over. . . . We made our *enemies* our *friends*. We healed their wounds and in the process, we lifted ourselves up.'

We were and we are *grateful* that in our democratic tradition, the military is ultimately under civilian direction of the President of the United States. We are thankful that you, Mr. President, are our Commander-in-Chief, and we are thankful for your leadership and vision as we commemorate the 50th Anniversary of the end of World War II. I speak for every Veteran here today and observing at home, when I say that you have truly shown us that a grateful nation remembers.

In behalf of all our veterans, living and dead, it is my honor to present to you the Commander-in-Chief, President William Jefferson Clinton:

God bless the President of the United States!"

We were invited to return on *Air Force One* to the mainland, but since the president's plane was stopping in California, we needed to get back to Washington for our immediate trip to Japan. Therefore General Ronald R. Fogleman, Chief of Staff of the U.S. Air Force, invited us to accompany him and Mrs. Fogleman on his well-appointed communications plane to Washington. Most interestingly, Astronaut Commander James Lovell and Mrs. Lovell were aboard also. He had given the main address at the concluding Honolulu service. We enjoyed this unhurried association with this fine couple, not least because of his *Apollo 13* fame.

Not all moments are as high as being invited to fly aboard *Air Force One*. There are, however, higher moments still: to be able to continue in service to the Living Lord, to learn the greater depths of prayer, to enjoy family and friends, to welcome the arrival of grandchildren, to celebrate a golden wedding anniversary and beyond, to honor a wonderful wife, and to embrace the gift of life as it is experienced during its ninth decade. I repeat, there *is* life after retirement.

13
Summing Up

Finally, there must be an end to all this. In autobiographical writing, how does one stop? I am not referring at the moment to what was once quaintly called the "article of death." As to that, I am ready for it but am not in any hurry about it. At the same time I do have a curiosity about what we call life everlasting and do not shrink from the experience at God's time. This kind of writing has been far more difficult and demanding than I had thought. What, with many interruptions, it has taken far longer than I had expected. It has proved a kind of catharsis and at the same time has been therapeutic. Sometimes it has been a kind of act of penitence, for how can one examine one's life and be entirely satisfied? We live by God's grace and forgiveness. So the writing is an act of thanksgiving.

By now I can look back on more than sixty years of ministry and am in my fortieth year of episcopacy. It has been wide-ranging and of immense variety. Sometimes I can discern lines or threads that run through my whole life and presently I shall touch on these. Already I have mentioned the roles of missionary and evangelist, which I have preferred to ecumenist and social activist. Actually the distinctions are not sharp and clear. In fact, these various roles blend and meld into one another.

Some autobiographies seem to conclude by gathering up

the things one has forgotten to mention earlier. Or they consist of appropriate literary quotations. My father-in-law speaks in a final chapter of his spiritual autobiography about "What Life Has Taught Me—So Far," and proceeds to list thirty of life's lessons, and what lessons they were! Others allow the conversation simply to taper off or grind down. Still others comment upon the broad atmosphere of the times in which their lives have been cast.

This suggests to me that I ought to glimpse again at the world into which I was born. One often hears cited the Chinese curse: "May you live in interesting times!" That seems aptly to apply to my generation. Or one could complain as Polycarp did in the second century: "My God! In what a century have you caused me to live!"

My whole life has been set in the midst of excitement, turmoil, and rapid social change. For I was born into a more or less static world. It has proved to be one of dramatic shifts. I was born into a world of the horse and buggy, which has become one of supersonic speed and space exploration. As a child I marveled at making out the features of the man *in* the moon; now we can speak of man *on* the moon. I was born in a large world; it is now one of shrunken dimensions. As a child I was accustomed to kerosene lamps; we are now in the promise and threat of a nuclear age. I was born in a world of Western domination; now it is marked by scores of newly independent nations. The once mighty overseas British Empire whose aggregate population once numbered more than a billion on six continents is now reduced to thirteen small islands outside the United Kingdom, whose numbers total only about two hundred thousand people. How moving it was to hear the

British military band play upon its withdrawal from Hong Kong on July 1, 1997, the hymn "The Day Thou Gavest, Lord, is Ended," with its reference to "earth's proud empires" passing away.

It seems almost trite to refer to the host of innovations that have marked my years: radios, television, computers, and all the rest. Some of these developments have proceeded at such a pace that I now seem almost "out of it." One's thoughts turn to "good old days." Yet any temptation to indulge in nostalgia is erased as we cling to conveniences that make modern life what it is. "Good old days" tend to be the product of faulty memories.

The Income Tax in the United States was launched in the year in which I was born; the Federal Reserve system was also inaugurated. The next year saw the start of the Great World War of 1914–18. I have lived through World War II, the Korean conflict, Vietnam, the Gulf War, and lesser engagements in which our country has been involved directly. Beyond that, it is said that our world has not been free of war *somewhere* throughout my whole lifetime—or even perhaps for centuries. In addition, the Cold War raged throughout my entire active work as bishop and continued beyond that, until the eventual collapse of the USSR and its satellite countries. My generation lived through the Great Depression and it has left its stamp upon us.

When we look more closely at the current American scene, it is far from reassuring. Extreme poverty for some, outrageous wealth for others, hunger, homelessness, and drug addiction only begin to touch the borders of our concerns. Long accustomed to fear the nuclear threat, and supposed external enemies, we suddenly find the real enemy within: collapse of values, self-indulgence, pronounced social and economic inequality, violence on our streets and in our hearts, decay of institutions and infrastructure. One may observe also the decay and corruption of language: note the trend toward speaking of the health *industry*, the sports *industry*, the gambling *industry*, and even the prison or funeral i*ndustry*. Moreover, we too easily forget that what hurts others hurts us all. In the recent musical, "Miss Saigon," one of its most telling lyrics is entitled "The American Dream," which for many has largely faded. Our early ventures into exploration and conquest of outer space only serve to underline our failure in conquering inner space—ourselves. Alexis de Tocqueville decades ago spoke admiringly of America as a caring society organized to be mutually helpful. Oft cited is his investigation into the secret of our nation's greatness. He concludes: "America is great because America is good. When America ceases to be good, America will cease to be great."

But we have no reason for despair. Ours has been the best of times as well as the worst of times. Barbara Tuchman's *Distant Mirror* refers to fourteenth century Europe, in which we can see ourselves, the period of the black death. Ours too is an ailing century complete with its own form of plague; namely, AIDS. Yet that same time period could produce a St. Francis of Assisi, not to mention a Thomas Aquinas. So, I repeat, we ought not be excessively pessimistic, for our society also has its redeeming features.

When the worst has been said of our day, we must still give heed to Tuchman's evaluation of it: "One of humankind's better moments." Ours has been a period of aroused conscience and of awakening consciousness. Some may say that humanity is mostly callous, but before our very eyes we can see the emergence of multitudes of those who care. "Everybody everywhere matters." The fact is, that even if the option were open to me, I would choose no other period in history than the one in which I have been placed.

Eunice's father frequently addressed youth groups in many parts of the world. He often challenged them to think about the three basic decisions of their lives: (1) the choice of a philosophy or faith or life-style; (2) the choice of one's life work or vocation; (3) the choice of one's life partner, which could include the decision to remain single, an honorable alternative. While I was still comparatively young, by age twenty-seven, I had made all three decisions. Once again, even if I could, I would not change any one of them. Moreover, having made these basic decisions, thereafter many other things have followed as consequences, a kind of chain reaction was set in motion.

Already I have said a good deal about my conversion experience, my turning from idols to serve the Living God. The Christian is called to a life of holiness, of being set apart, not the holiness of *escape* but of *engagement* in the real issues of the real world. As Paul put it variously: we are "called to be saints," "to belong to Jesus Christ," "to be God's dedicated people," "to be those whom God helps to put wrong things right." This is treacherous ground to tread upon for I know full well how repeatedly and sorely I have fallen short. Nevertheless, I know that my intention has been to be pleasing to God. When my certificate of consecration as bishop was framed, I was asked to choose a quotation of Scripture to be placed on the mat. It was 2 Chronicles 16:9: "For the eyes of the Lord run to and fro throughout the whole earth to show himself strong in the behalf of them whose heart is perfect toward him" (KJV).

It is, of course, one thing to make a decision as to one's own life. It is another to be steadfast in this decision. This requires disciplined devotion, daily one must "maintain the spiritual glow" (Rom. 12:11 Moffatt). Indeed, until I have engaged in daily devotion there is a kind of gnawing within me until the need is satisfied. So one is sustained in the art of Christian living: by public and private worship, by the Word, by one's own prayer and the intercession of others, and by service and caring. We are sustained too by the massive infrastructure of society that makes contemporary life possible. My call to be a missionary has been a kind of call within a call. To use Paul's phrase, my vocation to ordained Christian ministry has been a "necessity laid upon me." To become a missionary to India has proved to be the single most important fact about my life. Perhaps it is not too much to use an old phrase: "If God calls you to be a missionary, don't stoop to be a king." This privilege I would not exchange for anything. My life has been enriched beyond measure by it. For me it is a matter of pride to recall that I have been honored to be a missionary of Jesus Christ toward the end of the great modern period of mission endeavor. My role as bishop has just been a further development or extension of more basic vocational choices. In my endeavor to be obedient to this summons, it has meant almost constant joy along the way.

The tasks are not in the end burdensome. My satisfaction has often derived not from what one *has to do* in vocational fulfillment, but in what one *gets to do,* a fine distinction. Then I have discovered something about Christian maturity: the stage by which we are no longer burdened by carrying our faith; rather, our faith carries us.

Clearly I must say more about my third decision: my life partner. In one sense it is hard to speak of this. After nearly sixty years of life together, there is such a mingling of lives that even separate identity seems somewhat obscured. What one does both do. It has occurred to me that these very memoirs should be entitled *We Did It Together.*

We have had a good marriage. To suggest that it has never been under strain would not be speaking truth. We have had stresses, but have endured and have made the discovery that marriage gets better with time. My testimony is that I have experienced fulfillment through Eunice and through our children and grandchildren.

Eunice and I are by no means alike. Her background of having been born and brought up in India stands in stark contrast to my own more conventional beginnings. Recently, I learned of a group called Global Nomads International. It is for children of American parents who have been reared in another culture. This is true of missionary children so that Eunice could be a charter member of such an organization, which seems to be a kind of "support group" for those who have been traumatized by their unconventional experience as children. On the other hand, she apparently does not need such support. Never have I heard her complain about her childhood. Rather, she has felt greatly enriched by her bicultural beginnings. I know that I too have very often profited by this as we have lived in southern Asia and Africa. She has been able immediately to grasp the meaning of events that was hidden from my eyes.

Once the two of us subjected ourselves to a Myers-Briggs test as to personality types. Eunice came out ISTJ (for *Introversion, Sensory, Thinking, Judging*). This, being roughly translated, points to a person decisive in practical affairs, who is dependable, who keeps her word, and who is uneasy about financial instability—a fair portrait of my spouse! The test revealed that my type is described as INFP (for *Introversion, Intuition, Feeling, Perception*). Again, being interpreted, this means one who is decisive in practical affairs, who prefers to work with possibilities and relationships rather than just facts, who is sensitive as to people's feelings and enjoys pleasing people, and who is flexible and spontaneous. To all of this, I must plead guilty. So, we are quite different in type but nevertheless we get along well together. My wife has proved understanding of the heavy demands that have often been put upon me. She has tried to relieve many of the pressures to which I was subjected and has all too often shielded me from stresses by taking them upon herself. We have been good friends and colleagues and traveling companions. Eunice has been supportive in every possible way. She has at the same time been my most constant, stern, and usually constructive critic, often snatching me back at the very brink of what might have been disastrous decisions.

Through it all she has had a life of her own. She has shown a knack for friendship and has always maintained her own circle of friends. She does not like to speak in public but does so with competence and great acceptance.

Like her mother before her, she does not favor demonstrative affection or piety. Yet she possesses warmth and manifests a mature and quiet faith. While in Boston she researched and wrote a small book entitled *Drug Abuse: Summons to Community Action*. This was in 1971 when our society was just being alerted to this problem. Under the auspices of North Conway Institute, which, under the leadership of the Reverend David Works, has dealt with substance abuse, fifty thousand copies of her book were distributed. Her emphasis was that to cope successfully with the drug problem *all* the forces of community—educational, social, medical, police, political, business, and religious—must attack it together and simultaneously. This approach seems to me to be valid still.

In this narrative I have already referred to our three children. We had our family a little later than some do for we were in our thirties before we had any children, but they have developed well. Any parent nowadays has to swallow hard at some of the decisions their children make along the way, but we have been blessed with good relations with our children. They have all done well and we are proud of them. Our oldest daughter, Anne, is a clinical psychologist, working for the past ten years in the federal government, and currently working with the U.S. Department of Health and Human Services in their Center for Mental Health Services. She is committed to a new initiative to reduce violence in America's schools by fostering the healthy development of all children, providing adequate mental health services, and encouraging resilience.

Our next daughter, Jan, served for twenty years with U.S. Office of Interpol, rising to the level of acting director. Transferred to a new agency, she became director of ICITAP (International Criminal Investigative Training Assistance Program), under the U.S. Justice Department. This program is for the training of police in more humane methods in emerging democratic countries. This took her to such places as Haiti, Albania, Bosnia, Liberia, Ukraine, and a long list of other troubled countries. She has had to deal with pronounced gender bias in her work, but has advanced to executive level, showing great administrative and leadership skills. Currently she is with the Department of State in USAID.

Our son, Stan, is an architect currently teaching with his wife at Oberlin College. He is a gifted teacher and highly creative in his approach to his work—possessing skill in combining theory and practice. He has earned his Ph.D in architecture at Columbia University. He enjoys life in the broad field of art and design, linked with the practice of architecture and consulting in the field.

Each of the three has two children, giving us six grand-children. Both Anne and Jan had early marriages that ended in divorce. Anne is happily married now to Dr. Robert Younes, a medical doctor. He has shown great social concern; he was a Peace Corps volunteer in Africa and is currently on the board of St. Jude Hospital in Memphis, a role to which he gives great devotion. They have two children, Nicholas, a junior in high school and Nora, whom they adopted as a baby from Chile, now in grade school. Jan has not remarried and has done a remarkable job, we think, of rearing her two daughters, Christine, just graduated from Bucknell College, and Kathryn, from Colgate University. Stan's wife, Patricia, a professor of Art

History at Oberlin, is a specialist in Impressionism and women in art. Their two girls are Adrienne, a student at Smith College, and Alice, in grade school. We are very proud of all of them and they are a delight to us. We are fortunate that our two daughters live nearby us in the Washington, D.C., area, and our son about six hours away by car.

Somehow as I write this I recall words I encountered somewhere: that our children and grandchildren expect as much from us as we expect from them; a kind of reciprocity of great expectations!

There is another dimension of our lives together. It has to do with our pets: with us it was dogs. In our first years in India we were enriched by Spotty, a mixture of cocker spaniel and fox terrier. He was bright and cheerful, a rapid learner. Then came an Alsatian or German shepherd, Scarlett. She was beautiful and far from being jealous of her, Spotty was her protector. Later, after our children arrived, there came two collies: Lassie and her son, Laddie, both sheer delights. Finally there was another German shepherd, Ricky (Rikki Tikki Tavi). He was protector of our family. These dogs were all models of loyalty. We are convinced that they thought they were people and we recall them with deep appreciation.

A bit earlier I alluded to certain themes that have been threaded through my life, or better, *our* lives. Woven together they doubtless form its tapestry and texture. In fact, these threads help to hold our lives together. One of these threads is India, a fact that I have consistently emphasized. Even as these words are penned India is celebrating its golden anniversary of independence: marveling in the fact that an advanced degree of democracy has been maintained, while remaining mindful of goals and ideals still to be realized in that complex society. We return there again and again to drink afresh from the riches India has to share with those who are receptive. We were especially pleased that in the Jubilee year of 1997 our good friend K. R. Narayanan was elected president of the world's largest democracy and that he with his Burmese wife, Usha, share the palatial residence that once housed the viceroys of India. We have been honored by visiting them there.

Without elaboration, another strand is Gandhi and all that Gandhi stood for. Then there is the missionary thread, the ecumenical thread, and the global thread. Others are of a more personal nature: empathy, the deep feeling for others, loyalty, persistence, and most of all the obligation for sharing. One could put it this way: that in our travels we are exposed to situations about which we must *act* to effect change. A lifelong practice has been that if we encounter a need—a task that needs to be performed—it is not open to us to ignore it. Either we must act, or upon more mature reflection, decide not to act. If a challenge confronts us about which we *can* do something, then we *must* do something. For the Christian is on duty all the time.

To speak in this way is to ride for a fall. For one cannot hide shortcomings; how again and again we fail others by failing to hear their need, whether spoken, or, more important, unspoken. For we let people down and overload them with work, all the while remaining insensitive to what we are doing. So we must become conscious of both what we have done and what we have left undone. The fact is that I have not been a good steward of many of the gifts God has given me. Though a Wesleyan, who is supposed to be strictly accountable for the use of time, I have failed miserably. No wonder I was once addressed so deeply by a clock tower in a monastery at Suzdal in Russia where not merely the hours were struck *but every minute.* Before this I have confessed my failure to achieve real mastery in so many of the subjects I have studied. This is true of Indian languages; a failure that means one does not "get inside" another culture adequately. Once again, though I regard myself a man of peace, have I been so with sufficient passion and consistency?

Though good music appeals to the very depths of my being, I have not given myself to its study and cannot read a note. Thanks be to God, then, for such a woman as Mrs. Harris Childs in New York, for seeing to it for several years that Eunice and I were exposed to the best in music at Carnegie Hall and the Metropolitan Opera. Likewise I could lament my limited exposure to great art and literature. I find myself wishing I had done more with poetry. But having said all this, I refuse at this stage to succumb to regret and remorse, but rather to look toward my visions and dreams that I have had in abundance.

> Maybe this is a time to let John Bunyan speak for me:
> There's no discouragement
> Shall make him once relent
> His first avowed intent
> To be a pilgrim.

So speaks the pilgrim—the missionary: I gladly sing with him.

This I can say for, as I have repeatedly emphasized, I

am a child of the church. In her arms I was baptized. By her ministry, expressed by devoted laypersons and pastors, I was nurtured and helped along the way long before I was aware of it. By her life-transforming good news, I was awakened in Jesus Christ. How fortunate I have been to be caught up in her ministry and her mission! How favored too I have been to come along when the church has been renewed in so many ways, when joy in the celebration of worship has been recovered, when the hope of unity of the Body of Christ has been rekindled! By God's goodness I trust that I shall some day die in her bosom. Finally, as a child of the church, I strongly affirm her faith in life eternal, for in Christ we know that death is not the end.

At the same time, much of my ministry has been during a period in which the church has been under assault and, like most of the other institutions in Western culture, has been subjected to sometimes seething criticism. If the church has been first to face the onslaught, is it not precisely because in its sentinel position of guardian of society it is exposed at the frontiers? By the same token, it has been the first to recover and to be able to point the way to restorations of the other institutions. This may be the point for me to register my deep concern about those who seemingly desire to use the church to further their own one-issue agendas. This approach both distorts and finally destroys.

Though at times I have found myself in the position of the loyal opposition, my criticism of the church has been constructive, like criticizing one's Mother, which the church is. Without any effort to invent fresh language for my criticism, it is basically that the church has very often been so caught up in its horizontal dimension of *diakonia,* social criticism and service, that its vertical dimension of *koinonia,* fellowship and communion with God, has been obscured. This confusion has hampered the effectiveness of its concomitant responsibility of *kerygma,* demonstrating and proclaiming the good news. This criticism also applies equally to the World Council and National Council of Churches. This same factor has contributed to the widening of the gap between so-called mainline and evangelical churches. Others have said this more effectively than I have, but I too must voice it.

Having done so, my confidence is still that it is *Christ's* church, not ours; and the forces of evil shall not prevail against it. I am frequently recalled to what T. S. Eliot declared long ago: "There shall always be the Church and the World and the heart of man, shivering and fluttering between them: choosing and chosen."

What I have just written pertains to the discussion that has raged within the ecumenical movement almost since the beginning, what is the agenda to be: the church's or the World's? No voice has been lifted more often in the debate than that of W. A. Visser't Hooft. In an address at Uppsala in 1968 he made the oft-quoted remark: "It must become clear that church members who deny in fact their responsibility for the needy in any part of the world are just as much guilty of heresy as those who deny this or that article of the faith." It is less well known that Visser't Hooft himself later counterbalanced that statement with: "And church members who deny that God has reconciled men to himself in Christ are just as much guilty of heresy as those who refuse to be involved in the struggle for justice and freedom for all men and who do nothing to help their brethren in need." If a serious discussion of these sentences could be mounted between the two factions of the church to which I have just alluded, then we will have taken a major step toward bridging the gap that separates us.

Regarding agenda, surely the real question before the church is: "What does the Lord require of you?" To my mind the response would be to keep on doing much that we have been doing: declare God's Word everywhere to all, lift up the hearts of people, probe with them the mystery of being, give direction and hope in life's great moments, be guardian of the sacred, uphold the great values, defend the poor, seek peace, combat the hateful rebellion against our Creator that is racism, be a voice to the voiceless, support the weak, stand firm for justice, care for God's good earth, and affirm life eternal. Is this a mere "laundry list"? If so, then this would be a sign of how hard our hearts have become. Well, enough of that!

The fact remains that I look forward with hope and find that I am not too much a captive of the past. There are some advantages in growing older. One can within limits pretty much do and say what one wants to. You are no longer a threat to anyone any more. You are sustained by the great books you have read, by the colleagues and acquaintances you have made worldwide along the way, by repeated affirmations and intercessions by others, by exemplary figures who have expended themselves in the name of God and service of humankind. The faces of many of them come before me at this very moment and I am grateful.

Among them would be the more than one thousand men and women I have ordained as ministers of Jesus Christ. To speak of friends is to remind me that I am not aware of having any enemies and if I did, I should immediately set about trying to turn them if I could into friends.

One practice I have pursued. It is to give thanks to God and to others. So I have written thousands of letters of appreciation. Moreover, almost invariably I have tried to thank those who have spoken or performed in public. I say that I have never heard a poor sermon. If the preachers are not at their best, so much the more do they need some commendation. There is, I think, a necessary eucharistic pattern in life—a need of forever giving thanks. The central rite of Christians is rightly the Eucharist.

It has often been noted about Paul that he had the practice of saying "Finally," but he keeps on. There comes a time when one says "Finally" and means it. Therefore, I conclude with these words which I have used elsewhere:

IF I HAD IT TO DO OVER AGAIN

Let me cite no less a theological authority than Marilyn Monroe. She was once asked whether or not she would change anything if she had it to do over again. Her answer reportedly was: "No." She was doubtless a realist and probably spoke the truth for more of us than we would care to admit.

On the other hand, if we *do* find ourselves musing, "If I had it to do over again," we surely are talking nonsense unless from the moment of such an insight, we do do it differently.

Sometimes I say to myself that if I could begin my ministry again, I would emphasize healing more. Teaching and preaching, yes, but Jesus' ministry, which we share and continue also, involved healing. So lately I have been stressing the healing dimension—I who once longed to be a surgeon!

Now let me list some things that I would do over again, if I had it to do over again:

1. I would choose a mentor. Or are we chosen *by* mentors? Probably both. Then too we may have several mentors. One of mine was Ralph E. Diffendorfer, long chief foreign missions executive among Methodists. From him I learned administration, staff work, and corporate decision-making; that is, in addition to what I learned courtesy of Uncle Sam, as an officer for more than four years in the U.S. Army during World War II.

2. Then I would choose again to be a missionary. Or is one chosen to be a missionary? I have emphasized the great privilege of becoming a missionary of Jesus Christ. It has colored and accented my whole life and I would accept nothing in exchange for it. Just imagine being a missionary during a period in which the whole church was recovering and redefining what it is to be in mission!

3. I would continue the practice of having a theological adviser. In fact, I have had several of them; Walter Muelder and John Godsey among them. I mean a professional theologian to whom I could go to ask the questions one is dying to ask but never had the opportunity. One of mine was the late Professor Carl Michalson. An example:

I once asked him, "Carl, what is meant by the 'new hermeneutic'?" His reply: "You know the old hermeneutic—our interpreting Scripture? Well, the new hermeneutic is: how Scripture interprets us." It was worth a semester's seminary course and I moved light years ahead as a practicing theologian. I recall a debt also to Paul Tillich, who said that existentialism is the contemporary theologian's good luck. I have not been an existentialist, but have profited from this insight.

4. I would join a discussion group with colleagues and contemporaries after the manner I have referred to in this narrative. Here again I have been a part of several and have alluded to them earlier. All of these were invaluable. Don't try to go it alone.

5. I would do more writing. Public speaking is more thrilling, but writing is at the same time more precise and more enduring.

6. Keep a journal. I have done so for half of my active ministry. Samuel Pepys's position is still secure but at least I can account in retrospect for where I was—even if I didn't quite know at the time!

7. Develop and persist in sound devotional habits. For me, this has taken a long time to establish. Most helpful has been the use of *The Daily Office* by the Joint Liturgical Group in the United Kingdom. It helps me to pray.

8. Study and teach the Bible. This I have done for more than sixty years. No other practice has proved more valuable.

9. Do not neglect the ecumenical dimension. This development during "our time" was as unexpected as it was unprecedented. It is not a small thing. What a privi-

lege to have known leaders across the whole Christian spectrum and beyond! We are under obligation to see that this flame does not flicker. Above all, get to know your counterparts wherever you are.

10. Keep in tune with the real issues. And keep involved in them. Be and be seen to be a part of the solution to these issues.

11. Be *open*. If I were asked to name the most important spiritual dimension, I should say openness. This helps one to be positive, a part of solutions rather than a part of our problems.

12. To me it has proved helpful to practice what I call the "stewardship of ideas." If an idea comes to me, I write it down. Then, it does not leave my desk until I have put it into use; or, upon more mature reflection, have deliberately decided I should set it aside.

13. Frequently I feel self-condemned for not having given a fuller place to my spouse and family. This seems a common ailment in our calling.

14. Once again I have failed to involve myself adequately in some systematic sport or exercise program. Walking or hiking is the closest I have come to this. I do enjoy watching football. Then I would say that it helps when we can regard our vocation as also an avocation. How fortunate when one *enjoys* one's work!

15. Get to "know the territory"—and the "troops." Travel is essential and I confess that I have always enjoyed travel.

16. Honor the laity. This I have tried to do.

17. Cultivate a lively sense of the presence of God in your life. I've noted that the most acutely spiritually

attuned persons I've known have not hesitated to acknowledge this: God's active presence. For me it has been more operative in retrospect than in prospect. Like Joseph to his brothers I can say: "You meant it for evil, but God meant it for good."

18. Whatever our particular task or focus may be, we must rely on our friends. The story is told of the late Lord Michael Ramsey, former Archbishop of Canterbury, that during his final months he was asked what he did when he was not reading, writing, praying. The prelate replied: "I think of my friends." So say all of us!

19. Nowadays I often reflect on the fact that being Christian is lifelong and worldwide; it is history long. There is no lifting of the mandate to love our neighbors, even our enemies, as long as life and health endure. It could almost be said that we are under a life sentence! But the yoke is easy.

20. My erstwhile elder colleague and friend was Bishop Herbert Welch. He spoke of the "Welch quadrilateral" for longevity: (1) moderation in work; (2) prohibition of worry; (3) trust in God; (4) a little play along the way. Then maybe we shall reach the stage of life to which Rabindranath Tagore refers: We raise the sail and are borne along on the winds of God.

Finally, a little humility helps. I once heard the late Lord George McLeod tell of a session at a Scots' Kirk determining to remedy the excessive wear of the stone steps to the church by turning the stones over—only to discover that frugal ancestors had already thought of that two centuries before!

Index